Reading
Organization
Theory

Albert J. Mills is Director of the PhD in Business Administration (Management) in the Sobey School of Business, Saint Mary's University. He has served on the editorial board of the Canadian Review of Sociology and Anthropology (1996-8), a special editorial board of the Administrative Science Quarterly (1996-7), the Board of Standing Conference on Organizational Symbolism (2000-05), and the Executive of the Administrative Sciences Association of Canada (1999-2005). Mills is currently a member of four editorial boards, including *Leadership, Organization, Organization and Management History*, and *Tamara* (the Journal of Critical Postmodern Organizational Science).In addition to a number of journal articles, he is the author, co-author, and co-editor of eight books, and has edited/co-edited special issues of the Canadian Review of Sociology and Anthropology (1999: on "organizational crisis"), and Culture and Organization (2002: on "exploring the gendering of organizational culture"). To date, he has taught in Britain, the United States, Canada, the Netherlands, Hungary, Macedonia, Slovenia, Kuwait, Finland, and Vietnam. He has presented numerous academic papers at international conferences in Canada, the UK, Ireland, the United States, Mexico, Brazil, Poland, the Netherlands, Denmark, Finland, France, Australia, and Hungary.

Tony Simmons has pursued an undistinguished career at Athabasca University (Alberta), where he spends much of his time writing correspondence courses in sociology for distance education students and teaching special needs students in prisons, reserves and other outreach locations. He is presently working on another book – on the practical uses of social theory for the global age. Tony Simmons currently lives in Edmonton with his cat, Reilly, where he continues in a struggle to align his practice with his theory.

Jean Helms Mills is Associate Professor of Management in the Sobey School of Business at Saint. Mary's University. Prior to her academic career, she worked in the airline industry for seventeen years. Luckily she has been able to combine her interest in aviation with her research interests. Currently, Helms Mills is a co-investigator on a three year Social Sciences and Humanities Research Council grant (SSHRC) studying "The Gendering of Organizational Culture Over Time: Case Studies of Selected US Airlines". She has presented her work at numerous national and international conferences and is the author of "Making Sense of Organizational Change" (Routledge, 2003) and co-author of three other books. Dr Helms Mills has numerous scholarly publications. In addition, she is the Associate Editor (The Americas) for the journal "Culture and Organization" and the Vice President of Communications for the Administrative Sciences Association of Canada (ASAC).

Reading
Organization
Theory

A Critical Approach
to the Study of Organizational
Behaviour and Structure

Albert J. Mills, Tony Simmons and Jean Helms Mills

UNIVERSITY OF TORONTO PRESS

Previously published by Garamond Press Ltd. (an imprint of Broadview Press) © the authors, 2005

Library and Archives Canada Cataloguing in Publication

Mills, Albert J., 1945–
Reading organization theory : a critical approach to the study of organizational behaviour and structure / Albert J. Mills, Tony Simmons and Jean Helms Mills. —3rd ed.

Includes bibliographical references and index.
ISBN 978-1-55193-053-4

1. Organizational sociology. I. Simmons, Anthony M. (Anthony Michael), 1945– II. Mills, Jean Helms, 1954– III. Title.

HM131.M542   2005   302.3'5   C2005-904610-4

We welcome comments and suggestions regarding any aspect of our publications—please feel free to contact us at news@utphighereducation.com or visit our Internet site at www.utphighereducation.com.

North America
5201 Dufferin Street
North York, Ontario, Canada, M3H 5T8

2250 Military Road
Tonawanda, New York, USA, 14150

ORDERS PHONE: 1-800-565-9523
ORDERS FAX: 1-800-221-9985
ORDERS E-MAIL: utpbooks@utpress.utoronto.ca

UK, Ireland, and continental Europe
NBN International
Estover Road, Plymouth, PL6 7PY, UK
ORDERS PHONE: 44 (0) 1752 202301
ORDERS FAX: 44 (0) 1752 202333
ORDERS E-MAIL: enquiries@nbninternational.com

The University of Toronto Press acknowledges the financial support for its publishing activities of the Government of Canada through the Canada Book Fund.

Printed in Canada

Contents

CHAPTER 4

CHAPTER 5

CHAPTER 7

KNOWLEDGE AND POWER IN THEORIES OF ORGANIZATION: THE ORGANIZATIONAL WORLD AND THE MANAGERIAL PARADIGM 233

INTEGRATED CASE: THE WESTRAY MINE EXPLOSION 247

THE WESTRAY MINE EXPLOSION: TEACHING NOTE 263

Acknowledgments

Books are deceptive. They carry three sets of names – the author(s), the book title, and the publisher. Hidden from view, buried deep in the text, is the contribution of many other people whose energy, intellectual stimulation, and tireless efforts were no less important in bringing the book into being. For our part we would like to thank Carol Agócs, Peta Tancred, Jerry White and Stewart Clegg for a wealth of useful and encouraging comments of earlier drafts. Terry Morrison (the former President of Athabasca University) and Paul Dixon (the former Dean of the Sobey Business School at Saint Mary's University) for much needed financial assistance. Val Delorme, Sandra Fougere, Sue Helms, and Carol Schafer who gave much of their time to the technical side of the production: Steve Schafer, whose library assistance exceeded the call of duty; Kelly Maher for her research for earlier editions of the book; Margaret Anderson whose wonderful drawings have helped to simplify and make clear a number of otherwise complex ideas; Peter Saunders of Garamond Press for his continued commitment and suggestions for improvement.

We would also like to thank colleagues old and new whose intellectual exchanges have somehow found their way into the text: the Bradford *Work and Organization Research Group* – Judith Foreman, Dave Hooper, Paul Iles, Tom Johnson, Glenn Morgan, Jules Piscarne, and Liz Shorrocks; our friends and colleagues from the Faculty of Administrative Studies at Athabasca University — Peter Chiaramonte, Andy Khan, and Richard Marsden, the Department of Commerce at Mount Allison University — Gina Grandy, Peter Sianchuck, Roger Wehrell, the School of Business at Acadia University – Conor Vibert, Kelly Dye, and the Sobey School of Business — David Wicks, Shripad Pendse, Kevin Kelloway, Hari Das, Terrance Weatherbee, plus the first five cohorts of the Sobey PhD programme.

To Megan – *Albert J. Mills*

For Sybil: who believed,
For Albert: who waited,
For Irene: who understood – *Tony Simmons*

To my aunt, Pauline Helms – *Jean Helms Mills*

Developing a Critical Approach to Organizational Study

This chapter discusses the need for a critical approach to organizational study and outlines the main elements of a critical approach. The chapter examines competing views (or paradigms) within organizational analysis, and explains how to deconstruct organizational texts, how to develop a reflexive research agenda, and how to "reach out and authorize" the reader in the process of writing-up research findings.

Alice in Organization Land

Once upon a time there was a girl called Alice. Alice, with her parents, had recently emigrated from Underdeveloped Land to the United States of Industrialization where she lived in one of the poorer neighbourhoods of a major city.

One day something miraculous happened. Alice was walking just outside the city limits when she tripped and fell down a large hole. The fall seemed endless but when she finally reached the bottom she was confronted by a strange looking man, with wire rimmed glasses, a blackboard and a large, voluminous book. "Hello little girl," he said, emphasizing the word girl, "welcome to Organization Land." As Alice stared in amazement the man opened the book, placed it on the floor and invited her to step into it. Reaching out his hand the man reassured Alice with these words, "A Willy Wonka world of chocolate this is not, but a land of reality made up of many wondrous things." Alice took a deep breath and stepped into the book and what she saw was truly amazing. She had stepped into a world where no one talked of class, race, ethnic background, or gender.

Everything was so white, so sanitized, so comfortable, so male that after a while the whiteness became too overbearing and no one seemed to under-

stand Alice. At first she thought that people had trouble hearing her but then it began to dawn on her that no one even noticed her. When suddenly she heard it. It was faint at first but the sound began to grow, "Girl, girl, girl," and as the noise grew louder it sounded increasingly menacing, Alice began to feel constrained, she could hardly breathe, she wanted to yell. Finally, she was able to close her eyes and let out a loud scream. As she opened her eyes she found her mother leaning over her bed; "Oh mummy," she cried, "I had a bad dream. I don't ever want to go to Organization Land." "My poor child," said the mother trying to comfort her, "it wasn't a dream."

INTRODUCTION

This book explains and develops a critical approach to understanding organizations. It can be read alongside mainstream organizational behaviour (OB) and organization theory (OT) text books. The book is aimed primarily at the student of organization across the various sub-divisions. It is not our intention to reinforce the existing fragmentation of the field into organization theory (OT), organizational behaviour (OB), and the sociology of organizations. We do not accept that organizational structure and behaviour can be understood without reference to one another. Nor do we accept that organizations can be simply understood as reflections of the broader society in which they are located or as social entities in their own right. It is our contention that organizations need to be understood as the outcome of several levels of abstraction that includes internal and external factors, structural and behavioural factors and various combinations of each factor. To that end the book's title is a reference to the theory of organization (in the broadest sense) rather than the more disciplinary and narrow organization theory.

The book has five key objectives. It aims to introduce you to:

i) A critical understanding of mainstream studies of organization (from Scientific Management through to Business Process Reengineering). The book is not a substitute for mainstream texts. It is assumed that you will either be familiar with or in the process of studying mainstream accounts of organization and that this book will challenge you to think about many of the assumptions involved in your course of study.

ii) An awareness that there are several, competing approaches to organizational analysis.

iii) The notion that issues of class, gender and race/ethnicity are *essential* features of organizational analysis.

iv) The viewpoint that organizations are *historically* constructed entities.

v) Ways of developing a critical approach to organizational analysis.

ORGANIZATIONAL STUDY AND THE NEGLECT OF CLASS, GENDER, AND RACE/ETHNICITY

The story of Alice in Organization Land is not a fairy tale. Pick up any OT or OB text book, turn to the index and try to find any reference to race, ethnicity, class, or gender. Chances are that you will find very little.[1] Yet the issues are not trivial. The workforce of the major industrial nations consists of large numbers of female workers, and people from different ethnic backgrounds. In Canada a Royal Commission on "Equality in Employment,"[2] reporting in 1984, listed 14 major "selected ethnic groups" which included "British, French, other European, Indo-Pakistani, Indo-Chinese, Japanese, Korean, Chinese, Pacific Islands, Black, Native People, and Central/South American." The Commission went on to state that there was evidence of widespread "systemic discrimination" against "native people, and visible minorities"[3] as well as "disabled persons" and women,[4] and added that:

> It is not fair that many people in these groups have restricted employment opportunities, limited access to decision-making processes that critically affect them, little public visibility as contributing Canadians, and a circumscribed range of option generally.(Abella, 1984: 1)

It is hard to believe that issues of this kind – even after the public scrutiny of a Royal Commission in Canada and employment equity legislation in the US, Britain, and Canada – have remained largely unspoken within OT and OB texts twenty years later.

It is only since the last decade of the twentieth century that business educators have begun to come to terms with the issues. In the United States the *US Commission on Admission to Graduate Management Education* named race and gender as two of the most pressing issues for business education in the 1990s. Commenting on the study, Commission member William Ouchi pointed out the shortcomings of existing approaches to management education:

> [An MBA class] has to be a heterogeneous group. For example, if you were in Southern California in the year 2000, you could not call yourself a sensible

person if you weren't fully committed to a diverse, multi-cultural workplace with full representation of Latinos, Blacks, Asian-Pacifics, and women. The way we currently approach that problem is to say that our entering students have to be able to do algebra II and calculus, and then do everything we can to compose a student body that will be sufficiently diverse from among those who have sufficient mathematics. Well, that's absolutely nuts. The world isn't saying, "Give us people who can do math, and then do the best you can to make them adequately diverse." The world is saying, "Your mission is to see that people of all races and both genders have equal access to the fruits of this society and to participation in the business community" (Ouchi, 1990: 38).

In the 1990s the *American Assembly of Collegiate Schools of Business* (AACSB) reacted to the issue by altering its accreditation rules. The AACSB, which plays a powerful role in the accreditation of business schools in the US and Canada, insists that to be AACSB-accredited a business school has to include a focus on race and gender in its curriculum.[5] In Canada, apart from the limited impact of the AACSB, business education has yet to deal with the issues of race, ethnicity and gender in a systematic fashion.

To continue our experiment, turn back to one of the organizational texts and now attempt to find references to the impact of organizations on the lives of people. Again you will find next to nothing despite the fact that the effects of organizational life have been linked to a lack of self esteem (Leonard, 1984); sexual harassment (LeMoncheck and Sterba, 2001); a sense of powerlessness (Foldy, 2002); a segregated work life (Greene, Ackers and Black, 2002); pay inequities (Gregory, Sales and Hegewisch, 1999); racism (Delgado and Stefancic, 2000); and physical injury:[6] the list is endless.

As a final experiment, look through the text and try to assess how much of it deals with experiences with which you are familiar. If your experiences are anything like ours you will have little to note down. It is hardly surprising that studies of organization strike so many students as boring and outside their interests and experiences. Many students are soon likely to feel that organizations are something that people serve rather than the other way around. If you are as Alice, you might run away, give up, or simply keep going just to obtain the credits. Don't despair, approached from a totally different perspective organizational analysis is one of the most important areas of study that you will ever undertake.

The aim of this book is not to turn anyone away from the study of organizations. On the contrary, through an exploration of class, gender, race/ethnicity and the impact of organizations on social and psychic life we hope to encourage a renewed interest in organizational analysis. To that end, the book encourages you to think for yourself and to provide information and ideas to help you find your own way. Above all else, the book sets out to provide you with the tools of analysis rather than simply an alternative view of organizations. The content does, of course, reflect our version of reality – our way of viewing organizations, but its purpose is to engage in dialogue with existing theories of organization in a way which will challenge you to think about organizations and how to study them.

In this chapter our central objective is to challenge you to think about the character of mainstream organizational analysis; to expose you to a number of alternative approaches; and to start you thinking about how you might begin to develop a critical approach. First we want to inspire an interest in the study of organizations.

WHY STUDY ORGANIZATIONS? GETTING INTERESTED

Welcome to the world of high-risk technologies. You may have noticed that they seem to be multiplying, and it is true. As our technology expands, as our wars multiply, and as we invade more and more of nature, we create systems – organizations, and the organization of organizations – that increase the risks for operators, passengers, innocent bystanders, and for future generations. [These systems include] nuclear power plants, chemical plants, aircraft and air traffic control, ships, dams, nuclear weapons, space missions, and genetic engineering. Most of these risky enterprises have catastrophic potential, the ability to take the lives of hundreds of people in one blow, or to shorten or cripple the lives of thousands or millions more. Every year there are more such systems. That is the bad news. The good news is that if we can understand the nature of risky enterprises better, we may be able to reduce or even remove these dangers. (Charles Perrow, 1984: 3).

We live in a time dominated by organizations. Organizations permeate nearly everything we do. They shape the way we live, the way we think, the way we are valued and the way we value ourselves. They offer opportunities for social improvement but they also threaten our very existence. In short, we cannot afford to ignore organizations and we cannot afford to ignore organizational behaviour.

Organizational Behaviour and September 11th

The story is well known.[7] In the United States, on September 11th 2001 a group of terrorists hijacked four commercial airliners. Two of the planes were deliberately crashed into the twin towers of the World Trade Center in New York, completely destroying the buildings and killing close to three thousand people. One plane killed around two hundred people when it was crashed into the Pentagon in Washington, D.C. The fourth plane, which became engaged in a life and death struggle between the hijackers and the passengers, crashed in a Pennsylvania field, killing all on board.

Among the central questions that people have been asking since these events are: Who did this and why? How was it possible? Is a similar group capable of doing this again? Is there any way we can guard against another such occurrence? Although these questions have been couched in political terms and certainly have political ramifications many of the answers are rooted in questions of organizational behaviour.

To begin with, the hijackers gained from a number of common organizational problems. In particular large bureaucracies, such as the Immigration and Naturalization Service (USINS), the Federal Bureau of Investigation (FBI), the Central Intelligence Agency (CIA) and the Federal Aviation Authority (FAA] failed to adequately identify and keep track of the hijackers as they entered and operated within the USA. These agencies also failed to coordinate their "anti-terrorist" activities or to share information. In addition, there is some evidence that, prior to September 11^{th,} surveillance of individual hijackers was thwarted due to conflict within the FBI and between the FBI, CIA, and other agencies[8]. It has since been argued that there needs to be closer cooperation between the various security and national defense agencies.

As early as January of 2001, Sandy Berger, the Clinton administration's National Security Advisor, was speculating that the new Bush administration would spend more time on terrorism in general, and al-Qaeda in particular, than on any other subject.[9] By the Summer of that year there were sufficient intelligent reports to concern government agencies that a major attack against US interests was imminent. That the attack was not averted was due, in the words of one commentator, to "a systematic collapse in the ability of Washington's national security apparatus to handle the terrorist threat."[10] In February of 2001, a future hijacker, Hani Hanjour, raised suspicions with the instructors of the Arizona flight school where he was registered. He was investigated by the FAA, who concluded that he was a legitimate student. Around the same time, and in an apparently separate investigation, FBI agent Kenneth Williams began probing the activities of suspected Islamic radicals enrolling in flying lessons at the Arizona flight school. In July he filed a report of his suspicions that al-Qaeda may be attempting to infiltrate US aviation for terrorist purposes. He sent his report to FBI headquarters and, ironically, to the New York field office. No action was taken. Williams' memorandum did not get past mid-level unit heads. The same time as Williams was preparing his report two more of the September 11 hijacker re-entered the US. Although known to the CIA as members of al-Qaeda, the Agency failed to pass on the information to the USINS until the end of August. That month the FBI bungled another potentially important break in the unfolding case. Tipped off by suspicions from the manager of the Pan Am International Flight Academy in Minnesota, FBI agents arrested a man who was involved in the planning of the September 11th attack. Despite the potential significance of this arrest, the case was never brought to the attention to top officials in Washington. When local FBI agents applied to FBI headquarters for authorization to search the man's computer for information on his links to other suspected terrorists they were turned down.

The overall problems of these various agencies were due in various parts to bureaucratic, structural, resource, and political constraints. All of these agencies are hierarchically structured and require those in the field to send special requests "up the line" to headquarters and top officials. As in the September 11 situation, this often takes months to get dealt with. Ironically, the FBI's counter-terrorism activities were hampered in this case by a decentralization of its activities to its 58 field offices, which were discouraged from sharing information with each other. In terms of resources the FBI has been described as "ill-equipped to deal with the terrorist threat. It had neither the language nor the analytical skills to understand al-Qaeda. [Its] information-technology dated to pre-internet days."[11] In party political terms there is some evidence that a major report on terrorism was rejected by the Bush administration because it was originally crafted for the Clinton government. Organizational politics also played a part because of the bureaucratic process of dividing up areas of interest and the creation specialisms. For example, there is some suggestion of a "power play" between those government departments charged with "functional" responsibilities (such as terrorism) and those charged with "regional" responsibilities (such as relations with Pakistan).

Moving beyond the intelligence agencies we have the airport authorities. Despite the establishment of numerous routine security checks the hijackers were able to takeover no fewer than four commercial airplanes from two major US airports, Logan (Boston) and Newark (New Jersey/New York).

Among the problems that have since been identified is the fact that airport security services lacked national standard and employed poorly paid, often untrained, agents.

Onboard the planes were flight crews who had been trained to avoid conflict with hijackers: prior to September 11th airline hijackings did not involve any deliberate attempt to crash the plane. Sadly, this form of training allowed the hijackers to carry out their objectives without a struggle. It was only in the fourth hijacked plane, where passengers – through use of cellular phones – were aware of the fate of the other hijackings that a struggle ensued. US air-crews are now being training to resist all hijacking attempts.

Finally, despite the fact that it was known that a number of planes had been hijacked at the same time, the US Air Force failed to respond quickly to inter-cept any in-bound Washington flight that may have threatened the White House or the Pentagon. Two Air National Guard planes from Otis Air Force base in Cape Cod, Massachusetts did manage to get to the airspace above New York before the second plane hit but they were hampered by lack of informa-tion. Here the problem was both resource-based and sensemaking. Due to the limited possibility of an air attack on the United States on September 11 there were only four fighter planes on alert to protect the whole of the north-east-ern part of the country. By the time the two planes had reached New York the first of the hijacked planes had hit the World Trade Center. Local air traffic controllers witnessed this but did not immediately connect it to information that at least one commercial airliner had been hijacked and was heading off course to New York. The idea that a plane could be hijacked and flown into a building just did not make sense on the morning of September 11. It was un-heard off so discounted. Instead the situation was initially reported as a light plane having crashed into the World Trade Center. Thus, the fighter pilots above New York were not aware that the hijacking and the World Trade Center crashes were connected. Had they known they may have been able to find the second hijacked plane that was on course for the same destination.

In brief, a number of cumulative organizational problems allowed a dedicated group of hijackers to achieve their aims of inflicting maximum damage on the United States.

But there were also positive organizational behaviours that prevented the trag-edy from being even greater. When evidence of hijacking first became clear to Air Traffic Control firm leadership ensured that the number of hijackings was minimized. Action was quickly taken to ground all existing commercial planes throughout the US, to get a number of planes in the air to land, and to divert all planes bound for the US from a foreign destination to land elsewhere. There is some evidence that the hijackers may have targeted more than four planes. Hundreds of planes landed safely that day without incident. On the ground numerous towns and cities responded quickly, efficiently, and often with great warmth and affection, to organize food and accommodation for the tens of thousands of stranded passengers. More than 250 aircraft, carrying close to 44,000 passengers were diverted to Canadian airports alone. In the small Canadian town of Gander (pop. 10,000), for example, thirty-eight aircraft were safely landed and the 6500 passengers accommodated and fed for several days.

In New York itself the Mayor, Rudy Giuliani, had to exercise extraordinary skills to deal with crisis and many have commented on the speed and efficiency of the New York fire service and police departments in dealing with the immediate situation.

The events of September 11th have had a tremendous impact on organizational life for many people in the period since. For one thing, numerous government agencies have restricted access to a range of information that was previously available,[12] the government has established a new Homeland Security agency that is tightening control on activities that were previously unrestricted, and at airports throughout the world numerous new and heightened security measures have been introduced.

OB is not a panacea for dealing with organizational crises, but an examination of the events of September 11th 2001 reveals that an understanding of organizational behaviour provides insights into how such tragedies happen and how best to deal with them. The study of OB can help us to understand where behaviour at work is problematic and where it is effective. It can provide important clues to future action and help us to make informed decisions about organizational directions. In short, OB involves the systematic study of behaviour at work that provides concepts, theories and models to help us make sense of a range of activities from the mundane to the critical.

The Organizational World

Because of a reliance by organizations on petroleum products the twentieth century has been called the "oil century," and its last quarter has been characterized as an era of "oil crisis" (Halberstam, 1986). This characterization ignores the fact that organizational arrangements preceded oil; that in order for oil to be extracted and utilized there had to be large-scale organizations to make it happen. The organization was the real symbol of the twentieth century, and the last quarter was more appropriately characterized as an era of organizational crisis. The importance of both oil and "organization" was highlighted during the Gulf War in 1991. While it may be argued that oil was a central issue of the war, and that the issue was resolved through conflict, this signalled a wholesale failure in the character of existing organizations. For example, the ability of the United Nations to prevent war, and the ability of the Canadian Parliament to remain committed to peacekeeping activities. The 2003 invasion of Iraq signalled the supreme importance of organization both in the failure of the United Nations to prevent the invasion and the ability of the US High Command to wage the war.

Organizations are not new but our idea of what an organization is, what its purpose is, has only developed over the past 100 years or so (Morgan, 1996b). Forms of organization have been a part of human social development from as far back as we know. Indeed, as early as 600 BC, there was in Greek society an association with characteristics, which are similar to those found in modern corporations (Hatton, 1990). Before the Industrial Revolution, in the mid-eighteenth century, the development of organizations to deal with specific tasks was restricted to relatively few areas of social endeavour – such as religion (churches), wars and taxation (armies), scholarly communities (universities) trade and colonization (merchant and craft guilds, and trading companies). Very few of these bodies dealt with large numbers of people. Where organizations touched the lives of many people, they did so in an irregular fashion, for example, as in the collection of taxes or the raising of an army

All that was to change with the Industrial Revolution and the widespread development of manufactories, which brought people together under one roof for purposes of production. The new factory organizations generated a host of other new organizations to deal with the distribution, sale, and regulation of goods. Political parties developed to protect the interests of different classes of people associated with the new means of production, and within the factories, trade unions began to develop as workers saw a need to protect their jobs.

Bound up with the proliferation of organizations came a new type of thinking – organizational thinking. Increasingly, an array of social problems and activities began to be dealt with through the development of organizations. The principles of factory organization were used to deal with other aspects of social life:

> Schools, hospitals, prisons, government bureaucracies, and other organizations thus took on many of the characteristics of the factory – its division of labour, its hierarchical structure and its metallic impersonality. Even in the

arts we find some of the principles of the factory. Instead of working for a patron, as was customary during the long reign of agricultural civilization, musicians, artists, composers, and writers relied on the mercies of the marketplace. More and more they turned out "products" for anonymous consumers. (Toffler, 1981: 45).

This situation has developed to the present day where we can hardly think of an aspect of our life without thinking about an organizational answer. Whether we are going to work or school, taking in a movie, getting a Big Mac, listening to a concert, or attending a hockey game we are involved with one organization or another.

The modern organizational world and capitalism have developed hand in hand. At its simplest, capitalism involves three major features that have become embodied within modern principles of organizations – i) ownership and control of organizations lies with very few persons; ii) production is for profit, with products offered for sale in competitive, market situations and iii) productive tasks are carried out by employees who rely on work as their only or major source of income. This has resulted in a number of organizational dynamics that centre on issues of control. For those in charge competition create pressures to control costs. Production for a market creates pressures on the producer to control uncertainties because a company can never fully predict how many or even whether enough people will buy the products. The hiring of employees – whose primary interest in the job is the wage they will receive – creates pressures to control organizational behaviour. This has helped to shape organizations as hierarchical arrangements, where decision-making is top down, and broken into departments, with various posts created to control employees (e.g., supervisors, personnel departments) and the market (e.g., marketing departments). Interpersonal relationships within organizations are largely impersonal, manipulative, mistrustful, and mediated by money.

The soul destroying aspects of organizational life were long ago captured in the works of the founding group of sociologists – Emile Durkheim, Karl Marx and Max Weber. Durkheim believed that modern organization was destroying a sense of community and was atomizing individuals to the point where unable to relate to others and the broader society (see for example, Durkheim, 1957; 1964). In a similar vein, Marx saw organizations as alienating and soul destroying, preventing individuals from realizing their full human and social potential (see Marx, 1967; Marx and Engels, 1940). Weber predicted an ever increasing bureaucratization of life to the point where people's lives would be drab, impersonal and soulless (see Weber, 1947; 1967): he called this "the iron cage of bureaucracy." Both Durkheim and Marx were optimistic in believing that it was possible to transform the organizational world. Durkheim believed that over time organizational arrangements could create a new sense of community but only if organizations were limited in size (to a few hundred persons), and only if workplace relationships were organized along more democratic lines. Marx's optimism rested on the assumption that capitalist forms of organization would – through revolution – be replaced by socialist forms which, in turn, would encourage a "withering away" of organizational arrangements as we know them (Marx and Engels, 1967). Weber, on the other hand, was extremely pessimistic, confident that the inevitable spread of bureaucracy would be hastened not hindered by the rise of socialism.

Durkheim's vision of the small organization was ill-placed in the twentieth century world of large scale organization. But in 1917 the Russian Revolution breathed new life into Marx's dream of a classless society. From its founding in 1922, the Soviet Union served as a model to many people seeking an alternative to capitalism. It is a model that has been argued and fought over for the last seventy-five years but with the ending of the Berlin Wall and the collapse of Communist governments throughout Eastern Europe in the 1990s, it became clear that Weber's worst bureaucratic fears had been realized.

The ending of decades of Communist rule in Eastern Europe was hailed as a victory for capitalism, "the end of history" (Fukuyama, 1989) but that is a travesty of reality. It is not a victory but a clarification of a fundamental crisis in humankind's ability to organize. Rigid bureaucratization in the East led to economic shortages, widespread environmental pollution and eventual political collapse, but that does not hide the fact of poverty,[13] mass unemployment, widespread environmental pollution, and recession in the West. That capitalism is successful is but a testimony to the fact that capitalist organizations continue to thrive. It does not speak to the thousands of businesses that go bankrupt each year,[14] to the corruption and greed at various levels of government and business;[15] to industrial conflict;[16] nor to industry-related social and environmental disasters.[17]

The situation looks bleak, but that is the bad news. The good news, as Charles Perrow rightly says, is that we may be able to do something about it. To take an active interest in the study of organization is an important starting point but begin with a healthy scepticism. Healthy, in this case, means not being discouraged or overwhelmed by what seems a daunting task. Remember these three things; i) always dare to dream; without a vision we will succumb to the darkness; ii) there are examples of alternative modes of organizing, we need to search them out; and iii) never be afraid to think small. The big picture consists of many images, and it may be that effecting a small change will contribute to overall change. Scepticism means being prepared to question the value of organizing as a way of dealing with social problems: it means accepting the possibility that an absence of a (formally constituted) organization may be the alternative to a given way of organizing.

OUTLINING A CRITICAL APPROACH

Healthy scepticism is the basis of a critical approach to organizational analysis, but what is a critical approach? There is no one correct answer to this question. Definitions, like beauty, are often in the eye of the beholder. Our definition is a framework, rather than a prescription, to guide you through the rest of our analysis and discussion. We define a critical approach as one that takes as its starting point a concern to address those aspects of organizational arrangements that have a negative impact on people, e.g., low self-esteem, discrimination, pay inequities, stress and anguish, etc. In contrast to mainstream organizational analysis that concerns itself with the efficient use of people for formal organizational ends, (e.g., effectiveness, profitability, organizational growth), a critical approach sets out to uncover the ways in which organizational ends can be detrimental to people.

Through an examination of two contrasting definitions of organizational behaviour we can see the difference between a mainstream and a critical approach. The first quotation is from a mainstream text.

> Organizational behaviour … is a field of study that investigates the impact that individuals, groups, and structure have on behaviour within organizations, for the purpose of applying such knowledge toward improving an organization's effectiveness, (Robbins, 1989: 5).

Note how the author's definition of organizational behaviour is constructed around concern with organizational effectiveness. Implicit in this approach is support for the status quo; existing patterns of organizational ownership and control go unchallenged. Now look at the second quotation taken from a critical approach.

People in organizations are frequently treated in organization theory as either sources of social psychological "problems" or as embodiments of individual needs and dispositions. We eschew this perspective ... in favour of one which stresses the reality of structural divisions in society: notably sexual and class divisions. These are not only of major importance in their own right but are also significantly interrelated. As practices they are in large part reproduced by organizations, particularly in their recruitment strategies and work design. There isn't thus a clear link between labour markets, organization structure and forms of discrimination in society ... (Clegg and Dunkerley, 1980: 6).

In this second quotation the authors' central concern is the impact of organizations on the lives of people, specifically, the relationship between organizations and discrimination. Implicit within this approach is the need for social and organizational change. Unlike the first author who talks about people in an undifferentiated way, these authors talk about people's location within sex and class differentiated groups. Indeed, a hallmark of a critical approach is a focus on organizational disparities of power and opportunity and how this affects women, persons of colour, aboriginal peoples, and/or the working class.

A focus on redressing organizational disparities of power and opportunity is only the starting point of a critical approach. At least four main elements are involved in the process of critical organizational analysis, processes which are as elemental as any school work – comprehension, reading, writing, and acting.

Comprehension: The Many Faces of Organizational Analysis

The first thing to know about any theory of organization is that it is rooted in a particular set of assumptions and way of looking at the world. The work of an organizational researcher is shaped by his or her assumptions about the nature of organizations, and by what he or she hopes to achieve (e.g., organizational efficiency, employment equity, etc.). Thus, understanding the underlying assumptions of a theory of organization can better help us to identify and assess what it has to tell us about people in organizations.

Returning to the two quotes above, we can see that Stephen Robbins studies organizational behaviour in order to "improve an organization's effectiveness." If we look more closely at Robbins' underlying assumptions we find that he believes in the right of managers to "plan, organize, lead, and control" the behaviour of others:

Managers get things done through other people. They make decisions, allocate resources, and direct the activities of others to attain goals ....

Every organization contains people, and it is the manager's job to direct and coordinate these people ....

After the goals are set, the plans formulated, the structural arrangements delineated, and the people hired, trained, and motivated, there is still the possibility that something may go amiss. To ensure that things are going as they should, management must monitor the organization's performance. Actual performance must be compared with the previously set goal. If there is any significant deviation, it is the management's job to get the organization back on track. This monitoring, comparing, and potential correcting is what is meant by the controlling function (Robbins, 1996: 5-7).

There is no questioning of who does what or who should decide the goals, Robbins accepts that organizational managers decide the goals, make the plans, and ensure that other people carry them out.

Stewart Clegg and David Dunkerley, on the other hand, begin with a totally different set of assumptions. As we can see from the quote above, they are interested in understanding how organizations contribute to discrimination by "reproducing sexual and class divisions through recruitment strategies and work design." By questioning the nature of organizations and the way they are run Clegg and Dunkerley set out to address sexual and class divisions in society.

The role of a researcher's underlying assumptions can also be illustrated by reference to the Canadianized versions of the Robbins' textbook.[18] In 1999 Nancy Langton of the University of British Columbia Canadianized Robbins' US textbook and made some important changes. Langton's approach to the text was influenced by the fact that she is a feminist scholar whose research interests include "women and management issues," "pay equity," and "gender equity" (Robbins and Langton, 2004: xxii). Although the Robbins and Langston textbooks still ultimately focus on managers and efficiency they broaden the definitions to allow us to consider that other people may be affected by organizations and may play a role in organizational behaviour. For example, in the 2003 textbook we are told that "OB is for everyone" and that the study of OB is not only "for leaders and managers of organizations [who] often set the agenda for everyone else" but also for employees, entrepreneurs and self-employed people who may "play a proactive role in achieving organizational success" (Robbins and Langton, 2003: 5). We are also told that OB is not just focussed on business organizations but "is relevant beyond the employment situation" and can also be important for those working in daycare centres, voluntary groups, and community organizations (Robbins and Langton, 2003: 4). And OB is not just about understanding the impact of behaviour on management defined outcomes but also on how behaviour impacts on those involved. Thus, OB can be defined as: "a field of study that investigates how individuals, groups, and structure affect and are affected by behaviour within organizations" (Robbins and Langton, 2004: 3). Although none of these works challenge the status quo they are a genuine attempt within mainstream thinking to broaden the field beyond just efficiency and profitability.

Earlier we divided studies of organization into two broad categories depending on their desired outcome or focus: "mainstream" – concerned with organizational efficiency and improvement, and "critical" – concerned with the negative impact of organizational arrangements on people. If we look closely at different theories within each of these broad categories we will find that there are a number of other important distinctions that can be made. This generates at least six main approaches to the study of organization – managerialist, actionalist, radical, feminist, racioethnicity, and post-modernist.

The Managerialist Approach: This approach focuses primarily on the organizational manager and his or her concerns, such as efficiency, effectiveness, profitability, goal attainment, etc. As we can see from the Robbins' quotes above, this approach studies organizational behaviour and structure from the manager's viewpoint.

The managerialist approach to the study of organizations is the oldest and most established of all the approaches. It is sometimes also referred to as the "mainstream" approach because of its predominant acceptance and use in the fields of OB and OT. This dominance is reflected in the great majority of OB and OT textbooks, which represent the managerialist approach as the only approach. This makes it harder for other approaches to gain acceptance as they are, by definition, outside of the mainstream.[19]

What we currently refer to as Organizational Behaviour (OB) and Organization Theory (OT) developed out of a concern with organizational efficiency. Early researchers – such as Frederick Taylor, Henri Fayol, Frank and Lillian Gilbreth, and the Hawthorne Studies researchers – were concerned with finding ways to improve the tasks, behaviour and attitudes of employees to achieve greater efficiency.

Historically, as we discuss in Chapter 3, OT and OB developed out of a set of scholarly pursuits which were designed to assist the development of capitalist enterprises. *Scientific Management* for example, arose out of the needs of employers to increase their employees' efficiency Similarly, the *Human Rela-*

tions approach to organizational behaviour developed out of the concerns of the Western Electric company to improve productivity at their Hawthorne Works in Chicago.[20] These studies and many others contributed to the development of organizational disciplines that were *managerialist* in nature, that is, that take the defined needs of those in charge of organizations as the starting point for the development of research foci and projects.

The Actionalist Approach: This approach focuses on the organizational member and how he or she understands the meaning of organization. It takes its name from the work of David Silverman's (1970) "action frame of reference," which argues that to understand organizations we need to understand the meanings that people attribute to their actions.

This approach is similar to the managerialist approach, in that it is concerned to *document* rather than *challenge* the status quo of existing organizational power arrangements. However, instead of being concerned with managing or improving attitudes and behaviour the actionalist approach is concerned with comprehending how people's beliefs and understandings of a situation help to create an ordered situation. The actionalist approach is similar to that of anthropology, where the behaviours of a group of people are studied to contribute to our knowledge of human behaviour. While the anthropologist tends to study aboriginal peoples, the actionalist researcher studies people in "modern" organizations. Schein (1992; 1987) calls this the "ethnographic approach". A managerialist approach, on the other hand, focuses on analyzing how certain attitudes and behaviours contribute to an organization's efficiency. Schein (1992; 1987) calls this the "clinical approach."

The Radical Approach: This approach takes as its starting point a concern to understand and change the alienating and/or exploitative effects of organizations on people. It covers a range of perspectives from "radical structuralist" to "radical humanist" (Burrell and Morgan, 1979). The difference between the two approaches is a reflection of a major schism in the radical left political groups of the 1960s and '70s. While both ends of the radical spectrum view organizations as spheres of domination and are prepared to challenge managerialism head on, structuralists have been concerned with the *exploitative* character of organizations as "modes of production" or class systems, while humanists have focused on organizations as processes of *ideological* domination. In terms of methodology, radical structuralists are akin to the managerialist approach in taking a *realist* view of life, but humanists are akin to the actionalist approach in focusing on human subjectivity in the creation of meaning: unlike the actionalist approach, radical humanists argue that the negotiation of meaning involves power, with the view of the few dominating the understandings of the many.

The Feminist Approach: In more recent years we have seen the development of feminist organizational analysis which takes as its focus the impact of organizational arrangements on women, and seeks to address issues of gender-based discrimination.

This approach also includes a range of perspectives from the mainstream to the critical. Feminist approaches akin to the mainstream approach accept the underlying managerialist assumptions but seek to *include* more women in the process of management. Feminist actionalist perspectives seek to *add* women's understandings of reality to studies of organization. Radical feminist perspectives seek to *change* the character of organizational arrangements to end the domination of women by men.

Feminist organizational analysis is not simply a female clone or revision of male-developed approaches, it stands as a vibrant new approach on its own. This is especially true in the face of the demise of the old, political left and the continued development of the women's movement, new feminism, and poststructuralist feminism.

The Racioethnicity Approach: Until recently studies of organizations ignored or marginalized issues of race and ethnicity. The almost deafening silence on race and ethnicity has led to the development in recent years of a body of work that focuses on the experiences of people of colour and aboriginal peoples within organizations. This racioethnicity approach[21] seeks to identify and address the discriminatory aspects of organizational practices that serve to exclude certain people from organizations, and from important professional and managerial positions within organizations.

Some racioethnicity research accepts the underlying managerialist assumptions of organizational study and seeks to find places within the system for people of colour. Much of this work has found a place in the recent "diversity management" fad. Other racioethnicity research is focused on challenging the racist (or "post-colonialist") notions inherent in the concept and power structures of organizations and seek to establish different, non-racist, ways of organizing.

The Post-Modernist Approach: This approach is very different from all the others in that *its starting point* is the questioning of underlying assumptions and viewpoints. The postmodernist approach seeks to *expose* the underlying assumptions of organizational theories and practices. It does this in order to encourage people to free themselves from different forms of organizational control.

From a conservative or mainstream postmodernist perspective, this type of analysis can assist managers to identify outmoded attitudes and behaviours, which inhibit their ability to question and challenge themselves and others. The "enlightened" manager is then in a better position to develop more innovative ways of working; ways that may even challenge and question the way the organization does business and the power structures of the organization.

From a radical postmodernist perspective, this type of analysis sets out to reveal organizational and management studies as "disciplinary practices," or powerful sets of ideas rooted in workplace assumptions and associated practices, that serve to define what is ideal or appropriate workplace behaviour. It is argued that disciplines such as Organizational Behaviour (OB), Organization Theory (OT), Human Resources Management (HRM), and various other business subjects shape how managers and employees alike develop ideas about the "ideal" or "typical" employee or manager. These ideas have a powerful influence on who is hired, who is fired, who is promoted and who is passed over. This viewpoint has as a central concern the exposure of the impact that theories of workplace behaviour have on people's sense of self and their ability or power to influence their sense of worth, self-esteem and identity.

By understanding that there are competing views of organizations, rooted in different assumptions and world-views, we can resist accepting as given any particular focus, set of concerns, or "evidence." It also probes us to examine our own underlying assumptions, as we approach the task of critical organizational analysis. Reviewing the various approaches to organizational analysis, we include as *critical* any approach which focuses on organizational change as a means of addressing human oppression. This would include radical, feminist, racioethnicity, and post-modernist theories of organizations.

Reading: Deconstructing the Text

Shulamit Reinharz (1988) argues that most scholarly writing is "embedded" within a dominant perspective, which is capitalist in orientation, as well as patriarchal, homophobic, racist, and ageist. That is, it reflects the thinking of dominant, white, heterosexual, males in society: "to treat scientific writing not only as a source of information as defined by the author, but also as a text revealing something about the author" (p.168).

Figure 1.1: Different Approaches to the Study of Organizational Behaviour and Structure

APPROACH	FOCUS	CONCERN
Managerialist [also known as "mainstream," "functionalist" or "clinical"]	The manager	To understand how behaviour and structure contributes to organizational improvement (e.g., productivity, job satisfaction, growth, survival, etc.)
Actionalist [also known as "interpretive" or "ethnographic"]	The "organizational member"	To understand how people develop a "sense" of organization through a series of behaviours and negotiated meanings, and how that "sense" or understanding contributes to the development and maintenance of the organization.
Radical [sometimes divided into "radical humanist" and "radical structuralist"]	The "worker"	To redress the "exploitation" or "alienation" of workers by exposing how their behaviour and thoughts are shaped and controlled by the structures of organizations and the ideological dominance of those in charge.
Feminist	Women	To identify and address processes of sexual discrimination through study of the impact of individual men, groups of men, and maculinist values and ideas on organizational behaviour, structure and practices.
Racioethnicity	People of colour	To identify and address processes of racial discrimination through investigation of the impact of race and ethnicity, racist and ethnocentric values on organizational behaviour, structure and practices.
Post-Modernist	The individual "subject"	To expose the study of management and organization as a set of ideas rooted in particular notions of work and people.

By reading not only the content, but the underlying assumptions beneath the surface of any text, we can uncover the author's value system and way of looking at the world. This will put us in a much better position to evaluate the book and its contents.

Reinharz indicates a number of ways of approaching the task of *deconstruction*. That is, of attempting to uncover the underlying assumptions of a work:

> Although the passive voice of much scientific writing hides the author's voice to a large extent, clues can sometimes be found in introductions, conclusions, and asides (ibid).

Reinharz suggests that the task of uncovering hidden assumptions involves a thorough examination of texts:

> not in terms of their major arguments, but rather in terms of their asides, illustrations and examples. [Looking] not at what the authors Thought needed explaining, but at what they thought did not – that is, their taken-for-granted assumptions. [This] is a first strategy … facing the preconceptions squarely. Examples writers use reveal the images with which they think and build their arguments. The examples writers offer can be likened to Thematic Apperception Test pictures used by psychologists to trigger their subjects' way of looking at the world [p.163].

Using Reinharz' guide to deconstruction, we are able to get to the bottom of any given OB, Management, or OT text and uncover the hidden assumptions involved. To see how this works in practice, we have drawn examples from texts that are widely used in the US and Canada.

Taken-for-granted Assumptions

In the opening chapter of one text, under a section titled, "What is an Organization?" the author relates the importance of organizations to the everyday life of the reader:

> We know organizations are there because they touch us every day. Indeed, they are so common we take them for granted. We hardly notice that we are born in a hospital, have our birth records registered in a government agency, are educated in schools and universities, are raised on food produced on corporate farms, are treated by doctors engaged in joint practice, buy a house built by a construction company and sold by a real-estate agency, borrow money from a bank, turn to police and fire departments when trouble erupts, use moving

companies to change residences, receive an array of benefits from government agencies, spend forty hours a week working in an organization, and are even laid to rest by an undertaker (Daft, 2001: 5).

At one level this statement is a fairly innocuous listing of areas of social life, which can be related to organizations. It is constructed to show us how organizations impinge on various aspects of our lives. Yet, when we look further into the statement it would seem that its purpose is to convince us of the importance of organization theory, rather than the significance of organizations in the *lives* of people. The overwhelming majority of the text is devoted to the attainment of organizational effectiveness and efficiency.

If we examine the list closer, we find that there are a number of taken-for-granted examples that are somehow meant to be generic and appropriate to all readers. But the fact is that people do not all stand in the same relationship to organizations; many people are not fortunate enough to receive a university education, to buy a house, borrow money from a bank, or be engaged in full-time paid employment. Some people prefer to have their children born and educated at home, some people are more likely to be the subject of police attention, and some people will spend more time resisting organizational control, rather than being in control of organizations.

The author's statement is completely devoid of disparities that arise out of class, ethnic and, gender positions. To take one of those issues – gender, the author's list fails to note that it is females who bear children, while the doctors involved in the delivery are usually males; and that males are more likely to receive a university education and to become a university professor. Furthermore, the task of buying groceries is usually done by women, while it is mainly males who own and manage corporate farms, construction firms and government agencies. The staff of police and fire departments are usually male dominated, and the professions of the priesthood and undertaking are almost exclusively male. Generally, full-time employment remains more characteristic of males than females.

Silences, Exclusions, and Deletions

On race/ethnicity, gender and class, most organizational behaviour, management, and organization theory texts suffer from one or another of three problems:

(i) they have little or nothing to say on race, ethnicity, gender, or class;

(ii) when race, gender, ethnicity and class are mention the issues are often trivialized;

(iii) discussion of race, class, gender and ethnicity is framed from the perspective of the white, male manager.

Race and ethnicity: a review of 107 major business textbooks published between 1959 and 1996 found that only seven dealt with race and ethnicity at "a substantial level", the rest had virtually nothing to say (Mills and Helms Hatfield, 1998: 57). Two of the textbooks that dealt with race and ethnicity were published in the 1980s while five were published after 1995. Clearly the more recent texts are an advance on what has gone before but issues of race and ethnicity tend to discussed through the notion of "diversity management", which is framed from the perspective of the white, male manager (Prasad and Mills, 1997).

In updating this book we reviewed ten of the most popular OB, OT and Management textbooks in use in Canada that were published in the 21st century. We found that four make no reference to race, ethnicity, or even diversity management, one devotes only twelve lines and another less than a page and a half to diversity management. The other four textbooks devote anything from several pages to a whole chapter on diversity management, and one includes a "focus on diversity", which runs through the book. Of the six books that discuss diversity management all assume that "diversity" refers to everyone other than white males. When textbooks talk about managing diversity we need to question who is doing the managing and who is it that is being managed. The following example seems to suggest that it is the white male who is being encouraged to manage women and minorities: "Management can use a number of strategies to help reduce the effects of workplace stereotypes [by selecting] enough minority members to get them beyond token status. [And by encouraging] teamwork that brings minority and majority members together" (Johns and Saks, 2001: 84-85). In varying degrees, the authors of the six textbooks mention humanitarian reasons for "valuing diversity" but they all give centre stage to discussion of the business advantages.

Class: To be clear, the mainstream OB and OT textbook is written from the perspective of the manager. When the business student reads an OB or an OT textbook he or she is being invited to view the organizational world through the eyes of the manager and the employer. From this perspective the employee is seen as problematic. By studying OB and OT you will be able to see how to lead and structure the behaviour of employees, how to motivate, teach, and communicate with them and, above all, how to improve *their* performance. It is not surprising that you are not invited to see the world through the eyes of the employee, except where it might impact on the bottom line (e.g., where diversity, or lack of it, threatens to make the company less competitive). For example, in a text by Johns and Saks (2001) there are recurring sections called "You be the manager" where students are invited to solve a case as if they were the manager. Robbins and Langton's (2003: 5) contention that "OB is for everyone" does not go beyond management control. Instead they view employees as "moving beyond their traditional function of providing labour and play a more proactive role in achieving organizational success... Managers are increasingly asking employees to share in their decision-making processes rather than simply follow orders." How this works in practice can be seen in a Robbins and Langton (2004: 6-7) example of employment at Westjet. Here they state that at "Westjet Airlines Ltd. employees are given lots of freedom to manage themselves... For instance, flight attendants are directed to serve customers in a caring, positive, and cheerful manner. How do they carry that out? It's up to them." Had Robbins and Langton focussed on the employee, in this case the flight attendant, they may have found that Westjet's demands for a specific type of emotion labour leaves little room for employee decision-making and can be highly problematic in terms of emotional and psychological pressures. Arlie Hochschild's (1983) classic study of emotion labour in the airline business provides tremendous insights to the impact of behavioural requirements of the psychic life of those involved, (see also Kane, 1974; Mills, 1995).

Gender: The review of 107 business textbooks published between 1959-1996 mention above also found that "the overwhelming majority – including 18 published in the 1990s – [had] little (65) or nothing (37) to say about women, gender or even sex differences. Only five texts ... discuss the issue of gender in any depth.... The majority of references to gender differences are introduced by way of discussion of employment equity legislation or the "growing number of women in the work force" – with women being depicted in each case as a departure from the male work norm; something of note for male managers." (Mills and Helms Hatfield, 1995: 55).

A more recent review of 128 business textbooks published between 1960 and 2000 examined the extent to which the vast feminist research on work, management and organization is reported. The review found some positive but also some disquieting findings. On the positive side the review concluded that feminist organizational research is being cited in mainstream business texts, and increasingly so since the early 1990s. On the negative side the review concluded, (i) "The majority of selected feminist work was not cited in any business textbook;" (ii) "A substantial number of business textbooks continue to ignore gender;" (iii) "The great majority of those business textbooks that cite feminist research do so in a cursory manner;" and (iv) "Business textbooks take longer to cite feminist organizational research than research from other mainstream organizational approaches" (Mills, 2004). Research on the impact of masculinity on management is entirely absent from the business text.[22]

Examples

Examples are an important learning tool. If the author can find a good example they can more easily get their point across. The problem comes where the example serves to undermine the general point the author is trying to make. Johns and Saks (2001: 83), for example, make the point that "One of the most problematic stereotypes for organizations is the gender stereotype. Considering their numbers in the workforce, women are severely underrepresented in managerial and administrative jobs." Certainly a good point but one that is undermined later on when they quoting approvingly the work of "Wardrobe engineer" John T. Molloy, who argues that the clothing worn by organizational members sends clear signals about their competence, seriousness, and ability to be promoted:

> For [that] reason, Molloy strongly vetoes sweaters for women executives. Molloy stresses that proper clothing will not make up for a lack of ambition, intelligence, and savvy. Rather, he argues that the wrong clothing will prevent others from detecting these qualities. To this end, he prescribes detailed "business uniforms," the men's built around a conservative suit and the women's around a skirted suit and blouse (Johns and Saks, 2001: 320).

Through this example Johns and Saks (2001) reinforce rather than challenge the deep-rooted stereotypes that they had earlier questioned.

Asides

Throw away lines, or asides, tend to reinforce deep-rooted attitudes by giving the appearance that some things are "normal." For example, in attempting to explain the relative success rate of female compared with male entrepreneurs the following texts reinforce the notion that women are *inherently* different from men in their psychological make-up or character:

> Women tend more toward transformational leadership, while men tend more toward transactional leadership (Starke and Sexty, 1995: 400).

A Royal Bank of Canada study estimates that one-quarter to one third of all businesses worldwide are owned by women, and that women now account for half the increase in new businesses each year. Between 1991 and 1994, firms led by women created jobs four times faster than the average of all Canadian companies. Women are more conservative than men in running a small business, and their failure rate is lower than that of men (Griffin, Ebert and Starke, 2002:199).

Women feel less pressured than men to achieve quick results. They a little more cautious, less apt to "shoot from the hip," so they make fewer mistakes. They also accept advice more readily than men, who may have a macho image of having to know it all (Nickels, McHugh, McHugh and Berman, 1994: 172).

Without being preceded by any discussion of gender and socialization, or without any attempt to problematize the notion of gender, statements of this kind – however intended – support the notion that women are *naturally* more conservative than men and than men are *naturally* macho in their behaviour.

Language and Metaphor

Unlike in previous decades, current text books tend to use "gender-neutral" prose but several gendered terms continue in use, such as the use of "middle-men" and "channel captain," and "supersalesman" in one of the texts we examined. Analysis of the various metaphors used, however, indicates a heavy emphasis on male-associated notions of competition and warfare drawn from sports and the military, e.g., from the same text we find the following – "New Technologies *Threaten* Canada Post," "This is forcing the big name national brands … *to fight back*." (Our emphasis, authors).

Illustrations

Finally, we can tell a lot about assumptions by the types of illustrations that a text uses – including photographs, graphics, and cartoons.

Photographs: A study comparing photographic images of males and females in five leading business textbook found that men constituted approximately 76% of all managers, 63% of all professionals and 71% of all non-salaried employees, e.g., construction workers, office clerks, etc. (Mills, 1997a). Of ten textbooks published in the 21st century (see above) the photographic images show men as constituting 71% of managers, 62.5% of professionals, and 51.5% of other non-managerial employees.

Graphic representations: While most of the texts in Mills' 1997 study appeared unproblematic in the use of graphics, one text, in particular, made extensive use of stick figures to illustrate such things as an organization chart, levels of management, functional organization, and span of control – in each case the stick figure is unambiguously male. This was also true of one of the 21st century texts that we examined, which uses stick men on the cover and at the beginning of each chapter (see Moorhead, Griffin, Irving and Coleman, 2000).

Cartoons: Cartoons appear in three of the texts studied by Mills (1997). In a total of twenty-five cartoons males appear in all of them while females appear in 13 (52%); of all the characters shown sixty-two (76.5%) are male and only nineteen (23.5%) are female; eighty-five percent (40) of all managers and professionals are shown as males. Despite the inclusion of some women we are left with the impression that women are not a normal part of the business world (Mills, 1997). In the 21st century texts five or ten used cartoons. In a total of 43 cartoons men appear in all but one (98%), while women appear in only 16 (37%). Just under 83% of managers depicted are men.

Regardless of intentions, silences, asides, examples, taken-for-granted assumptions, and illustrations serve to reinforce stereotypical notions about the respective worth and place of people in organizations depending on their colour, gender, and class origins. By deconstucting the text we can learn something about the character and application of a particular approach to the study of organizations.

Acting: The Praxis of Research

Understanding the different theoretical perspectives and underlying assumptions of various approaches to the study of organizations is one part of developing a critical perspective, developing your own research strategy is the other part.

As we saw earlier in the chapter, much of OT and OB research has developed out of management concerns with efficiency and effectiveness. Management research develops out of direct and indirect responses to perceived management needs. In the first case, research develops in response to specific management needs, as in the case of Western Electric and their Hawthorne Works. In the second case, research aims at answering broad management concerns, for example, motivation, leadership, structure: in this case, researchers usually build on existing theories and attempt to validate or improve on them, to contribute to improved management practice.

Critical organizational research, on the other hand, has arisen out of the concerns of, or with, the organizationally powerless, the less powerful, and the dispossessed; from this perspective, researchers identify and address organizational factors which create or enhance discrimination. Thus, the critical theorist is interested in exposing disparities of power, inequities, degradation, and factors which inhibit human growth, dignity, and potential. Often times critical research arises out a researcher's experiences with or as a member of a disaffected group – women, people of colour, working class.

Here are two contrasting examples of research agendas. The first is a management theorist – Edgar Schein, and the second is by a critical theorist – Ivan Illich.

In his book on *Organizational Culture and Leadership* Schein (1985) is eager to distinguish his "clinical" approach from that of an "ethnographic" one. According to Schein, ethnographers, "for intellectual and scientific reasons," bring to the situation "a set of concepts or models that motivated the research in the first place." The groups being studied "are often willing to participate but usually have no particular stake in the intellectual issues that may have motivated the study" (p. 21):

> In contrast, a "clinical perspective" is one where the group members are clients who have their own interests as the prime motivator for the involvement of the "outsider," often labelled "consultant" … in this context….
>
> Consultants also bring with them their models and concepts for obtaining and analyzing information, but the function of those models is to provide insight into how the client can be *helped*…
>
> I believe that this clinical perspective provides a useful counterpoint to the pure ethnographic perspective, because the clinician learns things that are different from what an ethnographer learns. Clients are motivated to reveal certain things when they are paying for help that may not come out if they are only "willing" to be studied. (Schein, 1985: 21-22).

Schein's ingenious use of the term "client" masks that organizational clients will invariably be management, but the "groups" being studied will almost certainly be employees.

Ivan Illich's interest in organizations was inspired by a different set of concerns – neither clinical nor ethnographic. Illich experienced the oppressive nature of organizations as a child in his native Austria. Anti-Semitic laws forced him – as "a half-Jew" – to flee the country at the age of 15: although his father was Catholic his mother was Jewish. After the Second World War, now a catholic priest, Illich came to the United States and, instead of taking up his theological studies at Princeton University, asked to be assigned to a Puerto Rican parish of New York. Illich had become instantly interested in the plight of the Puerto Ricans and in the next few years worked tirelessly to improve their lot.

His interest in the Puerto Rican people led him to an appointment, in 1956, as the vice-rector of the Catholic University at Ponce in Puerto Rico. That appointment led to involvement on the school board that governed the island's entire educational establishment and here "he was exposed to a new and puzzling vocabulary with terms like 'development,' 'human resources,' 'manpower planning'" (Caley, 1988: 4). Illich came to the conclusion that "planning" was a "new species of the sin presumption":

> The idea of planning as presumption, or pride, as a way of defending ourselves against surprise and against dependence on others would be central to Illich's later analyses of all modern systems (Caley, 1988: 4).

The more Illich was exposed to the school system the more doubts were raised in his mind. Here he explains to David Caley (1988: 4-5) the process which led him to write *Deschooling Society*:

> [It] was quite evident that after ten years of intensive [...] development of the school system in the country which at that moment was a showcase for development ... around the world, in Puerto Rico, schooling was so arranged that half of the students who came from the poorer families had a one in three chance to finish five years of elementary education, which were compulsory. Nobody faced the fact that schooling served, at least in Puerto Rico, to compound the native poverty of that half of children with a new interiorized sense of guilt for not having made it. I therefore came to the conclusion that schools inevitably are a system to produce dropouts, to produce more dropouts than successes, because since the school is open to 16 years, 18 years, 19 years of schooling, it never closes the door on anyone. It produces a few successes and a majority of failures. School really acts as a lottery system in which those who don't make it don't just lose what they had paid in, but for all their life they are stigmatized as inferior.... Schooling I increasingly came to see as the ritual of a society committed to progress and development, creating certain myths which are a requirement for a consumer society.

We can see from this statement that Illich's research was fuelled by an involvement with the poor and a general concern for what institutions can *do* to people. It led Illich to advocate a non-organizational alternative to learning.

Illich's (1981) approach in many ways summarizes the development of critical research – involvement, concern, reflection, action. The foci for many critical researchers arise out of their own experiences, out of involvement with disaffected groups or in struggles to bring about positive change in people's lives. Concern to address the issues that are thrown up in acts of resistance and protest has helped to clarify research foci for many critical researchers. In this way, critical research addresses issues that confront people. The act of writing then becomes a process of reflection and guidance for further action and involvement; this in turn will throw up answers to the questions asked, raise new questions, encourage new research. This process we call praxis – the translation of experiences into ideas, the testing out of those ideas through new experiences, and further reflection on the new experiences. This is the essence of a critical approach.

Writing: Reaching Out and Authorizing

The process of critical research involves a classic irony. It takes place in the context of traditional organizational forms – often with a need to satisfy values rooted in the very organizational problems that the researcher sets out to analyze and review. Grants are usually awarded only to those who appear to be "playing the game," to be operating within the same broad assumptions that inform those in charge of research moneys. For example, a large US corporate-funding body was reluctant to fund a major study of black women in the workplace unless the study included white women. To get the grant the researchers were forced to alter their research plan. In another case, a US federal funding agency refused to fund a conference on feminism and organizational science unless the conference included "prominent," (white) male management theorists from a list provided by the agency.

Organizational constraints play an ever more stringent role when it comes to "disseminating" or writing-up the results of research. Usually the researcher has to find an "approved" academic journal or conference, through which to publish the results. Academic journals in particular but also books contain assumptions about authorship. The writer is expected to adopt an "objective," and "detached" style of writing. In reading the work the reader is in a passive role in which s/he is being talked to by the expert – the author. In effect, the reader is "de-authorized."

This process has obvious implications for the critical writer. The content of the work – which sets out to review inequities – is undermined by a form that helps to recreate inequities. Critical researchers have found various ways around this. In some cases research has been undertaken for groups, such as feminist organizations and trade unions, who usually expect the results to be disseminated in the form of reports and articles in the organization's own press or newsletters and in other cases research has been disseminated through the presses of environmentalists, feminists, socialists, other radical groups and even the columns of the national press. These avenues are important for reaching out to those whom the critical researcher is working with or for.

For the critical researcher in the academic world, whose existence often depends on "academic publication," some efforts have been made to establish journals that publish radical material, for example, *Feminist Review*, and to resist – often unsuccessfully – pressure to publish in prescribed journals. In recent years efforts have been made to address the issue of "authority" in publishing, that is, to write in a way that attempts to authorize and include the reader. This style of writing is still rare but includes an effort by the writer to share something of his- or herself with the reader, to share their doubts about some of the things they are writing about, to avoid "speaking" in a way that indicates a one-way relationship of authority-reader, to raise questions rather than simply to provide answers.

To write in a way that authorizes those reading a work is far from easy but is a surely an important consideration in reporting critical research findings and ideas. For an example of this style of writing you may wish to look at Jane Flax (1990), who attempts to resolve many of the problems of authorship by sharing much about her struggles and concerns in writing the book – including the tragic death of her husband, and by writing in the form of "conversations," that is, counterpoising different views on theories rather than attempting to determine the "truth" in each. In this way those reading the book are involved in the process of making up their own mind. And she reminds us that she is:

> not a neutral participant in or a disinterested facilitator of these dialogues. At least three purposes motivate their evocation: a desire to grasp certain aspects of the texture of social life in the contemporary West; a fascination with questions of knowledge, gender, subjectivity, and power and their interrelations; and a wish to explore how theories might be written in postmodernist voices – nonauthoritarian, open-ended, and process-oriented....
>
> The conversational form of the book represents my attempt ... to (find) one way (among many possible ways) to continue theoretical writing while aban-

doning the "truth" enunciating or adjudicating modes feminists and post-modernists so powerfully and appropriately call into question (Flax, 1990: 3-4).

The book ends appropriately enough with "No Conclusions," a chapter devoted to raising as many doubts about the process of knowledge as the issues in focus:

> A fundamental and unresolved question pervading this book is how to justify – or even frame – theoretical and narrative choices (including my own) without recourse to "truth" or domination […] I do not find it helpful to think about this question in terms of a search for "less false" representations [….] Rather I would argue it is both necessary and difficult to displace truth/falsity with problems of meaning(s)… It is also possible that such yearning for meaning itself reflects experiences in this culture and outmoded ways of thinking. Perhaps it is better only to analyze desires for meaning and to learn to live without grounds (Flax, 1990: 222-3).

Like Flax, we are not neutral or disinterested parties. The object of this book is not to replace one set of truth claims with another but to encourage a questioning of the basis of organizational truth claims.

KEY TERMS

The following are key terms used in the chapter. The review questions below are designed to strengthen your understanding of the terms. Many of the terms are defined in the text of the chapter. The definitions of those in italics found in the *glossary of terms* at the end of the book.

actionalist approach	*ethnicity*	post-modernist approach
authorize	feminist approach	praxis
class	*gender*	*race*
critical approach	mainstream	racioethnicity approach
deconstruction	managerialist approach	radical approach

REVIEW QUESTIONS

The following questions are designed to strengthen your understanding of the chapter, and to encourage you to develop a broader knowledge of critical writ-

ing on organizations. Write short notes in answer to each question. The assignments are designed to allow you to reflect on what you have read so far. The
further study questions, marked "FS," are designed to help you to extend your
knowledge and understanding through long-term study and extra reading.

Q1. Briefly define each of the following terms, and say how each can be relevant to
an understanding of how organizations operate:

- class
- gender
- race
- ethnicity
- praxis

*Assignment: Now turn to the glossary at the end of the book and compare your
definitions.*

Q2. What is meant by a "critical approach to organization study"?

*Assignment: Write down five key factors which would define a "critical" approach and
say how that would differ from a mainstream OB or OT approach.*

[FS: read a chapter or article from the non-fictional lists on pages 29-30. Note how
the author(s) defines his/her approach and compare it with the definition outlined in
Chapter 1 of this book].

Q3. Briefly define each of the following approaches:

- managerialist
- actionalist
- radical
- feminist
- racioethnicity
- post-modernist

*Assignment: Write short notes on each approach and compare and contrast any two –
stating what the major differences and similarities are.*

[FS: read any *one* of the following chapters or articles, and then (a) attempt to assess
which approach is being taken, and (b) detail the problems involved in attempting to
classify research into given "approaches."

Rosabeth Moss Kanter (1977) *Men and Women of the Corporation* Chapter 8.
New York: Basic Books.

Gibson Burrell (1984) "Sex and Organizational Analysis," *Organization Studies*, 5 (2): 97-118.

Gareth Morgan. (1986) *Images of Organization*, Chapter 5. London: Sage.

Linda Smircich (1985) "Is the Concept of Culture a Paradigm for Understanding Organizations and Ourselves?" in P.J.Frost, et al. (eds.) *Organizational
Culture*, pp.55-72. Beverly Hills, CA.: Sage.

Q4. Outline a racioethnicity approach to the study of organizations.

Assignment: In developing a racioethnicity approach, what key factors would be most relevant? List and discuss at least five factors.

[FS: Read one of the articles from the 1990, Volume 11, issue of the *Journal of Organizational Behavior* and, (a) note down five factors which, in your opinion, marks the approach as racioethnicity, and then, (b) compare this article with the article or chapter that you read for question 3. How do the approaches differ? What are the main factors which distinguish one approach from the other?]

Q5. What is meant by the term "deconstruction" and how is it applicable to reading organizational and management theory?

Assignment: From any mainstream organization or management text, analyze some of the pages, chosen at random, and state (a) what you think is absent or silent, (b) what the taken-for-granted assumptions are, and (c) what kinds of message do you get from the illustrations, asides, and/or examples utilized.

Q6. What is the use of studying organizations?

Assignment: Choose a current news item and state how an understanding of organizations might help to address the problem in question.

INTERNET EXERCISES

Q1. Find three strikes that have affected productivity in Canada, the UK, and the US since 1997. How have they been resolved? What was lost, what was gained?

Q2. What is the breakdown of child poverty numbers according to province? What are the unemployment numbers according to province? What conclusions can be drawn, if any?

EXERCISE 1.1

The Paradigms Exercise

Outline: The exercise involves breaking the class into groups representing different organizational approaches. They are then shown a ten minute clip from the movie, *Norma Rae* which they are asked to view and respond to from the point of view of their assigned approach★.

Purpose: The object of this exercise is to strengthen students' understanding of each of the different approaches to organizations and to encourage them to reflect on the relationship between approach and outcome.

Preparation:

(1) Everyone in the class should read the following short introduction to the movie segment from *Norma Rae.*

Introduction to the film clip from the movie, *Norma Rae:*

This Academy Award winning film – staring Sally Field and Ron Leibman – is set in a small mill town in the South. The film focuses on a union organizer from New York (Leibman) who comes to the mill to organize, and the mill-hand Norma Rae (Field) who works with him to organizer her co-workers.

In the selected scene we see the company attempting to divide the employees by pinning up a notice that claims that black workers are behind the union and are seeking to control it. This leads to acts of violence against some black workers. Norma Rae tells the union organizer about the notice and he instructs her to copy it down. He argues that if they can get details of the notice they can use it to take legal action against the company.

Norma Rae attempts to remember the notice and copy it down later but she fails. She is finally forced to stand in front of the notice-board and copy down the offending notice word-for-word. At this point management ask her to stop and, when she refuses, she is taken to the manager's office and fired.

Undeterred Norma Rae returns to the shop floor, writes the words "UNION" in large letters on a piece of cardboard and then, standing on a bench, holds the notice high above her head for all to see. In response, the employees – one by one – switch off their machines in an act of solidarity and support.

Finally, the local sheriff arrives and arrests Norma Rae, and the scene ends.

(2) Divide the class into six groups.

(3) Each group will be assigned to play the role of a group of researchers representing one of the six organizational approaches – managerialist, actionalist, feminist, radical, racioethnicity, post-modernist.

---

* *Note: any suitable case, movie, or television programme can be substituted for Norma Rae.*

(4) The class will then be shown the ten minute clip from the movie, *Norma Rae*, and asked to do the following task:

The Task:

(i) As a group put yourself in the mind-set of a researcher in the assigned organizational approach, i.e., try to think as that person would.

(ii) Watch the video from the point of view of researchers in your assigned approach, i.e., try to view it as they would view the situation.

(iii) Following the viewing discuss what you saw and answer the following questions:

(a) What were the major problems in the workplace that led to unionization and the arrest of Norma Rae?

(b) What improvements would you make to the workplace?

(iv) Report your findings to the class.

(v) During the report-back session other groups should be encouraged to respond from the perspective of their assigned approaches.

Time Limit: 25 minutes for group discussion and 5 minutes report-back time for each group.

CASE ANALYSIS

Get the students to read the Westray Case in advance of the class.

Break the students into groups and assign each group a particular paradigm.

Ask the groups to analyse the case from the point of view of their assigned paradigm and answer the following broad questions:

(a) What were the main problems in the mine that contributed to the eventual disaster?

(b) What could have been done to prevent the disaster?

Time limit: 30 minutes for group discussion an 5 minutes report-back time for each group. Follow up discussion with a general question:

(c) What can we learn from the different paradigms when analyzing organizations?

USEFUL WEB SITES

<http://gilbrethnetwork.tripod.com/gbooks.html>
<www.refdesk.com/factgov.html>
<www.statscan.ca>

FURTHER READING

Here are selected readings. They provide further insights into some of the key points that we have been making, and to encourage creative thinking. Read any or all at your leisure.

On the impact of organization upon our ways of thinking and of living:
Alvin Toffler, (1981). THE THIRD WAVE. Glasgow: Pan.
Gareth Morgan, (1996b). IMAGES OF ORGANIZATION, Chapter 1

Literary images of organizational impact:
Franz Kafka, THE TRIAL
Arthur Miller, DEATH OF A SALESMAN
—— ALL MY SONS
George Orwell, 1984
John Le Carré, THE SPY WHO CAME IN FROM THE COLD
Margaret Atwood, THE HANDMAID'S TALE

The non-organizational alternative:
Ivan Ilich, (1981). DESCHOOLING SOCIETY

An overview of competing approaches:
Gibson Burrell and Gareth Morgan, (1979). SOCIOLOGICAL PARA-DIGMS AND ORGANIZATIONAL ANALYSIS
W.G. Astley and A.H. Van de Ven, (1983). CENTRAL PERSPECTIVES AND DEBATES IN ORGANIZATIONAL THEORY

Albert J. Mills and Stephen J. Murgatroyd, (1991). ORGANIZATIONAL RULES
Stephen R. Corman and Marshall S. Poole (eds.) (2000). PERSPECTIVES ON ORGANIZATIONAL COMMUNI-CATION

On feminist approaches:
J. Hearn, D.L. Sheppard, P. Tancred-Sheriff and G. Burrell (eds.), (1989). THE SEXUALITY OF ORGANIZATION
A.J. Mills and P. Tancred (eds.), (1992). GENDERING ORGANIZATIONAL ANALYSIS
I. Aaltio and A.J. Mills (eds.), (2002). GENDER, IDENTITY AND THE CULTURE OF ORGANIZATIONS

On racioethnicity approaches:
C.P. Alderfer and D.A. Thomas, (1988). "The Significance of Race and Ethnic-ity for Understanding Organizational Behaviour"
Ella Bell and Stella Nkomo, (1992). RE-VISIONING WOMEN MANAGERS' LIVES.
Marta B. Calás and Linda Smircich, (1992b). USING THE "F" WORD: FEMINIST THEORIES AND THE SOCIAL CONSEQUENCES OF ORGANIZATIONAL RESEARCH

Stella Nkomo, (1992). THE EMPEROR HAS NO CLOTHES: REWRITING "RACE IN ORGANIZATIONS"

P. Prasad, (1997). "The Protestant Ethic and the Myths of the Frontier: Cultural Barriers to the Practice of Organizational Diversity"

Anshuman Prasad, (1997a). "The Colonizing Consciousness and Representations of the Other: A Subaltern Critique of Ideology in the Petroleum Industry"

P. Prasad, A.J. Mills, M. Elmes and A. Prasad (eds.), (1997). "Managing the Organizational Melting Pot"

On post-modernist approaches:

S.R. Clegg, (1990). MODERN ORGANIZATIONS. ORGANIZATION STUDIES IN THE POSTMODERN WORLD

J. Hassard and M. Parker (eds.), (1993). POSTMODERNISM AND ORGANIZATIONS

D.M. Boje and R.F. Dennehy, (1992). MANAGING IN THE POSTMODERN WORLD: AMERICA'S REVOLUTION AGAINST EXPLOITATION

B. Townley, (1994). REFRAMING HUMAN RESOURCE MANAGEMENT. POWER, ETHICS AND THE SUBJECT AT WORK

D.M. Boje, R.P. Gephart and T.J. Thatchenkery (eds.), (1996). POSTMODERN MANAGEMENT AND ORGANIZATION THEORY

R. Jacques, (1996). MANUFACTURING THE EMPLOYEE

Mary Jo Hatch, (1997). ORGANIZATION THEORY: MODERN SYMBOLIC AND POSTMODERN PERSPECTIVES

On developing a critical methodology:

Shulamit Reinharz, (1988). FEMINIST DISTRUST: PROBLEMS OF CONTENT IN SOCIOLOGICAL WORK

Marta Calás, (1992a). RE-WRITING GENDER INTO ORGANIZATIONAL THEORIZING

E.L. Bell, T.C. Denton and S.M. Nkomo, (1992). WOMEN OF COLOR IN MANAGEMENT: TOWARDS AN INCLUSIVE ANALYSIS

Liz Stanley and S. Wise, (1983). BREAKING OUT: FEMINIST CONSCIOUSNESS AND FEMINIST RESEARCH

Sandra L. Kirby and K. McKenna, (1989). EXPERIENCE, RESEARCH, SOCIAL CHANGE

Paul Feyeraband, (1975). AGAINST METHOD

G. Morgan (ed.), (1983). BEYOND METHOD

Mats Alvesson and K. Skoldberg, (1999). REFLEXIVE METHODOLOGY: NEW VISTAS FOR QUALITATIVE RESEARCH

Mats Alvesson and Stan Deetz, (2000). DOING CRITICAL MANAGEMENT RESEARCH

Mats Alvesson, (2002). POSTMODERNISM AND SOCIAL RESEARCH (Buckingham, Open University)

Stephen Linstead, Liz Fulop and Simon Lilley, (2004). MANAGEMENT AND ORGANIZATION: A CRITICAL TEXT, London: Palgrave MacMillan.

On case analysis and other learning activities:

A. Mikalachki, D.R. Mikalachki and R. Burke, (1992). GENDER ISSUES IN MANAGEMENT

Gary Powell, (1994). GENDER AND DIVERSITY IN THE WORKPLACE: LEARNING ACTIVITIES AND EXERCISES

—— (2004). MANAGING A DIVERSE WORKFORCE: LEARNING ACTIVITIES

END NOTES

1. A study of 107 Management, OB and OT textbooks that were widely in use in the USA and Canada between 1959 and 1995, found that prior to the mid-1980s twenty-one texts (81%) had nothing to say about race and ethnicity and the remaining five (19%) made only a passing reference to the subject; since 1985 twenty-seven texts (45%) had nothing to say about race, thirty (50%) mentioned the subject in passing and only three (5%) dealt with the subject in any depth. In regard to gender thirty (34%) texts, including nine that were published in the 1990s had nothing to say. Of the remaining texts all but a handful discuss gender in more than a cursory fashion (Mills and Helms Hatfield, 1998). In an up-dated study of 128 texts published between 1960 and 2000 it was found that despite the growth of feminist studies of organization and discrimination very little of that research was reflected in management textbooks (Mills, 2004).

2. More commonly referred to as "The Abella Commission" after its chair, Judge Rosalie Silberman Abella.

3. In 2001 there were just under 1 million people (or 3.3%) in Canada who were classified as persons of "aboriginal identity." "Visible minorities" in Canada numbered just under 4 million people, or 13.4% of the population. Of these the largest ethnic groups are "Chinese"(over 1 million people, or 3.4%), "South Asian" (over 900,000 or 3%), and "Black" (just under 700,000 or 2.2%). See Statistics Canada on line <http://www.statcan.ca/english/Pgdb/demo41.htm>.

4. In 2001 women constituted 51% of the population of Canada. See Statistics Canada on-line <http://www.statcan.ca>

5. Arguably, the influence of AASCB accreditation rules has influenced the production of textbooks, many of which now include sections on "workplace diversity." In recent years the organization has broadened its efforts to university accreditation in Australia, Europe and Canada. In 1997 the AACSB changed its name to the Association to Advance Collegiate Schools of Business, dropping the word "American" in order to appeal to an audience beyond the US.

6. For example, between 1980-1999, on average, 52% of Canadian employees took time off because of work related injuries <http://info.load-otea.hrdc-drhc.gc.ca> and yet OB/OT text books have had little or nothing to say on this.

7. Compiled from a variety of sources including <http://www.fromthe wilderness.com/free/ww3/02_11_02_

lucy.html>; Michael Elliot, "Secret History of the September 11 Failure," *The Sunday Telegraph*, Sept. 1, 2001 edition, pp. 14-17; Ted Bridis, "FBI Admits it missed suspected terror e-mail," National Post, (Canada), 30 August, 2002 edition, p. A10; Gavin Hewitt, "Nasty's voice cracks: "I don't know what we could have done to get there quicker," *The Sunday Telegraph*, Sept., 1, 2001 edition, p.9; Jim Defede, "An oasis of community in a world of upheaval," National Post (Canada), 31 August, 2002 edition, p. B1; Clarke (2004).

8. See for example the following website devoted to news coverage of events leading up to the crisis <http://www.fromthewilderness.com/free/ww3/02_11_02_lucy.html>.

9. See Elliot, op cit.

10. Michael Elliot, op cit., p.14.

11. Ibid.

12. See <ombwatch@ombwatch.org>.

13. The United States and Canada have the two highest rates of child poverty of any "developed" nation and the rate is on the increase. "Since 1989, when the House of Commons passed a unanimous resolution to "…seek to eliminate child poverty by the year 2000", poverty among children has increased by 21%. (As of 2003) one in six children, or1,139,000 children, still lives in poverty in Canada." <www.campaign2000.ca>.

14. Bankruptcies in Canada have been steadily rising since the mid-1980s when approximately 10,000 companies went out of business each year (Schafer, 1997). In 2001 the total number of business bankruptcies for Canada was just over 4 billion<http://strategis.ic.gc.ca/>. Consumer Bankruptcies went up by 7.2%, Canadian Business Bankruptcies dropped by 7.6% <www.bankruptcycanada.com>. Commenting on the fact that bankruptcies are a growing fact for individuals as well as businesses Bankruptcy Canada.com notes that: "One of the most significant changes in bankruptcies over the last few years is the remarkable decline in business bankruptcies and the even more remarkable increase in the consumer bankruptcy rate. The chart, below illustrates this. In the years 1990 to 2002 business bankruptcies declined 19%, while consumer bankruptcies, in the same period increased a whopping 83%!" (ibid).

15. From "Watergate" in the 1970s and "Whitewater" in the 1990s, to "Enron" at the beginning of the twenty first century, scandals have been associated with the highest levels of government and business in the United States. Canada has had more than its own share of government scandals. One of the worse cases occurred in 1996 and led to the arrest of twelve members of former Saskatchewan premier Grant Devine's Conservative government. Of the twelve arrested six were found guilty and jailed for defrauding taxpayers of more than $837,000. In 2000, Jane Stewart, then Minister of Human Resource Development of Canada (HRDC), was involved in a scandal concerning the mismanagement and misspending of funds for job creation programmes. At the time of writing, the Liberal government of Paul Martin has

been racked by a sponsorship scandal. The Auditor General's Report for 2004 indicated that senior federal government officials responsible for advertising and sponsorship contracts for Via Rail, Canada Post, the RCMP, the Business Development Bank of Canada and the Old Port of Montreal, had not only wasted money but had shown disregard for rules. The result was the mishandling of millions of dollars in the period since 1995 to the present. The Auditor General went on to comment: "I think this is such a blatant misuse of public funds that it is shocking. I am actually appalled by what we've found." The Report led to calls for a public enquiry and resulted in the immediate firing of former Minister of Public Works Alfonso Gagliano, from his position as the Canadian Ambassador to Denmark.

In terms of corruption, the business world has not been left behind – as witnessed by the activities of the chief executives of Enron in 2001, or the fall of Barings Bank in the mid 90's. These cases of business corruption have done for the new millennium what Watergate did for political corruption in the 1970s. Sadly the much publicized arrests of Ivan Boesky (insider trading) and Michael Milken (corrupt junk bond deals) did not put an end to stock market crime or corrupt trading practices. In October 1996, for example, the US *Federal Bureau of Investigation* (FBI) cracked down on stock fraud by arresting 46 "securities fraud suspects" in Manhattan – including Canadian Daryl Buerge of Cam-Net Communications Network, Inc., who

was charged with conspiracy to commit securities fraud. According to Michael Don, the President of Securities Investor Protection Corp., stock fraud has become a permanent part of the North American securities landscape: "over the last decade there has been an average of six failures a year in US. securities firms and almost all of them as a result of fraud" (quoted in the Financial Post, October 19/21, 1996). More recently, in 2004, we have witnessed the trial of Martha Stewart for fraud and insider trading. In Canada, as a result of the arrest of Daryl Beurge, the Vancouver Stock Exchange suspended trading in Cam-Net shares. Two years earlier the previous president of the company, Robert Moore, had been cited for trading millions of dollars worth of shares without filing insider trading reports. Insider trading and other corrupt trading practices hit Canadian headlines on several other occasions in 1996. In February the chairman of B.C. Hydro, John Laxton, was fired for insider-investment, while in August the *B.C. Securities Commission* found former premier Bill Bennett, his brother Russell and lumber baron Herb Doman guilt of insider trading. In November the Veronika Hirsch case hit the headlines. In August Hirsch, a fund manager at AGF Management Ltd., was recruited by rival Fidelity Investments Canada Ltd. to run their *True North Fund*, but three months later she was the centre of a trading scandal when it was reported that she had engaged in unethical practices by not disclosing a personal trade that had netted her a quarter of a million dollars.

In 1996 and more recently in 2004, both the US and the Canadian military, plagued by a series of problems that included murder, torture, sexual harassment, and hazing, joined the front ranks of institutional scandals.

16. The Commission for Labour Cooperation reported that strikes in Canada had on average resulted in 2.3 million "person-days lost" per year due to 394 work stoppages during the period1989-2002. (The Commission for Labour Cooperation, 2003). That figure, which resulted from 394 work stoppages, took into account the growing large-scale strikes that hit Canada during the last five years of the century: in 1995 a dispute over job security closed down Canada's rail system; in 1996 a large-scale strike hit General Motors Canadian plants as close to 30,000 autoworkers struck over outsourcing and job security; in 1997 it was the turn of airline pilots at four of Air Canada's feeder airlines in Nova Scotia, Quebec, Ontario and B.C., this time over seniority rights.

17. Environmental pollution is perhaps *the* most serious issue facing the world today. Concerns with "global warming," damage to the ozone layer, the destruction of the rain forests, and numerous other threats to the environment have led, in recent years, to several high-level conferences of different governments from across the globe. In 1997, industrialised nations got together to form the Kyoto Accord, which proposed to limit world gas emissions that are thought to be the cause of the overheating of the Earth's atmosphere. Although Canada agreed to the ratification of the Kyoto accord and has promised to reduce emissions over the next 10 years, the US has refused to sign the accord because, according to George W. Bush, it will harm the US economy. Not surprisingly, the biggest opponents to the accord are car manufacturers.

In the meantime pollution continues to be a serious problem. In Canada one of the chief contaminants is PCBs. The problem with PCB storage is that the longer they remain intact the greater the risk of disasters, such as the 1988 fire at a PCB storage warehouse in St-Basile-le-Grand, which led to the evacuation of the town. Concerns surrounding the safe disposal of PCBs again came to the attention of the Canadian public in a big way in 1996. Early in the year, testing at the Sydney, Nova Scotia tar ponds identified nearly 45,000 tonnes of PCB-contaminated sediment instead of the 13,000 tonnes that had been expected. Although the tar ponds have been described as one of Canada's worst toxic waste sites, nothing has been done to compensate or remove residents who live near the ponds (Canadian Press Newswire, June 23, 1996). By August 2001, 36 sewage outfalls were still pouring 13 million litres of untreated waste into the ponds daily. In December 2001, a federal and provincial report concluded that the tar ponds were as safe as any other urban part of the province <http://cbc.ca/news/indepth/background/tar_ponds.html>. In 2004, the clean up is far from complete The tar ponds, which have been described as one of Canada's worst toxic waste sites are finally being cleaned up, in what is being called by the Nova Scotia government as "Canada's most ambitious environmental remediation project <http://www.gov.ns.ca/stpa/>.

18. "Canadianization" refers to the process where a Canadian (or Canadian-based) scholar transforms an existing US textbook to make it more appropriate to Canadian audiences. This can involve anything from changing the places names (e.g., from Chicago to Toronto), the cases, and the examples, through to a major rewrite to capture Canadian social and political life (e.g., inserting Canadian terms, history, geography, bilingualism, Canadian ways of relating to other countries, etc.).

19. The almost total exclusion of other theories of organization led Gibson Burrell and Gareth Morgan (1979) to write a book arguing for acceptance of other approaches as equally legitimate ways of viewing organization. The book has since had a powerful influence on the categorization of different approaches according to their underlying assumptions: classifying theories as functionalist, interpretive, radical humanist and radical structuralist.

20. Rose (1978) provides a fascinating history of management thought and the links with capitalist development and interests.

21. The term "racio-ethnicity" was coined by Cox (1990).

22. For an understanding of some of the problems of men and masculinities see Collinson and Hearn (1996), Maier (1997), Miller (2002), Mills (1998a), and Wicks and Mills (2000).

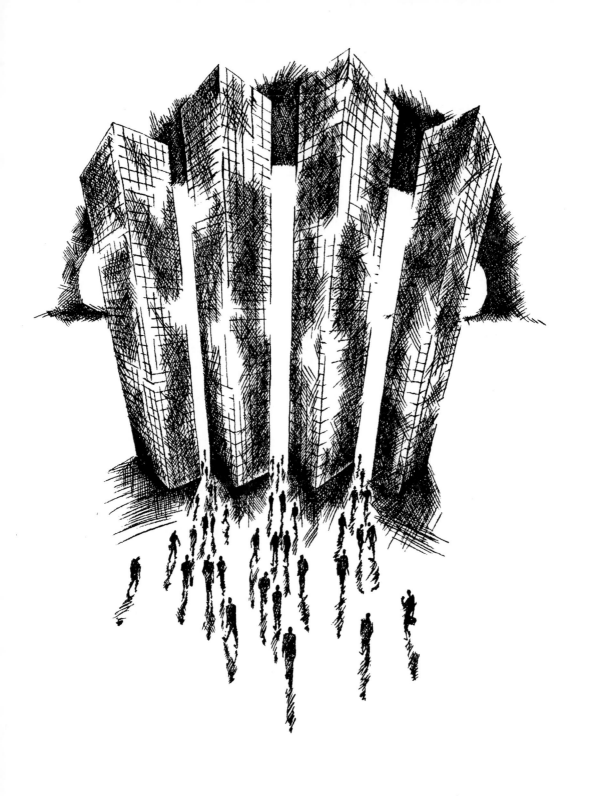

CHAPTER 2

Understanding Bureaucracies: The Age of the Organizational Giants

This chapter examines the character of the bureaucratic phenomenon and its implications for understanding the nature of modern organization. By way of an historical framework, the reader is encouraged to analyze the relationship between social thought, social divisions, and organizational structure. The objective is to provide the reader with a basic vocabulary of organizational analysis (viz. rationalization, bureaucracy, centralization, hierarchy, etc.) while challenging him/her to think about the impact of bureaucracy upon social structure (the way we organize), organizational outcomes (efficiency), and social life (our sense of self, identity, public/private divisions).

The Dark Side of Bureaucracy[1]

On May 3rd of 2001 the Ontario Government announced the introduction of mandatory drug testing for welfare recipients. Recipients were also tested for literacy skills. Those who refused to cooperate with either the drug testing or literacy programs were refused assistance. The program had previously been announced in "Blueprint," the election platform of the Progressive Conservative Party of Ontario, where it was argued, "It's common sense — you can't get off welfare and hold a job if you're addicted to drugs."

The measure was opposed by a number of organizations including the Canadian Civil Liberties Union, the Ontario Federation of Community Mental Health and Addiction Programs, the Psychiatric Patient Advocate Office (PPAO), and the Canadian Union of Public Employees (CUPE).

The issues raised included concerns about the "intrusiveness of the test-ing," the "arbitrary" nature of the testing that was "imposed on one class of people," the problem of "tying a person's income to their cooperation with mandatory drug testing." CUPE pointed out that caseworkers were "ap-palled by this latest attack on Ontario's most vulnerable citizens," arguing that "drug testing is an abuse of human rights." The union argued that if the government was "really serious about helping people on welfare, it would reduce the number of families each caseworker has to work with each and every day. If there were more caseworkers, they'd be able to assist people get the counselling and training they need."

INTRODUCTION

For many members of our society, bureaucracies – especially government bu-reaucracies – are objects of resentment, and even of fear. As the story above shows, even a lawful and commonplace activity such as applying for welfare assistance, can become an intimidating and demoralizing experience for those who make these applications. For in this bureaucratic world, welfare officials and welfare applicants, (or recipients), meet each other on very unequal terms: the former possesses all the power and authority while the latter possesses none. It is a world in which bureaucrats exercise very real power over the lives of their clients, and where the final word of these officials often acquires the force of law. Because of this political inequality, welfare applicants often find that they must humble themselves before officials, and tolerate violations of their privacy and self-respect that would be unthinkable in any other social situation.

Of course, the welfare department is not the only bureaucracy where the lines of authority are clearly drawn between bureaucrat and client, or where the lives of individuals may be deeply affected by the decisions of bureaucratic of-ficials. Other bureaucracies in our society may exercise powers, which are far greater than those of the welfare bureaucracy.

The Department of Indian and Northern Affairs, for example, has tradition-ally administered and controlled all aspects of the lives of registered Indians in Canada. It has exercised the power to confer or to withhold registered Indian status, to disburse treaty payments, and to provide funding for local bands. In earlier times, Indian agents, as officials of the Indian Affairs bureaucracy, also exercised the power to grant voting rights, to ship Indian children off to residential schools, to keep alcohol off the reserves, and even to authorize the travel of Indians away from the reserves. Looking back on the colonial aspects of Indian policy in Canada, many of us would be tempted to say that the traditional power that the Indian Affairs bureaucracy exercised over Indian people was nothing less than totalitarian in its scope and application (Ponting, 1986; Ponting, 1997; Ponting, Gibbins and Siggner, 1980).

Similarly, the Department of Immigration, as another government bureaucracy, has also exercised tremendous power over the lives of individuals. This has included the power to issue or withhold admission rights to individuals at ports-of-entry; the power to facilitate family re-union; and the power to issue and enforce deportation orders. Consequently, resentment and fear of this bureaucracy has not been uncommon among those immigrants who have experienced first-hand the arbitrary use, or even abuse, of power at the hands of immigration officials.[2]

Whether we use the dramatic examples of Welfare, Immigration, or Indian Affairs; or whether we use the more benign examples of Revenue and Taxation, or Motor Vehicles, there is no doubt that bureaucracies wield considerable power in our society. They have become a force to be reckoned with. And although most of our examples have been drawn from government bureaucracies, it should not be forgotten that private sector bureaucracies can also make decisions which, in some circumstances, may make or break our lives in different ways. One has only to think about the power which banks and insurance companies exercise over our financial lives; or the power exercised by large corporations such as Canadian Pacific, General Motors, Imperial Oil, or Air Canada over the livelihoods of hundreds of thousands of Canadian workers. There is no escape from the power of bureaucracies in the modern world. For as one observer has suggested:

> Bureaucracy is like sin – we all know something about it, but only those who practice it enjoy it. Ordinary people tend to be against both, and experts on the subject tend to become obsessed, so that some see bureaucracy everywhere as fanatical clerics see sin up every back alley. If you hold that all sex is sin, you simply mean you wish you had never been born; if you believe all bureaucracies are degenerate you are simply registering a protest against modern society (Chapman, 1961)

In this chapter, we shall look at some of the different images of bureaucracy which have appeared at various times in the writings of both popular and scholarly authors. Bureaucracies have been lambasted and lampooned, but they have also been celebrated and idealized. Some writers have seen them as dark and sinister forces carrying the seeds of totalitarianism and oppression. Other writers have seen them as models of rationality and efficiency, which characterize the evolution of modern organizations. But whether they are viewed as forces of light or forces of darkness, most images of bureaucracy have, until recently, told us little or nothing about the role of gender, ethnicity or class in modern organizations. Most of the work on organization and bureaucracy has remained strangely silent in these important areas. Part of the task of this chapter is to speak to these traditional silences of organizational theory.

But in order to begin our discussion, let us start by looking at the impact that large organizations have had on the lives of all of us, not only in this country, but all over the world.

LIVING IN A BUREAUCRATIC WONDERLAND

Modern organizations are an inescapable part of our everyday experience. Whether we live in crowded cities or in outlying rural parts of the country, all of us remain dependent upon organizations for most aspects of our lives. Many of us belong to a number of different organizations such as trade unions, chambers of commerce, political parties, churches, ethnic organizations, school boards, hunting and fishing societies, or provincial motor associations. Membership in these organizations helps to give our lives meaning and purpose.

We don't have to join organizations, however, in order for them to exercise a pervasive influence over our lives. We depend upon organizations for the production and distribution of essential goods and services, for our information, communication and transportation; indeed, for all activities which require the cooperation of groups and individuals in our society. Only an imaginary Robinson Crusoe, isolated and entirely self-sufficient, could remain independent of the pervasive web spun by organizations in the modern world.

Today, the role of large organizations in our society, in both the public and private sectors of our society has increasingly come into question. And while no one can deny that the efficiencies of these large organizations have made possible the unprecedented economic and technological development of the twentieth century, there is a growing popular awareness that the tremendous power and influence wielded by these organizations may already be threatening some of our basic social and political values, especially those of individual liberty and political democracy.

Although the nightmare visions of George Orwell's *1984* and Aldous Huxley's *Brave New World* have, so far, failed to materialize in our society, the disturbing growth in the control which centralized bureaucratic organizations exercise over our lives leaves little cause for complacency. Most of us are unaware of how much information about our personal finances, taxes, travel, politics, hospital records, telephone calls and citizenship status is routinely collected and shared among the giant corporations and public bureaucracies in our society. Indeed, the ability of modern organizations to collect and store essential information on individuals led one writer to refer to these modern trends as "friendly fascism" (Gross, 1985). Whether we like it or not, most of us now live in societies in which many aspects of our lives are controlled by large organizations.[3]

Large organizations have played an important part in the development of both capitalist and socialist societies. In our own society, we have seen the trend towards the growth of big business on a national and international level. Sometimes the growth of big business is accomplished by swallowing up competitors through corporate take-overs or other amalgamations. When this happens, we often begin to talk about the development of monopolies, or even oligopolies, in certain industries where a few large corporations have become dominant. Many consumer advocates, and even some economists, have warned that when a few big businesses take control of an industry, competition becomes a thing of the past. With the decline of real competition in the marketplace, the power that consumers once had to shop elsewhere is slowly lost, for where else can you go when one or two large companies run the only game in town? Even without fully realizing it, the traditional characterization of the "free enterprise system" – as a system based on "free and fair competition," has long been undermined by the growth of big business and its market dominance.

In the former socialist societies, large organizations played an even greater role in the political, economic and technological development of those societies. Large, state-run organizations were used by socialist governments to rapidly industrialize underdeveloped regions of their countries, sometimes bringing impressive material achievements to those societies. At the same time, those same state-run organizations also helped to build up harsh police states and oppressive bureaucratic regimes. The crumbling of the Berlin Wall, and the fall of the Communist governments in Eastern Europe and the USSR have shown how hated these regimes were. If anything helped to bring about their downfall it was the all-pervasive nature of the state bureaucracies.

WHAT IS BUREAUCRACY?

Virtually all large organizations in the modern world are run as bureaucracies. These may be government-run bureaucracies such as Revenue Canada or the Department of Indian and Northern Affairs; corporate bureaucracies such as The Bay, or Air Canada; or even non-governmental bureaucracies such as the Roman Catholic Church or Alcoholics Anonymous. What all these institutions have in common is that they are run according to bureaucratic principles of organization.

When people hear the term "bureaucracy", they are likely to think of all the bad experiences they have had with large organizations, especially with government agencies. Trying to collect an unemployment cheque from a Canada Employment and Immigration Centre, filling in tax returns for Revenue Canada, nominating relatives for immigration to Canada: most of us have had some frustrating and time-wasting experiences with government bureaucracies. It's hardly surprising then, that for many people the term "bureaucracy" conjures up images of "red tape," lost files, unanswered letters, forms in triplicate, unsympathetic officials, and general hassles with authority. More than anything else, the term "bureaucracy" has come to mean inefficiency.

Within mainstream organization theory, however, the term, "bureaucracy", has a more technical and a more neutral meaning. It refers to the way in which an institution is organized irrespective of whether it is a government agency or a private business. Part of the meaning of the term, "bureaucracy," can be seen from its roots in "bureau" (a writing desk, or an office), and "cracy" (a form of government). A shorthand definition of bureaucracy could well be: "government by the paper-pushers," as well as "government by office holders."

When mainstream theorists talk about bureaucracy what they have in mind is a large and complex formal organization, which is organized through an elaborate division of labour, under a hierarchical structure of authority, and which operates according to explicit rules and procedures. While this is a rather general definition, it shows how theorists are mainly concerned with the principles of organization, which characterize bureaucracies. Bureaucratic organization has developed as something of an enigma in the modern world. On the one hand, bureaucracies have suffered from a bad press, with many people associating bureaucracy with inefficiencies. Yet, on the other hand, we have witnessed a tremendous growth in the development of bureaucratic organization by the very fact that managers have associated bureaucracy with organizational efficiency, i.e., the ability to process a large number of organizational factors, within a relatively short time. The high degree of routinization, specialization, formalization, and standardization that can be obtained through bureaucratic organization has allowed managers to achieve certain tasks in ways that reduce duplication (each person has a specific function to perform), training and orientation (each person learns a standard and formal way of doing things), costs (the cheapening of jobs by breaking them down into routine elements), time (routinization and standardization assists people to undertake their tasks in a simple and quick way), and control (bureaucratic rules and regulations replace the need for a series of overseers and supervisors). As we shall see later, these "efficiencies" are often achieved at great human costs to employees. The dilemma is that without bureaucracies the processing of a number of services would make life more difficult and cumbersome for many of us.

An every day example of a bureaucracy in Canada is the Motor Vehicles Branch run by provincial governments. These offices are streamlined for processing large numbers of people and large amounts of information on a routine basis. Although hundreds of motor vehicle applications are made every day, for most of us, this transaction only takes a few minutes to complete. When it comes to the mass processing of people and information, bureaucracies are often the most efficient organizations for the job.

This is not to deny that some people do experience problems when dealing with bureaucracies – especially with government bureaucracies. But when we think of the large numbers of people, and the enormous amounts of information which are processed every day in an efficient and routine manner by most government bureaucracies, the problem cases may be seen as exceptions to the general trend of efficiency within these organizations. We shall return to the problems of bureaucracy later in this chapter.

NOW TURN TO EXERCISE 2.1 AT THE END OF THE CHAPTER

THE BIRTH OF BUREAUCRACY IN CLASSICAL
ORGANIZATION THEORY

The growth of large bureaucracies in the modern world first attracted the attention of prominent European social thinkers during the nineteenth and early twentieth centuries. Karl Marx, Max Weber and Robert Michels were all keenly aware that in modern industrial societies, there had been a rapid growth in the size and complexity of organizations. At the same time, however, each of these social thinkers had his own views about the future of bureaucratic organizations in modern society.

Karl Marx believed that the growth of bureaucracy in government and the civil service was directly related to the rise of the capitalist state. The real purpose of the state and its bureaucracy, he believed, was to defend the economic interests of the capitalist ruling class against the attempt of other social classes – especially the working class – to seize political power. For Marx, then, the state bureaucracy, including the bureaucrats who worked as part of it, was seen as an essential part of the system of capitalist domination, which would disappear after the overthrow of capitalism and the victory of socialism. Marx expected that the state bureaucracy would diminish and eventually disappear from socialist society because the working class would take over direct control of its own political and economic institutions. Bureaucracy, for Marx, was a sign that workers were alienated from the centres of economic and political power, which were being run by the capitalist class in its own interests. With the introduction of socialism and the advent of a democratic working class government, Marx believed that the working class would run its own affairs directly, and thus the need for bureaucracy would disappear (Marx, 1999; Marx and Engels, 1967).[4]

Other Marxists such as Lenin also believed that the growth of bureaucracy in modern society was a temporary and transitional phase, which would come to an end with the victory of socialism. In fact, Lenin predicted that eventually, under communism, there would be a "withering away of the state," or, in other words, the gradual disappearance of the bureaucratic institutions of government (Lenin, 1927; 1992). When we look back today, however, at the development of socialism in the USSR and in Eastern Europe, it is clear that Marx' and Lenin's forecasts were unrealistically optimistic and even utopian in their expectations.

If the Marxists were overly optimistic about the eventual disappearance of bureaucracy, Max Weber was decidedly more pessimistic in his outlook. He believed that the growth of large bureaucracies in the modern world was part of a general historical trend towards greater rationalization – by which he meant the tendency for people to evaluate events, circumstances, and other people in calculative terms, the logic of mean-ends in which people weigh up and value things according to a perceived balance of what they put in against what they can get out of a situation. For Weber, this found its supreme expression in the development of organizational forms, bureaucracies, in which the logic of calculability is translated into its organizational form- efficiency, i.e., the drive to achieve the maximal ends with the least expenditure of time and energy. This drive for efficiency, in turn, according to Weber, reinforces the process of rationalization (Weber, 1948; Weber, Parsons and Giddens, 1992). As we shall see later, Weber's concept of "rationality" has since been challenged as reflecting male-associated values (Martin, 1990).

Max Weber believed that in the modern world – characterized by the logic of rationality – all organizations are under constant pressure to become more and more efficient. This is true not simply for business enterprises or governments, but for all organizations in society including churches, universities, political parties, the armed forces, dating services, and even the local McDonald's.[5] In a culture of rationalization no organization remains untouched by the constant pressures for greater efficiency.

Weber suggested that most organizations adapt to the pressures for greater efficiency by introducing bureaucratic principles of organization. The bureaucracy is the hallmark of efficiency in modern society and is the best example of an organization based on what Weber calls the "rational-legal" type of authority.

In addition to analyzing the bureaucracy in terms of efficiency, Weber was also interested in it as an institution of authority. Unlike other types of authority which are based either on traditional hereditary institutions like the monarchy, the nobility and the church, or on the personal authority of charismatic individuals like religious prophets or political leaders, the bureaucracy is based on the institutions of rational-legal authority. This last type of authority, according to Weber, is distinguished by its use of impersonal rules of administration, and by the fact that authority is linked to office held rather than to the person of the office holder. The bureaucracy, more than any other institution, epitomizes this rational-legal form of authority.

According to Weber, the modern bureaucracy is based on a set of organizational principles, which distinguish it from more traditional forms of organization. Taken together, these principles provide a complete description of a hypothetical bureaucracy, or what Weber calls "an ideal-type," although he concedes that it is unlikely that any actual bureaucracy in the real world would follow all of these principles.

Weber's ideal type of bureaucracy is a hypothetical model, or a template, which can be used to study actual organizations in the real world. When examining modern organizations, we can always see how closely they correspond to, or depart from, the general principles of bureaucratic organization outlined in Weber's hypothetical model.

Weber suggested that the modern bureaucracy was run according to a general set of principles, which distinguished it from earlier, or pre-modern, organizations. He outlined six general principles of bureaucratic organization.

1. EACH OFFICE IN A BUREAUCRACY HAS A CLEARLY DEFINED SPHERE OF COMPETENCE; AND BUREAUCRATIC OFFICIALS ARE ONLY SUBJECT TO AUTHORITY WITH RESPECT TO THEIR OFFICIAL OBLIGATIONS.

In other words, all bureaucracies are organized around a specialized division of labour. The work of a modern organization is divided among all its members, so that each member performs a highly specialized task. Canada Post, for example, divides its work among letter carriers, mail sorters, counter clerks, supervisors and so on. Everyone becomes a cog in the organizational machine.

2. OFFICIALS IN A BUREAUCRACY ARE ORGANIZED IN A CLEARLY DEFINED HIERARCHY OF OFFICES.

In other words, besides having a specialized division of labour, bureaucracies also have a system of authority, which flows downwards from the top of the organization. This is the official chain of command in which the highest officials in the organization have the most authority. All officials in the organization give orders to those immediately below them, and accept orders from those immediately above them. In other words, all bureaucracies are arranged in an elaborate pecking-order.

3. ADMINISTRATION IS BASED UPON WRITTEN DOCUMENTS; THE BODY OF OFFICIALS ENGAGED IN HANDLING THESE DOCUMENTS AND FILES, MAKE UP THE "BUREAU" OR "OFFICE".

In other words, bureaucracies are run according to an elaborate set of written rules and regulations. These may be manuals of technical instruction which have to be followed to the letter, as in the case when auto mechanics, or computer technicians, service and repair high technology equipment. Or there may be procedural or policy manuals used by government officials to process applications for unemployment benefits, accident compensation, immigrant visas, child allowances, and so on. Bureaucracies are notorious for their paperwork, and for following written rules and regulations to the letter. But it should be noted that written rules are designed for efficiency (everyone can learn the same rules), and for equity (everyone is treated according to the same rules). There are supposed to be no favourites in bureaucracies: everyone is treated the same.

4. ADMINISTRATION IS BASED UPON GENERAL RULES AND REGULATIONS WHICH ARE ENFORCED IN AN OBJECTIVE AND IMPERSONAL MANNER.

In other words, people who work for bureaucracies, whether for the Motor Vehicles Branch, or for The Bay, relate to each other primarily as office-holders and only secondarily as individuals. This means that people are defined first and foremost in terms of the jobs they do rather than who they are as people. People may come and people may go in a bureaucracy, but the jobs remain to be done as long as the organization survives. All of this results in the fact that people usually treat each other in a formal and impersonal manner because it is their jobs, which bring them together rather than friendship, or common interests. Similarly, people who work in bureaucracies usually try to treat their clients, (members of the public), in a formal and impersonal manner – as "cases" rather than as unique individuals. If everyone is to be treated the same, then everyone will be treated impersonally.

5. CANDIDATES ARE APPOINTED ON THE BASIS OF TECHNICAL QUALIFICATIONS, BY EXAMINATIONS OR DIPLOMAS, CERTIFYING TECHNICAL TRAINING.

In other words, people who work for bureaucracies are normally hired because of their training, qualifications and experience for the job: their technical expertise. Most bureaucracies will claim to hire people on the basis of their knowledge and their skills, and not for their personal qualities.

6. OFFICES WITHIN A BUREAUCRACY ARE VIEWED AS PROFESSIONAL CAREERS. PROMOTION IS BASED UPON SENIORITY OR ACHIEVEMENT, OR BOTH.

In other words, bureaucracies offer their members the chance for long-term careers. With the proper training and experience, it is usually possible for staff to move up the rungs of the organizational ladder. Workers in a bureaucracy are heavily dependent upon the organization for their long-term employment. The bureaucracy may protect its job security through seniority rules, and may even open up new career paths to other positions within the organization.

For Max Weber, then, these six principles of organization typified the modern bureaucracy, and distinguished it from more traditional forms of organization found in pre-modern societies. This is not to suggest that Weber believed that all modern bureaucracies are organized according to each and everyone of these principles; only that these principles are represented in the typical bureaucracy.

THE BUREAUCRATIC IMAGE: THE ORGANIZATION AS MACHINE

In constructing his classical ideal-type of bureaucracy, Weber gave birth to an image, which has continued to dominate the field of organization studies. This is the image of the organization as a machine, made up of a set of mutually interdependent human parts, which work together in a systematic and orderly way to achieve a number of formally defined goals (Morgan, 1996b).

Looking back at the history of Organization Theory, we can see just how compelling this image of organization has been. Indeed, no writer since the time of Max Weber has managed to escape its influence, and most have accepted its overall validity, even when they have quarrelled with its details. The image of the bureaucracy as an organizational machine has become established as a *leitmotif*, or dominant theme, of most traditions of Organization Theory. It is an image, which emphasizes a number of mechanistic properties of the bureaucratic organization including, among other things:

- calculability
- rationality
- technical expertise
- knowledge
- impersonality
- uniformity

Underlying all of these different properties, however, it is the conception of efficiency, which really defines the modern bureaucracy for Weber, and sets it apart from earlier form of organization. But as several commentators have noted, Weber's conception of efficiency was derived from examples of the authoritarian institutions of his own time – particularly the modern army, and the Catholic Church.[6] It is for this reason that Weber's notion of the ideal-typical bureaucracy rests on the embedded values of hierarchy, inequality, conformity, determinism and objectivity. For Weber, then, the notion of efficiency is understood within an authoritarian structure of social relations.

This has been the great appeal of Weber's work for subsequent generations of management theorists, and is part of the explanation for the remarkable longevity of Weber's image of bureaucracy. At the same time, however, the authoritarian assumptions of his ideal-type have also created problems for later theorists who have sometimes struggled to reconcile this mechanistic image of the formal structure of organizations with the reality of the informal network of social relations which is also a part of most organizations.

Most large organizations in modern societies are run along bureaucratic lines in order to achieve the goal of maximum efficiency. In the modern world, efficiency has become the name of the game: the universal standard which is used to measure the performance of all organizations – in both the public and the private sectors of the economy and society.

DEBATING THE BUREAUCRACY: DILEMMAS OF MODERN ORGANIZATION THEORY

In Max Weber's writings, the image of the bureaucracy as a machine found its most eloquent expression, although other writers such as Frederick Winslow Taylor (1911), and Henri Fayol (1949) had already used this image in their own studies of organizations, several decades before Weber's work became known outside Germany.

For management theorists, viewing the organization as a machine implied that it could be redesigned (for greater efficiency and productivity), in much the same way as other machines, which were stripped down and reassembled in the workshops. The appeal of the machine image to the early schools of Scientific, and of Universalistic, Management lay in the assumption that all aspects of the organization – especially its formal structure – were wholly amenable to managerial supervision and control. According to this image, individual workers were seen as just so many cogs in a machine that could be manipulated and replaced depending upon the operational needs of the organization. The machine image proved a powerful one in management circles, and its legacy may still be seen today in some aspects of organization theory,[7] and in some updated versions of the policies of Scientific Management. Old theories never really die; it is only their advocates who slowly fade away (Jacques, 1996).

During the 1930s and 1940s, these earlier management theories of organization began to lose ground to a new generation of organization theorists who owed more to sociology and social psychology than to engineering. Beginning with the Hawthorne Studies conducted by Elton Mayo (1933), and his associates (Roethlisberger and Dickson, 1939), and followed shortly after by Chester Barnard's (1938) study of the executive, the image of the organization as a machine gradually gave way to that of the organization as an organism, and as a social system. The discovery of the influence of informal work groups, and the new emphasis on cooperative rather than authoritarian styles of management, paved the way for the Human Relations of management studies. Although it was still motivated by the interests of effective management and organizational efficiency, the Human Relations school brought a new emphasis to bear on the importance of humane leadership, as well as cooperation and communication between management and workers. The iron fist had all but disappeared into the velvet glove.

The rise of the organism, and the decline of the machine, as alternative images of organization produced a new generation of behavioural studies of bureaucracy. Weber's image of the bureaucracy as a rational and efficient form of organization was successfully challenged throughout the decades of the 1930s, 1940s and 1950s by a number of writers who sought to demonstrate the dysfunctional, inefficient and irrational features of bureaucratic organizations. Writers like Robert Merton (1940), Alvin Gouldner (1954), Seymour Martin Lipsett (1950), Philip Selznick (1949), Victor Thompson (1961), among others, undertook a series of studies of actual bureaucracies and found that, in many empirical cases, bureaucratic behaviour was often very different from that suggested by the traditional image.

Many of these studies showed that officials working within bureaucracies were not always motivated by the dispassionate and impersonal norms of bureaucratic behaviour suggested by Max Weber. Bureaucrats often had their own personal interests in mind, and their own professional axes to grind, all of which detracted from the rational and efficient running of the organization. At the same time, other studies demonstrated how the rationality and efficiency of a bureaucracy could also be impaired when officials became over-preoccupied with rigidly following the rules.

This debate over the effectiveness of the bureaucracy as a form of organization continued well into the 1960s, and has never really ended. It marked the point at which modern theorists of organization began to seriously question the ideal-typical model of bureaucracy in the light of what was being learned about actual bureaucratic organizations. What became clear from many of the empirical studies done during this period was that bureaucracies did not always live up to their textbook reputations as models of rationality and efficiency: like everything else, they had their upsides and their down sides.

The up side of bureaucracy – its advantages as a form of organization – has been recognized since the time of Max Weber. Bureaucracies, which are run along objective and impersonal lines, and which are based upon a technical division of labour, are well adapted to meet the goals of maximum efficiency. When compared to pre-industrial bureaucracies (of ancient China, Egypt, Rome, South America, Medieval Europe, etc.) the modern bureaucracy has to a great – although not complete – extent, replaced traditional values, which were based on personal, familial, ethnic or regional loyalties with the modern values of objectivity and efficiency. It was this transition from traditionalism to modernity that Max Weber described as the process of rationalization.

By the middle of the twentieth century, however, organization theorists had become familiar with many of the down sides of the bureaucracy – its limitations and shortcomings as a model of organization. Several major problems of bureaucracies came to light during this period.

Rigidity

Bureaucracies can sometimes appear inflexible and inefficient when dealing with unusual, exceptional or atypical cases. This is because bureaucracies are organized, first and foremost, to process large numbers of people, and large amounts of information, with the greatest possible efficiency. For most cases, the standard rules and regulations work well enough. However, what works well for the large majority of typical cases may not work well for a sizeable minority of exceptional or unusual cases. Thus, a passport applicant who is unable to produce a birth certificate, for example, may find the bureaucrats at the Passport Office unwilling and unable to process his/her application in a routine manner. There may be a considerable delay in resolving this type of problem. Or someone who has taken paternity leave may find the bureaucrats at the Canada Employment and Immigration Commission most unhelpful when applying for U.I.C. benefits if the normal rules cannot be easily applied.

To a greater or lesser extent, most bureaucracies are streamlined to process large numbers of similar cases but are often less prepared to deal with unusual or idiosyncratic cases. Most of us can vividly recall the occasional "hassles" we have had with bureaucracies, but we tend to forget the countless times they have provided us with (relatively) efficient routine service – as when mailing a letter, registering an automobile, registering for a course, or making an airline reservation.

Goal Displacement

In some bureaucracies, the goals of individual bureaucrats, or of the departments they work for, may become more important than the official goals of the organization. Robert Merton (1940) showed, for example, how the goal of obsessively following rules and regulations may become more important to the individual bureaucrat than the broader goals of the institution. Merton defined this as the problem of "bureaucratic ritualism," in which the means (of accomplishing goals) came to displace the goals themselves.

Most of us have probably experienced this problem in one form or another. Anyone who has waited patiently (and unsuccessfully) for service in a department store in which the store assistants appear more concerned with tidying their display units than with serving customers, has witnessed an example of goal displacement. Or again, anyone who has tried to register for university courses only to be told that class quotas have been filled, or that prerequisites are necessary, has probably felt that the broader goals of education are being displaced by the strict enforcement of bureaucratic rules and regulations.

Another American sociologist, Philip Selznick (1949) has also described how goal displacement in organizations may arise when the goals of particular departments, or sections, begin to override the official goals of the organization as a whole. In universities, for example, the loss of funds through government cutbacks may lead to the growing importance of external fund-raising as a central activity of the institution. Some departments within the university may begin to define their goals in entrepreneurial and business terms, which may conflict with, or even partially displace, the more traditional academic goals of the university as an institution of higher learning.[8] Most large and complex formal organizations, whether located in the public or private sectors, are vulnerable to some degree of goal displacement.

Impersonality

Many people who work for bureaucracies, or who are clients of bureaucracies, find them to be impersonal and uncaring institutions.[9] The story, which opens this chapter describes how welfare applicants, or recipients, are often intimidated in their dealings with welfare officials. This may often be the case when people in emotional situations are dealt with in an insensitive bureaucratic manner. Sexual assault victims and immigrant applicants, among others, may also experience the impersonality of the bureaucracy. This problem may be further exacerbated when differences of ethnicity and gender are also involved. Ethnic and gender inequalities often combine to make bureaucracies very unpleasant places for immigrants, native people and women.[10]

Empire-building and Self-perpetuation

One of the most famous critics of bureaucracy was the popular author C. Northcote Parkinson, who argued that bureaucrats have a vested interest in making work for themselves in order to justify hiring assistants and, thereby, increase their own statuses (Parkinson, 1957). He believed that this tendency towards empire-building was endemic to all bureaucracies. In a similar vein, Lawrence Peter – a one time professor at UBC – argued that officials in bureaucracies are normally promoted beyond the level of their competence to do the job. These conclusions have become enshrined in popular folk wisdom as "Parkinson's Law" (Parkinson, 1957) and the "Peter Principle" (Peter and Hull, 1969).

Most bureaucracies will continue to stay in business long after their basic goals have been achieved, and after their original usefulness has been outlived. A good example of this is the North Atlantic Treaty Organization (NATO), which is no longer concerned with the collective military security of the Western alliance since the collapse of communism in the USSR and the rest of Eastern Europe. Today, the goals of NATO have been redefined as those of encouraging greater political and ideological cooperation between the "two Europes."[11] Another example of a bureaucracy which changed its goals to stay in business is the National Foundation for Infantile Paralysis (US). It was originally established to fight poliomyelitis, but today it campaigns against arthritis.

Resistance to Change

Bureaucracies may also acquire a certain amount of institutional inertia which make them unsympathetic, or even resistant, to change. In his study of the first CCF provincial government in Saskatchewan, Seymour Martin Lipset (1950; 1971) described how upper class senior civil servants conspired to retard and to resist many of the progressive reforms which were introduced by the new social democratic government. Although the government had passed the new reforms, senior civil servants were able to frustrate and obstruct their implementation.[12] Similarly, top civil servants in the UK also conspired to obstruct the implementation of reforms passed by the post-war Labour government (Benn, 1988; 2000; 1995). In Canada, Warren Allmand has described the opposition he encountered from top officials in his ministry when he attempted to introduce reforms into the Department of Indian and Northern Development.[13]

Secrecy

Bureaucracies may also attempt to conceal information from the public domain. This is particularly true of government bureaucracies, which may claim that public disclosure of information is contrary to the interests of national security.[14] Thus, when the British civil servant, Clive Ponting, revealed that the Argentine warship, the Admiral Belgrano, had been sunk outside of the Falklands' war zone, he was prosecuted for a breach of the Official Secrets Act. The Nixon administration similarly withheld information about its unauthorized bombing raids into Cambodia by also invoking national security interests (cf. Shawcross, 1979).

Private bureaucracies may also suppress information when disclosure is felt to be inconvenient or embarrassing. During the oil shortage of the 1970s, for example, US oil companies were reluctant to supply information about current supplies, and about the amount of proven oil reserves.

Anti-democratic

Ever since the time of Max Weber, bureaucracy has been seen as incompatible with the ideals of democracy. This is because hierarchy remains the great organizing principle of bureaucracy, and stands opposed to the most basic assumptions of democracy. Weber, himself, was well aware of the authoritarian potential of bureaucracy and in his later life wrote pessimistically about the "iron cage" of bureaucratic organization.

It was left to Robert Michels (1949), however, to more fully document the anti-democratic tendencies of modern bureaucracies. Michels concluded that all large bureaucratic organizations would eventually succumb to the "iron law of oligarchy." He meant by this that all large organizations – whether political parties, corporations, government bureaucracies, or even trade unions – would, sooner or later, fall under the domination of oligarchies, i.e., small ruling elites. He concluded that all bureaucracies were destined to undergo this concentration and centralization of power and authority at the top of their organizations.

These debates produced some important new theoretical and empirical insights, and showed that the classical textbook image of bureaucracy was unable to do justice to the range of complexity and variation which existed between actual organizations in the real world. Today, debates over the future of bureaucracy continue to preoccupy organization theorists. Some writers, like Warren Bennis (1966), have predicted that bureaucracies will become organizational dinosaurs and are already on their way to extinction. This is because bureaucracies are basically rigid and inflexible organizations which performed efficiently when the demand for goods and services was unchanging, but are unable to adapt to the needs of a constantly changing marketplace. Bureaucracies may have been good for standardization and predictability, but are poorly adapted for innovation: certainly the trend across Eastern Europe at the current time is to dismantle many of the large bureaucracies that characterized and ran the former communist states.

This view has been challenged, however, by other writers such as Robert Miewald (1970) who maintains that the news of the death of bureaucracy has been greatly exaggerated. Bureaucracies, in his view, have already shown that they can be flexible and can adapt to new situations. Many bureaucracies have long ago dispensed with the older machine-like image of organization in favour of new images and structures which emphasize professionalism and collegiality rather than authority and supervision.[15] The development of quality circles in Japanese factories is only one example of how new forms of bureaucracy are no longer so heavily dependent upon hierarchy as a fundamental principle of organization.

At the same time, however, although these and other studies succeeded in disclosing some of the dysfunctions and problems, which were never shown in the idealized textbook image of bureaucracy, most theorists and managers still remained committed to the most basic assumptions of the bureaucratic model of organization. Notwithstanding its blindness to some of the disadvantages of bureaucracy, the basic assumptions of the Weberian model continued to be accepted by most mainstream theorists within the field of organization studies:

> The Weberian structure has been built upon, rationalized, adjusted, twisted and modified for the past forty years, but its essential assumptions still govern the popular conception of organizations and administrators in our colleges and universities, the research that is undertaken in the field, the development activities that produce our most usable and used technologies, and the way we talk about our workplaces (Clark, 1985: 51).

While these debates have illuminated many different aspects of bureaucracies, and have helped to advance our understanding of organizations, it is from its silences and its omissions that we are best able to define the present limits of modern organization theory. Among these silences have been the topics of power and inequality in bureaucracies, which, until recently, have been largely neglected by modern organization theorists. This neglect has made it difficult to speak of other topics such as race, ethnicity, gender and class which are, of course, intimately connected with the issues of power and inequality. It is to address these silences that we now turn.

STANDING IN THE SHADOWS: BUREAUCRACIES AND MINORITY GROUPS

One of the most neglected areas in the study of bureaucracy has been the position of so-called minority groups within and in relation to these organizations. Standard accounts in OB and OT have paid scant attention to the position of women, ethnic groups, or other minorities in terms of their relations to the majority group which runs most bureaucratic organizations. This neglect can be partly explained by the fact that many writers in the OB and OT tradition subscribe to the prevailing image of bureaucracies as rational organizations which are administered by impersonal and objective rules and procedures. Under these conditions, there would appear to be little room for favouritism, nepotism, or other forms of non-rational evaluation – such as sexual or racial discrimination. For all intents and purposes, the bureaucracy functions as a meritocracy in which rewards are wholly determined by technical competence.

According to this image of the bureaucracy, the ethnicity or gender of those who work within bureaucracies is of minor concern compared to their formal and technical qualifications. People are supposedly judged on what they do within the organization, rather than who they are – in terms of their gender or ethnicity (or social class). Consequently, some writers have suggested that bureaucracies – because of their commitment to impersonal and objective norms – help to break down traditional status divisions between people, such as gender, ethnicity and class, and thereby contribute to a levelling of social differences. In fact, Max Weber, himself, advanced this argument in the course of his writings on bureaucracy:

> The development of bureaucracy greatly favours the levelling of social classes and this can be shown historically to be the normal tendency. Conversely, every process of social levelling creates a faourable situation for the development of bureaucracy; for it tends to eliminate class privileges, which include the appropriation of authority as well as the occupation of offices on an honorary basis or as an avocation by virtue of wealth. This combination everywhere inevitably foreshadows the development of mass democracy (Weber, 1947: 340).

Because of the general acceptance in mainstream OB and OT of this heavily idealized image of the bureaucracy, very little attention has been paid to the experiences of minority people organized within a majority setting. Only now is this beginning to change, and those who have stood for a long time in the shadows of bureaucracy are at last becoming subjects of serious study.

Part of the impetus for the growing interest in, what may be called "organizational minorities" comes from recent attempts by critical organization theorists to re-introduce the issues of power, authority, inequality, and conflict back into mainstream OB and OT.[16] This theoretical reorientation, as much as anything else, has helped to focus attention on the inequalities of power and status, which exist in bureaucracies, and on the experiences of those who suffer them.

One of the early consequences of studying organizational minorities has been to shatter the image of the impersonal and objective bureaucracy. It is clear from the experiences of many minority groups that bureaucracies have usually mirrored the prejudices of the larger society. In the United States, for example, Blacks were forbidden to carry the mail until 1865, because of their perceived threat to national security. It was not until 1869 that they were allowed to work in the federal bureaucracy.[17] Similarly, it was not until 1967 that outright discrimination against women in the federal bureaucracy was ended by a presidential executive order. This, and other evidence, of the historical and contemporary discrimination against women and other minority groups in the US federal bureaucracy, has prompted one critic to completely disavow the "merit myth" which continues to underlie the traditional view of bureaucracy:

> The myth which makes public employment almost synonymous with "civil service," asserts that virtually all public servants have been chosen largely on the basis of merit, evidenced by objective written tests and other scientifically determined criteria, and that only the "best and brightest" survive this fair selection process to be appointed to and promoted within federal, state and local government jobs. The facts, however, are that most public employees today are not under a civil service or merit system, and that overt discrimination against racial-ethnic minorities and women, preferential treatment for others, and covert "scientific" techniques, have combined to produce an unrepresentative "meritless" bureaucracy (Kranz, 1976: 204).

Indeed, as Kathy Ferguson (1984) has argued, the very character of bureaucratic rationality has served to operate as a set of principles against which women have been judged unfavourably as potential members of the bureaucracy. A "discourse of bureaucracy" – with its stress on rationality, objectivity, and impersonality, developed alongside a "discourse of domesticity" – which stressed emotionality, subjectivity, and familial values. Historically, bureaucratic principles, in contrast to domestic principles, became associated with males and maleness and served to exclude women (seen as having domestic and thus inappropriate characteristics) from the bureaucracies or to restrict them to the lower levels.[18]

Other writers have also rejected the idealized picture of the bureaucracy and have pointed to the persistent under-representation of women and ethnic minorities as evidence of institutionalized discrimination within these organizations. Indeed, as Gideon Sjborg (1983: 276) laconically remarked:

> [...] one does not have to be a Marxist to recognize that bureaucracy is the single most important means for sustaining class differences in modern society.

Rosabeth Moss Kanter's (1977) now classic study of the private bureaucracy helped to draw attention to the inequitable distribution of power in the bureaucracy and its impact on the largely powerless women (and men). Kanter revealed how women more than men are concentrated at the lower rungs of the organization and have less opportunities than men to rise in the organization. She called this the "opportunity structure" which serves to signal to women (and some men) that they are not fully valued members of the organization.

In Canada, there has been no shortage of evidence to suggest that bureaucracies have often failed to uphold the universalistic standards envisaged by Max Weber. Examples of institutionalized discrimination in various forms have been uncovered in studies ranging from francophones in public sector and private sector bureaucracies (Beattie, 1975), women in work organizations (Abella, 1984) as well as immigrants and visible minorities in the labour market (Bolaria and Li, 1988; Gupta, 1995; Li, 1983; Ramcharan, 1982; Thiessen et al., 1996a; Mirchandani, 1998). In fact, the degree of inequity which has been observed, in both public and private sector employment, between the dominant white, Anglo-Saxon, middle-class male group and subordinate minority groups caused one authority to label the whole of Canadian society – and the institutions within in – as a "vertical mosaic" (Porter, 1965). In terms of women, Nicole Morgan's (1988) study of the Canadian Public Service provides a classic example of the inequities prevalent within bureaucratic organizations. Morgan details the fact that it took two world wars and various government degrees for women to gain entrance to the Canadian Public Service (women were only 30% of the service by 1939 and only 44% two decades later) and to develop into a stable part of the bureaucracy but that, in the process, they have been subjected to numerous discriminatory recruitment and promotion practices which was consolidated in the development of "women's work" within the bureaucracy and the restriction of women to the lower levels of the hierarchy. Even today the ghettoization of women's work continues as an aspect of the Canadian Public Service and few women have yet been recruited to the upper echelons.[19] The response of government bureaucracy has been to deal with the issue in ways which have crystallized rather than challenged the problem: in the establishment of government positions and policies to deal with "women's issues" the notion that there are specific gender areas or concerns within the bureaucracy has been strengthened (Grant and Tancred-Sheriff, 1992).

Most of these studies were completed by scholars outside of the disciplines of OB and OT in such areas as sociology, history and political science. Only very recently have organization theorists begun to study the relations between majority and minority groups within an organizational setting. Of the few Canadian organization studies that presently exist in this area most have focused on gender relations in organizations[20] – an issue we look at in greater depth in Chapter 5. Within Canadian OB and OT there has been very little done on ethnic relations within organizations,[21] which is surprising given the official ideology of multiculturalism in this country. It is to partly rectify this omission that we turn to a more detailed discussion of ethnicity in Chapter 6.

KEY TERMS

authority	bureaucracy	calculability
division of labour	efficiency	formalization
hierarchy	impersonality	power
rational-legal authority	traditional authority	charismatic authority
rationality	routinization	specialization
standardization	uniformity	rigidity
goal displacement		

REVIEW QUESTIONS

Q1. Define bureaucracy.

Assignment: *Now turn to the glossary at the end of the book and compare your definitions.*

Q2. Briefly define each of the following terms, and say how each relates to the notion of bureaucracy:
- hierarchy
- specialization
- standardization
- impersonality
- formalization

Assignment: *Now turn to the glossary at the end of the book and compare your definitions.*

Q3. Briefly discuss some of the ways in which bureaucracies may be said to be efficient, or inefficient. Try to provide some examples from your own life experiences.

Assignment: *Apply the readings to some real life situations.*

Q4. Briefly define each of the following terms and say how they relate to the debate on bureaucracy:

- goal-displacement
- rigidity
- uniformity
- routinization
- division of labour

 Assignment: *Now turn to the glossary at the end of the book and compare your definitions*

INTERNET EXERCISES

Q1. Compare and contrast the employment guidelines for McDonald's, Disney, and a government agency. Can you find examples of the successful or unsuccessful application of these policies?

Q2. Find two to three online job application forms for government and non government positions. How do they compare? What signs of bureaucracy are imbedded in the questions?

EXERCISE 2.1

This exercise is designed to make you think about the significance of bureaucracies in your own life. Do the tasks individually and then discuss your findings in small groups.

A. On a sheet of paper:

1. Itemize the contents of your wallet, purse, or pocketbook.

2. List the number of documentary items (e.g., ID cards, credit cards, etc.) which link you to bureaucratic organizations.

3. Distinguish between those items which are voluntary, and those which are compulsory.

B. On the same sheet of paper:

1. Make a list of all the compulsory links that you have with bureaucracies.

2. Now, make a list of the ways in which the voluntary links you have with bureaucracies also have some compulsory aspects to them.

3. Briefly discuss how the bureaucratic items in your wallet, purse, or pocketbook would differ if you were of a different gender. How would they differ if you were an aboriginal rather than a non-aboriginal Canadian?

For the first part of the exercise, it is only necessary to examine the contents of your wallet, purse, or pocketbook. You will find that there are a surprising number of documentary links to large bureaucratic organizations contained in your immediate personal belongings. In trying to establish how important these items are for you in different situations – i.e., when opening a bank account, when joining a public library, when writing a cheque – you are also showing how much control some of these bureaucracies exercise over your life.

C. For the second part of the exercise, you should try to think of as many compulsory documentary links that you have with bureaucracies. These can include anything from birth to death certificates: bureaucracies are interested in documenting you from the cradle to the grave. Then try to think of the compulsory aspects which are often involved even in your voluntary links to bureaucracies. This may include the obligation to return library books, to pay your charge account bills, and so on. By putting together your compulsory and voluntary links with bureaucracies, you will begin to see just how much of your life is organized around these giant institutions.[22]

CASE ANALYSIS

Turn to Part II (Critical Approach section) of the Westray case and do Group Exercise B: Dialectical tension in theory and practice, and the five related questions.

USEFUL WEBSITES

<www.mcdonaldization.com>
<http://www.faculty.rsu.edu/~felwell/Theorists/Weber/Whome.htm>
<http://psychology.about.com/cs/bureaucracy/index.htm>
<http://www.systems-thinking.org/bop/bop.htm>

FURTHER READING

On the impact of bureaucracy upon our ways of thinking:

Gareth Morgan, (1996). IMAGES OF ORGANIZATION, Chapter 1

George Ritzer, (2000). THE MCDONALD-IZATION OF SOCIETY

On the impact of corporate bureaucracy on moral behaviour:

Robert Jackall, (1988). MORAL MAZES: THE WORLD OF CORPORATE MANAGERS

Bethany McLean and Peter Elkind, (2003). THE SMARTEST GUYS IN THE ROOM: THE AMAZING RISE AND SCANDALOUS FALL OF ENRON

Literary images of the impact of bureaucracy on social life:

George Orwell, 1984

Aldus Huxley, BRAVE NEW WORLD

Margaret Atwood, THE HANDMAID'S TALE

The impact of corporate and public bureaucracy on women:

Rosabeth Moss Kanter, (1977). MEN AND WOMEN OF THE CORPORATION

K.E. Ferguson, (1984). THE FEMINIST CASE AGAINST BUREAUCRACY

Nicole Morgan, (1988). THE EQUALITY GAME

Judith Grant and Peta Tancred, (1992). A FEMINIST PERSPECTIVE ON THE STATE

Clare Burton, (1992). MERIT AND GENDER: ORGANIZATIONS AND THE MOBILIZATION OF MASCU-LINE BIAS

Graham Lowe, (1987). WOMEN IN THE ADMINISTRATIVE REVOLUTION

Albert J. Mills, (1997a). GENDER, BU-REAUCRACY AND THE BUSINESS CURRICULUM

David H.J. Morgan, (1996a). "THE GENDER OF BUREAUCRACY"

Mike Savage and Anne Witz, (1992). GENDER AND BUREAUCRACY

On the bureaucracy and efficiency debate:

Derek S. Pugh and David J. Hickson (eds.), (1997). WRITERS ON ORGANIZA-TIONS

Derek S. Pugh (ed.), (1997). ORGANIZA-TION THEORY

END NOTES

1. Information compiled from: CUPE news bulletin (16 Nov. 2000) <http://cupe.ca/www/news/2228>; Psychiat-ric Patient Advocate Office position paper (14 Dec. 2000) <http://www.ppao.gov.on.ca/pos-arc-man.html>; and Workfare Watch, bulletin #12, May 2001 <http://www.welfarewatch.toronto.on.ca/wrkfrw/PDF/Bulletin%2012.pdf>.

2. One nightmare case was that of Ri Song Dae. Ri had been a low level bureaucrat in the North Korean government of Kim Jong II when he decided to flee the country and defect to Canada. With his wife and six year old son, Ri entered Canada in August 2001 and filed a formal claim for refugee status for the whole family. Four months later, under some pressure

from the North Korean government and her parents, Ri's wife returned to North Korea. She was duly executed in April 2002, as was her father. Nonetheless, in September 2003 the Canadian Immigration and Refuge Board rejected Ri's application for refugee status and ordered that he be deported to North Korea. The Minister responsible admitted that there was no evidence that Ri had committed atrocities. However, he was deemed guilty of crimes against humanity by dint of the fact that he had served in the Government of North Korea. Reporting on the case, Boston Globe reporter Jeff Jacoby commented that "Canadians express pride in their country's humanitarian values, but it has been hard to detect any of those values as this case has moved through the Canadian bureaucracy." After widespread news coverage throughout North America and protests in Canada Ri was finally granted permission to stay in the country permanently. On March 3rd "Public Safety Minister Anne McLellan granted him permission to stay in Canada indefinitely, since his life would be in danger if he were deported." (The International Herald Tribune on line, 9 March 04 <http://www.iht.com/articles/509236.htm>.

3. In case these concerns seem unduly alarmist, it is worth noting that, prior to the implementation of the Privacy Act, similar sentiments were expressed by the Federal Privacy Commissioner in Canada:

"Invasions of privacy that once seemed plausible only on the pages of George Orwell's novels may soon be realities in Canada, the Federal Privacy Commissioner warned Tuesday (July 13, 1993)… It's not a question of paranoia (Bruce) Phillips said in his annual report. People are being denied employment, people being denied credit, people losing their jobs, people losing reputations because of information being collected and used about them without their knowledge and consent". (*Edmonton Journal*, July 14, 1993). Since 2001, the Office of the Commissioner carries out investigations that establish whether individuals have had their privacy rights violated and/or whether they have been accorded their right of access to their personal information <www.privcom.gc.ca>.

4. For a more detailed explanation of the Marxian perspective on bureaucracy, see Mouzelis (1975).

5. McDonald's is a prime example of bureaucratization. This organization has taken standardization and formalization to a fine art – detailing through a series of rules and regulations every aspect of the production process, from the exact way that burgers are to be cooked down to the requirement that employees smile (Morgan, 1996b; Ritzer, 1996). Some critics argue that this peculiar McDonald's version of bureaucracy is spreading to greater aspects of social life (Drane, 2001; Hayes and Wynyard, 2002; Ritzer, 1996), but at least one critical theorist is prepared to argue that there is something of value in McDonald's approach to fast food (Parker, 2002).

6. See Clark (1985: 48) who claims that, "The language of bureaucracy has several nested layers. It is militaristic,

mechanistic, sexist, capitalist, Western, and rationalistic." See also gender critiques of bureaucracy by Savage and Witz (1992), Ferguson (1984), Mills (2001), and Mills and Ryan (1997b).

7. See for example discussion of Business Process Reengineering (BPR) – (Hammer, 1990; Hammer, 1995; Hammer and Champy, 1993; Harrington, 1991).

8. For Canadian examples of this tendency see Newson and Buchbinder (1988), and Turk (2000).

9. For a vivid account of the impersonal and intrusive character of government agencies when dealing with unemployed people, see Burnman (1988) and Neil (1992).

10. For a shocking account of one native woman's experience with the welfare bureaucracy in Western Canada see Campbell (1973). Purich (1986) documents the treatment of aboriginal peoples under Canada's bureaucratic laws for dealing with "Indians."

11. The beginnings of the NATO strategy to deal with the post Cold War world are discussed in NATO review, 1991. In 2004 the organization defined itself as "an alliance of 26 countries" committed to "safeguard the freedom and security of its member countries by political and military means. During the last fifteen years, NATO has also played an increasingly important role in crisis management and peacekeeping." <http://www.nato.int/home.htm>.

12. See also Bendix (1974).

13. A former minister during the 1970's, Montreal M.P., Warren Allmand, recalls friction between himself and the Department's bureaucrats because he initiated an open-door policy with native leaders. "There was a whisper campaign going on behind my back by bureaucrats. They said I was listening more to the Indians than my officials and I wasn't doing my job." "Indian Affairs' $2.5 billion buys a lot of red tape." Jack Aubry, Ottawa Citizen, quoted in *Edmonton Journal*, Nov. 4, 1990.

14. For a useful reviews of secrecy in government see Rogers (1997), Theoharis (1998), Vincent (1998), and Rozell (2002).

15. Professor Henry Minzberg (1979) of McGill University has characterized bureaucracies into three types – the "machine bureaucracy," the "professional bureaucracy," and the "divisional form" of organization, which combines "machine bureaucracy" with semi-autonomous divisions.

16. Cf. Best and Kellner (1991, 1997); Burrell and Morgan (1979); Clegg and Dunkerley (1980); Clegg (1989); Clegg, Hardy, and Nord (1996); Ferguson (1984); Bell, Denton, and Nkomo (1992); Prasad et al., (1997).

17. For a revealing account of the racist practices and policies traditionally employed in the British civil service to exclude Black candidates see Harris, (1991).

18. For a feminist critical reading of the concept of "rationality" in organization theory see Mumby and Putnam (1992).

19. By the end of the twentieth century women comprised 50.5% of all workers in the federal public service, while their work force availability is 48.7% (Treasury Board Secretariat, 1999). Although their representation in the service is

now equal to that of their general work force availability, "many issues facing women remain unresolved" (Treasury Board Secretariat, 1999: 14). Note also that the above figures indicating reasonable representativeness hide the large numbers of women in traditional roles (e.g., administrative support, nursing, human resources) and the very low representation in non-traditional roles (e.g., science and technology, information technology, upper management). Women represent 84% of the Administrative Support workers, 14.2% of Operational workers (a category that includes correctional services, firefighters, general labour and trades), 24.7% of Technical workers, and 32.2% of Scientific and Professional workers. In 1998 women represented 24.3% of the Executive positions in the public service sector. For recent analysis of women in the public service in Canada see Gorber (2001) and Nehmé (2001).

20. Cf. Agócs (1989), Agócs et al., (1992); Cullen (1997); Mills and Chiaramonte (1991); Mills and Tancred (1992); Prasad et al., (1997); (Mirchandani, 1998); Mills and Helms Mills (2004).

21. The work of Mighty (1991; 1997), Mirchandani (1998; 2004), and Konrad, Prasad and Pringle (In press) are rare examples.

22. We are indebted to Derek Sayer, Department of Sociology, University of Alberta, for the idea for this assignment.

CHAPTER 3

Calling the Shots:
How Theories of Organization
Relate to Managers

This chapter examines some of the ways in which the topic of management has been conceptualized in Organization Theory and Organizational Behaviour and how these conceptualizations have been deeply coloured by the managerialist perspective of the discipline. The chapter begins with an exploration of management as "the fourth factor of production," and goes on to trace the relationship between the development of big business and the growth of management theory. Attention is paid to the impact of management and organization theory on the character of class struggle - in particular the development of scientific management and the "deskilling" debate. The chapter ends with an examination of management as practice.

Speedy Taylor and Management Theorizing

Frederick Winslow Taylor (they called him Speedy Taylor in the shop) was born in Germantown, Pennsylvania.... The early years he was a machinist with the other machinists in the shop, cussed and joked and worked with the rest of them, soldiered on the job when they did. But when he got to be foreman, he was on the management's side of the fence.... He couldn't stand to see an idle lathe or an idle man.

Production went to his head and thrilled his sleepless nerves like liquor or women on a Saturday night. He never loafed and he'd be damned if anyone else would. Production was an itch under his skin....

He was impatient of explanation, he didn't care whose hide he took off in enforcing the laws he believed inherent in the industrial process....

There's the right way of doing a thing and the wrong way of doing it; the right way means increased production, lower costs, higher wages, bigger profits: the American plan (from the novel, The Big Money, by John Dos Passos – quoted in Davis and Scott, 1964: 79).

The verb to manage, from manus, the Latin for hand, originally meant to train a horse in his paces, to cause him to do the exercises of the manege [...] Like a rider who uses reins, bridle, spurs, carrot, whip, and training from birth to impose his will, the capitalist strives, through management, to control. And control is indeed the central concept of all management systems, as has been recognized implicitly or explicitly by all theoreticians of management (Braverman, 1974: 67-68).

INTRODUCTION

It is not possible to get very far in a course on Organization Theory (OT) or Organizational Behaviour (OB) without encountering the topic of management. Management occupies a special place in the hearts and minds of organization theorists and, if they are to be believed, its importance to the operation of the modern organization can hardly be overestimated. Indeed, for most writers, management is not only the single, most important factor involved in the running of an organization, it is the all-encompassing factor which influences all other aspects of organizational life. This has led many contemporary theorists to refer to management as "the fourth factor of production," in a way that rivals in importance the three other traditional factors of land, labour and capital.[1] Such an emphasis on the importance of management should come as no surprise in a discipline which has evolved from a largely managerial viewpoint.

In this chapter, we shall examine some of the ways in which the topic of management has been conceptualized in OB and OT and how these conceptualizations have been deeply influenced by the managerial perspective of the discipline. There is, in effect, something of a self-justificatory character to much of the writing on management which has come out of the mainstream traditions of Organization Theory and Organizational Behaviour. In spite of attempts by management theorists to establish their field as an objective, or even as a "scientific" branch of knowledge, much of the contemporary writing on management theory has never really lost its ideological character, i.e., its tendency to legitimize and to routinize the perspectives of management within the organization. This has resulted in a typically one-sided and incomplete understanding of management in much of what passes for studies of organization and management today. Part of the task of this chapter is to show how this narrow definition of the field has obscured our understanding of some of the broader historical, and more critical issues related to management in modern society. There is more to the study of management than managers, themselves, would have us believe. And if OB and OT are to become more than simply an apologia for managers, the time has come for some of the broader theoretical issues of modern management to be raised in a critical and historical perspective.

In its essentials, as the chapter's opening quotation by Braverman makes clear, the most basic problem facing all managers is the problem of control, i.e., how to ensure the compliance and/or the cooperation of subordinate individuals within an organization. If managers are to run their organizations effectively, they need to be able to control the behaviour of those over whom they exercise authority and responsibility. The problem of control, therefore, defines more than anything else the central challenge faced by managers everywhere, irrespective of organizations they manage.

Very few of the definitions of management offered in the literature, however, reduce the matter to such stark and simple terms. The task of management is more commonly seen as that of bringing together different resources for the purpose of accomplishing definite organizational goals. In this type of definition, the image of a manager as a controller of (potentially) recalcitrant subordinates is replaced by that of a manager as a broker for obtaining and coordinating the different institutional resources necessary for the effective operation of the enterprise or organization (cf. Edwards, 1979). The strong implication of this image, of course, is that the real job of manager is to bring together, or to assemble, a set of complementary – or non-antagonistic – elements that can be combined, in order to realize the goals of the organization. There is no hint in this type of definition that the interests of any of the elements may actually be in opposition to each other, or that the relationship between them may be defined primarily by differences of power. Instead, it is usually implied that the role of management is to combine these elements into an effective functional unity that is based upon a common set of underlying interests. According to this view, an important function of management is to ensure that all elements of the organization become aware of their underlying common interests and act in accordance with these interests. This is what we may call the "functional," or "consensus" view of management, and it is this view that is typically represented in most introductory definitions of the field:

> Management is the process of achieving organizational objectives in an effective and efficient manner through planning, organizing, leading, and controlling… Getting things done with people and other resources and providing direction and leadership are what managers do (Boone, Kurtz and Knowles, 1999: 155).

In this and similar definitions, the view of the manager as an agent of social control is largely supplanted by one in which the manager is seen more as a juggler of different human and material resources. As has been the case for many other subjects in OB/OT the issues of power, conflict and inequality are generally down played, and the interests of management are largely identified with the interests of the organization as a "functional whole."

The important thing to recognize about this image of management, besides the fact that it largely eschews any reference to the issues of power, conflict and inequality, is that management is seen as the only agency that is capable of bringing together the different elements of the organization. It alone can rise above the particular interests of each constituency in order to serve the operational needs of the total organization. Thus, it is only the interests of management that are fully identified with the interests of the organization as a whole. And it is for this reason that the factor of management in viewed by many organization theorists as the essential fourth factor of production which, because of its uniquely universal view of the total organization, has become the most vital and important component in the running of the modern organization.

> No job is more vital to our society than that of the manager. It is the manager who determines whether our social institutions serve us well or whether they squander our talents and resources (Mintzberg, 1975: 61).

What is true of business enterprises is also true of government departments, and of non-profit organizations. Management is usually seen as that vital and creative spark which alone can bring together and coordinate the resources needed for the effective running of these organizations. As long as there are organizations there will always be a need for their specialized management, for without management – it is implied – these resources will remain unorganized and unproductive. This sense of the universal and eternal need for professional management is well captured by Dale (1978), in a quote from the Fabian Socialist, Sidney Webb, which appears at the beginning of a textbook on Management Theory:

> Under any social order from now to Utopia a management elite is indispensable and all-enduring […] The question is not: "Will there be a management elite?" but "What sort of elite will it be?"

The point of examining these traditional definitions of management from a critical perspective is not to suggest that they are entirely without merit, or that they paint a totally false picture of what managers do. There is no reason why the practice of management should not be seen as the task of juggling various resources in an effort to combine and coordinate them for the realization of organizational goals. From a managerial perspective, it makes good sense to define the functions of management in these, or similar, terms. The point is, however, that such definitions offer a very partial, one-sided, and incomplete understanding of the practice of management, an understanding which remains thoroughly wedded to a managerial perspective and agenda.

As we shall see in the next section of this chapter, part of the problem with the consensus view of management is its tendency to overlook the lessons of history and to focus, almost exclusively, on the search for practical techniques of "successful" management. This has resulted in the degradation of theory in much of what passes for mainstream OB and OT. The absence of any critical or historical perspective has blinded much of OT/OB to the significance of the issues of power, conflict and inequality, and has reduced it at times to the level of a managerial ideology where its only remaining functioning is to serve as a practical guide for managerial action. But, as we shall see, this consensus view tells us very little about the historical rise of professional management, or about the class origins of managers as a social group. In order to throw more light on these and other questions, we need a theory of management that is more than simply a guide to practical action; we need a theory which is both comparative and historical and which is free from the narrow administrative focus which underlies the practical interests of managers as a social group. What we need is a critical-theoretical perspective on Organization and Management Theory.

THE VISIBLE HAND: BIG BUSINESS AND THE
MANAGERIAL REVOLUTION

There are very few mainstream OB or OT textbooks that question the need for some kind of top-down management structure with its resultant hierarchical division of authority. For the vast majority of writers in the managerial tradition, the social functions of management and the social status of managers are largely self-evident, and require no special explanation or justification.[2] Indeed, as one writer suggests, it isn't only management theorists who feel this way:

> If you asked most social scientists why work is run by bosses and managers and not by workers, they would likely tell you that such organization is "necessary" or "inevitable" or perhaps "efficient". Some proclaim, for example, that the hierarchical organization of work is a necessary corollary of modern production technology. others assert that while hierarchy may not be necessary, it is efficient, making possible more profits for the employer, higher wages for the workers, and greater production for society than alternative arrangements can provide (Edwards, 1979: vii).

For writers who have remained locked in a managerial perspective, and especially for those without any understanding of the lessons of history, such assumptions are accepted as entirely natural and unproblematic. In order to examine these assumptions from a more critical perspective, however, it is important to see how the practices of management have changed over the course of recent history and how they can be understood, not so much as universal imperatives of all organizations, but as strategies used by powerful social groups to maintain direction and control over changing organizations.

While there is general agreement that management, in one form or another, has been practiced in all civilized states, including those of ancient civilizations (cf. Wren, 1987), most theorists today identify the rise of what has sometimes been called "systematic management" with the modern age of industrialization (ibid). The roots of modern management practices can be traced back to early development of industrial capitalism, and to the greatly increased need for a disciplined work force that was associated with the origins of factory production. Many writers today, however, believe that the real turning point in management practices came with the growth of big business at the end of the nineteenth century and the beginning of the twentieth century. With the growth of ever larger and more complex organizations – especially business enterprises – the age of the individual entrepreneur slowly gave way, in the early twentieth century, to the age of the professional manager. By the end of the second decade of the twentieth century, it had become clear to so many observers that the days of "the rugged individualist" tycoons of industry and commerce – the Fords, Mellons, Duponts, Carnegies, Rockefellers – were numbered, and that in their places a new breed of corporate owners and directors was emerging. The age of the individual entrepreneur was passing and a new age of corporate ownership and control had already begun to replace it.

The transformation of competitive capitalism into the later stage of monopoly capitalism brought with it important changes in the management and control of large-scale businesses and industrial enterprises. During the early part of the twentieth century, individual entrepreneurs still played an active role in the management and supervision of their companies. It was not uncommon, for example, for Henry Ford to visit the shop-floor of his factories in order to assess the efficiency of his machines, and the performance of his work-force (Lacey, 1986). But by the end of the 1920s, this kind of personal, or paternalistic, intervention by owners of large companies had become increasingly uncommon, and increasingly improbable.[3] The transformation of ownership from individual into corporate hands was accompanied by the rise of a new class of professional managers whose businesses they managed. The rise of this new class of professional managers during the opening decades of the twentieth century is often referred to as "the managerial revolution."[4]

Some writers have suggested that the managerial revolution also resulted in a transfer of power from the traditional class of owners to that of the professional salaried managers, leading in the words of one interpreter to a "decomposition of capital" (Dahrendorf, 1959:41-48) i.e., a shift of power from a narrow elite of owners to a broader constituency of managers, owners, shareholders and other "stakeholders." This interpretation has been challenged by other writers who have argued that boards of directors, rather than managers, have retained their ultimate power to direct and control the companies they own.

One of the more important interpretations of the managerial revolution is provided in the work of the economic historian, Alfred Chandler.[5] In his book, *The Visible Hand*, which won him the Pulitzer Prize for History, Chandler describes the formative years of modern capitalism. He suggests that between the years 1850-1920, a new type of economic institution emerged in the United States, the multi-unit firm, which was controlled by a new class of managers operating under new conditions of capitalist production. Chandler shows how the causes of this expansion in the size and complexity of industrial and commercial firms during the years of his study were to be found in changes in demand which brought about the growth of mass markets, technological change, and high volume production.[6]

Chandler's analysis of the growth of economic organizations in the early part of the twentieth century has far-reaching implications for an understanding of the managerial revolution,[7] and of the systems of managerial hierarchy which have become established in all types of productive enterprises, and, by extension, into all formal organizations in the modern world. Chandler records that when organizations began to move away from small owner-controlled enterprises towards modern multi-unit business corporations, a new class of managers appeared. These new salaried managers, who gradually displaced many of the earlier entrepreneurial owner/managers, began to transform the structural arrangements of the industrial and commercial businesses in which they worked. According to Chandler, the role of management was central to the development of the new organizational structure which came to dominate the multi-unit firms in the opening decades of the twentieth century. He suggests that, "the visible hand of management has replaced Adam Smith's invisible hand of market forces."

The most significant of these structural changes was the introduction of a more decentralized corporate structure, which allowed for a much greater specialization of management functions. This was typically represented in the key distinctions between the general offices, divisions, departments and field units. These changes laid the foundations for the modern system of hierarchical management that, in its essentials, remains with us today.[8]

The importance of Chandler's historical analysis of the rise of the multi-unit firm, and of the corporate management structures which corresponded to it, lies in the fact that we are able to see more clearly how modern forms of management have actually evolved. There is nothing "inevitable" or "natural" about the way in which these structures came into existence; they emerged in response to a particular set of historical conditions which marked the transition from a family, or finance based capitalism, to a maturing managerial capitalism. If history teaches us anything, it is that no structures are fixed or permanent, and that everything is subject to flux, change and transformation. The managerial structures, which today appear so unalterable and so stable, could tomorrow be brought down by historical events as surely as the fall of the Berlin Wall. This historical understanding of the roots of modern management is a useful and necessary corrective to many mainstream OT/OB texts that often seem to assume that present structures of management are the only rationally conceivable ones in the modern world.

Further insight into the evolution of modern systems of management, and of the changing forms of workplace supervision and control which grew out of these systems, is to be found in the recent work of labour process theorists (cf. Burawoy, 1979; 1985; Edwards, 1979). In his pioneering text on the changing structures of workplace relations Richard Edwards (1979) describes three different systems of workplace control that have evolved since the Industrial Revolution. The appearance of each of these systems at different times in the course of the last hundred years illustrates the continuous attempts by managers to adapt to the ever-changing conditions of work, and to the problems of its supervision and control. What is of particular value in this approach, (and in the work of other labour process theorists), is the development of a genuinely historical perspective with which to study the evolving forms of labour-management relations. An historical approach can often serve to move us beyond the orthodox assumptions of contemporary management principles to a point where they can be more easily questioned and critiqued.[9]

In his own work, Edwards identifies three systems of workplace control that, he suggests, can be distinguished from each other in terms of how work is directed, evaluated, and disciplined. What he calls "simple control," (and which still survives in many workplaces today), was characteristic of small owner-manager firms with tight and often highly personalized systems of workplace supervision. These systems flourished throughout most of the nineteenth century, but were progressively displaced by the growth of big business in the early twentieth century, and by the increasing size and complexity of the workplace. Under the system of simple control, work-forces were normally small and bosses were usually close and powerful. In these situations, the treatment of workers was often arbitrary, and reflected the personal styles and temperaments of individual foremen and supervisors. Because many of these early businesses were family enterprises, workers were often subject to the petty tyranny, and paternalistic authority of bosses who were part of the family business.[10]

With the growth of big business, systems of simple control were soon overtaken by systems of technical control. In place of the highly paternalistic forms of supervision which had characterized the small family firm, big businesses were now able to control workers through the introduction of new technology. Nowhere was this more apparent than in the Ford Motor Company when, in 1914, Henry Ford installed the first form of assembly-line production: the chain-driven "endless conveyor" to assemble magnetos. The advent of assembly line production meant that workers could now be directly controlled by the technology. The machinery, itself, directed the labour process and set the pace and rates of work. Under these conditions, the supervision of workers underwent some changes. Foremen no longer initiated the work tasks as the machinery now did this. Instead of directing the labour process, foremen were now responsible for monitoring and evaluating the flow of work.

> The actual power to control work is thus vested in the line itself, rather than in the person of the foreman. Instead of control appearing to flow from boss to workers, control emerges from much more impersonal "technology" (Edwards, op cit: 120).

The growth of automation, and of the systems of technical control which corresponded to it, created the conditions for the managerial revolution. This first generation of professional managers increased their control over the workplace by controlling the ways in which the jobs of workers were designed. Many of these early managers came from highly technical backgrounds: some were industrial design experts, others, systems engineers or industry economists. Their most lasting achievement, as we shall see in the next section, was the creation of the classical schools of management theory, including the school of Scientific Management. But as Edwards shows, systems of technical control were unable to solve all the labour problems of production and, in fact, began to generate some new ones. More than any previous system, the technical system of control carried with it the danger that workplace conflicts could erupt into broader and more general plant-wide struggles between labour and management. When all workers were locked into an assembly line, labour conflicts could easily escalate to include the whole plant. Work stoppages, plant sitdowns and accelerated drives for unionization throughout the 1930s, all increasingly defined the limits of technical control in modern industry.

These experiences led several major companies to move beyond purely technical systems of control, and during the post-War period the first examples were seen of new bureaucratic systems of control. Unlike technical control, which is embedded in the physical and technological aspects of production, and is built into the design of the machines, bureaucratic control is embedded in the social and organizational structures of the firm and is built into job categories, work rules, promotion procedures, discipline, wage-scales, definitions of responsibility, and so on. As Edwards (1979: 131) suggests, "Bureaucratic control establishes the impersonal force of "company rules" or "company policy" as the basis for control."

Originally, in companies like Polaroid and IBM, bureaucratic control of the workplace was introduced as a way of avoiding unionization, and the whole adversarial collective bargaining model that became established in the 1950s. With the advance of unionism in many industrial sectors, however, bureaucratic systems of control began to incorporate unions into the structures of workplace control through the rules and regulations laid out in many collective agreements. Unions were obliged to honour the terms of these agreements and to discipline any of their members who were found to be in violation of these terms.

The real success of the system of bureaucratic control, however, resided in the power it gave to management to comprehensively determine all aspects of the corporate occupational structure. Managers became responsible for how jobs were classified, how job descriptions were defined, how wage and salary rates established, how hiring and promotion procedures were adopted, and virtually every other aspect of the organization of the labour force. This form of control was extended to all sections of the labour force including blue collar and white-collar workers, as well as to managers themselves. Unlike previous forms of workplace control, bureaucratic control was comprehensive in its coverage of all members of the work force, and regulated every aspect of their lives on the job.

Today, in most work organizations, managers normally use some combination of each of these three systems of control to exact cooperation and/or compliance from their subordinates. Like everything else, management systems have undergone major changes over the past one hundred years or more in order to maintain and extend control over their work forces.

In the early days of "Scientific Management" control was achieved through a twofold strategy of job redesign and attitude change on the part of workers and managers:

> [In] its essence scientific management involves a complete mental revolution on the part of the workingmen.... And it involves an equally complete mental revolution on the part of those on management's side....

> The great revolution that takes place in the mental attitude of the two parties under scientific management is that both sides take their eyes off the division of the surplus as the all-important matter, and turn their attention towards increasing the size of the surplus until the surplus becomes so large ... that there

is ample room for a large increase in wages for the workmen and an equally large increase in profits for the manufacturer (Frederick Taylor, 1912).

Although the essence of scientific management involved deskilling work, through the redesign of tasks, Taylor had hoped that the resulting efficiencies (and associated bonuses) would lead to a "revolutionary" change in workplace attitudes. In fact, the "efficiencies" that came to be associated with scientific management led to greater labour unrest and a US Senate inquiry into Taylorism.

Following the initial problems with "scientific management" management, theory became more focused on control through "human relations," involving attempts to involve employees in the control process. The Hawthorne studies, for example, encouraged managers to build on workers' sense of workplace solidarity to establish a great commitment to the company. This trend was strengthened in the early post-war years of full employment, widespread education, and rising expectations, and can be seen in popular management theories of control that focused on "democratic management style" (Lewin, Lippitt and White, 1939; McGregor, 1960), "participative management" (Argyris, 1957; Coch and French, 1948), "socio-technical systems theory" (Trist, 1981; Trist and Bamforth, 1951), "individual needs theories of motivation" (Maslow, 1998; Maslow, 1943; McClelland, 1961), the "quality of working life" (QWL) movement (Ondrack and Evans, 1984; Susman, 1972; Susman, 1976), organizational development (OD) (Brown and Covey, 1987; Porras and Robertson, 1992), organizational culture (Peters and Waterman, 1982; Schein, 1992; Schein, 1990), "empowerment" (Kanter, 1979; Kotter, 1990; Kotter, 1996), and "total quality management" (TQM) (Deming, 1986; Juran, 1988).[11]

The humanization trend reached something of a zenith in the QWL movement that, to some extent, questioned the basic scientific management philosophy of deskilling labour. Advocates of QWL had begun to realise that:

> there are economic and organizational conditions under which extreme job fragmentation and low worker discretion are not the most productive/profitable modes of structuring work [; that] rationalization entails some degree of despecialization, destandardization, and restoration of workers' discretion. These departures from Taylorism … can cut labour costs and reduce the time required to produce or process an item … (Rinehart, 1986, p. 509).

Nonetheless, although apparently focused on "the quality of working life," some critics argue that QWL led to "uncompensated work intensification, labour elimination, and the weakening of organizations to protect workers from management and to enable them to improve the quality of working life" (Rinehart, 1986, p. 522).

The more recent trends in management, the balanced scorecard, six sigma, and in particular, re-engineering, very much resonate with the changed conditions of the times. Re-engineering is a theory that emphasizes the restructuring of the workplace through a focus on workflow or process; companies are encouraged to organize around outcomes not tasks. At a time when unemployment is relatively high, trade union membership is on the decline, and communism has collapsed as a world force, we may have predicted the rise of new theories of management that focus on work processes, rather than people, on cutting rather than improving jobs, and, in the case of re-engineering, on a complete "revolutionary" capitalist transformation of the workplace, rather than any incremental improvements (see Hammer, 1990; 1995; Hammer and Champy, 1993). For example, the Nova Scotia Power Corporation was structured around given jobs and skills such as meter installer, meter reader, and bill collector. After a programme of re-engineering, which identified "specific services to the customer" as important outcomes, all three jobs were combined so that the new "customer service field representatives," or CSFRs, could more efficiently service customer needs. The problem is that meter reading, meter installation and debt collection are three very different tasks involving different skills (e.g., the electrical knowledge involved in meter reading) and different emotional labour (e.g., meter reading versus debt collection). The combining of these tasks has since caused various problems for employees and customers alike (Helms Mills, 2003a).

That much of the humanism has gone from this new form of management can be seen in the language of re-engineering and its adherents: "Don't automate, obliterate" argues Michael Hammer (1990), "You either get on the train, or we'll run over you with the train" (Hammer 1993: 33). It is a language that is very reminiscent of Frederick Taylor, with the gurus of re-engineering referring to themselves as "revolutionaries," arguing that "the Re-engineering Revolution profoundly rearranges the way people conceive of themselves, their work, their place in society" (Hammer, 1995: 321). It would appear that the argument has come full circle!

NOW TURN TO EXERCISE 3.1 AT THE END OF THE CHAPTER

READING BETWEEN THE LINES: MANAGEMENT THEORY
AND CLASS STRUGGLE

One of the fundamental paradoxes of OT and OB is the idea that a science of organization can be built up from the particular perspective of managers. Organizations, of course, especially work organizations, are composed of workers as well as managers. Why is it that the "applied sciences" of organization have been developed for the benefit of managers, rather than workers? Why is it that managers, rather than workers, are seen to represent and embody the interests of the organization as a whole? Most OT and OB textbooks take it for granted that management has a rightful monopoly over the production and application of systematic knowledge about organizations.[12] Apparently, it comes with the territory. The job of being a manager involves learning about organizations, and how to increase their efficiency, productivity and profitability. The job of being a worker involves doing what you are told.

Today, the "science" of management is no longer paralleled by any comparable "science" of "workmanship."[13] The truth is, that many of the practical sciences of "workmanship" are passing into extinction. Traditional trades are falling into disuse, and more apprenticeships are being terminated. The accumulated knowledge of (usually male) generations is gradually being lost and forgotten, while a sizeable number of women have been recruited into the ranks of management but no comparable developments have occurred in the spread of designated skills and skilled employment among women workers. This is the real story behind the rise of management science. It is a story in which the struggle for greater knowledge and control of work by management has always been at the expense of workers – a reduction in the skills of (mainly male) workers while supporting the continued exclusion of women from the skilled ranks:[14] Braverman (1974) refers to this process as "deskilling." When reading between the lines of OT and OB therefore, it is useful to bear in mind that the different theories of management, so neatly presented in the major textbooks, usually emerged from a background of struggle and confrontation between labour and management. For managers, the search for knowledge of the general principles of work organizations has always been motivated by the desire for greater control over the work-force.[15] In other words, the search for knowledge in OT and OB has remained inseparable from the struggle for power.

The history of organizational studies over this century has seen the rise and fall of a number of different theories of management. During the earlier part of this century, many of these ideas were developed by individual men and women[16] who were themselves, either business people, or who had strong interests in business affairs – especially in the state of management-labour relations. Most of these early contributors to what is now known as OT and OB came from business backgrounds and included men like the French industrialist, Henri Fayol; the GM executive, James Mooney; the Vice-President of Johns-Mannville, Alvin Brown; the British chocolate executive, Oliver Sheldon; the New Jersey Bell Telephone Company President, Chester Barnard; the British management consultant, Lyndall Urwick; and, of course, Frederick Winslow Taylor of the Bethlehem, and the Midvale Steel Companies. In fact, it has only been over the past forty years or so that academics have overtaken businessmen in their contributions to the field of study.

No one who has ever opened a standard textbook in OT and OB can fail to have been impressed by the variety of different theoretical perspectives currently represented in this field. The historical development of the field has left behind a legacy of theoretical pluralism that continues to define the discipline up to the present day. The story behind the emergence of these different "schools" of management theory is inextricably linked to the continuing struggle of managers to expand their scope of control over the workplace, and to increase the productivity and profitability of business enterprises under the changing historical conditions of production. Each of the different schools of management theory, therefore, may be thought of as a separate landmark in the continuing struggle for power between labour and management, a struggle that – with temporary reversals – has seen labour in constant retreat.

This is not the way that management theory is normally depicted in most of the standard textbooks. To read many of these accounts, it almost seems as those management theorists have only been motivated by the disinterested search for knowledge and/or efficiency for its own sake, than by the pursuit of larger profits. But as we shall see throughout this chapter, the development of management theory has rarely been undertaken simply as an academic exercise. At stake has always been the issue of power: how to invest managers with more power – in the interests of greater efficiency, productivity, profitability, or general organizational effectiveness; and how to strip power from the workers – in the interests of exacting their cooperation and/or compliance in the process of production.

THE PERIODIZATION OF THEORY AND THE ILLUSION OF PROGRESS: THE CASE OF SCIENTIFIC MANAGEMENT

There are two problems of history in mainstream OB and OT textbooks. The first problem is that a history of the development of management thought is rapidly disappearing from OB and OT texts as we move into the 21st century. It is as if the past has no bearing on the present: as we shall see throughout this book, the social context in which OB and OT developed and continues to develop has an important bearing on what it has to say. On the other hand, where the OB or OT text does deal with a history of management thought it is usually presented in such a way as to imply, if not openly state, a progressive unfolding of ideas. We shall deal with the lack of history elsewhere. In this section we turn to the peculiar history of management theory that appears, however embedded, in mainstream OB and OT textbooks.

Prior to the 21st century most OB and OT textbooks included at least a small review of past theories of management (cf. Donnelly, Gibson and Ivancevich, 1987; Wren and Voich, 1984). Sometimes these would be dedicated chapters or sections of chapters devoted to the development of management theory (e.g., Starke and Sexty, 1995) or sometimes the history would be embedded in a review of specific areas of thought such as motivation (e.g., Schermerhorn, Templer, Cattaneo, Hunt and Osborn, 1992). Today, we are more likely to find the embedded version of history. In all of these cases, however, the growth of management thought is illustrated in historical terms, beginning with the earliest known examples of management practices (e.g., motivation) and ending with the latest examples of modern management theory – exemplified in contingency theory, business process reengineering, total quality management, the balances scorecard, etc.

This almost ritualistic invocation of the founding figures and early pioneers of management theory serves a number of important functions in the teaching of modern management studies. Like any other branch of organized knowledge, it is designed to show students how the contemporary principles and practices of management owe something to the insights of earlier writers who were precursors of the modern study of organizations and management. More than this, however, the historical developmental approach to the study of management theory, (especially when introduced near the beginning of a text), creates the impression – one might even say the illusion – that the evolution of management thought may be understood as a linear progression from relatively underdeveloped to more fully developed ideas. In other words, that theories of management, much like the popular conception of physical theories of the natural sciences,[17] have progressed through different stages of growth and maturation on their way to becoming a fully-fledged "science" of management.

This linear conception of the growth of management theory acquires a special importance when comparing the "less enlightened" theories of management that flourished during earlier parts of the century with the supposedly more enlightened and more rational systems of analysis and decision-making that prevail today. In the case of Scientific Management, for example, which is commonly acknowledged to be one of the earliest traditions of systematic management, many standard textbooks will describe both its theoretical contributions and its limitations, before showing how these limitations were later addressed by other theoretical perspectives, such as the Human Relations School.[18] Similarly, the partial truths of the Human Relations School are then typically shown to be later superseded by more fully developed schools, such as the Contingency school, for example.

What is often overlooked in the "rational reconstruction"[19] of the history of management theory is the disproportionate influence that some of these early theoretical schools have exercised upon the subsequent development of management thought, and the important role that they have continued to play in shaping modern management practices. This is particularly true of Scientific Management, which, in spite of its discredited reputation in some academic quarters, continues to be a powerful influence in the management of many organizations. Contrary to the illusion created by the rational reconstruction of management theory, the theory and practice of Scientific Management have not been universally consigned to the scrap-heap of history, in favour of more enlightened and more humanistic forms of management. Scientific Management, in many ways, has established the domain for all later systems of management, and its principles and practices are still embedded in the management systems of many modern business enterprises (Jacques, 1996).[20]

Although the historical periodization of management theory may seem to imply that earlier theories have been progressively superseded by later theories in the general march towards a "science of management," many management theorists still acknowledge the seminal and continuing influence of Scientific Management ideas upon the entire field of management studies. This is made particularly clear in a strong statement by the doyen of modern management theory, Peter Drucker (1986: 280), which cuts straight to the heart of the matter:

> Personnel Administration and Human Relations are the things talked about and written whenever the management of worker and work is being discussed. They are the things the Personnel Department concerns itself with. But they are not the concepts of the actual management of worker and work in American industry. This concept is Scientific Management. Scientific Management focuses on the work. Its core is the organized study of work, the analysis of work into its simplest elements and the systematic improvement of the worker's performance of each of these elements. Scientific Management has both basic concepts and easily applicable tools and techniques. And it has no difficulty proving the contribution it makes; its results in the form of higher output are visible and readily measurable. Indeed, Scientific Management is all but a systematic philosophy of worker and work. Altogether it may well be the most powerful as well as the most lasting contribution America has made to Western thought since the Federalist Papers.

Drucker is not alone in emphasizing the powerful influence that Scientific Management has exerted on subsequent generations of management theorists. Other writers have also defended Scientific Management against its academic critics, and have tried to rehabilitate it among contemporary students of management theory. Thus, after dismissing such charges against Scientific Management as economism, authoritarianism, exploitation, anti-unionism and dishonesty, Locke (1982: 22-23) concludes his assessment of Taylor, the "founding father" of Scientific Management, by claiming that Taylor's ideas were not only, "right in the context of his time [...] but that most of his insights are still valid today."

In some ways it almost seems as though the ideas of Scientific Management have come full circle. They were certainly received with enthusiasm by business groups during the early decades of the twentieth century, and were even introduced into such giant companies as Dupont and General Motors (Wren, 1987). Later, however, these ideas came under critical attack from labour groups, academics and finally from government, culminating in a Congressional Inquiry into Scientific Management in 1911.[21] Today, to judge from its coverage in contemporary textbooks, Scientific Management has been rehabilitated, and many writers now openly acknowledge its seminal influence on the development of the theory and practice of professional management. The ideas of Scientific Management have never really gone out of style, at least for businessmen and managers, for Taylor always asserted the primacy of their interests in the control of work: to him, this was the bottom line of all systems of management.

However, although most OT and OB texts discuss the origins of Scientific Management, and show its significance for the further development of management theory, virtually none of these mainstream interpretations demonstrate any real understanding of what the practice of Scientific Management has done to the traditional skills and crafts of the (largely male, skilled) labour force, and how, in many cases, women have been crudely used as agents of deskilling.[22] The implications of Scientific Management have, like those of all other theories of management, only been understood from a managerial perspective. It is important, however, to be able to view the consequences of Scientific Management — both in theory and in practice — from the perspective of those at the bottom of the organization, as well as those from the top. In other words, we are entitled to ask: what has Scientific Management, (or any other school of management, for that matter), meant, not only for managers, themselves, but for the workers who have been subjected to its system of control?

Scientific Management, along with the "Universalist" tradition of the French industrialist, Henri Fayol, is normally classified within the Classical school of management theory which emerged at the turn of the century. These theories of the Classical School had several things in common:

1. They view organizations as machines, which is to say, they focus on the formal structure and the design of organizations — the formal, or official status of managers and workers, and the technical design of jobs in the workplace.[23] Their emphasis reflects the engineering interests of men like Taylor and Fayol, who pioneered these early theories of management.

2. They attempt to develop a universal set of principles of management that could be applied to any organization. Both Taylor and Fayol were committed to the goal of developing a general set of principles of management that would form the basis for a "science" of management. Later theorists would reject this Universalist approach in favour of "contingency," approaches to the study of organizations.

From the beginning, it is clear that Taylor was preoccupied with how to increase the efficiency of the workplace. He believed that the tendency of workers to engage in what was known as, "systematic soldiering," that is, in the restriction of their output, constituted the greatest single obstacle to efficiency.[24]

In order to eliminate the problem of soldiering, Taylor saw that it was necessary for managers to greatly increase their control over workers, and over the labour process, and to redesign jobs in ways that stripped workers of any remaining independence they may have had on the job. As is well known, Taylor accomplished these goals through analyzing different jobs in order to determine the most efficient way to perform them, and through redesigning these jobs by breaking each of them into simple tasks, and assigning workers to perform each of these fragmented tasks. By increasing the division of labour, and by transforming work from a complex set of skilled operations into a simple set of repetitive tasks, Taylor hoped to increase the efficiency and productivity of the workplace, and the general effectiveness of the total organization.

In order to achieve these goals, Taylor recommended that the reorganization and redesign of work should be done according to the basic principles of Scientific Management:

1. Managers should control the conception of work, while workers should be responsible only for its execution. In other words, managers should make all the decisions regarding the planning and design of work, while workers should only be responsible for the implementation of these decisions. Taylor introduced a radical distinction between mental and manual labour which was to transform the face of the modern workplace.

2. "Scientific" methods should be used to analyze, and to design all jobs. Taylor was one of the earlier (though not the first) to use "time and motion" studies of workplace efficiency.

3. Detailed instructions should be given to each worker of how to perform his or her job. Workers should follow these instructions to the letter as they represented the one, "best," "scientific" way of performing the task.

4. The "best" workers should be selected to perform each type of job. In practice, this often meant replacing skilled craftsmen (sic) with unskilled workers, who would be more dependent upon management for instructions.

5. Workers should be fully trained by management to perform their jobs; with management monopolizing technical knowledge and having responsibility for training workers to perform their jobs competently and efficiently.

6. Finally, work performance should be regularly monitored by management to ensure that standard procedures of work were being followed.

These, in a nutshell, are some of the basic principles that underlie Taylor's system of Scientific Management, and their contribution to the history of management thought is commonly discussed in OB and OT texts. What has received far less attention is the impact that Taylorism has had on the occupational and educational status of workers in the modern period. Contrary to the popular textbook view, Taylorism was much more than simply an early theory of management; to be later superseded by more enlightened theories of management. In its own way, Taylorism set its seal upon all later theories of management by showing how important it was for managers to increase their control over the labour process. It was only by securing control over the way in which work was done that management could effect the transformation of the modern workplace.

For Taylor and his colleagues, the transformation of work meant, above all else, the destruction of independent "workmanship" with its accumulated tradition of craft skills, and the corresponding monopolization and control of work by management. The advent of Taylorism, therefore, heralded the dawn of modern management. And while later theories of management drew attention to the neglected social aspects of the workplace, it was Taylorism which encouraged the drive that is now prevalent in many workplaces to turn managers into absolute controllers of work, and workers into the passive servants of the new production processes.[25] The consequences of this "deskilling," or "degradation" of work has been well documented (Braverman, 1974; Leonard, 1984).

Although the ideas of many personnel administrators today have usually been influenced by supposedly more humanistic theories of management, the principles of Scientific Management still underlie the organization and design of the workplace in many modern enterprises. This is particularly true for those industries where there is a straightforward task to perform; where the goal is to mass produce the same product again and again; where precision and standardization are deemed important; and where there is a management demand for a work-force that is compliant and easily disciplined. These conditions may be found in a number of enterprises, but nowhere are they so evident as in the fast-food industry. If you really want to see the principles of Scientific Management in action today, go down to your nearest McDonald's, A&W, Burger King, Kentucky Fried Chicken, or similar fast-food outlet. In all of these establishments, the principles of F.W. Taylor are as alive today as on the day he first introduced them. All this is apparent from the way in which managers plan and direct every detail of the work process. Workers are told what to do, managers tell them exactly how to do it. Every aspect of the work of preparing and serving hamburgers is outlined in a detailed manual of instructions.[26] Workers are expected to follow these instructions to the letter, in the interests of standardization and efficiency. Only the "best" candidates for this type of work are hired: usually young men and women of high-school age, with minimum qualifications and skills, or recent immigrants who, employers hope, will be most prepared to work under constant pressure for minimum wages due to their desperate need for a job.

Far from being a discredited and long forgotten blip in the early history of OB and OT, the principles of Scientific Management have become embedded in the modern workplace. Indeed, the separation of the planning and direction of work from its actual performance, and the corresponding rise of professional managers as a distinct social group (some would even define them as a distinct social class)[27] owe much to those principles, first articulated by Taylor. Later theoretical schools emerged to focus on other aspects of management theory, which had been neglected by Scientific Management theorists, including the "human dimension" of work organizations, the rational decision-making processes of managers; and the Contingency approach to organizational change. None of these schools, however, seriously questioned the fundamental division of labour presupposed in all applications of Scientific Management, namely the separation of the conception of work from its execution. It was not until very recently that some management theorists have begun to look beyond this traditional way of organizing work. Nonetheless, newer approaches to organizational management – particularly Business Process Improvement or reengineering – continue to build work practices which privilege workplace structures and processes at the expense of employee initiative and creativity.

MANAGEMENT IN PRACTICE: WHAT MANAGERS REALLY DO

The question of what managers really do, and whether it is adequately represented in the traditions of OT and OB, has preoccupied a number of writers over the past decades. Some writers have argued that management theory has played a useful role in helping us to classify, analyze, and even to explain the complex set of activities that are typically performed by all managers. Other writers have suggested, however, that these theoretical descriptions of management bear little resemblance to what managers actually do during the course of their working days. What are needed in the opinion of the latter, are more empirical studies of managers at work, and less theoretical studies.

One of the earliest attempts to classify the work of managers was made by the French writer Henri Fayol, pioneer of the early school of Universalist management theory. Fayol suggested that the work of management could be broken down into five distinct activities:

- Planning
- Organizing
- Commanding (or directing)
- Coordinating
- Controlling

This attempt to reduce the practice of management to a set of all-inclusive categories was typical of many of the early classical theorists who, as we have already seen, were primarily interested in developing general principles of management. Fayol's classification of managerial work was later revised by another of the classical theorists, Luther Gulick (1937), who proposed an amended typology:

- Planning – deciding on what things to have done, and how to do them in order to accomplish the goals of the organization.
- Organizing – establishing the formal structure of the organization and implementing an efficient division of labour in the work-force.
- Staffing – recruiting and training staff members to perform the different functions of the organization.
- Directing – providing leadership to the organization by setting goals, making decisions and implementing them through instructions and orders to subordinates.
- Coordinating – making sure that the different parts of the organization work harmoniously together to fulfil a common set of goals.
- Reporting – keeping informed about all aspects of the organization through records, research and inspection.
- Budgeting – engaging in the financial planning, accounting and control of the fiscal life of the organization.

Today, some OB and OT texts (cf. Boone et al., 1999; Moorhead et al., 2000) further reduce these earlier classifications of management work to a set of four or five, which generally include some combination of the following elements:

- Planning
- Organizing

- Motivating
- Controlling
- Leading

In these respects, we can see that the earlier attempts of the classical theorists to formulate a systematic and universal classification of the work of management have continued to influence many modern writers in organizing their ideas for contemporary students of management.

Ironically, Gulick's reference to "budgeting" has disappeared almost totally from later classifications. Arguably budgeting is a key element of the practice of management.[28] Without budgeting responsibility, it could be argued, a manager is a manager in name only, and is actually an administrator, or senior clerk.[29] Certainly we can note a trend in many large corporations for functions previously undertaken by middle management to be taken on by, on the one hand, senior management (tasks demanding less drudgery, faster response time) and on the other hand low paid clerical staff (more routine work, not as prioritized).[30] This can be seen in the current trend of large corporations (e.g., British Airways) to create "flatter organizations," i.e., to cut out several layers of middle management.

Other writers have rejected the classical approach, and have argued that the abstract formal categories that have been used to classify the functions of management have very little relevance to what managers really do. In place of broad theoretical generalizations, these critics suggest, what are needed are more empirical studies of how managers actually spend their working days. Most managers, unlike the theorists who write about them, do not divide up their working day into different times for planning, organizing, budgeting, etc:

> If we ask a managing director when he is coordinating, or how much coordination he has been doing during the day, he would not know, and even the most highly skilled observer would not know either. The same holds true of the concepts of planning, command, organization and control (Carlsson, 1951).

In an influential article published several years after Carlsson's groundbreaking work, Henry Mintzberg (1975) dismissed as "folklore," the classical view of management. According to Mintzberg, Henri Fayol's categories have about as much relationship to what managers really do as a Renaissance painting has to a Cubist abstract. Based on his own study of five chief executives over a five-week period, and on the evidence of other similar studies, Mintzberg concluded that the practice of management could not usefully be reduced to the broad Universalist categories favoured by classical theorists. Contrary to the "folklore" of classical theory, Mintzberg found that the daily activities of the managers he studied were characterized by brevity, variety and discontinuity.

During the course of their workday, managers had a large number of brief, informal, two-person contacts, either over the telephone, or through unscheduled meetings. Most of their time, however, was taken up with a relatively small number of scheduled meetings that tended to last for lengthy periods of time. Mintzberg also discovered that his managers much preferred "soft" information – especially by word of mouth – to the "hard" information of written documents and computerized information systems. The reason for this was that this kind of information, obtained through gossip or hearsay, was likely to be more up-to-date than information obtained through more formal channels: "Today's gossip may be tomorrow's facts."

Mintzberg (1975: 60) concluded that the spontaneous, intuitive and generally informal methods of work adopted by most managers during their workday bore little resemblance to the highly rationalized and deliberate functions of management outlined by the classical theorists:

> If there is a single theme that runs through this article, it is that the pressures of his job drive the manager to be superficial in his actions – to overload himself with work, encourage interruption, respond quickly to every stimulus, seek the tangible and avoid the abstract, make decisions in small increments, and do everything abruptly.

In place of the classical functions of management, therefore, Mintzberg suggested that it is more useful to view the work of management as involving the performance of a number of different roles:

- Interpersonal roles, which include,
    1. Managers as figureheads.
    2. Managers as leaders.
    3. Managers as liaison officers.

- Informational roles, which include
    4. Managers as monitors
    5. Managers as disseminators
    6. Managers as spokespeople.

- Decisional roles, which include
  7. Managers as entrepreneurs
  8. Managers as disturbance handlers
  9. Managers as resource allocators
  10. Managers as negotiators.

Several other researchers have also concluded that the classical view of management bears little relationship to what managers actually do at work. Most of these studies have shown that managers do not methodically plan their days around the classical functions of management – at least, not in any systematic sense. These functions are normally performed in jumbled and fragmented ways, as the typical manager struggles to pack a multitude of different activities into the limited time-span of a single day. The evidence from Sweden (cf. Carlsson, 1951), the United States and Canada (cf. Helms Mills, 2003b; Mintzberg, 1973; 1983; Sayles, 1964), Great Britain (cf. Delbridge, 1998; Lawrence, 1984; Stewart, 1988), and Germany (cf. Lawrence, 1984), is all fairly consistent on most of these points. The greater part of the typical manager's day is spent on informal discussions which are usually unplanned, and are often only between two people. With the exception of scheduled meetings, most managers are unable to spend more than thirty minutes on any project without interruption or diversion. The vast majority of contacts that the manager has with other personnel in the organization last less than five minutes. Subordinates initiate most of these contacts; superiors initiated less than five percent.[31]

The results of these empirical studies have convinced some critics of OT and OB, that if students are to learn anything useful about the management of organizations, they should begin with an understanding of how managers actually spend their time, rather than by learning about how classical theorists think that managers should spend their time. Management, for these writers, is not simply a science, but also an art, which cannot easily be reduced to a set of broad abstract principles.

In closing this chapter on management and its relationship to OB and OT, we should not lose sight of the fact that managers are real individuals who run organizations in our society. Beyond its importance as an historical phenomenon, therefore, or as a series of theoretical schools, or set of administrative practices, the institution of management remains a way of life for those whose job it is to plan, direct and supervise the work of others. In this sense, we can even regard the institution of management as part of a culture, in much the same way as recent theorists have begun to study organizations as cultural systems (Martin, 2002). Like all cultures, the management or corporate culture of any organization contains its own values and philosophies, its rituals and symbols, its myths, and its legendary or heroic figures. Every major organization seems to have a celebrated cultural hero: Wardair had its Max Ward; Chrysler its Lee Iacocca; McDonald's its Ray Kroc; Trump its Donald Trump; Mary Kay Cosmetics its Mary Kay Ash, and so on.

Today, some of the more traditional features of management culture in our society have fallen into disrepute. This is especially true of the tendency for managers to be drawn from a relatively narrow cross-section of society from which women and minority groups have been largely excluded. The traditional management culture has remained resolutely androgynous and ethnocentric, as well as middle class in nature; the overwhelming majority of individuals working in top management positions have – until very recently – been white males. This patriarchal dominance, with its corresponding exclusion of women and minorities, has left a very strong imprint on the management culture of organizations in our society, although it is an imprint which has been largely overlooked in mainstream texts of OB and OT (Mills, 2004).

Until recently, many of the least desirable aspects of the managerial culture were assumed to be inevitable features of the corporate world. Many writers on OT and OB have taken for granted the need for managers to be aggressive and competitive in their attempts to successfully scale the corporate ladder. Everyone knows, so it would seem, that the corporate world is often a ruthless jungle, and in order to survive in it successful managers must demonstrate the necessary qualities of aggression, competition, and ruthless ambition. Life at the top of many organizations is invariably stressful and often characterized by loneliness, fear, anxiety, and insecurity.[32] But according to the received wisdom, this is the way the world is, and only those who can demonstrate these gladiatorial qualities can hope to prevail in the corporate culture of management.

More recently, however, some feminist critics of mainstream (and malestream) OB and OT have questioned the inevitability of these predatory aspects of the corporate culture. In their view, the climate of competition, aggression, loneliness and fear which often typifies the corporate culture owes more to the resolutely "male ethos" of life at the top of the organization than to any other institutional imperative. According to this view, the dominance hierarchies associated with so many organizations in our contemporary corporate structure derive from the patriarchal structures of male power and authority. It is these gendered structures, rather than any more general organizational imperative, which breed the gladiatorial qualities so often associated with managers – both male and female – within our organizations. The real force of this feminist critique of traditional OT and OB lies in its implication that, with a radical redirection of organizational values, away from competition, aggression, hierarchy, and individualism, towards cooperation, empathy, equality and reciprocity, our organizational cultures could be transformed into more humane and fulfilling sets of social relationships. This is the great challenge of thinking our way beyond present structures and values in order to actively reshape our institutions. We shall return to some of these issues when looking ahead to the future of OT and OB in the final chapter of this book.

KEY TERMS

budgeting	deskilling	Scientific Management
bureaucratic systems of control	directing	"time and motion" studies
classical approach	informational roles	simple control
commanding	interpersonal roles	staffing
"consensus" view of management	managerial revolution	Reporting
controlling	managerial viewpoint	systematic soldiering
coordinating	organizing	planning
corporate culture	technical control	universalist tradition
decisional roles	re-engineering	

REVIEW QUESTIONS

Q1. What is management? And how do we know?

Assignment: In answering this question, read one account each from the universalist, feminist, from the postmodern, and from the Mintzberg approaches. (see the text and Further reading for guidance to the literature); compare the approaches of each. What do each say about what managers actually do? What do each say about how management should be studied? What difference does gender play in "what managers do"?

Q2. Briefly define each of the following terms, and discuss their contribution to our understanding of management.
- consensus view of management
- classical approach
- universalist tradition
- managerial viewpoint

Assignment: Now turn to the glossary at the end of the book and compare your definitions.

Q3. What is meant by the term "the managerial revolution" and what does it tell us about the practice of management?

Assignment: In answering this question, you should review the appropriate sections of the chapter

Q4. Briefly define each of the following terms and try to provide examples of each from your own work and/or educational experience(s).
- bureaucratic systems of control
- simple control
- technical control

Assignment: Review the appropriate chapter sections, and apply to your own work and/or school experiences.

Q5. What is meant by the terms "deskilling," and "degradation of work," and how may these terms be related to gender and skill in the workplace? Give some examples from your own experience(s) or observations to show how these terms may be applied to different work and/or school situations.

Assignment: Review the appropriate chapter sections, and check your definitions with the glossary at the end of the chapter.

Q6. Briefly define each of the following terms and say how classical theorists relate each to the "practice" of management:
- Budgeting
- Commanding
- Controlling
- Coordinating
- Directing
- Organizing
- Staffing
- Reporting
- Planning

Assignment: Now turn to the glossary at the end of the book and compare your definitions.

Q7. What is the corporate culture of an organization and how does it relate to management?

Assignment: Read any mainstream OB or OT account on management and the role of corporate culture. Now, compare the account you have just read with any feminist accounts of management. How do the two approaches compare? What do feminist accounts tell us about corporate culture and how it might be changed?

Q8. Briefly define "re-engineering" and describe its similarities and differences compared to scientific management.

Assignment: Read the discussions in the chapter and in the glossary of terms on scientific management and re-engineering and attempt to say what differences and similarities you can find.

INTERNET EXERCISES

Q1. Find three organizations online that make specific reference to their corporate cultures. How do they do this and what conclusions, if any can you draw from this information.

Q2. Find 3 companies that have introduced TQM, Re-engineering, and The Balanced Scorecard and compare the role of management in each of these.

EXERCISE 3.1

This exercise is designed to make you think about the significance of management as a set of practices- its impact upon the lives of people generally and your life in particular. Do the tasks individually and then discuss your findings in small groups.

A. From the list below indicate which of the activities you are involved in, on an ongoing, or regular, basis. Indicate whether you manage the activity alone or whether someone else manages for you. On a separate sheet of paper indicate the type of actions involved in managing the activity. (An example is given of a "checking account at the Bank"). Try to be as detailed as possible when describing the kind of managing activities involved.

Example

Activity	Yes/No	Self Managed	Other Managed
Bank Checking Account	Yes	Keeping track of the day-to-day transactions, making payments, ensuring that monies received are paid in record keeping	Bank manager – official recording of accounts; ensuring that account is "in balance"

Activity	Yes/No	Self Managed	Other Managed
Bank Checking Account			
Bank Savings Account			
Owning a car			
Driving a car			
Enrollment in a course of higher education			
Preparing for an examination			
Sitting an examination			
Membership of a social club			
Committee member or organizer of a social club			
Being part of a group of friends			
Being a father or mother to young children			
Being a father or mother to grown children			
Being a member of a family			
Being part of a community organization			
Being a member of a choir			
Being a member of a native band organization			
Being a member of a church			
Being a member of a music band or group			

Activity	Yes/No	Self Managed	Other Managed
Being a member of a sports group			
Being an organizer of a community organization			
Being the leader of a music group/band			
Being a native band leader			
Being an employer			
Being an employee			
Responsibility for child care			
Dating			
Going to the movies, the theatre, or some other activity			
Being a brother or sister			
Eating out in a cafeteria or restaurant			
Going to the doctor for medical advice/treatment			
Going to the hospital for medical treatment			
Going to confession			
Going on strike or engaging in other forms of organizational disputes			
Editing a student newspaper			
Writing for a student newspaper			
Being disciplined by school, university or employer			
Reading a book			
Writing an essay or other assignment			
Buying household groceries and other items			
Other activities not listed above			

B. Now, in small groups discuss your lists, and attempt to summarize the following questions:

1. As a group, how much of your regular activity is self managed and how much of it is managed by others? (You might indicate which activity is wholly self-managed; wholly other managed, or involves a combination of self and other management).

2. Now examine the forms of control used in managing different types of activity and attempt to classify activities according to the dominant form of control. What is the range of control experienced by group members? (Give examples). What is the form of control that is most experienced by group members? (Give examples).

3. Is the range and/or form of control most experienced different depending upon a person's gender, ethnic/race, or class background? What does your answer tell us about managerial control?

4. What is the central different between forms of self-control and other control?

5. Are any specific forms of control associated with some activities but not others?

6. Which activities, if any, could be managed differently and under what circumstances?

CASE ANALYSIS

Turn to the Westray case.

1. How would you characterise the dominant mode of control at the mine?

2. What does the case tell us about the process of management and managing?

Turn to Part 1 and answer the questions in module 1 on Leadership.

USEFUL WEBSITES

<http://www.henrymintzberg.com/>

FURTHER READING

On the history of management thought and development:

Stewart Clegg and David Dunkerly, (1980). ORGANIZATION, CLASS AND CONTROL

Gareth Morgan, (1996b). IMAGES OF ORGANIZATION

Albert J. Mills and Stephen Murgatroyd, (1991). Chapter 1, ORGANIZATIONAL RULES

Michael Rose, (1978). INDUSTRIAL BEHAVIOUR

D.A. Wren, (1994). THE EVOLUTION OF MANAGEMENT THOUGHT

Literary images of management control:

A.J.Cronin, THE STARS LOOK DOWN

John Dos Passos, (1946). THE BIG MONEY

Upton Sinclair, (1946). THE JUNGLE

The non-managerial alternative:

Ivan Ilich, (1981). DESCHOOLING SOCIETY

Michel Foucault, (1979). DISCIPLINE AND PUNISH

On the impact of management theory on the conceptualization of women workers:

R.L.Feldberg and E.N Glenn, (1979). MALE AND FEMALE: JOB VERSUS GENDER MODELS IN THE SOCIOLOGY OF WORK

Marta Calás, AN/OTHER SILENT VOICE? REPRESENTING "HISPANIC WOMEN" IN ORGANIZATIONAL TEXTS

On the neglect of gender in labour process theories:

Scott Davies, (1990). INSERTING GENDER INTO BUROWOY'S THEORY OF THE LABOUR PROCESS

Peta Tancred-Sheriff, (1989). GENDER, SEXUALITY, AND THE LABOUR PROCESS

On the problem of "women in management":

Marta Calás and Linda Smircich, (1992b). USING THE "F" WORD: FEMINIST THEORIES AND THE SOCIAL CONSEQUENCES OF ORGANIZATIONAL RESEARCH

On the resistance of female employees to management control:

Anna Pollert, (1981). GIRLS, WIVES, FACTORY, LIVES

Susan Porter Benson, (1986). COUNTER CULTURES. SALESWOMEN, MANAGERS AND CUSTOMERS IN AMERICAN DEPARTMENT STORES

Robyn Thomas et al., (2004). IDENTITY POLITICS AT WORK: GENDERING RESISTANCE, RESISTING GENDER

On management and people of colour:

Ella Bell and Stella Nkomo, (1992). RE-VISONING WOMEN MANAGER'S LIVES

Anshuman Prasad and Pushkala Prasad, (2002). OTHERNESS AT LARGE. IDENTITY AND DIFFERENCE IN THE NEW GLOBALIZED ORGANIZATIONAL LANDSCAPE

On the application of management theories and the outcomes for people:

Pat Armstrong, et al., (1997). MEDICAL ALERT: NEW WORK ORGANIZATIONS IN HEALTH CARE

Erica Foldy, (2002). "MANAGING" DIVERSITY: IDENTITY AND POWER IN ORGANIZATIONS

Nanette Fondas, (1997). FEMINIZATION UNVIELED: MANAGEMENT QUALITIES IN CONTEMPORARY WRITINGS

P. Prasad, A.J. Mills, M. Elmes and P. Prasad, (1997). MANAGING THE ORGANI-ZATIONAL MELTING POT: DILEM-MAS OF WORKPLACE DIVERSITY

James Rinehart, (1986). IMPROVING THE QUALITY OF WORKING LIFE THROUGH JOB REDESIGN: WORK HUMANIZATION OR WORK RATIONALIZATION?

Robyn Thomas and Annette Davies, (2002). GENDER AND THE NEW PUBLIC MANAGEMENT

Robyn Thomas et al., (2004). IDENTITY POLITICS AT WORK: GENDERING RESISTANCE, RESISTING GEN-DER

END NOTES

1. See Wren (1994: 36). The economist, Alfred Marshall also subscribed to the view that management – or, what he called, "organization" – should be treated separately from the other factors of production. In this regard, he suggested that:
   "The agents of production are com-monly classed as land, labour and capital [...] it seems best sometimes to recognize organization apart as a distinct agent of production" (cited in Dale, 1973: 157).

2. It can be argued that current manage-ment and organization theorists favour moves to employee "empowerment" as a less hierarchical approach (cf. Robbins and Langton, 2004). As we saw in Chapter 1, the notion of em-powerment is highly problematic and usually refers to a process where senior management set the direction of action and behaviour leaving employees to decide how to implement management directives (Foldy, 2002).

3. In this regard Max Ward was something of a modern anachronism. Ward ran his Canadian airline, Wardair, like his personal fiefdom, Intervening in everything from general management decisions to the degree of starch that went into his aeroplane table cloths. In the end, partially as a result of Ward's entrepreneurial style, Wardair suc-cumbed to corporate takeovers by Pacific Western Airlines (PWA). Now, following the acquisition of Canadian Airlines by Air Canada, Wardair is only a distant memory in the archives of Canadian aviation. (For Max Ward's own story see Ward, 1991).

4. Cf. Berle and Means (1967), Dahrendorf (1959), Burnham (1941), Galbraith (1978) and Chandler(1977; 1984). James Burnham, a disillusioned Trotskyite, became impressed by the fact that alongside the growth of professional management in the West, in Soviet Russia – with its bureaucratic state control – a new class of profes-sional managers had developed to run state enterprises "on behalf of" the state.

5. See Rinehart (1986: 100-107) and Krahn and Lowe (2002) for the Cana-dian terms of this debate.

6. This explication of Chandler's ideas is indebted to Pugh et al. (1983: 50-54).

7. Chandler makes a distinction between horizontal and vertical growth – see Wren (1987: 82-83).

8. Another writer whose work has paralleled that of Chandler in some respects is that of Oliver Williamson (1975). The thesis of the managerial revolution was also anticipated in the writings of Karl Marx, who was quite prescient in his analysis of the growth of professional management, as the following quotation reveals:
"Just as the first capitalist is relieved from actual labour as soon as his capital has reached that minimum amount with which capitalist production, properly speaking, first begins, so he now hands over the work of direct and constant supervision of the individual workers and groups of workers to a special kind of wage-labourer. An industrial army of workers under the command of a capitalist requires, like a real army, officers (managers) and NCO's (foremen, overseers), who command during the labour process in the name of capital. The work of supervision becomes their established and exclusive functions"(Marx, Capital I. Cited in Nichols and Beynon, 1977: 30).

9. Burowoy (1979:12), arguing for the significance of the historical perspective, states that, "Industrial sociology and organization theory proceed from the facts of consensus or social control. They do not explain them. It is necessary, therefore, to break with the transhistorical generalities of industrial sociology and organization theory and to dispense with metaphysical assumptions about underlying conflict or harmony [...]. To do this we must restore historical context to the discussion."

10. Wren (1987:43), provides some graphic examples of the kinds of dictatorial management practices which prevailed throughout much of the early period of industrialization. In some cases, corporal punishment was used to discipline – especially child labourers. Fining was also a common practice against workers who had violated the rules of the company in some way. It is of interest to note, however, that in these early paternalistic family enterprises, punishment could just as easily be exacted for supposedly moral transgressions as for breaches of industrial discipline. This is made clear from the following set of sanctions which were posted in the factories of Samuel Oldknow, considered one of the more progressive employers of the late eighteenth century:
"That when any person, either Man, Woman or Child, is heard to CURSE or SWEAR, the same shall forfeit One Shilling -And when a Hand is absent from Work, (unless unavoidably detained by sickness, or Leave being first obtained), the same shall forfeit as many Hours of Work as have been lost; and if by the Job or Piece, after a Rate of 2 [shillings] 6 [pence] per Day – Such Forfeitures to be put in a Box, and distributed to the Sick and Necessitous, at the discretion of their Employer."
This rule was posted December 1, 1797 and is reprinted in B.W. Clapp (ed.), Documents in English Economic History, Vol. 1. London: G. Bell and Sons, 1976:387. Capitals from the original.

11. For an account of the negative impact of TQM on the Canadian health care system see Armstrong et al., (1997).

12. In recent years the focus of attention has shifted to "knowledge work" (Bahra, 2001; Blackler, 1992; Dierkes, 2001; Newell, 2002; Ray, Quintas, Little and Open University., 2002; Sanchez, 2001; Senge, 1994). This has resulted in a shift that encourages managers to give employees greater leeway to develop and exercise their knowledge. For some, this new "view of organizations, which lets people grow and develop, contrasts sharply with those early Taylorist principles of organizational design, which embraced principles of speed, repetition, cost efficiency, and above all conformity" (Ellis and Dick, 2000: 119). Indeed, the contrast is an important one. Nonetheless, attempts to manage knowledge take management control to new and more problematic areas of an employee's sense of self. Further, as the following definition indicates, the notion of knowledge is being defined from a narrow management perspective: Knowledge management refers to "any structured activity that improves an organization's capacity to acquire, share, and utilize knowledge that enhances its survival and success" (McShane and Von Glinow, 2000: 19). For critical readings on knowledge (1972; Foucault, 1980)and knowledge management see (Bratton, Helms Mills, Pyrch and Sawchuk, 2004; Easterby-Smith and Lyles, 2003; Griseri, 2001; Styhre, 2003).

13. To date, the struggle between management and labour has traditionally been represented as a struggle between groups of males – the male manager and the skilled male worker. This debate misses the fact that women have traditionally been excluded from management and from position and definitions of skilled work (cf. Cockburn, 1985; 1991). Labour process and management theorists alike have been guilty of ignoring gender from their analyses (Davies, 1990; Tancred-Sheriff, 1989).

14. Not only have women been excluded from many skilled jobs but very few female-dominated jobs have – regardless of skill requirement – been classified as "skilled". Cf. Cockburn, op cit.

15. Tancred-Sheriff (1989) argues that in the labour process women have been used as a form of "adjunct control" in which their sexuality has been used by organizations as a form of mediation between the business and its clients.

16. Several women have made important contributions to OB and OT, but until recently their contribution has been neglected (Tancred-Sheriff and Campbell, 1992). Dr. Lillian Moller Gilbreth, who, with her husband Frank Gilbreth, pioneered the system of Scientific Management, during the early decades of this century; Mary Parker Follet, who was another proponent of Scientific Management, later played an important part in presaging the development of the Human Relations School. In later years Joan Woodward played a central role in the development of the contingency approach to management.

17. For a critique of this popular view of science, see Kuhn (1970); Feyerabend (1975).

18. For example, in his review of Scientific Management, Robbins (Robbins, 1990: 35) concludes with a qualification which is typical of many historical interpretations:

"In retrospect, we recognize that Taylor offered a limited focus on organizations. He was looking only at organizing work at the lowest level of the organization – appropriate to the management job of a supervisor […]".

Similarly, Nelson and Quick (2000: 469-470) refer to Scientific Management as a "traditional" approach and argue that it's "fundamental limitation […] is that it undervalues the human capacity for thought and ingenuity." They then go on to look at a number of more modern and enlightened approaches.

19. This term was originally used by Imre Lakatos (1972) to describe the inductivist, or incremental view of modern science in which the history of science is portrayed as the gradual and inevitable progress towards the truth. Lakatos has criticized this received view as inconsistent with the way in which the history of science has actually developed. For further critical discussion of the inductivist historiography and epistemology of science see Kuhn (1970) and Feyerabend (1975).

20. This is at its clearest in business process reengineering (cf. Hammer, 1990; 1996; Hammer and Champy, 1993).

21. See, Hearings before Special Committee of the House of Representatives to Investigate the Taylor and other systems of Shop Management under authority of House Resolution 90, Washington, D.C., US Government Printing Office, 1912.

22. While Braverman (1974) revealed how female workers were used by managers as cheap labour to perform the newly deskilled tasks of previously skilled male workers, it was left to Cockburn (1985) to remind us that the notion of "skill" is itself a gendered concept and that Scientific Management helped to strengthen the tendency to exclude women from categories of skilled work.

23. See Morgan (1996b: Chapter 2) for an excellent discussion of how the Classical school of management drew its inspiration from the image of the organization as a machine. Morgan shows how the machine metaphor is far from dead in the modern world, but continues to inform ideas about management in many modern business enterprises.

24. Taylor's obsession with the problem of soldiering in the workplace has been observed by many writers. Krahn and Low (1988: 105) for example, quote Taylor as saying that, "There could be no greater crime against humanity than this restriction of output." Even given the seriousness (and self-righteousness) with which Taylor looked upon industrial efficiency, this statement seems quite obsessive in the degree of its exaggeration. Braverman (1974: 98) also shows the importance that the problem of soldiering had for Taylor in a quotation which reveals just how central this issue was to him:

"The greater part of systematic soldiering […] is done by the men with the deliberate object of keeping their employers ignorant of how fast work can be done. So universal is soldiering for this purpose, that hardly a competent workman can be found in a large establishment, or under any of the ordinary systems of compensating labour, who does not devote a considerable part of his time to studying just how slowly he can work and still convince his employer that he is going at a good pace. The causes of this are, briefly, that practically all employers determine upon a maximum sum which they feel it is right for each of their classes to earn per day, whether their men work by the day or piece."

25. Although some OB and OT textbooks suggest that the principles of Scientific Management presupposed the full cooperation of workers in the "scientific" reorganization and redesign of their jobs, Taylor (1967: 83), himself, was never in any doubt about how such cooperation should be secured:
"It is only through enforced standardization of methods, enforced adoption of the best implements and working conditions, and enforced cooperation that this faster work can be assured. And the duty of enforcing the adoption of standards and of enforcing this cooperation rests with management alone [...] All those who, are proper teaching, either will not or cannot work in accordance with the new methods and at the higher speed must be discharged by the management."

26. Some indication of how precisely McDonald's workers are trained in the details of fast food preparation and service can be seen from the following description of the operating manual used in all McDonald's franchises:
"It told operators exactly how to draw mill shakes, grill hamburgers, and fry potatoes. It specified precise cooking times for all products and temperature settings for all equipment. It fixed standard portions on every food item, down to the quarter ounce of onions placed on each hamburger patty and the thirty-two slices per pound of cheese. It specified that french fries be cut at nine-thirty seconds of an inch thick. And it defined quality controls that were unique to food service, including the disposal of meat and potato products that were held more than ten minutes in a serving bin. The manual also defined those specialized production techniques that made the operation of McDonald's like an assembly line [...]." Cited in Love (1986: 141-2). See also Morgan (1996b), and Ritzer (1996). A similar account is offered by Ester Reiter (1986; 1990), based on her own experiences as a fast-food worker for Burger King. But perhaps the quintessential example of Taylorist principles comes from the slogan which was popularized by the management of Kentucky Fried Chicken in the form of the acronym, KISS: Keep It Simple Stupid. Surely, there has never been a more parsimonious expression of the basic principles of Scientific Management!

27. See Burham (1941); Dahrendorf (1959); Berle and Means (1967); and in the context of the East European managers, Djilas (1982).

28. Mills and Murgatroyd (1991: 122-124), for example, argue that "accounting rules" are an essential element of the functioning of organizational management.

29. Kanter (1977; 1979) and Pfeffer (1992) have noted the relationship between power and resources. Kanter has noted that many managers in large corporations have little discretion over resources and, as such, are powerless – managers in name only. Pfeffer, on the other hand, described power as the most important resource for managers to have.

30. We are grateful to Peter Saunders for these observations about the centrality of budgeting.

31. To date, in true gendered fashion, studies of what managers do have almost exclusively focussed on males. Judi Marshall (1984) has made an important study of female managers that after 20 years is still one of the few studies of what women managers do.

32. Many examples of the predatory aspects of the corporate culture of management exist. The following comments taken from the reminiscences of one former CEO provide a vivid illustration of life at the top for many managers.

"Fear is always prevalent in the corporate structure. Even if you're a top man, even if you're hard, even if you do your job – by the slight flick of a finger, your boss can fire you. There's always the insecurity. You bungle a job. You're fearful of losing a big customer. You're fearful so many things will appear on your record, stand against you. You're always fearful of the big mistake[…]
The executive is a lonely animal in the jungle who doesn't have a friend. Business is related to life. I think in our everyday living we're lonely" (Terkel, 1974: 406).

CHAPTER 4

Creating the Psychic Prison

The central objective of this chapter is to challenge the reader to think about the impacts of organizational arrangements on the way persons come to relate to each other and come to view themselves and other persons. To this end the chapter explores the relationship between the construction of human subjectivity and social factors that contribute to the construction of organization life. The chapter then examines six important critical approaches to the understanding of the psychic life of organizations - critical theory, humanist, Marxist, Postmodernist, psychoanalytic, and feminist. The chapter ends by suggesting a synthesis of critical approaches.

Work and Identity – An Interview With Sharon Webb[1]

Sharon Webb was born on her parents' tobacco farm in Ontario in the late 1950s. It was a very traditional environment in which the men worked the land and the women cooked and cleaned. From an early age, Sharon's father impressed on her the importance of the relationship between work and sense of self, constantly warning his children that if they didn't grow up like him they "were going to be nothing but ditch-diggers." It was a message which he directed more at his sons than at Sharon. He had a different message for her: "You're going to get pregnant, you're going to get married and you're going to be stupid." This might have moulded her into his image of her but he was a harsh man who had little time for his children and that fuelled in her a determination to resist.

She left home at fourteen and entered the world of work where she faced many challenges to her sense of self and identity. As a parts' truck driver, for example, Sharon faced many problems. The company that she came to work for had never hired a female driver before and was in the process of contesting accusations of discrimination when Sharon applied for the position. She was hired but it was made clear to her that she wasn't wanted. To impress on her that it was a "man's job" they made her pick up sixty pound cylinder heads as part of the job. She later found out that the men were expected to use forklifts to pick up the cylinder heads. Next her driving skills were questioned. If she didn't complete her deliveries in a certain time she was told, "We'll find someone more capable." Then her supervisor prohibited her from talking with anyone else in the workplace: "I got so mad and I used to cry. And I thought, No, I'm not giving in, I'm not giving in to this bullhead. Oh, and I'd be so mad – I'd get in my truck, I'd bawl my eyes out half way across the city and then calm down again."

Any attempts that she made to learn more about the job were met with hostility: one time she was in the office attempting to learn something about computing and was "literally torn out of the office" by the supervisor and told, "That's not your job and you're not to learn anything that I don't teach you. If you're caught in here again you're fired." On other occasions she was demeaned when the supervisor attempted to show her "how to hold a pencil correctly" to improve her efficiency and when she was expected to "wash toilets, empty ashtrays, do the garbage"- jobs not connected with the employment of a parts' driver. Sharon was also sexually harassed but "warned off" her male colleagues. She had more problems with the male customers: "They'd say, here's a hot little number working in here – she must service everyone. They'd try it because there's people out there who think that all the time." Eventually Sharon was forced to quit this job. She moved on to other work and other sets of organizational experiences.

INTRODUCTION

Organizations are human creations. Persons establish them for given and changeable ends, and they employ or recruit other persons to help achieve those ends. The activities of the people involved become linked and regularized through various processes of co-ordination and control. In time these activities create a sense of something objective, something standing above the members of the organization; a sense of structure, of organization, is created. In turn, the "objective" *sense* of organization helps to create the illusion that organizations are places devoid of human subjectivity and emotion: worries, concerns, dreams, desires, family, and sexuality are expected to be submerged in the day-to-day activities of the organization and its goals.

This feel of the organization is a familiar one, but it is not the only impression. People do not leave their selves behind when they come to work. The workplace is charged with emotionality, family concerns, sexuality, worries, hopes and dreams: try as they may, persons cannot divorce their selves from the workplace. Organizations are composed of people with diverse psychological needs and behaviours, which inevitably come to influence and be shaped by, working relationships.

In describing her work experiences Sharon Webb said that "most of the jobs that [she] found unpleasant had to do with the people [she] had to work with, not the work itself." In her job as a parts' truck driver she confronted questions about her womanhood, her physical capabilities, her intelligence, her skills, her ability to learn, and her moral values. She had to survive an organizational context where "real women" were those who appeared weak, got pregnant, and were primarily committed to home and family. It was an organizational context where overt displays of heterosexuality were an expected sign of masculinity and femininity.

The specifics of such non-task related experiences are peculiar to Sharon Webb, but the experiences themselves are a general part of everyday work life. The experiences were not incidental to Sharon's job. Her ability to complete her work tasks and earn a wage was framed by non-task experiences. That Sharon was able to survive tells us something about her psychological strength and the ability of persons to resist organizational pressures. But not everyone is capable of resisting pressures. In part, this may have something to do with the fact that not all organizational pressures are experienced as negative; in part it has to do with the individual strengths of the people involved; in part it has to do with the fact that most organizational experiences confront us as "normal"; but largely it has to do with the fact that, at an individual level, most people have little or no organizational power.[2]

Organizations have come to exert a powerful influence over people's lives. Power, social status, income, and wealth are often gained in and through organizations. Those whose relationship to the modern organization is tenuous ("housewives"), disrupted ("unemployed"), undeveloped ("preschooler"), or terminal ("retirees") find themselves labelled as somehow less than whole persons. For those inside the organizational world, hierarchical relationships determine various material, social, and psychological outcomes.

That organizations can have a powerful influence on the way people come to think about themselves and others has rarely been of interest to organizational theorists and managers. Where there has been a focus on the psychological well-being of persons in organizations, it is linked with a concern to improve organizational goals. Indeed, much of OT/OB theory has served to reinforce managerialist views of the role of organizations and the persons who serve them (Clegg, 1981). That is why we examine the role of OT/OB theory in the following section of this chapter.

To uncover the links between organizational structures and personality we need to go beyond traditional OT/OB theory. Through an examination of critical theory, humanist, Marxist, Postmodernist, psychoanalytic feminist and racioethnicity studies of organization, the remainder of this chapter sets out to introduce a range of alternative theories and to identify some of the key relationships between organization and personality.

PSYCHIC PHENOMENA AND ORGANIZATIONAL BEHAVIOUR

An interest in the psychology of people at work began in the early stages of the development of OT and OB. Scientific management theory developed at a time when employers believed in the absolute right of managers to command and the employees to obey. This was reflected in the work of Frederick Taylor, the originator of Scientific Management theory. On the surface Taylor's theory of management has nothing to do with psychology but his implicit views of human nature play a central role. Taylor viewed the employee as a simple organism who responds to reward and to threat, noting that "one of the very first requirements for a man who is fit to handle pig iron as a regular occupation is that he more nearly resembles in his mental makeup the ox than any other type" (quoted in Steers, 1981: 374): this notion of human nature became an important factor in the way Scientific Management was applied and how employees were treated (Rose, 1978).[3]

It was the Hawthorne Studies that began to focus on the psychological aspects of employees. The series of studies commissioned by Western Electric at its Hawthorne Works (Chicago), beginning in the mid 1920s and ending in the mid 1930s, was motivated by management concerns with low productivity and high turnover. Unlike Taylor, the Hawthorne researchers drew on explicit theories of human personality – including the work of Durkheim, Pareto and Freud; theories which were used to legitimize the development of specific forms of workplace control. What was implicit throughout the Hawthorne research is a view of women as psychologically inferior to men (see Chapter 5).

Durkheim's theory of social solidarity was used to argue that the modern workplace fulfills a need in people for group solidarity (Roethlisberger and Dickson, 1939). Workplace control was seen not as some undemocratic series of dictates but as an important form of social integration in an otherwise fragmented society. Pareto's elitist theory of leadership was used to legitimize a view of employees as "irrational," and thus in need of the "rational" leadership of the modern manager. From this viewpoint management was not simply a right but an important form of social leadership. Freud's work on neurosis was used to explain that negative behaviour and attitudes at work were not so much due to dissatisfactions with the work as to deep-seated, psychological problems rooted in unresolved family and childhood factors. To this end the Western Electric company, for a time, required all their Hawthorne employees to undergo psychoanalytical counselling sessions to "help" them to see that certain of their attitudes were problematic and interpersonal rather than work related (Rose, 1978).

This elitist view of human nature had a major impact on the development of theories of organizational behaviour and was no doubt aided and abetted by the fact that it struck a cord with existing management views and needs, and by the misappropriate classification of this school of thought as "Human Relations"!

After World War II, a concern with psychological aspects of the workplace developed in a number of directions – focusing on motivation, leadership style, resistance to change, organizational climate, psychological well-being and satisfaction, and, more recently, organizational culture. The sheer number of studies on the relationship between psychological factors and organizational outcomes led, in North America, to the development of Organizational Behaviour as a specific area of study distinct from Organization Theory and its focus on the relationship between structural arrangements and organizational outcomes.

The development of OB and OT has been somewhat paradoxical. Although primarily concerned with the *management* of behaviour, most modern OB/OT textbooks express a concern for the psychological needs of employees – discussing issues such as stress, discrimination, and values. While the concern with people's needs is genuine enough it is usually subordinated to the ends of efficiency and profitability (Rinehart, 1986). As the following examples illustrate, the focus on psychological and/or social needs has become a tool for achieving organizational ends:

Stress: As you might expect from the discussion of psychological and physical problems, stress can affect performance. In part, performance decreases can be attributed to those psychological or physical impediments that prevent top performance. But there are indirect effects as well. For example, there seems to be at least some relationship between stress and absenteeism and turnover.... Regardless, there are high potential costs to replacing employees or dealing with underperformers who stay (Sweeney and McFarlin, 2002: 262).

Values: Organizations can mould their workplace by hiring people with similar values and/or aligning individuals' jobs and values.... Studies have shown that when individual values align with organizational values the results are positive.... Shared values between the employer and the organization also lead to more positive work attitudes, lower turnover, and greater productivity (Robbins and Langton, 2004: 75)

Diversity: Making all types of employee feel included and an important part of the organization can contribute to several positive organizational outcomes.... [An] organization's ability to attract, retain, and motivate individuals from diverse backgrounds (age, gender, ethnicity, etc.) helps it achieve and sustain competitive advantage in a variety of key areas (Konopaske and Ivancevich, 2004: 218).

In all three cases above, the authors' concern for people is lost in a greater concern with efficiency and productivity. Stress, values, and a sense of self (diversity) are all *things* to be manipulated. There is little consideration of the potential disruption and dislocation of the persons involved, or of the real problems involved in coping with discriminatory workplaces. Nor is there an apparent awareness of the paradox of concern with human growth in a context of unequal power relations.

Rarely do OT and OB studies question existing arrangements of power and control (cf. Hardy and Clegg, 1996). Even the language used masks organizational power relationships. On the one hand references are made to "people," "groups," "individuals" or even "organization members" but less often to "employees" or "workers." However, as the quotes above make clear, there is a vast difference between a person and an employee – "person" suggests someone with a high level of free will, while "employee" suggests a relationship involving limited discretion. On the other hand, endless references are made to "the organization" rather than to owners, chief executives, senior managers, shareholders, or boards of directors.

This gives the impression that a greater entity, or a greater good, rather than the narrow interests of those in control, is behind the needs of increased efficiency and profitability. Thus, the manipulation of stress is not due to the interests of shareholders or senior executives but to the "organization's standpoint." And the need to capitalize on diversity arises not from the viewpoint of those in control of the organization but from the "organizational perspective."

The issue of control, and its impact on personality, is left out of accounts in studies of organizational behaviour (Rinehart, 1986). Thus, it is not surprising that, apart from "diversity management" (see Chapter 6) most OB and OT studies also leave out of account issues of gender, ethnicity/race, and class. Much of OT/OB research fails to take the gender of their subjects into account in their findings and to date has largely neglected non-white workers as subjects. Likewise blue-collar workers have received only a fraction of the attention given to white-collar, professional and supervisory staffs. Industrial work – with its technological means of control (e.g., the conveyer belt), its payments-by-results system of motivation, and its clear lines of authority – seems a less appropriate area for studying the improvement of techniques of motivation and leadership, or of human growth! What we are left with is an area of study concerned, at best, with the psychological well-being of the non-manual, white, male employee.

By ignoring issues of control and its dimensions of class, gender and race OT and OB have contributed to, rather than exposed, the nature of organizational power and its impact on our sense of self. In the next section we explore the relationship between organizational power and personality through a review of seven critical approaches to organization.

NOW TURN TO EXERCISE 4.1 AT THE END OF THE CHAPTER

IMAGES OF THE PSYCHIC PRISON

[The] idea of organizations as psychic prisons [is a] metaphor [which] joins the idea that organizations are psychic phenomena, in the sense that they are ultimately created and sustained by conscious and unconscious processes, with the notion that people can actually become imprisoned or confined by the images, ideas, thoughts, and actions to which these processes give rise. The metaphor encourages us to understand that while organizations may be socially constructed realities, these constructions are often attributed an existence and power of their own that allow them to exercise a measure of control over their creators (Morgan, 1996b: 215).

An interest in the relationship between the development of the self and modern organization can be traced back to the work of Marx, Weber, and Durkheim (see Chapter 1) but, with few exceptions, none of these concerns have been developed within the OB/OT literature. The most thorough-going development and syntheses of Marx' and Weber's ideas were undertaken outside the emergent OT/OB fields by the *Institute of Social Research* (ISR*)*. Founded in Frankfurt (Germany) in 1923, the ISR was established to undertake interdisciplinary research concerned with grasping "the ultimate causes of (the) processes of (social) transformation and the laws according to which they evolve."[4] Marxist in orientation, the Institute attracted a number of radical scholars interested in research into the nature of capitalism and its transformation. Scholars who came to work at the ISR include Max Horkheimer, Theodore Adorno, Erich Fromm, Wilhelm Reich, and Herbert Marcuse.

Critical Theory

The broad theoretical perspective which developed at the ISR became known as the "Frankfurt School" or "critical theory" and was shaped by several factors – including the rise of fascism in Germany and the development of Stalinism in the Soviet Union. Those factors led many of the critical theorists to broaden their interest in the transformation of capitalism to encompass issues of personality development and the impact of bureaucratization on social life. Events in Germany and the Soviet Union were revealing that, given the right conditions, increasingly large numbers of persons were able to act in a cold, heartless and brutal manner. To make sense of the impact of organization on personality, critical theorists drew primarily on the work of Weber, Marx, and Freud.

The issues and debates generated by critical theory are complicated and outside the focus of an introductory text[5] but three areas of discussion raise important questions about the relationship between personality and organization and warrant our attention. The first area of discussion – on "consumption"- deals with the issue of economic power and dehumanization and suggests that in capitalist organizations people are treated as "things" or commodities. The second area of discussion – on "bureaucracy"- deals with the issue of ideological power and organizational behaviour and suggests that bureaucratic rules encourage people to internalize narrow bureaucratic ways of thinking and acting: people *become* bureaucrats. The third area of discussion – on "personality"– suggests that capitalism is a system that stifles creativity and human growth and rewards repressive and authoritarian behaviour.

On Capitalism and Consumption: Critical theorists argue that capitalism reduces persons to the level of "things."[6] Capitalism is defined as a system in which goods are produced not for immediate consumption but as items for sale on the market. For example, Albert Mills once worked in a factory that canned vegetables, but the green beans that he and his co-workers spent hours preparing were not viewed by the multinational company as vegetables to be eaten, so much as products to be sold. Similarly, the productive capacities of persons are viewed as commodities for sale. In order to live, the great majority of us have to sell our labour power (or workplace *abilities*) to an employer. Employers are in business to make a profit and are more likely to hire a person for what they can do (abilities, skills, etc), rather than who they are (i.e., personality). Personality, except where it has a direct bearing on the job, is normally irrelevant to the employer. Thus, workplace relations take on a thing-like quality, with employee contributions to the organization being valued as a commodity. This can be seen in the everyday phrases such as "he was worth employing," "her productivity is too low," "he isn't producing enough." When Albert Mills applied for the job at the canning factory, for example, he was hired for his capacity to labour for 14 hours per day, rather than who he was as a person. At no time did the company show any interest in the shop floor people they employed. An incident at the canning factory that illustrates the notion of people as commodities occurred when one of the employees fell asleep at his work. The supervisor responded by having all the seats removed from the work area, leaving employees to stand for 14 hours. It took a strike to force the company to replace the seats and to recognise that they were employing people and not machines.

According to critical theorists, the employee is surrounded by a world of things, and as a result begins to see him or herself as a thing. Many persons find it hard to escape the feeling that they are just a cog in the wheel, a faceless number who is ultimately replaceable. You may have noticed, for example, that in some organizations numbers are permanently fixed on office doors while names appear on temporary fixtures. The process is exacerbated by the fact that employees have little or no control over the work process, that the nature of their work is specialized and separate from the work of others, that employees are placed in a competitive relationship with other employees, and that the nature of work usually involves tasks which inhibit creative and autonomous thinking. In short, the nature of capitalist production inhibits the ability of the employee to experience his/herself as a creative and meaningful human being. This process is further compounded by the organizational character of the workplace which is increasingly bureaucratic in nature.

On Instrumental Reason and Bureaucracy: On the face of it bureaucracy is a particular form of organizational structure, defined by a combination of specialization, standardization, formalization and centralization (see Chapter 2), a neutral instrument of organization. Yet critical theorists argue that bureaucracy is not simply a way of organizing but is also a way of thinking and acting that is far from neutral in its impact on employees.

Max Weber contends that bureaucracy is a form of organizing that arises out of, and depends on, a form of rational, calculative thinking. The modern world, according to Weber, is characterized by instrumental reasoning whereby persons act according to a series of means and ends calculations and this has contributed to the development and efficiency of the bureaucracy form of organization (see Chapter 2). Building on the work of Weber, the critical theorist Herbert Marcuse (1970) argues that bureaucracy is not simply a form of organizational structure that is neutral in its functioning and outcomes: it is a form of organizational life which forces persons to think and act in narrow ways. Bureaucracy, according to Marcuse, affects employees in three crucial ways: (i) domination;, (ii) atomization, and (iii) the destruction of creative thought and reflexivity.

Domination: Within a system of private ownership and control instrumental reasoning, or means-end calculability serves the ends of the powerful within the organization. The relationship between capitalist and worker, manager and managed, profit and wages are masked by a complex system of organizational rules and regulations. For example, at two of Albert Mills' former employers – *Wilson's Ropery* and *Gaskell and Chambers Hotel and Barfitters* – those in charge decided the rules and the systems of work, with a view to maximizing profit. In the rope factory the system of control was clear; Mr. Wilson gave direct orders to Mills and his co-workers. In the bureaucratic offices of Gaskell and Chambers control was indirect, with those in charge directing much of the work through a series of company rules and regulations. Bureaucratic structures appear to the worker as a neutral organizational form; a scientifically devised means for achieving certain ends. It masks the control behind the rules and allows people to be controlled and to control the activities of others. At Gaskell and Chambers, for example, people did not need to be given a direct order to follow the dictates of those in charge; they followed the rules and regulations and made sure that other people did so too. Because of the apparent neutral experience of rules they often take on a life of their own, becoming ends in themselves; rules, in other words, become important for their own sake rather than the ends they are supposed to serve.

Bureaucratic control, according to Marcuse, influences not only domination of the body but of the personality. Bureaucratic rationality, by reducing every-thing to calculable dimensions, shapes how we are viewed as persons. The pro-ductive activities of the employee are not viewed from a human perspective which marvels at what a person can achieve, instead they are judged from a narrow set of performance measures designed to assess whether the person is a "good" employee. Those in charge of the bureaucracy do not judge employees for their humanity but for their ability to perform certain tasks ; to be "moti-vated, guided and measured by [external] standards" (Marcuse, 1941, quoted in Held, 1980: 67). In other words, we are hired for our workplace abilities which become associated with *who* we are, and then our abilities are judged in a number of ways that further shape how we are viewed as persons. If, for exam-ple, a worker's productivity is judged as below average then that person may be labelled "lazy"; if a person makes an error they may be viewed as "careless"; if a person refuses to work overtime they may be judged as lacking commitment, etc. We come to be viewed through the narrow lens of our ability to be the "good worker" rather than the "good person."

Atomization: A key aspect of bureaucracy is specialization in which a whole task is broken down into numerous elements to be completed by a mul-titude of different people. Each person in the bureaucracy is assigned one small, often routine, part of the overall process. Marcuse contends that this process of "atomization" is not simply structural but is psychological in its outcomes. At-omization has several negative affects on the employee: work is experienced as fragmented, knowledge of the overall process becomes remote, and there are fewer opportunities for mental and reflective labour. Atomization means that work relations and power relations are experienced, through rules and regula-tions, as neutral and impersonal. People come to judge themselves according to their relationship to the rules rather than to who they are as persons. For exam-ple, studies of the cause of the 1986 explosion of the Challenger shuttle – which resulted in the death of seven astronauts – indicate that when some people opposed the fatal launch they were told to "take off your engineering hats and put on your management hats" (Maier, 1997). In other words, people were being encouraged to forget their broader humanity and judge the dangers involved through a narrow managerial lens.

The Death of Creative Thought: The combination of impersonal domination and atomization helps to create a set of work experiences which encourage narrow, rigid thinking and which, as a consequence, help to inhibit the development of creative thought and action. This can, as other critical theorists have argued, lead to the arrest of personality development and the rise of the authoritarian personality (Adorno, 1969). Kanter's (1977; 1979) work on bureaucratic organization and power, for example, suggests that a lack of power encourages "rules mindedness"; that people who lack power and authority often resort to a petty use of rules and regulations to gain some importance in the job. Other studies of bureaucracy (see Chapter 2) indicate that rules and regulations often substitute for initiative and independent thought.

On Personality Development, Sexuality, and Authoritarianism: Following Marx, many of the critical theorists argue that persons have innate capacities for creativity; that through productive activity persons *create* their world and in so doing *create* themselves. Historically, however, productive activity has not been freely engaged in but instead has been subordinated to the needs of private ownership and control: as a result the individual has become a "worker" and his/her labour activity has been engaged in the production of things. This "unfree" labour has led to the development of a world which appears alien and beyond the comprehension and powers of the individual. Instead of feeling in command of the process of creativity, the modern worker experiences powerlessness and a distinct lack of creative abilities (Leonard, 1984).

Concern for understanding human subjectivity led several of the critical theorists to the work of Freud, and, as a result, the concepts of "life instinct" and "repression" became central to the analysis of organizational realities. In their various ways critical theorists argued that a striving for life – sexual and self-preservation instincts – is at the core of a person's being and the more that this instinct is suppressed the more distorted and disturbed, the less creative and human the person is likely to become. Capitalist organization is seen as playing a more or less direct role in the process of repressing the life instinct. Horkheimer, for example, argues that organizations repress the life force (or libido) to ensure sufficient energy for production but that this tends to reduce persons to the status of mere functionaries of economic mechanisms and enforces suffering on a massive scale. The experience of repression causes feelings of guilt and/or inadequacy and increased aggression towards self and others (Held, 1980: 44). As we shall see in Chapter 5, many organizations prohibit shows of emotionality – including "displays" of homosexuality (Shilts, 1993); an "over concern" with family issues, such as child-care needs, etc. (Wilson, 2002); and heterosexual office romances (Mainiero, 1993).

Focussing on sexuality – by which he meant genital sexuality[7] – Wilhelm Reich argues that capitalist organization represses sexuality and in the process blocks people's impulses for liberating experiences:

> It was not until relatively late, with the establishment of an authoritarian patriarchy and the beginning of the division of the classes, that suppression of sexuality begins to make an appearance. It is at this stage that sexual interests in general begin to enter the service of a minority's interest in material profit; in the patriarchal marriage and family this state of affairs assumes a solid organization form[....] The moral inhibition of the child's natural sexuality [through the formation of a strong super-ego], the last stage of which is the severe impairment of the child's genital sexuality, makes the child afraid, shy, fearful of authority, obedient, "good," and "docile"[....] It has a crippling effect on man's rebellious forces because every vital life-impulse is now burdened with severe fear; and since sex is a forbidden subject, thought in general and man's critical faculty also become inhibited (quoted in Held, 1980: 117).

This process results in rigid, conservative and reactionary thinking that, for Reich, is characteristic of capitalist organization but which was at its apex in Nazi Germany.

In attempting the explain the rise of fascism and the appeal of the Nazis, Reich and Adorno developed Freudian analyses. Adorno's work centred on the issue of ego weakness and narcissism. Adorno believed that capitalism had progressively weakened the position of the father as an authority figure and that as a result the growing child develops a weak ego and the inability to keep in check a striving for gratification. The person become self centred and absorbed (or "narcissistic"). Such a person becomes susceptible to powerful, organized agencies. This happens through two powerful mechanisms – (i) the provision of an outlet for repressed urges, and (ii) identification with a strong leader.

Repressed urges: Certain groups encourage the release of repressed urges and allow the transfer of energy to the service of the group. The Nazis, for example, attracted recruits by encouraging the use of violence and destruction. In today's world organized soccer hooliganism and the rise of neo-Nazism in Europe have attracted a number of young followers bent on destructive activity.

Identification and leadership: In Freudian theory the central mechanism for transforming human energy or libido into a bond between follower and leader is identification. The self-absorbed person with a weak ego is often prey to the attractions of a strong leader. Identification involves an essential, primitive narcissistic aspect, one which makes the "beloved object part of oneself." The authoritarian leader becomes, according to Adorno, an enlargement of the subject's own personality. Thus, strong narcissistic impulses can be satisfied by identification and idealization of a leader (Held, 1980: 135).

To date, the works of the critical theorists remain the most thoroughgoing analysis of the relationship between personality and organization. In recent years a growing number of studies have revived interest in the relationship between organizational realities and human personality – revisiting many of the issues raised by critical theory. Humanist approaches have taken up the issue of the impact of organization on personal growth. In contrast to the pessimism of critical theory, Humanism takes psychological well-being rather than neurosis as its starting point. In a similar way, Marxist analyses, while retaining a focus on the transformation of capitalist organization, have tended to turn away from Freudian explanations of psychology, turning instead to phenomenological approaches. Here the emphasis is on understanding how the human actor's view of the world is constructed and can be transformed through action rather than through psychoanalysis. In many ways psychoanalytic approaches to organization are the direct heirs of critical theory.

The work of Christopher Lasch and Manfred Kets de Vries, for instance, utilizes psychoanalytic theory to explain the problems and dangers of modern organization. Lasch focuses on the relationship between capitalist organization and narcissism, and Kets de Vries focuses on the impact of neurosis on organizational management. Post modernism has revived an interest in the relationship between organizational arrangements and the self but has questioned the use of essentialist concepts of the self. While critical theorists focused on the impact of organization on the (pre-existing) self postmodernists argue that the self is created in and through organizational discourses. Feminist theory, with its focus on women's liberation, is concerned with the impact of organization on the construction of discriminatory (gendered) selves. To this end, it has questioned an over-reliance on orthodox Freudian concepts and essentialist notions of the self which lay the blame for discrimination on women themselves.

Humanist

Within mainstream organizational behaviour analysis of the impact of organizational arrangements on human growth and personality has been limited to a small group of humanist psychologists. Foremost among these psychologists is Abraham Maslow and Chris Argyris.

Maslow's work, like that of Max Weber, has been bastardized by most OB/OT texts and reduced to a parody. Successive generations of students have come to associate Maslow with little more than the "hierarchy of needs" theory of human motivation, a theory – they are informed – that has not been verified and is of little predictive value for managers (Arnold, Cooper and Robertson, 1998).

If we look at the body of Maslow's work we find a concern with the human condition. That concern has been both applauded and questioned by feminists. Betty Friedan (1983: 319), for instance, praises Maslow's early work on women and his argument that "high dominance" women were more like "high dominance" men than low-dominance women. And she points out that as early as the 1930s Maslow was arguing that "either you have to describe as 'masculine' both high-dominance men and women or drop the terms 'masculine' and 'feminine' altogether because they are so 'misleading.'" Dallas Cullen (1992; 1997), on the other hand, makes a convincing argument that Maslow's work on dominance drew on masculinist views of reality that reinforced malestream notions of behaviour.

Unlike many other psychologists of his day or the earlier critical theorists, Maslow was interested not so much in "illness" (for example, neurosis) but in "wellness." He wanted to know what keeps people mentally healthy. From that starting point, he came to believe that there were a number of fundamental needs – physiological, security, social, esteem, and self-actualization – that had to be satisfied if people were to be psychologically healthy. Implicit in Maslow's hierarchical ordering of needs is a theory of maturation and development. That is, as we grow from infant to adult, moving through various processes of socialization, we acquire a number of socially defined needs beyond our basic physiological needs. Maslow was acutely aware that people do not always respond to needs in a hierarchical fashion, that some needs can be influenced by social situations (e.g., a person may starve themselves to death on a point of principle). Maslow's theory of needs could have served as a fundamental critique of the nature of organization had he used it as a measure of the contexts in which personality develop. His description[8] of the nature of self-actualization, for example, stands in sharp contrast to what is possible in the confines of hierarchically arranged organizations:

> A musician must make music, an artist must paint, a poet must write, if he is to be ultimately happy. What a man can be, he must be. This need we may call self-actualization…It refers to the desire for self fulfillment, namely, to the tendency for him to become actualized in what he is potentially [...] the desire to become more and more what one is, to become everything that one is capable of becoming (Maslow, 1943, p. 382).

Certainly, three decades earlier, research in Alberta on the Blackfoot Indians led Maslow to conclude that competitiveness within American culture was harmful.[9] Yet Maslow chose to work within the system, advising management how to alter some of their systems of work to allow employees greater degrees of freedom within existing constraints of power and control. And, despite his willingness to concede that people are not ultimately constrained by a hierarchical process of needs, he nonetheless continued to stress the hierarchical nature of psychological needs.[10]

In the application of Maslow's work to OT /OB, two important areas of research have been left out of account – his work on knowledge and inquiry, and on dominance and sexuality. Besides the five needs noted in the hierarchy of needs model, Maslow's research suggests two further needs – (a) freedom of inquiry and expression needs, and (b) a need to know – a need for curiosity, learning, philosophizing, experimenting, and exploring (Hoffman, 1988). It is not clear why those needs did not form part of Maslow's final model, but had they been included, they could – with their emphasis on control and domination – have contributed to a more critical examination of the existing character of modern organizations.

Maslow's work on domination was not made much of by Maslow himself, and, for reasons which are not entirely clear, he appears to have suppressed much of his thoughts on sexuality and female psychology.[11] From initial work with primates extended to studies of people, Maslow became convinced that "dominance" was an extremely important force in social relations, arguing that a dominance drive was a key determinant of social behaviour and organization (Hoffman, 1988: 69-70). If, as Maslow contends, people develop different dominance needs, this has important implications for organizational research. For instance, to what extent are organizational arrangements a reflection of the dominance needs of those who came to found and control them? To what extent do hierarchical arrangements encourage and provide expression for dominance needs? Had Maslow developed these ideas, he may have been able to further our understanding of the relationship between organizations and authoritarian behaviour.

Maslow's work on sexuality provides some clue to the potential relationship between organizations and dominance. He felt that the influence of social values, in shaping male-female relations, had an important impact on dominance feeling that it affected daily life at work as well as in marriage. He observed that, "The very definite training that most women in our culture get in being "ladylike" (non dominant) exerts its effect forever afterwards" (quoted in Hoffman, 1988: 234-5).

Maslow was essentialist in his believe that "definite inborn psychological differences exist between men and women,"[12] and that "male and female basic needs must be fulfilled prior to self-actualization." But he also believed that self-actualization involves a synthesis of traits associated in North American culture with both masculinity and femininity – an aspect of the concept of self-actualization that OB/OT accounts have been completely silent about! Despite his belief in the existence of some innate psychological differences between men and women Maslow nonetheless recognized the role of male-dominated cultural forces in holding back the potential for female self-actualization, arguing that because our western culture denigrates the feminine modes, "our conceptions of the universe, of science, of intelligence [and] of emotion are lopsided and partial because they have been constructed by man." Continuing in this vein, he went on to say that, "If only women were allowed to be full human beings, thereby making it possible for men to be fully human" then western culture might finally generate a balanced, rather then male, approach "to philosophy, art, science." Unfortunately, these words were confined to a letter to a friend which concluded with the statement, "If ever I get up courage enough to write anything on the subject I shall send you a copy"(quoted in Hoffman, 1988: 234-5).[13]

The work of Chris Argyris also raises important questions about the relationship between personality and organizational structure. Argyris's work focuses on human maturation and growth, arguing that as people move from infancy to adulthood they move from (i) passivity to increasing activity; (ii) dependency to relative independence; (iii) limited to various ways of behaving; (iv) limited to deep rooted interests; (v) short to long time perspectives; (vi) being in a superordinate position to aspiring to occupy an equal position as an adult; and (vii) a lack of awareness of self to awareness and control over self. As persons mature and grow a great deal of their time is spent in organizations but, as Argyris notes, the existing structures of those organizations do not encourage maturation; they do not permit persons to use their capacities and skills in a mature and productive way. For Argyris, far too many jobs in modern industry were so fragmented and specialized that they prevented workers from using their capacities and from seeing the relationship between what they were doing and the total organizational mission (Schein, 1980: 68). Argyris's solution to this problem was to argue for "participative management," that is, to allow employees a say in the decision-making processes, without dismantling the existing systems of power and control.

The work of Maslow, Argyris and others has been influential in drawing attention to human needs and growth but the impact of their observations has been weakened by a commitment to change *within*, rather then *of*, the existing frameworks of power, and, to some extent, of notions of "human" development premised on male-associated characteristics and processes of development (Cullen, 1992; 1997; Gilligan, 1982).

Marxist

The work of Peter Leonard (1984) occupies an interesting position within Marxism in that it straddles the humanist/structuralist (Burrell and Morgan, 1979) schism that has characterized Marxist thought since the development of critical theory. In *Personality and Ideology* Leonard combines a focus on the structural imperatives of capitalism with a focus on human agency and subjectivity. Unlike critical theory, Leonard attempts to synthesize the social psychology of George Herbert Mead with the political economy of Marx.

At its simplest, Mead argues that *the self* is socially constructed. We are not born with a particular self or personality, rather, we develop a sense of self through interaction with others. Interaction includes the capacity to relate to symbols and part of that process involves the designation of the self with a symbol. Thus, the person becomes an object in his/her own world (Leonard, 1984: 71). The process through which the self is developed involves a relationship of "I" to "me." The "I" refers to the process of thinking and acting, whilst the "me" refers to the reflective process. The "me" represents the organized attitudes of others, which confronts the "I," which in turn is worked on by the "I." Thus, Mead's view of the self is fairly complex and suggests a self, which is never finally formed but is always to some degree in a state of flux and mediation. Mead's approach, however, lacks an adequate theory of the social order in which symbolic interaction takes place. Leonard sets out to correct this by utilizing Mead's psychology to an understanding of historical materialism. In this way, argues Leonard, we can analyze how the self – for the large majority of working people – develops in contexts, in which the "I" is confronted by more powerful symbols and actors.

In capitalist society social relations centre on production and reproduction, and are based on class, gender and ethnic domination. Thus,

> contexts are penetrated by meanings, definitions, and "common sense" assumptions which reflect the ideologies through which a class, gender, ethnic group or other collectivity maintains its internal coherence, makes sense of the world, and either legitimates its dominant position in the social order or validates its resistance to domination (Leonard, 1984: 109).

Turning to the structure of personality and "use-time" in the process of production, Leonard argues that an important factor in the development of personality is how the person uses the time available to him or her for various kinds of activities. Under capitalism the necessity to labour predetermines the general distribution of use-time and the time utilized in labour is usually "abstract and does not, for most, allow the expanded development of capacities" (Leonard, 1984: 91).

> On the other side, the opportunity to develop capacities within personal, concrete activities are for many also restricted, except in so far as they further the interests of capital in maintaining labour power or increasing the consumption of commodities (ibid).

The structure of capitalist organization is such that the effect is one of "reducing the motivation to continue one's capacities, and so the personality will become 'stagnant and ossified.'" (Leonard, 1984: 98).

Despite his observations about the impact of work on personality Leonard is far from pessimistic about the potential for liberation, and argues that involvement in groups and activities that resist capitalism can help to stimulate creative contexts in which the self can develop, leading to a process of self and social emancipation.

The work of Leonard – along with that of Illich (1981), Clegg (1975; 1980), Burrell and Morgan (1979), and Benson (1977) – signalled an important and promising development in Marxist theory. This work was important not only in applying Marxist theory to an understanding of the relationship between organizational realities and personality but in attempting to do so through a synthesis of Marxist and phenomenological theories. But the promise ended with the series of events that rocked the communist world – beginning with *glasnost* in 1985 and continuing through the fall of the Berlin Wall, and, the subsequent break up of the Eastern bloc into several, often warring, States. Those changes, among other things, have led some to characterize the era as a crisis of Marxism, or "the end of history" (Fukuyama, 1989), that is, the irrevocable triumph of liberal capitalism. It has led numerous Marxists to search for alternative ways of thinking, with many being attracted to Postmodernist analysis (Burrell, 1994; Clegg, 1998; Morgan, 1996b). But the changes since the collapse of communism – an era of change unprecedented since the French and American Revolutions – have not heralded a triumph of capitalism as much as a collapse of modernity, as peoples and what were once nations struggle to rebuild a sense of self and identity. It is a time when now more than ever persons are questioning the old ways of viewing the world and, as a result, Postmodernist analysis has become attractive to a range of scholars.

Postmodernist

Over the last decade or so Postmodernist analysis has replaced Marxism and critical theory as the predominate school of radical thought.[14] In terms of organizational analysis, the work of Michel Foucault has been of particular interest to radical theorists,[15] and has much to say about the relationship between subjectivity and the development of particular forms of organization.

Foucault's work fundamentally challenges the modern(ist) notion of the individual as something essential, fixed, or "deep inside" us. For Foucault, the individual comes to *be* through a series of "disciplinary" and "confessional" practices – practices which, in the modern world, are organizational in form. Who we are and how we see ourselves is a product of the network of (largely) organizational practices within which we work and exist.

Foucault sees the development of modern society as a series of developments in which power, knowledge, and the body are closely inter-related. A concern with knowledge of, and over, the body characterizes the development of modern society. In the new manufactories of the eighteenth century new forms of knowledge assisted the emerging class of entrepreneurs to regularize the extraction of time and labour from the bodies of their work-force. Increasingly entrepreneurs and government took an interest in the control and regulation of the body. The state became interested in the health, numbers and condition of the population. This generated an array of new organizations and professionals concerned with translating and regulating the developing interest in the body. In the process concepts and practices of "normalization" were produced:

> These practices are supported and exercised by the state and by new bodies of knowledge, especially medicine and the human sciences. Under the humanistic rubric of the state's interest in and obligation to the creation and protection of the "well-being" of its inhabitants, global surveillance of its members is increasingly instituted. The state need experts to amass the knowledge it requires and to execute the policies said to effect and maximize this well-being and protection. Instances of such knowledge and associated practices include medicine, education, public health, prisons, and schools (Flax, 1990: 207).

Foucault calls these "disciplinary" practices – practices that are concerned with concrete and precise knowledge of the body, and as such constitute "biopower" in their outcomes of control. A major outcome of the nature and widespread existence of disciplinary practices has been, according to Foucault, the creation of the individual self; a constant placing of individuals in situations where they are forced to think about themselves and are simultaneously provided with the answers.

Alongside these practices,

> the individual subject is also created through confessional practices. The primary exemplars of these practices are psychoanalysis and psychiatry. These discourses produce sexuality as a dangerous force within us that can be controlled only by the person exercising surveillance upon her- or himself. Such surveillance is said to lead to both "self-knowledge" and freedom from the effects of these forces. However, in order to attain such self-knowledge and self-control, the individual must consult an expert whose knowledge provides privileged access to this dangerous aspect of the person's "self" (Flax, 1990: 208).

Thus, the modern(ist) era confronts us with powerful discourses in which notions of the "self" are primary – notions that create various senses of "self" in the image of the organizational practices from which they arise. In a world of dominant, organizational relationships this raises interesting and disturbing questions about the construction of self and reality: it has led several radical organizational theorists to study the relationship between organizational practices and subjectivity (Knights and Morgan, 1991; Knights and Willmott, 1999;

Nord and Fox, 1996). In particular they have been drawn to Foucault's "unique emphasis on the body as the place in which the most minute and local social practices are linked up with the large scale organization of power" (Dreyfus and Rabinow, 1982: xxii); to his theory of power – with its notion that power is everywhere and nowhere, "ubiquitous, but ultimately uncentred power relations" (Rattansi and Boyne, 1990: 18), not possessed by individuals, groups or functions but always a relationship that involves positive as well as negative outcomes; and by his argument that meta-narratives (that is, general or universalizing theories of how societies function) are but competing truth claims that threaten to replace one set of power relations with another. For the Postmodernist these three elements "provide a valuable means for comprehending the complexities of social control" (Ferguson, 1984: xii). They help to explain why it is that individuals comply with processes of power that may ultimately work against them, i.e., they are not simple victims of an all-powerful system but are contributors to a series of relationships through which power is created and maintained. These elements also help to explain how, through seeking radical change, individuals come to substitute one set of power relationships (e.g., capitalism) with another (e.g., communism) i.e., though acceptance of a particular theory of society individuals buy into a set of truth claims which serve as a new power influence over the way they come to view themselves.

Postmodernist ideas are currently proving attractive to a growing number of radicals but several critical questions about this viewpoint remain unanswered. The ultimate triumph of postmodernism may well depend on the responses provided to these questions.

Power: It has been argued that post modernism underestimates the role of power holders in organizations:

> While it would be extremely foolish not to recognize diverse forms and locations of power … (it) remains legitimate to talk of power "holders." That is, power is both a relationship and held by individuals or groups" (Thompson, 1991).

Self: The post modernist concept of the self as fragmentary has been challenged for failing to come to terms with,

> The fact […] that we live one life not several, our ability to choose which other "worlds" we wish to inhabit is very much dependent on our position in this world (Marx Memorial Library, 1992).

Radical change: Finally post modernism has been criticized for an inability to encourage radical change:

> Postmodernism [...] is recognized as having abandoned any attempt to make any sense of (change). David Harvey notes Postmodernism's: – "total acceptance of the ephemerality, fragmentation, discontinuity, and the chaotic. It does not transcend it or counteract it. Postmodernism swims, even wallows, in the fragmentary and the chaotic currents of change as if that is all there is" (Marx Memorial Library, 1992).[16]

Psychoanalysis

In the last decade or so a number of psychoanalytical studies of organization have drawn attention to the links between self and organizational reality, and in ways that are reminiscent of the early work of the critical theorists. Christopher Lasch's (1979) study of narcissism in American life raises a number of interesting questions for organizational analysis. Lasch suggests that there is a strong relationship between the way we come to conceive of ourselves and of organization:

> Every age develops its own peculiar forms of pathology, which expresses in exaggerated form its underlying character structure. In Freud's time, hysteria and obsessional neurosis carried to extremes the personality traits associated with the capitalist order at an earlier stage in its development – acquisitiveness, fanatical devotion to work, and a fierce repression of sexuality (Lasch, 1979: 87-88).

According to Lasch, our own time is characterized by a "culture of narcissism," signified by the widespread evidence of "borderline personality" disorders. In terms of clinical observations, patients who symptomize the malaise suffer from pervasive feelings of emptiness and a deep disturbance of self-esteem (Lasch, 1979: 89). Lasch's description of the general malaise of narcissism complements Foucault's notion of the construction of the self in suggesting that the end product of discourses concerned with self-knowledge is the creation of individual self obsession:

> Medicine and psychiatry – more generally the therapeutic outlook and sensibility that pervade modern society – reinforce the pattern created by other cultural influences, in which the individual endlessly examines himself for signs of aging and ill health, for tell-tale symptoms of psychic stress, for

blemishes and flaws that might diminish his attractiveness, or on the other hand for reassuring indications that his life is proceeding according to schedule (Lasch, 1979: 99).

Drawing upon the work of Kohut, Lasch contends that narcissism arises out of the "unavoidable shortcomings of maternal care" (Kohut, 1971) which results in the child coming to realize that s/he is not the centre of the universe, that the mother is ultimately separate from the child and not there solely for his/her total gratification. The resulting disappointment and frustration lead the child to strive to reverse the situation and "involves either creating a tyrannical idealized self-image or the incorporation of tyrannical idealized parent image for the self" (Walter, 1983: 262).

Far from containing narcissistic disorders the structure of modern society both reflect and encourages them. As Joel Kovel expresses it,

> [The] stimulation of infantile cravings by advertising, the usurpation of parental authority by the media and the school, and the rationalization of inner life accompanied by the false promise of personal fulfillment, have created a new type of "social individual." The result is not the classical neurosis where an infantile impulse is suppression by patriarchal authority, but a modern version in which impulse is stimulated, perverted and given neither an adequate object upon which to satisfy itself nor coherent forms of control.... The entire complex, played out in a setting of alienation rather than direct control, loses the classical form of symptom – and the classical opportunity of simply restoring an impulse to consciousness." (quoted in Lasch, 1979: 90)

Narcissism finds its expression in the modern organization in a number of ways:

> For all his inner suffering, the narcissist has many traits that make for success in bureaucratic institutions, which put a premium on the manipulation of interpersonal relations, discourage the formation of deep personal attachments, and at the same time provide the narcissist with the approval he needs in order to validate his self esteem.... The management of personal impressions come naturally to him, and his mastery of its intricacies serves him well in political and business organizations where performance now counts for less than "visibility," "momentum," and a winning record. As the "organization man" gives way to the bureaucratic "gamesman" – the "loyalty era" of American business to the age of the "executive success game" – the narcissist comes into his own (Lasch, 1979: 91-92).

In the organizational world the exteriors of offices, the interiors of offices, and the presentation of self within offices have come to symbolize narcissism, symbols that not only reward but require narcissistic behaviour (Walter, 1983).

The narcissistic organizational culture gives rise to a type of leader who "sees the world as a mirror of himself and has no interest in external events except as they throw back a reflection of his own image"(Lasch, 1979: 96). Such leaders are often more concerned with image than substance; advancing through the corporate ranks not by serving the organization but by convincing his associates that he possesses the attributes of a "winner"; in getting to the top he manipulates persons and symbols and, in an organizational culture created out of intersecting male values (Aaltio and Mills, 2002; Mills and Murgatroyd, 1991), many of those symbols utilize females and images of femininity:

> A graciously and perhaps even sumptuously decorated office reception of a company communicates opulence and self-assurance…. So too does the presence of a comely lady receptionist. These individuals are clearly not of goddess stature but are reminiscent of the nymphs who served as handmaidens to mythological gods in a variety of ways (Walter, 1983: 259).

The organizational "gamesman":

> avoids intimacy as a trap, preferring the "exciting, sexy atmosphere" with which the modern executive surrounds himself at work, "where adoring, mini-skirted secretaries constantly flirt with him. In all his personal relations, the gamesman depends on the admiration or fear he inspires in others to certify his credentials as a "winner."(Lasch, 1979: 93-94).

This type of leadership contributes to an organizational culture in which certain images of leadership and of masculinity are expected to be "mirrored"(Kets de Vries, 1989). For males the narcissistic organizational culture holds up images of certain types of male-associated behaviour that they are expected to mirror if they are to be deemed simultaneously successful and male. Mirroring is facilitated by excessive dependency between executives and subordinates: in these situations subordinates may come to identify excessively with the leader (Kets de Vries, 1989; 1989; 1991). In its extreme form this may involve over identification "to the point of madness," as in the case of the relationship between Henry Ford and his lieutenants – Liebold, Sorensen, and Bennett, and the FBI under J. Edgar Hoover (Kets de Vries, 1991). On the other hand, failure to mirror the appropriate behaviour can result in organizational/

sexual innuendo and rejection, as in the firing of an executive by Henry Ford II who deemed that the man's tight trousers signified a lack of manliness and, by implication, managerial competence (Iacocca, 1984).

What is striking about the psychoanalysis of organizations is its male reference points, reference points which are inherent in the way psychoanalysis is conceived (Lowe, Mills and Mullen, 2002), right down to the gendered way that maternal care is seen as the root of narcissistic development (Flax, 1990). It is far from clear to what extent narcissism can be said to be a characteristic of both males and females: indeed there is some evidence that gender constrained differences of experience between males and females (and between working and middle-class females) is associated with different forms of psychological distress and neurosis (Nahem, 1981), and "doing" is more likely to be encouraged in/associated with males than females, i.e., aggression and a striving for dominance will be characterized as male rather than female traits (Cullen, 1992; 1997). Nonetheless, psychoanalytic studies of organization indicate the type of dominant discourses within which male and female selves are constructed.[17]

Feminist

For women, organizational cultures present an entirely different set of problems about identity formation. Women are confronted with organizational discourses that not only shape notions of femininity (and of masculinity) but whose rules and practices are male dominated. From a feminist psychoanalytical perspective Jane Flax (1990: 120) argues that psychoanalytic theories "lack a critical, sustained account of gender formation and its costs to self and culture as a whole." Contending that children have acquired a "core identity" by the age of three, Flax urges a reconsideration of the mother-child dyad and the mother's power in the unconscious lives of men and women:

> This is an important step in the process of doing justice to the subjectivity of women and undoing the repression of experiences of ourselves as mothers and as persons who have been mothered (Flax, 1990: 123).

The significance for the mother-child dyad however should not be viewed separately from all the other social relations of which it is a part:

> Although part of the child's self is constitute through her or his internalization of the caretakers, in the process the child incorporates more than his or her experience of specific persons....To some extent the parents' entire social histories become part of the child's self. An adequate theory of human develop-

ment from an object relations perspective would have to include an account of all these different levels and types of social relations and their interactions, mutual determinations, and possible antagonisms. It would have to include an expanded concept of families – families not merely as a set of immediate relations among individuals but also as permeable structures located within and partially determined by her social structures, including those of production, culture, and race, class, and gender systems. (Flax, 1990: 124).

This perspective seems to suggest that the influence of organizational discourse on the shaping of gender identity is significant but more so in the early stages of core identity formation. Nonetheless she goes on to argue that disciplinary and confessional practices influence the way we categorize one another by gender and the way we come to view ourselves.

What is not clear from Flax's analysis is the extent to which involvement in any number of disciplinary and confessional practices influences, shapes, or modifies the core self and its gendered character. She does, however, offer the advice that a feminist deconstruction of the self would point to locating self and its experiences in concrete social relations:

A social self would come to be partially in and through powerful, affective relationships with other persons. These relations with others and our feelings and fantasies about them, along with experiences of embodiedness also mediated by such relations, can come to constitute an "inner" self that is neither fictive or "natural." Such a self is simultaneously embodied, gendered, social, and unique. It is capable of telling stories and of conceiving and experiencing itself in all these ways.(Flax, 1990: 232).

Feminist studies indicate ways in which people's sense of gendered self becomes shaped by organizational discourse. Blustein, Devenis and Kidney, (1989: 200), for example, found a relationship between "the exploration and commitment processes that characterize one's identity formation... and an analogous set of career development tasks." Marshall and Wetherall interviewed a group of male and female law students about their perceptions of the characteristics required to be a lawyer. What they found was that there tended to be a shared view about the masculine nature of the traits required to be a successful lawyer, and that this had different implications for male and female students:

Effectively, the relation between women and occupational identity became problematized, whereas the relation between men and occupational identity became normalized.... Women and lawyers were portrayed as dissonant, the identity relationship became a site of struggle but, in contrast, the masculine and the law became synonymous, with the masculine personality portrayed as identical with the legal personality. (Marshall and Weatherall, 1989: 121).

For some of the female respondents, this meant that becoming a lawyer involves learning to overcome feminine traits. Some of the other female respondents saw women as positive agents of change – improving the law through feminine characteristics. In either case, women were faced with gender and occupational identity as "conflict and a site of struggle" (Marshall and Weatherall, 1989: 123).

Gendered images of occupations and organizational realities are not simply reflected in the ideas of actors, reproduced by rote. It is through discourse that particular versions of reality and of self are produced/reproduced, modified and changed. As Marshall and Wetherall (1989: 125) argue:

> there is no one "true" representation of self and identity. At any given moment there will be varying possibilities for self-construction [... because] identities are actively negotiated and transformed in discourse and [...] language is the area where strategic construction and reconstruction of self occurs."

Continuing the theme of gender and identity, Wetherall, Stiven, and Potter (Weatherall, Stiven and Potter, 1987: 61-62) argue that notions of career are imbued with intersecting and contradictory discourses concerning gender and employment opportunities. Studying a group of final year university students, Wetherall et al. found that,

> Two particular kinds of talk tended to dominate participants' discourse about women in the workplace, careers and children. These could be called the "equal opportunities" and "practical considerations" themes. [Ibid]

The equal opportunities theme was a form of talk which endorsed liberal values of egalitarianism, freedom of choice for the individual, equally shared responsibilities, and so on. The practical considerations theme, on the other hand, combined notions of the reproductive role and maternal urges of females with supposed understandable employer reluctance to risk hiring females over men. This quotation from a male respondent illustrates the latter theme:

> I suppose you can always see how an employer's mind will work, if he has a choice between two identically qualified and identically, identical personalities, and one is male and one is female, you can sympathize with him for

wondering if the female is not going to get married and have children (Weatherall et al., 1987: 62).

These themes did not clearly represent differences of opinion between respondents but were often made by the same person. Wetherall et al. argue that "these contradictions may be responsible for the force and continuity of the ideology" that continues to maintain discriminatory differences between men and women, contradictions which help people – men and women – to "make sense" of a changing world in which gender notions remain strongly unchanged in the face of equity struggles and laws. Through the contradictions respondents were able to support the growing discourse of employment equity and yet, in a way that distanced themselves, explain why equity wouldn't work.

Racioethnicity

Influenced by the work of Edward Said, a relatively new group of "postcolonial" organization theorists are engaged in researching the impact of "imperialist" ideas on people of colour and the relationship between them and whites, within organizational contexts. Said's (1979; 1993) work focuses on the relationship between the practice of imperialism and identity formation among subject peoples, arguing that imperialism is a cultural as well as an economic practice that has shaped a series of negative images of subject peoples. Organizational researchers, building on Said's notion, have examined the cultural practices (e.g., language, ideology, motivational symbols, forms of communication, etc.) of organizations and their impact on organizational members, particularly people of colour. Pushkala Prasad (1997b), for example, argues that broad motivational ideas such as "the Protestant ethic" and "the myth of the frontier" are peculiarly Western ideas, imbued with Western notions of ideal work practices. In work settings where such ideals are stressed persons raised outside of those traditions are likely to be judged less favourably than those who readily conform to expectations. In a similar vein, Anshuman Prasad (1997a) argues that organizational studies have been shaped by a "post-colonial" lens whereby North American and European understandings of former "colonial peoples" have been shaped by those former relationships of power, i.e., that the history of colonial relations negatively colours the way that people of colour are viewed in western and western owned companies. More recently the Prasads have applied their postcolonial perspective to analysis of human relations practices (Prasad and Prasad, 2002).

The neglect of race and ethnicity within mainstream studies of organization has led Canadian researcher Joy Mighty (1991; 1997) and US researcher Stella Nkomo (1992) to, respectively, classify the practice of organizational behaviour as a form of cultural imperialism or an ethnic paradigm. From this perspective the researchers argue for a more inclusive analysis of behaviour in organizations that will take account not only of race and ethnicity but of the racist character of organizations and theories of organization. Other accounts of race and ethnicity question whether organizational studies (OB/OT) will ever be able to overcome ingrained ways of thinking. Marta Calás (1992), for example, argues that OB/OT is a way of thinking, with its own established language, thought processes, and practices that are constructed out of "Western humanistic discourse," i.e., it values people and activities according to Western standards.

Nkomo and Cox (1989) in the United States, and Mighty (1997) in Canada, have drawn attention to the multiple impacts of race, gender and immigration on people's experiences in organizations. The work of Bell and Nkomo (1992; 1992), through analysis of the different life-cycles and opportunities that each group of women experience, has been instrumental in developing understandings of the differences that black and white female managers face in the workplace. Bell and her colleagues (1992; 1992) have also studied the way that organizational structures contribute to the "reproduction of race relations within organizations.

SUMMARY

Radical theories of organization indicate several links between the structure of organization and the development of human personality and identity. The schools of thought that we have reviewed disagree — often fundamentally — on the specific influences of organization on human life but they share a basic concern with the potentially distorting and destructive outcomes of those influences. Each school of thought encourages us to analyze the relationship between how organizations are structured and our experiences of self: how we *become* women and men, black and white, middle class and working class; how we come to feel about ourselves and others; how we come to express ourselves; how we shape our sexual preferences and those of others around us.

Despite the varying differences between each radical school the overriding conclusion to be drawn is that we need a theory of organizations that focuses on structure and personality; focuses on the relationship between organizational and societal realities; incorporates issues of class, race, ethnicity, and gender; is concerned with issues of micro and macro power structures; is continually aware of and questioning competing meta-narratives (from radical as well as non-radical perspectives); has as its aim human liberation. Such a perspective – particularly in the face of Postmodernist critique – will not be easy but in the current debates between Marxists, feminists, Postmodernists, and racioethnicity scholars there is the promise of such a new perspective which will combine the radical intent of feminism, racioethnicity and Marxism with the scepticism of post modernism.[18]

KEY TERMS

identity	self	*subjectivity*
repression	rationality	*instrumental reason*
Postmodernism	critical theory	*bio-power*
authoritarian personality	*dominance*	*disciplinary practices*
self-actualization	psychic prison	*confessional practices*
narcissism	*mirroring*	*discourse*
life instincts/Eros	*post-colonial theory*	

REVIEW QUESTIONS

Q1. Briefly define "narcissism" and explain how a "culture of narcissism" can influence organizational personality.

Assignment: Compare your answer with the definition in the glossary of terms and the discussion in the chapter section on psychoanalysis.

[FS: For a broader understanding read Lasch *The Culture of Narcissism*, Chapters 2 and 3]

Q2. In what ways can organizational arrangements have an influence on gender?

Assignment: List and discuss three (3) organizational factors (for example, sexual discrimination) associated with gender. Explain how each organizational factor influences the way people view men and women.

[FS: For a broader understanding of the factors involved read Wetherall, Stiven and Potter (1987); Marshall and Wetherall (1989); and Ferguson (Ferguson, 1984: Chapter 1).

Q3. Write short notes on each of the following terms and say how critical theory relates them to organizations
- authoritarian personality
- repression
- Eros/life instinct

Assignment: Compare your answer with the definitions in the glossary of terms and the discussion in the section of the chapter on critical theory.

[FS: To gain a more in-depth understanding of the terms read Chapter 4 Held (1980) or any other work that summarizes critical theory and psychoanalysis].

Q4. List and discuss three ways that critical theory sees bureaucracy as affecting employees.

Assignment: Read Chapter 2 and the section on Instrumental Reason in this chapter and compare your answer.

[FS: For a more advanced understanding read Held (1980) and the Introduction Chapter 1 of Marcuse (1970)]

Q5. What did Maslow mean by the term "self-actualization" and to what extent is it attainable within the confines of the present structure of work?

Assignment: Compare your answer with the discussion in the chapter section on Humanism.

[FS: For a fuller understanding of self-actualization read Chapters 9, 13 and 15 of Hoffman (1988)]

Q6. What is the relationship between identity and use-time?

Assignment: Compare your answer with the chapter section on Marxism

[FS: For a fuller understanding of the relationship between identity and use-time read Leonard (1984: Chapter 4)]

Q7. Briefly define the following terms and discuss how they help us to make sense of organizations:
- bio-power
- disciplinary practices
- confessional practices
- subjectivity
- dominance
- discourse

Assignment: Compare your answer with the discussion in the Postmodernism section of the chapter.

[FS: For an in-depth understanding of these terms read Burrell (1988)]

Q8. What is "mirroring" and what can it tell us about the problems of organizational leadership?

Assignment: Compare you answer with the discussion of psychoanalysis section of the chapter.

[FS: For a greater understanding of mirroring read Kets de Vries (1989)]

Q9. Post-colonial theory argues that many organizational ideas are strongly influenced by western cultural values and that these values contribute to negative understandings of people of colour. What types of western ideas are prominent in mainstream OB/OT and what influence to they have on the employment of people of colour?

Assignment: Using a mainstream OB or OT textbook find 3 terms which are culturally biased and explain how the biases may negatively influence how people of colour are judged at work.

[FS: For an in-depth analysis of post-colonial theory read Edward Said (1993) and Anshuman Prasad (1997a)]

INTERNET EXERCISES

Q1. Find three organizations that promote diversity through different work family initiatives? Are they adequate and do they work?

Q2. Find online examples of the dark side of Disney's employment practices. How does Disney create a "psychic prison"?

EXERCISE 4.1

This exercise is designed to make you think about the relationship between organizations and how we see and feel about ourselves.

For this exercise you will need a notebook to use as a diary. Keep a diary of your organizational experiences during the next seven days. In terms of your self focus on the following factors:

self esteem − sexuality − identity

In terms of organizational experiences focus on the following factors:

hierarchy – Rules – structure – space

time – status – interpersonal relationships – task

Hierarchy – refers to levels of authority in an organization.

Rules – refer to written and unwritten, formal and informal, rules which guide and control behaviour in an organization.

Structure – refers to the way an organization organizes its affairs, for example, the extent to which it is formal, standardized, centralized, highly controlled.

Space – refers to the physical layout of a place and the ways that the space is used. For example, there is a difference between the way McDonald's and The Keg structure their organizational space. There is also a difference in the use of space – for example, some organizations – such as colleges – allow their employees free access to most aspects of the organization and other organizations – such as prisons and nuclear power station – restrict employees to a limit area.

Time – refers to the time span within which an organization operates, (for example, 9.00-5.00) and to the way time is used, (for example, the way an organization controls the use of time by requiring a certain level of speed, or expecting assignments and exams to be completed at certain times only)

Status – refers to the importance of one group over another.

Interpersonal-relationships – refers to the way persons relate to each other, for example, sharply, friendly, rude.

Task – refers to the actual duties or actions that a person carries out within an organization, for example, digging, reading, calculating.

Task #1: At the beginning of the notebook write some short notes on yourself.

A (i) *Self-esteem*: under this heading say something about how you feel about yourself and how you would ultimately like to feel about yourself. Using the following seven point scale, rate where you feel that you are usually:

1..............> 2..............> 3..............> 4..............> 5..............> 6..............> 7.............

| Senseof self: None | Very little | A bit | Some | Quite a bit | Very much | Complete |

A (ii) Now say something about how you usually feel. Write down ten adjectives that best describe you, for example, lonely, happy, restless, defensive, etc.

B (i) *Sexuality*: Under this heading write some short notes on your experience of yourself as a man or a woman. Write down ten adjectives that best describe the kind of woman or man that you are, for example, macho, gentle, strong, intellectual. Now write a brief note on the kind of man or woman that you would like to be.

B (ii) Write a brief note on how you see your sexual orientation; for example, heterosexual, bisexual, lesbian, gay. What makes you feel good about your sexuality, what makes you feel bad?

C (i) *Identity*: Under this heading write short notes on who you are. Write down ten adjectives that best sum up the kind of person that you are, for example, intelligent, athletic, driven, deep, etc. Note down the type of job that you would like to be doing if you had a free choice.

Task #2: Over the next week you will experience a variety of organizational situations at college, at work, in the stores, at a library, at an organized sporting event, at a political meeting, etc. Using the list of organizational factors above, note down each time an event or situation has a noticeable effect (e.g., makes you laugh, depresses you) and try to identify which factors were involved.

EXAMPLE:

DAY 1

Organization: Political Party Meeting

Incident: Turned up at meeting a few minutes late, made to feel inadequate and unorganized. Asked to make coffee during the meeting. Ignored when trying to put forward suggestions.

Feelings = depression, anger, weakened self-esteem, made to feel that I'm "only a woman," feel that I'm not seen as a real person with any direction.

Organizational factors: 1. Time – the meetings are always inconvenient as far as child-care arrangements are concerned; 2. Space – the men seen to dominate the meeting room; 3. Location – meeting above a bar reinforces my feelings of vulnerability as I have to negotiate drunks; 4) Status – as one of the few women involved I am made to feel somehow different and less than adequate.

Task #3: At the end of the seven days reflect upon your diary and write notes on your overall experiences. Compare notes with other students and in small groups discuss the following questions:

a) To what extent do organizations influence the way we feel about our selves?

b) To what extent do organizations contribute to the construction of our sense of self?

c) To what extent do we enter organizations with a developed sense of self?

d) What features of an organization are more likely to influence how we feel about ourselves?

e) What features are least likely to influence how we feel about ourselves?

f) How can we address some of the more psychologically damaging aspects of organizations?

CASE ANALYSIS

Turn to the Westray Case and answer the following questions:

1. Turn to Part II and answer the 5 questions for the section called "The Implications of Truth".

2. Using a feminist approach discuss the role of masculinity in the events that led up to the disaster.

3. Using a humanist approach what recommendations would you make for improving mine conditions?

4. Use a psychoanalytical approach to analyse the disaster. What are your five main conclusions?

USEFUL INTERNET SITES

<http://www.postcolonialweb.org>
<http://foucault.info/>
<http://psychclassics.yorku.ca/>
<http://www.marcuse.org/herbert/>
<http://www.uta.edu/huma/illuminations/marc.htm>

FURTHER READING

Critical theory:
Mats Alvesson and Stan Deetz, (1996).
CRITICAL THEORY AND
POSTMODERNISM APPROACHES
TO ORGANIZATIONAL STUDIES
Steve Best and Douglas Kellner, (1991).
POSTMODERN THEORY. CRITI-
CAL INTERROGATIONS
David Held, (1980). INTRODUCTION
TO CRITICAL THEORY

Humanist psychology:
Edward Hoffman, (1988). THE RIGHT
TO BE HUMAN: A BIOGRAPHY
OF ABRAHAM MASLOW

Marxism:
Peter Leonard, (1984). PERSONALITY
AND IDEOLOGY

Postmodernism:
David Boje, Robert Gephart and Tojo
Thatchenkery, (1996). POSTMODERN
MANAGEMENT AND ORGANIZA-
TION THEORY
Christopher Butler, (2002).
POSTMODERNISM: A VERY
SHORT INTRODUCTION
Martin Parker and John Hassard (eds.),
(1993). POSTMODERNITY AND
ORGANIZATIONS

Psychoanalytical theory:
Adrian Carr, (2003). SPECIAL ISSUE OF
THE JOURNAL OF MANAGERIAL
PSYCHOLOGY, VOLUME 17 (5)
Manfred Kets de Vries and Denny Miller,
(1984). THE NEUROTIC ORGANI-
ZATION

Feminist theory:
Iiris Aaltio and Albert J. Mills, (2002).
GENDER, IDENTITY AND THE
CULTURE OF ORGANIZATIONS
Kathy Ferguson, (1994). ON BRINGING
MORE THEORY, MORE VOICES,
AND MORE POLITICS TO THE
STUDY OF ORGANIZATION
Kathy Ferguson, (1984). THE FEMINIST
CASE AGAINST BUREAUCRACY

Racioethnicity:
Stella Nkomo, (1992). THE EMPEROR
HAS NO CLOTHES: REWRITING
"RACE IN ORGANIZATIONS"
Anshuman and Pushkala Prasad, (2002).
OTHERNESS AT LARGE: IDEN-
TITY AND DIFFERENCE IN THE
NEW GLOBALIZED ORGANIZA-
TIONAL LANDSCAPE.

END NOTES

1. Interview with Albert Mills for a study on "Women at Work". The name is a pseudonym.
2. For more on gender and resistance see Thomas et al. (2004).
3. For discussion on the gendered subtext of Taylorism and how it influenced our understanding of management, see Benschop and Doorewaard (1998).
4. Carl Grunberg, the Institute's first director, quoted in Held (1980: 30).
5. For a fuller discussion read Held (1980). See also Best and Kellner (1991) who attempt to up-date critical theory through a fusion with postmodernist theory.
6. Here critical theory draws heavily upon Marx's theories of alienation (1967) and commodity production (1999) and Lukacs' (1971) theory of reification.
7. This is a much narrower interpretation of Freud's concept than the notion of life instinct which encompasses numerous aspects of human strivings.
8. Disappointingly, Maslow utilizes the male dominant language and imagery of the time to describe self-actualization.
9. Maslow associated the Blackfoot emphasis on generosity with the high levels of "emotional security" that he found among members of the tribe (Hoffman, 1988).
10. Mills, Kelley and Cooke (2002) argued that Maslow's notion of hierarchy was influenced by contemporary capitalist values.
11. Cullen's (1992) analysis of Maslow's work on sexuality and dominance reveals a number of methodological

and, not least, sexist problems with the research. Cullen argues that Maslow's research methods involved elements of coercion in regard to the recruitment of "low esteem" female respondents, and that his notion of "self-actualization" was premised on a male notion of self fulfillment.
12. This worldview no doubt underlay his understanding of "self-actualization" (see Cullen, 1992).
13. Maslow was a complex theorist. As we have seen he could both appeal to and anger feminists. He expressed genuine concerns for human growth and development yet his work lend itself to capitalist notions of hierarchy and he himself lent his energies and his theories to companies in the pursuit of profit. He applauded the cooperative nature of the Blackfoot Indians yet developed a profoundly individualist theory of human needs. In 1952 Maslow signed an open letter to the government calling for the repeal of the McCarran Act (a law that restricted the activities of anyone suspected of communist sympathies and activities). Maslow's signature on the open letter was enough to invoke the suspicions of the Federal Bureau of Investigations (FBI): Maslow came under FBI surveillance in December of 1954 when "an anonymous source" informed them of Maslow's involvement in the open letter of 1952 (Federal Bureau of Investigation, 1954-1968). Maslow was followed, his house watched, neighbours interviewed, and the numbers of visitors' cars taken down. The FBI

concluded that "investigation did not indicate that he [Maslow] was a member of the Communist Party", nonetheless, the FBI file remained active for several years(Federal Bureau of Investigation, 1954-1968). By the 1970s Maslow had become a keen supporter of the Vietnam War and advocated that "draft dodgers" be locked up and severely punished.

14. It should be made clear that not all Postmodernist theory is radical in intent.

15. Cf. Burrell (1988; 1994); Clegg (1990; 1998; 1996). Other Postmodernist writers that has been of particular interest to radical organizational theorists include Derrida (cf. Calás, 1992), Deleuze, Lyotard, and Baudrillard (cf. Thompson, 1991).

16. For a fuller discussion on the problems of postmodernist thought see Best and Kellner (1991) and Butler (2002).

17. For further discussion on the application of psychoanalytical approaches to organization and management see Carr (2003).

18. We are currently in the stages of the development of new syntheses which include "post feminism" (Calás and Smircich, 1992b; Calás and Smircich, 1996) and "post-marxism" (Jameson, 1991), and "reconstructed critical theory" (Best and Kellner, 1991).

CHAPTER 5

Sex and Organizational Analysis

This chapter focuses on the significance of gender as a feature of organizational life. Issues of masculinity, sexual harassment, heterosexuality, sexuality, and power are explored. The main objective is to reveal the deep-seated nature of the gendered character of organizations, encouraging the reader to think more deeply about the relationship between organizational construction and sexual discrimination in its broadest sense (from employment equity to the gendering of self).

Sex, Power and Abuse at Abu Ghraib Prison[1]

In March 2003, citing the threat of "weapons of mass destruction," the United States and its allies attacked Iraq with military force. Using its own weapons of mass destruction the US and its "coalition of the willing" quickly destroyed the Iraqi army and took over control of the country. In May 2003 US President George Bush claimed that the war's objectives have been accomplished. The United States installed a Civilian Administrator, Paul Bremer, to run the country. In a policy of "de-Baathification," Bremer removed over 400,000 former members of the ruling Baathist Party from the police, army and civil service. Many Iraqis were jailed as suspected "terrorists" and active supporters of the former regime.

From the beginning, US interrogators used techniques of abuse as part of a strategy to gain information from Iraqi prisoners, and as early as May 2003 three US military police officers were discharged from service after they were found to have used excessive force on Iraqi detainees at Camp Bucca in Southern Iraq. Nonetheless, all manner of abuse continued to be used despite formal complaints from the Red Cross, Amnesty International, and even the US-appointed Iraqi minister of human rights. The International Committee of the Red Cross, for instance, complained of a number of human rights violations that included hooding, beatings with hard objects, threats against family members, being forced to stay in physically stressful positions for hours on end, and degrading acts. Abdel Bassat Turki, the US-appointed human rights minister, complained to Paul Bremer about the treatment of Iraqi prisoners, particularly female inmates who had been denied medical treatment and proper toilet facilities. Turki and other US-appointed Iraqi ministers also asked Bremer to investigate allegations of the raping of a female Iraqi prisoner. Failing to receive adequate responses to his complaints, Turki resigned his position in April 2004.

Prisoner abuse began to surface in January 2004 when a military policeman, Joseph Darby, reported his observations to the Army's Criminal Investigations Division. The issue went public in May 2004 when the media began to publish shocking accounts of sexual and physical abuse in the US-controlled Abu Ghraib prison in Baghdad. Investigation has since revealed that male prisoners were held in solitary confinement, stripped naked, and paraded in front of other detainees and male and female prison guards; forced to wear women's underwear on their head; sexually taunted and made fun of by female prison guards; forced to simulate oral sex with other male inmates; made to simulate sex with other male inmates; piled on top of each other; and forced to masturbate in front of female guards. To exacerbate the humiliation, the inmates were often photographed in these sexually abusive situations.

Pressured to respond to the ensuing widespread outcry, the US military laid the blame at the feet of a few prison guards that have subsequently been arrested and face count martial. In one case a high ranking officer used the opportunity to question the role of women in the military, suggesting that perhaps women should not be sent to combat zones.

Others, including high-ranking military officials, questioned how such abuse can occur and suggested that the fault may lay with a breakdown of command or, worse, the result of a deliberate policy of abuse. For example, Patrick Leahy, the Democratic Senator from Vermont, commented on the photographs, "All the guards are smiling, they're taking all these pictures because they know that nobody above them is going to object. They have to know that somebody up there is agreeing with them." Award winning journalist Seymour M. Hersh agrees, arguing that the "roots of the Abu Ghraib prison scandal lie not in the criminal inclinations of a few Army reservists but in a decision approved [in 2003] by Secretary of Defense Donald Rumsfeld, to expand a highly-secret operation." According to Hersh, the operation "encouraged physical coercion and sexual humiliation [...] in an effort to generate more intelligence about the growing insurgency in Iraq." Hersh goes on to suggest that the genesis of the sexual attacks on Iraqi men can be traced back to a study of The Arab Mind (by Raphael Patai), which was popular among pro-war conservatives. The study contends that Arabs are particularly vulnerable to sexual humiliation: "The segregation of the sexes, the veiling of the women ... and all the other minute rules that govern and restrict contact between men and women, have the effect of making sex a prime mental preoccupation in the Arab world," according to Patai. Any "indication of homosexual leanings, as with all other expressions of sexuality, is never given any publicity." Indeed, one government consultant has speculated that the photographing of naked male Iraqi prisoners may have been part of the process to coerce them into spying on their associates to avoid having the photographs made public.

In a similar vein, (unnamed) British military sources suggested, "the sexual humiliation of Iraqi prisoners [...] was not an invention of maverick guards but part of a system of ill-treatment and degradation used by special forces soldiers." This source claims that it is a technique that is referred to as R2I (short for, resistance to interrogation).

Amidst the furor over the scandal Kenneth Roth, the executive director of Human Rights Watch, commented: "In an odd way the sexual abuses at Abu Ghraib have become a diversion for the prisoner abuse and the violation of the Geneva Conventions that is authorized."

INTRODUCTION

The story of abuses at the Abu Ghraib prison dramatically illustrates the theme of this chapter, that is, the relationship between sex and power within organizations. A number of insights can be drawn from the story.

To begin with, the story simultaneously suggests that sex is an integral and aberrant aspect of organizational life. On the one hand, the use of sexuality seems widespread yet, on the other hand, its use is seen as contrary to military and prison practice. As we shall indicate throughout the chapter, both scenarios are accurate. Most organizations, including the military and prison services, contend that sex has no part of the "normal" functioning of their operations. It is something that is, and should be seen as, quite separate from organizational life. But, as shall see, they often go to great lengths to incorporate issues of sex in their structures and operations.

Second, the story reveals the links between sex and power. In the case of the male Arab prisoners we can see that US interrogators used sexual abuse to break down the prisoners' sense of self-identity and associated pride.

Third, the story centres on male dominant organizational control. Although women were involved they were either used by male superiors to denigrate the sexuality of male prisoners or, as in the case of the female officer in charge of the prison system in Iraq, circumvented. Brigadier General Janis Karpinski, the commander of the 800th Military Police Brigade, was ostensibly in charge of the Abu Ghraib prison but complained that the military structure was confused, with different military and government agencies exercising power over the prison. The situation was such that she claimed to have no idea who was operating in her prison system (Hersh, 2004). A subsequent report on the abuses, by Major General Antonio M. Taguba put much of the blame for the situation on Karpinski, accusing her of poor leadership and arguing that "she was extremely emotional during much of her testimony"(Copeland, 2004). Karpinski challenges this view of her leadership and wonders if a male officer would have been described as "emotional." Her argument is that the Abu Ghraib investigation is about scapegoating, and that the military command has decided that she is "disposable" (Ibid).

Fourth, the story indicates that organizational life cannot easily be separated from social life. A number of commentators have linked events at the Abu Ghraib prison to the 9/11 attack on the US, the political philosophy of the Bush administration, US socio-political assessments of the psychology of Arab peoples, the invasion and occupation of Iraq by US and allied military forces and increasing insurgency against the occupation forces (Burrough, Peretz, Rose and Wise, 2004; Goldenberg et al., 2004; Hersh, 2004; Saunders, 2004).

Fifth, the story suggests that the relationship between power, sex, and organization is complex and shifting. Thus, at one level sex and power are talked about in terms of the physical characteristics of the body (e.g., the nakedness of the prisoners). At another level the discussion is around sexual acts (e.g., the forced simulations of sex acts by the prisoners). A third level focuses on the relative power of men and women. A fourth level revolves around the relationship between organization and masculinity and femininity (e.g., the role of women in the military). A fifth level can be found in the discourse around sexual orientation and what constitutes appropriate or "normal" sexual relationships (e.g., Arab prisoners being forced to simulate both heterosexual and homosexual acts).

SEX AND ORGANIZATIONAL LIFE

To make sense of sex at work we need to begin by making a distinction between sex, gender, and sexuality. At its most basic level "sex" refers to the biological differences between men and women.[2] However, our notions of the nature of men and women are not restricted to biological differences. Through culture we come to associate women and men with varying sets of characteristics, for example, soft/rough, weak/strong. We refer to culturally acquired characteristics as "gender."

"Sexuality" is an important aspect of gender and refers to a person's sexual self; those aspects of a person that make them sexually attractive to another. Thus, a person is born with certain biological features (sex) and, using those features as a basis, people attribute particular characteristics (gender) to the person so that they are viewed as male or female. An important part of the process of becoming a man or a woman involves assumptions about the physical attractiveness (sexuality) of that person.

The process of becoming a man or a woman involves many stages and contexts in a person's life. Each stage and each context involves a number of power relations in which people are rarely equal. Definitions of womanhood and of manhood are often influenced and shaped by powerful forces in society. The US debate on gays in the military is a good example. The debate shows how powerful people in the armed forces and government managed, for many years, to shape an approved image of masculinity; one that was "rough," "tough" and decidedly heterosexual (cf. Shilts, 1993). More recently, the issue of same sex marriages has raised questions about traditional notions of marriage and the separation of church and state.

Organizations are powerful contexts in which people spend much of their lives. As such, they are important cultural sites which contribute to our understanding of what constitute men and women. This is achieved in any number of ways, ranging from decisions about what men and women are capable of through to the use of sexuality for organizational ends:

The association of types of work with "masculinity" and with "femininity": In 1981 the great majority of Canadian women were concentrated in clerical, or pink collar, or sales and service occupations, and in jobs that were generally low paying. This feminization of jobs had not improved much by 2002 with "70% of female employees working mostly in teaching, nursing and related health occupations, clerical positions, or sales and service" (Cooke-Reynolds and Zukewich, 2004). The position remained the same in 2003 (Disabled Women's Network Ontario, 2004). Each time an organization classifies a job as for "men only" or "women only" they are not only discriminating but they are helping to create narrow images of men and women. Steel work, for example, is so closely associated with men that steel work is seen in some communities as part of what it means to be masculine.[3]

The under-representation of women in the top echelons of organizational office-holding: When an organization fails to promote women to positions of management it is not only discriminating but, at the very least, is insinuating that leadership qualities are a masculine trait. In 1995 it is estimated that 52% of all Canadian women worked full-time but that figure had dropped to 44.5% by 2003 (Disabled Women's Network Ontario, 2004). Nonetheless, by 2002 women constituted 46.1% of the Canadian workforce (Disabled Women's Network Ontario, 2004) but only 33.7% of management positions (Catalyst, 2003). In Canada the number of women in management positions has improved in recent years (LeMoncheck and Sterba, 2001) but it still has a considerable way to go. For example, in the early to mid-1990s women constituted 17% of senior management positions (Statistics Canada, 1995), and less than one percent of the top executives at Canada's largest companies are women (Nemeth, 1993). A decade later "14 per cent of senior managers at large Canadian organizations are women. When you add medium-sized organizations, it is 20 percent" (Lorraine Dyke, Director of the Centre for Research and Education on Women and Work at Carleton University, quoted in Bufton, 2004). In the early 1990s women constituted around 6% of the boards of directors of Canadian companies (Bradshaw-Campbell, 1991). That percentage had grown to 9.8% by 2001 and 11.2% by 2003 (Catalyst, 2003). However, the proportion of companies with no women board directors has remained stable at around 51.4% for the first few years of the 21st century (Catalyst, 2003).

Pay inequities: When an organization pays a woman less than it does a man who is engaged in roughly similar work it is not only discriminating but it is contributing to the notion that womanhood is worth less than manhood. In Canada, in 1999 women were paid an average of 80 cents for every dollar earned by men (Statistics Canada, 2002). By 2004 the situation had improved to a point where the average female worker was earning 81.6 cents for every dollar earned by the average man (Disabled Women's Network Ontario, 2004). However, if we compare the earnings of men and women we find that women's earnings are at 63.9% of the average earnings of men, and that the gap had widened since 1997 (Disabled Women's Network Ontario, 2004). This is also true for women with university degrees who earned on average 75.9% of the average earnings of men with university degrees in 1995, but only 69.8% of the average men's earnings in 2003 (Disabled Women's Network Ontario, 2004). According to one estimate, almost one third of working women in Canada are low paid, compared to a fifth of working men (Disabled Women's Network Ontario, 2004).

The use of sexuality to sell products and services: An organization helps to shape public images of sexuality each time it uses sexuality to sell its products. On the whole, companies use young, white women and men to sell their products. By featuring certain kinds of women and men in their advertising, companies are not only selling their products but they are selling the idea that a person is not sexually attractive unless they conform to a certain look (Meehan and Riordan, 2002; Shields and Heinecken, 2002; Smith, 1998; Wolf, 2002).

The issue is clearly contentious. Late in 2004 a Saint Mary's University commerce student produced a "girlie calendar" as "part of a course in entrepreneurship" (Daily News Staff, 2004: 1). The calendar featured shots of young, mostly white, female students in various poses, ranging from "scantily-clad women in provocative poses to women wearing team uniforms" (Daily News Staff, 2004: 3). Responding to criticism of the project the business student who produced the calendar, admitted that some of the shots were "a little bit racy and provocative"(quoted in Daily News Staff, 2004: 3), including one shot where a female student is shown "tugging at her panties" and others of "the girls in their bikinis" (Daily News Staff, 2004: 3). The calendar caused controversy in the university and local community and led to a ban on sales within the university: originally sold on campus and local bars as part of the course project the student made "$4,000 in profits" (Daily News Staff, 2004). The Saint Mary's University student union paper – the Journal – ran a front page article on the issue titled: "Halifax University Girls: A Step Back" (Whitman, 2004) and "some SMU faculty voiced their disapproval". The university issued a statement that the "administration received many complaints about the calendar from students, faculty and staff" (Gillis, 2005). It banned any further sales from campus, due to a broad concern "about respect and equality from members of our community" (university spokesperson, quoted in Daily News Staff, 2004:3).

Sexual harassment: Acts of sexual harassment are among the clearest examples of sexual behaviour at work. Sexual harassment, in its most explicit form, involves *unwanted* attention of a sexual nature, whether through acts of a physical, verbal or otherwise suggestive nature: the overwhelming majority of cases involve the sexual harassment of a woman by a man. Studies of sexual harassment at work indicate that there is a relationship between the incidence and type of harassment and the character of the workplace itself (Giglio, 2003; O'Connell, 1999; Orser, 2001). Some workplace environments, for example, encourage or fail to discourage sexual harassment (Spence, 1999).

Power is a central issue in sexual harassment. Organizational arrangements create countless contexts of power inequity in which men occupy the majority or the only positions of power and authority. In many cases of sexual harassment organizational power is a factor where the woman is bothered by an organizationally more powerful male and/or has to rely on a male power structure to intervene to prevent harassment.

Prohibitions and norms against homosexuality: A central and recurring theme of organizational sexuality is heterosexuality. Signs of sexual preference other than heterosexuality are rarely tolerated within organizations.[4] Very little research has yet been done on homosexuality at work but what evidence there is indicates that gay women and men are usually expected to conceal their sexual preferences from organizational view (Schneider, 1982; 1984) and this places severe strains on the gay person (Irwin, Gay and Lesbian Rights Lobby (N.S.W.) and Australian Centre for Lesbian and Gay Research, 1999; Raeburn, 2004; Winfeld and Spielman, 2001; Zuckerman and Simons, 1996; Hall, 1990). When an organization discriminates against a person on the basis of their sexual preference they contribute to the suppression of sexual difference.

It should be clear from these various examples that sex is not only a constant feature of organizational life but also has numerous implications for organizational and personal outcomes. Yet, OB and OT has remained silent on the subject. As we saw in Chapter 1, organizational texts make little or no mention of sex, gender, or sexuality. In this chapter our central objective will be to challenge you to think about the relationship between sex, organization, and power, and about the implications of those relationships for organizational and personal outcomes.

NOW TURN TO EXERCISE 5.1 AT THE END OF THIS CHAPTER

SEX AND ACADEMIA

In 1986, the Association of Universities and Colleges of Canada passed a "Statement on the Status of Women in Canadian Universities," which pointed out the need for ... nstitutions of higher learning to assume a leadership role in ensuring equality for women in the workplace. Unfortunately, there is little evidence to suggest that Canadian universities have taken this responsibility seriously.... In general, universities appear to be no farther ahead than other organizations in ensuring equity for women [...] Little attention has been paid to the gender inequities in university management... However, it is not difficult to see that, just as in other organizations, women very seldom make it to upper management levels in Canadian universities. The number who have become university presidents is few indeed (Brindley and Frick, 1990: 1).

The pursuit of "knowledge," as with other pursuits, takes place in the context of power relationships (Chandler, Barry and Berg, 2004; Hearn, 2004; Husu, 2001). Universities are no less prone to the utilization of power to achieve decisions than many other organizations (Sinclair, 1995; Tudiver, 1999; Turk, 2000) Where universities differ from many other organizations is in masking the use of power behind claims of "scientific method" and "objectivity." (cf. Hearn, 2004; Husu, 2001).

Table 5.1: Percentage of Full-time Canadian University Professors by Gender, 2001-2002[5]

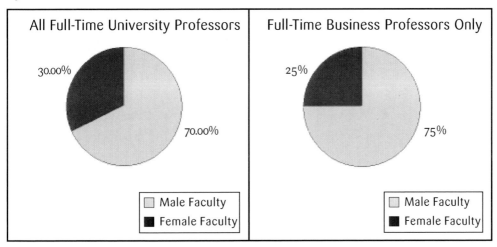

Percentages rounded to the nearest whole number.

Table 5.2: Percentage of Full-time Canadian University Professors by Rank and Gender, 2001-2002

1. All Professors

Full Professor		Associate Professor		Assistant Professor		Other	
Males	Females	Males	Females	Males	Females	Males	Females
84.0%	16.0%	67.2%	32.8%	59.2%	40.8%	46.1%	53.9%

2. Business Professors

Full Professor		Associate Professor		Assistant Professor		Other	
Males	Females	Males	Females	Males	Females	Males	Females
87.9%	12.1%	73.6%	26.4%	69.7%	30.3%	52.8%	47.2%

Almost two decades have passed since the Association of Universities and Colleges in Canada committed itself to increase the number of women in leadership roles (Brindley and Frick, 1990) yet by 2003 only 13.7% of university presidents were women, and their average compensation was 91.6% of men's (Stanley, Robbins and Morgan, 2004). It is not surprising that the growth of female leadership is slow because it reflects the inability of universities to promote women to senior faculty positions. For instance, women make up just over 15 percent of all Full Professorships (see Table 5.2) and 16 % of Canada Research Chairs (Canadian Association of University Teachers, 2004). Female professors constitute less than 29 % of all university professors (Table 5.1) and their average earnings were reported to be 85.5% of that of men's in 2003 (Stanley et al., 2004). We would note, however, that there has been some movement in the hiring and promotion of female faculty since 1995 when women constituted just over 23 % of all faculty and 11.1 % of Full Professorships (Mills and Simmons, 1999: 159). That the Universities, no less than other organizations, are male dominated means that a key aspect of the exercise of power involves a gendered dimension, that is, it reflects unequal power relationships between men and women (Bannerji, Carty, Dehli, Heald and McKenna, 1991).

Sadly, this appears to be just the tip of the iceberg. Various studies of Canadian universities have found widespread evidence of sexual discrimination to the degree that it could be described as an "incredible anti-woman ambiance"

(Dagg and Thompson, 1988; see also O'Connell, 1999) or a "chilly climate" for women (Prentice, 1996). Dagg and Thompson's (1988) study found a climate of sexism which included posters of scantily clad or naked women on university walls or orientation rituals that degraded women;[6] the use of course materials which made little or no reference to women, or which marginalized them; male professors who use derogatory terms for women, tell sexist jokes, and use images of women as sex objects to make a point in class; a relative lack of funding for feminist research; the under-funding and downgrading of women's studies programs; and widespread sexual harassment and sexual assault. Things had not essentially changed a decade later (Dagg and Thompson, 1988; Giglio, 2003; O'Connell, 1999). For women of colour, the universities and the school system as a whole present a double bind of racism and sexism (Carty, 1991; Hazell, 2002; Razack, 1998; Thiessen, Bascia and Goodson, 1996b).

Inequities and the Business School: One of the bastions of male dominance is the university business school. In Canada fewer than twelve per cent of the Deans of Canadian business schools are female,[7] and female faculty members constitute less than one in four of all business professors (see Table 5.1). Female business professors constitute a lower percentage of all faculty members, and each of the ranks when compared to female professors on the whole (see Tables 5.1 and 5.2). Nonetheless, Dr. Margot Northey (previously Dean of Queen's University Business School and one of the few female business school Deans in Canada) feels that, "In North America, women are making notable strides in business and in business schools" (quoted in Orator Magazine, 2002). In her opinion, female deans "all take pleasure in helping other women succeed, through support, advice and example. However I think the current emphasis on female role models can be overplayed, since females and males can and do learn from admirable individuals of either sex" (quoted in Orator Magazine, 2002).

In many business schools students are encouraged to "dress for success" and to develop an aggressive, competitive spirit. In a November 23, 2003 interview with the Halifax Chronicle Herald, Acadia University President Gail Dinter Gottleib was criticized for remarks she made suggesting that business school students at Acadia appeared to be dressed more for "flipping burgers" and fetching coffee." In defending her position, Dr Gottleib later said business students, like business people, should be held to a higher standard of dress. "…I want every business student who wants to walk from Wolfville onto Wall Street to have the best shot that they can…to be seriously considered for any type of professional job"(quoted in Hudson, 2003). Various critics of Gottleib argue that she singled out female students for comment by stating that only male students dressed appropriately. In her defence Gottleib contends that she thought that she was speaking off the record when she made certain remarks. Despite her concern to encourage women to appear more business-like Gottleib was pleased to accept the role of "crowning" the local beauty queen at the 2004 annual Apple Blossom Festival in nearby Kentville.

SEX AND ORGANIZATIONAL RESEARCH

An "anti-woman ambiance"(or, institutional sexism) is the context in which academic research is conceptualized, developed, funded, carried out, and disseminated; it is a context not dissimilar from other organizational contexts that the academic researcher encounters. The impact of institutional sexism can be seen in the bulk of organizational research which reflect sexist attitudes.

Reading through OB/OT research one is struck by the fact that women are either ignored or marginalized. It is as if the researchers were not so much occupants on an "ivory tower" as cloistered away in a monastic order. From the classic studies to current texts, gender has been neglected and ignored in studies of organization. This neglect has contributed to sexual discrimination by helping to normalize the idea that women are somehow peripheral to the public sphere.

The Hawthorne Studies provides a classic example of the way OB and OT ignores gender even where it is a major, and obvious, element in the workplace. The Hawthorne Studies played an important part in the development of OB OT as university disciplines- particularly in suggesting that people need social solidarity and leadership. But gender was a central variable that was left out of account (Acker and van Houten, 1974). Gender was a key factor in the research design itself. The two main groups studied were an all male ("Bank Wiring Room") and an all female ("Relay Assembly Test Room") group. The groups were studied in different ways. Study of the Bank Wiring Room involved observation of the existing work group: the men were free to continue their usual work practices, including autonomy to develop and maintain their own work norms. The "Relay Assembly Test Room," on the other hand, involved an artificially created work group; a small group of women was selected to take part in the experimental group situation. Unlike the men, the women were carefully recruited, closely supervised, and in numerous, told that they should improve their productivity:

> Group norms relating to productivity did develop in both work groups, but they developed in relationship to the external environment of each group and the external demands in regard to increasing productivity were different for the groups. Furthermore, the immediate external environment was controlled by males in both experiments. But maleness constitutes a different kind of external environment for a female group than for a male group because the effect of sex-based hierarchy of the larger society is added to the structuring of control in the organization. For the women's group, the relationship was between powerful males and weak females, that is, the females being weak, had to please the supervisors if they wished to stay in the test room, so they adopted the norm of increased production (Acker and van Houten, 1974: 156).

Sex based power differentials are evident throughout the research. The women selected for the experiment were young (around 20), unmarried, and, with one exception, living at home with their parents in traditional, first-generation immigrant families. All those in positions of authority and power – from supervisors to researchers – were men. When the young women were asked separately if they wished to participate in the experimental group, "it is not surprising that they all agreed" (Acker and van Houten, 1974: 153). In the published reports of the research there is more than a suggestion of paternalistic attitudes and manipulation by the researchers as evidenced, for example, in the repeated use of the term "girls" throughout the texts.

Acker and van Houten's (1974) analysis of the Hawthorne Studies indicates that sexuality is not only a feature of the workplace but of the study of the workplace itself. The disparities between the men's and the women's group were ignored in the research findings. For instance, the researchers failed to notice that it was the female group which increased output and the male group which restricted output. The findings of these studies went on, instead, to suggest that the results were applicable to all (genderless) employees.

> Since the research treatment was very different for the males and for the females, there still remains the question of whether the group of males would have responded similarly to the same combination of rewards and punishments. Of course we do not know (Acker and van Houten, 1974: 156).

French and his colleagues, in their now-classic participation studies, made a similar error of this kind. Lester Coch and John French carried out a study of a pyjama factory to study the effects of employee participation in decision-making on resistance to change. Their results, which indicated a positive relationship between participation and change, played an important role in influencing research into participation and "democratic work climates" (Coch and French, 1948). Twelve years later French attempted, without success, to replicate the earlier findings (French, Israel and Aas, 1960). Various reasons were offered to explain the difference in results but not that the original study involved female employees and the replication study involved male employees: the male subjects were less willing to accept the legitimacy of participation schemes, were more attached to norms of restricted output and, as a result, working practices were not "improved."

Where organizational studies have taken gender into account they have done so in a way that has trivialized it. The work of Blauner (1964) provides a prime example. Studying workplace alienation, Blauner analyzed the statements of male and female workers in different ways. When dealing with men Blauner interprets their activities and responses as being primarily job related, that is, he uses a "job's model" of analysis (Feldberg and Glenn, 1979). Thus, when men expressed discontent Blauner recorded this as valid expression of work-related dissatisfaction. When dealing with women Blauner interprets their activities and responses as being primarily related to their gender (but in the crudest biological sense), that is, he uses a "gender model." Thus, when women expressed discontent Blauner recorded this as being due to their "weaker physical stamina" and "family commitments."

Over the years a number of feminist studies have exposed the extent to which gender has been ignored in many of the leading studies of organization. Weber's theory of bureaucracy has been questioned for assuming that the underlying character of "rationality" is a universal, rather than a male-associated, characteristic (Martin, 1990). It has been argued that the male character of rationality explains why bureaucratic environments have served to inhibit female entry and opportunity (Ferguson, 1984; Morgan, 1988). Likewise, Crozier's (1964) study of bureaucracy has been challenged for ignoring gender in explaining organizational conflict (Acker and van Houten, 1974): although the machine operators were women and the maintenance workers, on whom the operators depended, were men, Crozier explained antagonisms between the groups in terms of bureaucratic structure. Herbert Simon's

(1997) "bounded rationality" model of decision making has been taken to task for ignoring the role of emotionality in organizational decisions (Mumby and Putnam, 1992) and Beynon and Blackburn's (1972) work has been criticized for using a gender model of explanation in determining female perceptions of work (Feldberg and Glenn, 1979). Doubt has also been cast on the generalizability of the pioneering leadership studies of Lewin, Lippitt, and White (1939): the studies, which indicated that employee productivity could be improved by a "democratic style of leadership" were based on experiments with ten years old boys (Mills, 1988b).

Radical theories of organization have not been exempt from the problem of gender neglect. Allen's (1975) Marxist analysis of organizations, and Burrell and Morgan's (1979) radical critique of organization theory provides no references to "men," "women," "sex," or "gender" in their indexes. Burawoy's (1979) contention that structure rather than gender determines workplace consent and resistance has been contested on the grounds that "gender matters not only for the structuring of the labour process, but also in interpersonal relations within the structure" (Davies, 1990). Silverman's (1970) action frame of reference, which challenged functionalist theories of organization by stressing the importance of the actor's perceptions, has been critiqued for its use of male reference points. Silverman, for example, argues that in understanding the worker we must see "his actions […] as the outcome of his perceptions of the various options open to him and of which alternative best meets his priorities at the time." But, as Clegg and Dunkerley (1980: 405) point out, this can also be applied to "her definitions, her actions, her perceptions of the various options open to her, and her priorities."

Finally, not only have women been ignored or marginalized within the various foci of research, they have been ignored as researchers. Sheriff and Campbell (1992) point out that the work of Mary Parker Follett presaged the transition from the Scientific Management School to the Human Relations School but there has been very little recognition of her pioneering role until very recently.

In summary, the neglect of gender by the great majority of organizational analysts has served to ignore some of the most crucial features of organizational life; led to an overlooking of organizational dynamics; contributed to the development of flawed methodologies; and, by far the most damning aspect, has contributed to sexual discrimination in the workplace.

Despite the widespread and deep-rooted relationship between sex and organizations research into that relationship has only begun to develop during the last three decades. In this last section of the chapter we want to raise some issues for further research, indicate examples of the type of research that is underway, signal some of the conflicts involved in the research strategies involved, and to help you to understand better some of the problems involved in this area of research.

Throughout the chapter we have indicated the various issues involved in research into sex and organizations. These can be summed up under four broad headings – *Equity Issues* (including sexual discrimination, employment equity), *Sexuality, Power and Authority Issues* (including women in management, resistance, sexual harassment and abuse, sexual preference, workplace romance), *Identity Issues* (including notions of self, self worth, and self esteem) and *Research Issues* (including implications for research and for the researcher).

Equity Issues

The issue of employment equity is a political one. Sex discrimination legislation has been, since the mid-1970s, a growing reality throughout the western industrial nations[8] and yet things have moved slowly. This has prompted some researchers to examine the workplace for clues to the bases of sexual discrimination so that we might better understand how to bring about change. This research has gone in various directions. At one level there is a wealth of descriptive analysis detailing the extent of sexual discrimination in the workplace. This is valuable in indicating the levels of inequities that exist and any trends or patterns of change. Research, at another level, is aimed at uncovering barriers to change.[9]

Barriers to Change

The direction of a research project depends on how the researcher views organization. To take four examples, organization is viewed as networks of communication, organizational cultures, systems of production or labour processes, and pathways to organizational careers.

Communication networks: some research focuses on the role of communication in inhibiting employment equity. Cava (1988), for example, focuses on effective male forms of communication to identify communicative strategies that will help women to be more effective in existing networks of communication. Cox (1986), on the other hand, is more interested in altering existing communication practices to ensure a successful "integration of women" into the organization. Cox identifies the problems for women of existing communicative strategies to encourage top management to alter their practices. Borisoff and Merrill (1985) develop this latter aspect by encouraging men and women at work to examine the nature of communicative strategies and their potential for effective organizational practice. In the process, they argue, people will find that some male-associated practices (e.g., interrupting) will be seen as ineffective and some (e.g., assertiveness) will be seen as effective: some female-associated practices (e.g., attentive listening) will be seen as effective and some (e.g., passivity) will be seen as ineffective. The aim is a fine mixture of effective male and female communication styles. Pearson's (1985) concern goes beyond the organization and is aimed at exposing the roots of gendered communication. Pearson argues that sexism in communications needs to be dealt with not only by weakening the hold of gendered practices in the workplace but also through fundamental changes in the way we socialize children.

In a different vein, Meissner (1986), Putnam (Putnam, 1982; 1983; Putnam and Fairhurst, 1985), Mills and Chiaramonte (1991), and Ashcraft and Mumby (2004) set out to reveal the role that communication plays in the construction of gender. Meissner argues that "communication reproduces dominance relations," indicating that inequities might be more effectively addressed through resistance to certain communicative practices. Putnam's research focuses on the socially constructed nature of organization and the centrality of communication to that process. Putnam (1982: 7) argues that we can free ourselves from the taken for granted assumptions that inhibit equity by understanding, "The specific grammars, codes, and recipes that determine appropriate human behaviour in specific contexts." Mills and Chiaramonte takes this one step farther. They argue that we need to understand the concept and practice of organization that precede organizational communication. They contend that strategies aimed at inner-organizational communication alone will not get to the heart of inequities because the very concept of organization per se is deeply gendered. Thus, a more effective long-term strategy should be aimed at altering the way we think and do organizing. Ashcraft and Mumby (2004: xii)) set out to pull together various insights in gender and communication in the development of what they call a "feminist communicology of organization" as a praxis for addressing workplace discrimination.

Organizational culture: The organization as a culture is another way of viewing organizations. Ironically, given that gender is a culturally devised phenomenon, there is little research on the relationship between organizational culture and sexual discrimination. Hofstede's (1980) international study of workplace values was among the first to link the notion of gender with organizational culture. Hofstede argues that countries differ in the dominance of masculine values and that this can be correlated with equity factors in the workplace. Hofstede classifies countries into high or low "masculinity" (or MAS) according to the extent to which respondents (of both sexes) "tend to endorse goals usually more popular among men (high MAS) or among women (low MAS)." Hofstede found that countries with high MAS scores have lower numbers of women in professional and technical jobs. It is not clear, however, whether lowered masculinity factors lead to enhanced opportunities for women at work or vice versa. Hofstede's work draws on traditional notions of masculinity and femininity and as such is seen as problematic, tending to reinforce rather than challenge traditional notions of gender (Mills, 2002b)

The work of Smircich (1985) shifted attention towards feminist analysis of organizational culture, arguing that, "A feminist perspective on culture calls for analysis and critique of the underlying gender basis of the production of knowledge and the prevailing social order." Two Canadian studies that were conducted in a feminist vein were the Abella Commission Report (1984) and Nicole Morgan's (1988) study of the Canadian Federal Public Service; both focused attention on the significance of culture for employment opportunities. The Abella Commission pointed the way in their description of the problem as "systemic discrimination":

> Rather than approaching discrimination from the perspective of the single perpetrator and the single victim, the systemic approach acknowledges that by and large the systems and practices we customarily and often unwittingly adopt may have an unjustifiably negative effect on certain groups in society [...]

The Report goes on to argue that systemic patterns of discrimination have "two basic antecedents":

> a) a disparately negative impact that flows from the structure of systems designed for a homogeneous constituency; and b) a disparately negative impact that flows from practices based on stereotypical characteristics ascribed to an individual because of the characteristics ascribed to the group of which he or

she is a member. The former usually results in a system designed for white, able-bodied males; the latter usually results in practices based on white able-bodied males' perceptions of everyone else (pp.9-19).

Morgan shows how prevailing social and political attitudes combine with organizational arrangements to create organizational cultures. Taking a broad view of the interrelationships between organizational and wider cultural factors, Morgan reveals how:

> some settings create possibilities for women to advance from entry-level to managerial positions while other settings have attempted to inhibit their advancement, or have relegated them to low-status, unskilled, part-time, and poorly paid jobs.

In a similar vein, Mills (1988a; 1996a; 2002a) and his colleagues (Aaltio and Mills, 2002; Aaltio, Mills and Helms Mills, 2002; Helms Mills, 2002; Helms Mills and Mills, 2000) study the combination of social and organizational features to examine the ways in which different rules of behaviour combine in the creation of an organizational culture and what the implications of different configurations are for sexual discrimination.

Outside the OB/OT literature, excellent studies of women's resistance to male culture have been carried out by Pollert (1981), Lamphere (1985), and Benson (1978; 1981; 1986).

Labour processes: Cockburn (1985; 1991), Lowe (1987), and Tancred-Sheriff (1989) focus on the organization as a system of production or labour process. Cockburn's historical analysis of the development of techniques of production indicates that the process is deeply gendered – with men controlling technology. Techniques of production – passed on from male to male in a series of training situations – create knowledge, power and status in the workplace and make the possibility of employment equity impossible unless "an autonomous women's movement inside and outside the trade unions can be created to develop women-only training and to transform the nature of technology and the relations of work." Lowe's work shows how the different relation of women and men to production techniques facilitates processes of "deskilling" which have transformed types of work from male to female dominated and, in the process, created low-paid and unskilled jobs. Tancred-Sheriff focuses on issues of control and explores how different managements have used female sexuality to facilitate control over clients and consumers.

Organizational pathways: Focusing on individual "pathways" to organizational careers, Gutek and Larwood (1987) and Brindley and Frick (1990) study successful women (and men). They collect information on the ways that women have become successful to understand how existing barriers can be breached by the next wave of female aspirants. Kanter (1977) takes a totally different approach by focussing on the organization as a structure and concluding that structural factors rather than gender differences account for much of the perceived difference between men and women at work. Kanter urges management to restructure in ways that can allow fuller opportunities to men and women.

Sex, Power, and Authority Issues

Within OB and OT research much of the focus on gender has been on the problem of (an absence of) women in management. This has generated an extensive literature of its own. The work of Gutek and Larwood (1987) and Davidson and Burke (1994) are examples of this kind of focus. Much of the women in management (WIM) research mirrors the broader inequities literature in attempting to describe and analyze barriers to women's entry into management. This literature has focused on the improvement of women within current hierarchical arrangements. For example, Morrison, White, and Van Elsor (1987) in the US, and Agócs (1989; 1992) in Canada identify ways that women might "break the glass ceiling" into top managerial positions. Within this framework research evaluates the role of mentors (Doyle, 2000; Duff, 1999), sex role stereotyping (Schein, 1994), leadership style (Powell, 1999), stress (Nelson and Burke, 2002), and the impact of family (McManus, 2000; Wolfe, 2001).

Much of the WIM literature is rooted in a "sex differences" approach which focuses on the difference between men and women as *essential* categories of person (Alvesson and Billing, 2002). Radical challenges to the WIM framework have come from various researchers, including Hearn and Parkin (1983; 1987), Wilson (2001), and Alvesson and Due Billing (2002; 1997), who take a "gender focused" approach. From this perspective the focus is on the ways that persons become seen as men and women and it is argued that the very issues of management and leadership themselves need to be questioned because they are as "gendered as they are problematic."

The WIM literature focuses on *positions* of power and authority but few studies take up the issue of the *exercise* of power and authority. From outside the WIM literature, Pollert (1981), Collinson (1996), and Knights (Kerfoot and

Knights, 1996; Knights and Willmott, 1999; Morgan and Knights, 1991) and colleagues draw attention to the ways in which sexuality is used as a form of control. Mills and colleagues (Helms Mills and Mills, 2000; Mills and Murgatroyd, 1991; Thomas et al., 2004) take up the issue of resistance to gendered organizational control – showing that women are not passive recipients of male notions of their value and worth.

The biggest area of WIM research into sexuality and power in organizations is focused on sexual harassment but a growing body of work is concerned with the relationship between sexuality and organizational outcomes. The literature of sexual harassment is far ranging and includes descriptive accounts (O'Connell, 1999); analysis of "sex-role spillover" that is, the extent to which people's non-work sex roles (husband/wife; father/mother) influence work roles (Gutek and Cohen, 1992), and the relationship between sexuality and power (Ashcraft and Mumby, 2004).

Other areas of sexuality research have looked at the contribution of organizational factors to the construction of particular types of sexuality (Hearn and Parkin, 1987; Mills, 1996a; Mills, 1996c), for example, the way women are expected to be caring as nurses but "sexy" as flight attendants; the impact of notions of sexuality on the way certain organizations have come to be constructed (Burrell, 1984; Mills and Ryan, 2001; Ranke-Heinemann, 1990), for example, the introduction of celibacy into the Catholic Church in the twelfth century; the contribution of organizations to acceptable images of sexual preference (Hall, 1989; Schneider, 1982; Schneider, 1984; Shilts, 1993), for example, the exclusion of homosexuality from organizational life; and the use of sexuality as a means of organizational control (Pollert, 1981), for example, the use of paternalist language by managers to control female employees.

Masculinity: In recent years attention has focused on the impact of masculinity on the ways that organizations become discriminatory (Collinson, 1988). The work of Collinson and Collinson (1989), for example, has documented the relationship between work practices and masculinity, showing how men are expected to act in certain work roles if they are to be accepted as "real men." Maier's (1991; 1998) work has revealed how forms of masculinity built around aggressive or competitive behaviour can influence organizational outcomes such as the events that led to the explosion of the Challenger Shuttle in 1986. Mills' (1998a) work focuses on explaining how certain professions (e.g., piloting) or occupations (e.g., engineering) contribute to forms of masculinity and combine to exclude women. Much of the recent work on masculinity owes much to a key article by Collinson and Hearn (1994), which argues for an approach to the study of gender, "which addresses the unities, differences and interrelations between men and masculinities" (p. 2). They contend that, "men and masculinities are frequently central to organizational analysis, yet [they are] rarely the focus of interrogation" (ibid). A number of other works have further developed the study masculinity at work, including Cheng (1996), Aaltio-Marjosola (1998), Wicks and Mills (2000), Mills and Helms Mills (2002), and Hearn (2002).

Race/Ethnicity and Sexuality: The relationship between sexuality, race/ethnicity, and organizational life has been greatly under-researched. The work of Nkomo (1992; 1989) and her colleagues (Bell and Nkomo, 1992; Bell, 1989; Bell et al., 1992) in the US, and Mighty (1997) in Canada are rare attempts to study these relationships through a focus on black women. Little or nothing has been done on Hispanic (Calás, 1992), Chinese, south Asian or native women but a number of good insights have begun to appear in recent postcolonialist accounts (Mirchandani, 2004; Prasad, 1997a; Prasad and Prasad, 2002; Prasad, 1997b; Sinha, 1987).

Identity Issues

A relatively new area of research deals with the impact of organizational arrangements on gender and sense of identity. As opposed to earlier research which focused primarily on the impact of sexist work practices on women's sense of self worth (e.g., Cooper and Davidson, 1984), this newer research is concerned with the impact of organization on the construction of a person's sexual identity, attempting to uncover the extent to which notions of "male/female," "masculine/feminine" are created by the organizational context (Aaltio and Mills, 2002; Hearn, 2002; Leonard, 1984; Thomas et al., 2004).

Research Issues

Gender focused research has helped to reveal some of the problems of the research act itself; as Acker and Van Houten's (1974) work indicates, sex is a research issue as well as a focus. The situation of male researcher and female subject is problematic. The male researcher all too often represents one more male authority figure and as such is in a powerful position viz. a viz. the female subject. Hearn and Parkin (1983) have responded to this question in part by combining the research efforts of a male and a female researcher. Hearn (1985)urges, "men concerned about sexism" to study male environments with the aim of unearthing the ways in which men "control and fix" those environments to the detriment of women (see also Collinson and Hearn, 1994; 1996). Similarly Maier (1991; 1997) advocates work with males to help men see that they too have a "self-interest in promoting gender equity."

The relationship of male researcher to female subjects is also problematic in terms of methodology. A number of female researchers have argued that a feminist approach to women in organizations needs to be rooted in the experiences of *being* a woman, and thus it is problematic if not impossible for a man to get at understandings born of a particular set of gendered experiences. This viewpoint is not uncontested and it has raised several questions. For example, if it is not possible for a man to understand a women is it possible for female researchers to understand male experiences except through the impact of those experiences on women? If gender is a phenomenon of males and females then cannot men and women equally be involved in gender research? If gender is a cultural phenomenon, and men and women social constructs, then isn't it contrary logic to exclude some persons from gender research because they are men? If, however, men are able to talk to the experiences of women doesn't that add to the furtherance of a male dominance in which women's sense of self is always being defined for them? These are difficult questions that are far from resolved.

The relationship of female researcher to female subject is also problematic if the research supports the existing male dominant character of organizations. Tancred-Sheriff and Campbell (1992) take issue with leading female researchers whose work, they argue, has lent itself to managerialism.

From feminist research outside of OB/OT two bits of fundamental advice are worth noting. Kirby and McKenna (1989) argue that the self – the gendered self – cannot and should not be divorced from the research act. Examination of self will help to keep in front of the researcher her or his own gendered nature and biases. Stanley and Wise (1983) argue that to reduce the power relationship between researcher and subject the researcher needs to work fully with groups of persons to develop a research strategy, that the research strategy should arise out of the needs, concerns, and perceptions of the group itself (see also Alvesson and Deetz, 1996; 2000; Hollway, 1989; Reinharz and Davidman, 1992; Warren and Hackney, 2000).

When attempting to make a case for greater equity it is difficult to avoid the temptation to draw together material which emphasises inequities while down-playing, or leaving out of account, that which indicates improvements in women's status in society. Student responses to previous editions of this text have brought home to us our own shortcomings in that regard. In particular two type of response have been particularly troubling. The first type of response argues that the book is outdated because employment equity is now "a fact of life"; indeed, some argue that it is the white male who is now the brunt of discrimination. The second type of response argues that the book is depressing in its (unintended) suggestion that few advances in equity have been made; students in this category are left wondering if employment equity is worth the struggle.

Four key points are worth making:

(i) there have been a number of positive developments in women's status in the workplace in recent years,

(ii) not all "developments" have been positive for women,

(ii) those positive developments did not arise naturally,

(ii) the great majority of women's rights have had to be fought for and *maintained* by a large number of courageous women (and men).

Positive Developments

Women in Canada constitute 50.4% of the population and since 1971 they have witnessed a number of positive developments in the workplace:

Legal developments: Since 1967 and *The Royal Commission on the Status of Women* there have been several legal developments designed to ensure greater equity for women in the workplace (see footnote 8).

Women in the labour force: Between 1971 and 2001 there was a substantial growth in the number of women over the age of 15 who have paid jobs – rising from 34% to 46% of all women in this category. At the same time the percentage of employees who are women rose from 44% to 71% (Cooke-Reynolds and Zukewich, 2004).

Women in "management and administrative" positions: Between 1972 and 2001 the number of "management and administrative positions" held by women in Canada rose from 17% to 35% (Cooke-Reynolds and Zukewich, 2004).

Women's earnings: In the early 1980s women in full-time employment earned approximately 64% of the average income earned by men; this figure rose to 68% in 1990 and 72% in 1993, dropped to 70% in 1994 and rose again to a new high of 73% in 1995. It rose to 81.6 in 2004 (Disabled Women's Network Ontario, 2004).

The industrial concentration of women: In 1982 77% of the female workforce was concentrated in a few female dominated industries, including nursing and related health occupations, clerical positions or sales and service occupations. This figure dropped to 70% in 1994 (Statistics Canada, 1995) but it has remained the same since that point (Cooke-Reynolds and Zukewich, 2004).

Women-led and women-owned businesses: Between the late 1970's and the early part of the 21st century the number women-owned businesses in Canada rose from just over 200,000 to 821,000 women entrepreneurs, "who contribute in excess of $18 billion to the Canadian economy every year."

Negative Developments

Clearly there have been a number of positive developments for women in the workforce and that fact should be applauded. This tells us that employment equity is worth fighting for. However, we cannot be complacent. Many of the gains also signal the extent to which equity has a long way to go (e.g., the gap between men's and women's earnings; the concentration of women in few industries) and there have also been a number of set-backs, including the roll-back of equity legislation in Ontario under the Harris government.[10] There are more women in the workforce than ever before but that has been accompanied by an increase in the stressors on women such as widespread incidences of sexual harassment (see above) the double bind of paid work and house work (Hochschild, 1989), increases in work-family role strain (Runte and Mills, 2002; Runte and Mills, 2004), and greater threats of lay-offs.[11] There are more women business owners than ever before but at a cost – self-employed women earn an average of 55% of the income of self employed men due to the fact that women work in less lucrative sectors and a higher percentage are part-time workers (Tillson, 1996).

As for the argument that it is now the white male who is discriminated against this is far from the truth. Women and visible minorities still continue to suffer far greater rates of discrimination than white men. When a woman or person of colour is hired or promoted to some positions there are still those who argue that it was due to the person's gender or colour and not there qualifications that got them the job. Rarely is it suggested that a white man is hired on the basis of *his* gender or *his* colour (Jacques, 1997). Yet the evidence suggests that in many cases that is the underlying reason why a disproportionate number of men are concentrated in some positions. One recent analysis of the myth of discrimination against white men provides a good example of the problem:

[A] 1994 Statistics Canada survey of 33,000 university and community college graduates found that two years after their 1990 graduation, visible minorities and women university grads had the edge in earnings. It seems a good argument for scrapping employment equity, but that's just half the story. The study goes on to show that many more members of the designated groups can't even get hired in the first place (Kaye, 1997: 69).

Clearly there *is* a need to continue the fight for employment equity. Women have made considerable gains over the last few decades but those gains had to be fought for and they have to be protected from erosion in the future. There is a place in that struggle for men and women because equity is an issue for us all. Even Dianne Francis (1996), the conservative columnist for *Maclean's* magazine admits that in terms of employment equity, women have "come a long way … and there's still plenty of distance to go." Colin Lindsay, the editor of the 1995 Statistics Canada report on Women in Canada, sums it up well:

Clearly, the situation for women has improved dramatically over the course of the last two decades. However, there are still very significant and substantial gaps left between most of the major social indicators for women and men" (quoted in Maclean's magazine, 21 Aug. 1995).

KEY TERMS

authority	employment equity	*femininity*
gender focused research	*masculinity*	*power*
sex based power	sex differences research	sexual harassment
sexual preference	sexuality	systemic discrimination

REVIEW QUESTIONS

Q1. Define sexuality.

Assignment: Check the definition of sexuality in the introduction of this chapter.

[FS: To improve your understanding of the term read and compare the definitions from the following articles and book chapters – Burrell (1984: 98); Hearn and Parkin (1987: 53-58); Mills (1996b: 323-25).

Q2. What is the relationship between sex, organization, and power?

Assignment: Read through your diary notes for exercise 5.1., and write brief notes on the following:- a) compared with when you first completed the exercise, how would you now assess the role and extent of sexuality in your organization? b) what general conclusions do you draw about the relationship between sexuality, organizations, and power? and c) if you had to repeat the exercise what, if anything, would you do differently, and why?

Q3. What are some of the main research issues involved in studying sex at work?

Assignment: Write short notes on each of the following problem areas – (i) methodology, (ii) definition, and (iii) understanding barriers to change. Compare your answer with the discussion in this chapter.

[FS: Read Hearn and Parkin (1987), Chapter 1, and (i) note down the main points identified as problem areas, and (ii) comment on each point, stating how it might be dealt with].

Q4. What is the difference between a "sex differences" and a "gender focused" approach to research?

Assignment: Compare your answer with the definitions in the "Sex, Power and Authority Issues" section of this chapter.

[FS: Read and contrast the following two studies of gender and leadership – Hearn and Parkin (1991) and Harriman (1985), Chapter 9. Write short notes on five major differences between each approach. Compare and contrast the approach of Wicks and Bradshaw(2002) with that of Alvesson and Billing (2002) on the issue of gender and organizational culture.

Q5. What part do masculinity and femininity play in organizational life?

Assignment: Compare your answer with the discussion throughout this chapter.

[FS: For a deeper analysis of the question read Mills and Murgatroyd (1991), Chapter 4; Collinson and Hearn , and/or Ashcraft and Mumby (2004)].

Q6. How can the study of sexuality and organizations help us to understand (a) sexual preference and (b) race/ethnicity at work?

Assignment: Compare your answer with the discussion throughout this chapter.

[FS: (i) Read Quinn (1977) and Hall (1989): what are the main similarities and differences between the two approaches?

(ii) Read Cox (1986): how do you think this study would differ if the focus had been on women of colour?].

Q7. Briefly define each of the following terms, and say how each might influence the way organizations operate:

- employment equity
- sexual discrimination
- systemic discrimination
- sexual harassment

Assignment: Now turn back to the chapter and compare your definitions.

INTERNET EXERCISES

Q1. Find the websites for three universities, in three different countries, that offer MBA programmes. Are there differences among the three in how they refer to students? Specifically, are students thought of as customers, clients, or students? Discuss the implications of this from a managerialist and radical approach.

Q2. Find the pay equity policies for Canada, UK, and USA. How do they differ and how are they the same?

EXERCISE 5.1

This exercise is designed to help you to arrive at your own conclusions about the nature of the relationship between sexuality, organization, and power.

For this exercise you will need a notebook to serve as a diary:

A. Power, Authority and Gender Divisions

Find out the sex composition (i.e., relative numbers of men and women) of (i) your university/college administration, (ii) the faculty as a whole, (iii) the faculty in which you are studying. Note down the results in your diary, and leave space for comments. Over the next week note down – one way or another –

any events, actions, or policies that suggest to you that the sex composition of the authority structure has/has not a significant influence on the life of the organization.

B. Observations

Over the period of a week keep a diary of your observations within the university or college. Try to observe as many aspects of college life that you can:

- Note down the graffiti from the toilet walls – does it tell you anything about some people's concern with sexuality?
- Look at notice boards – can you learn anything from the types of events and activities that are advertised? For example, how many of the activities encourage direct participation by men and women equally? How many activities are sex-typed, i.e., for men or for women only?
- Read the student newspaper, and sum up the extent to which it reflects sexual concerns.
- Look through the university or college calender – count the photographs and note down the respective percentages that include males and which include females; compare the number of photographs of men and women in which the person in depicted in a passive role, e.g., sitting, observing, and those which depict an authoritative role e.g., lecturing, administrating, directing, etc.
- At the various break, arrival and departure times spend time reflecting upon the conversations around you. Note down your thoughts. How much of the discussion revolves around things sexual? To what extent do you think they have a bearing on any of the other activities of the college?
- Observe relationships – both inside and out of the classroom. How are people relating to each other? Is there a sexual dimension and, if so, what role do you think it plays in the way things are organized or done?
- Pay attention to issues of sexual preference. To what extent to any or all of the things you note down reflect a concern with heterosexuality?

At the end of the week's observing write down some general conclusions about the role and extent of sexuality in your institution.

EXERCISE 5.2

This exercise is designed to get you to think about the use of sexual imagery and its impact on the institution and the people involved. Research the issue of the "Halifax University Girls Calendar." Drawing upon accounts of the calendar, make a list of all the arguments that people made for and against the production of the calendar. In small groups discuss the following questions: (i) What impact, if any, did the calendar have on Saint Mary's University? (ii) What impact, if any, did the calendar have on any of the people involved? (iii) Should the calendar have been produced as part of a university project? (iv) Should the calendar have been produced at all? (v) Should the calendar have been sold on the university campus?

As a group try to come to some consensus and then present your conclusions to the class with detailed points that support your argument.

CASE ANALYSIS

Turn to the Westray Case and answer the following question:

What role did masculinity contribute to the disaster?

Now look at the For Your Eyes Only Case and answer the case questions.

USEFUL WEB SITES

<http://www.swc-cfc.gc.ca/about/about_e.html>
<www.caut.ca>
<http://www.chrc-ccdp.ca/>

FURTHER READING

An overview of issues of sexuality:
David Collinson and Jeff Hearn, (1996). MEN AS MANAGERS, MANAGERS AS MEN
Jeff Hearn and Wendy Parkin, (1987). "SEX" AT "WORK"
Jeff Hearn et al., (1989). THE SEXUALITY OF ORGANIZATIONS
Barbara A. Gutek, (1985). SEX AND THE WORKPLACE

An overview of issues of gender and organization theory:
Mats Alvesson and Yvonne Due Billing, (1997). UNDERSTANDING GENDER AND ORGANIZATIONS
Joanne Martin, (2000). "HIDDEN GENDERED ASSUMPTIONS IN MAINSTREAM ORGANIZATIONAL THEORY AND RESEARCH"
Albert J. Mills and Peta Tancred (eds.), (1992). GENDERING ORGANIZATIONAL ANALYSIS

END NOTES

1. Sources for this story include, Borger and Harding (2004),Goldenberg (2004a; 2004b) , Goldenberg et al., (2004), Hersh (2004), International Committee of the Red Cross (2004) Klein (2004), Leigh (2004), and Saunders (2004).

2. Oakley (1972) makes this distinction but Rakow (1986) argues that "sex," itself, is a socially constructed concept and should be considered part of the concept of gender.

3. In 1980 a successful complaint to the Ontario Human Rights Commission forced the Stelco steelworks in Hamilton to recruit females. A major study of the changes in the industry found that a number of male steelworkers felt their "manhood" as well as their jobs to be under threat due to the entry of women into the industry (Livingstone and Luxton, 1989).

4. In a highly publicized case in 1987 the Canadian airline Wardair attempted to prevent one of its male flight attendants from wearing an earring. The company argued that it was bad for business because passengers would associate the earring with homosexuality and, by association, AIDS. The company lost the case. Delwin Vriend, a lab instructor at Edmonton's King's University College, fared less well. In 1995 Vriend was fired for "his on-the-job flaunting of his homosexuality." An Alberta court found that Vriend's rights had been violated under the province's Individual's Rights Protection Act (IRPA) but this was overturned, in February 1996, by the Alberta Court of Appeal who ruled that homosexual rights were not covered under the IRPA. Commenting on the case, Dave Chatters, the Reform Party MP for Athabasca, stated in a radio interview that discrimination against homosexuals as a group was acceptable under some circumstances, such as schools (British-Columbia Report, v.7/38, May 20, 1996). The same year that Vriend was fired the Supreme Court of Canada denied a "homosexual claim to old-age spousal benefits," voting 5-4 that legislative discrimination in favour of heterosexual marriage remains permissible (British-Columbia Report, v.7/38, May 20, 1996). In the 2004 Abu Ghraib prison scandal Iraqi prisoners were "humiliated" by being forced to simulate homosexual acts. This tells much about the homophobic thinking behind this policy.

5. Tables 5.1 and 5.2 are adapted from The Canadian Association of University Teachers Almanac of Post-Secondary Education in Canada (2005: 16-17).

6. The authors cite a ceremony by the University of Toronto engineering students which involves an assault on a life-size inflated female doll. In 1990 there were similar incidents at the University of Alberta which led to the setting up of an enquiry. In one incident engineering students put on a "skit-night" at which some of the males were said to have shouted at a female student, "shoot the bitch," a remark which – following the shooting deaths of the fourteen female students at the Montreal Polytechnique in

December 1989 – was in unusually poor taste. In 2003, one of the authors of this book, who taught at a "wired university," constantly had to deal with computer "wallpaper" that featured naked or nearly naked women and men.

7. The website for the Canadian Federation of Business School Deans <http://www.cfbsd.ca/> lists only five females among its membership.

8. The UK there are the Equal Pay (1970, 2001,2003) and Sex Discrimination Acts (1975, 1986, 2003) <http://www.pfc.org.uk/legal/sda.htm>; in the US the Equal Pay Act (1963) <http://www.eeoc.gov/policy/epa.html> and provisions against sex discrimination in the 1964 Civil Rights Act <http://usinfo.state.gov/usa/infousa/laws/majorlaw/civilr19.htm>; and in Canada a 1984 Royal Commission on Equity in Employment led to the Employment Equity Act (1986) <http://laws.justice.gc.ca/en/E-5.401/48801.html>.

9. The Report of the Task Force on Barriers to Women in the Public Service (1990), provides an excellent annotated bibliography of both studies on the extent of sexual discrimination and on how to uncover barriers to change. See also, Consulting Group on Employment Equity for Women (1995).

10. Mills (1997), in a case study of British Airways in the period 1945-60, shows how equity programmes can be set-back by developments within organizations.

11. In March of 1997 it was reported that while unemployment figures remained at 9.4% 46,000 women lost their jobs while 7,000 men gained new jobs. In the year 1996-7 women had gained 5,000 jobs overall but men had gained 108,000: in the words of Judy Rebick, host of CBC Newsworld's Face Off, "That means restructing is driving women out of the full-time workforce" (quoted in the Halifax Daily News).

CHAPTER 6

Out of Sight, Out of Mind: Race, Ethnicity and Organization Theory

This chapter examines the increasing significance of ethnicity in modern organizations. It begins by exploring several examples of ethnocentric and racist barriers which have traditionally excluded ethnic minorities from membership in some representative organizations in our society, and how ethnic communities have mobilized to bring pressure on these organizations to end their discriminatory practices. The central objective of the chapter is to help the reader to identify some of the issues and problems involved in the study of race, ethnicity and organizational analysis. To that end, the chapter provides an introductory analysis of key debates on ethnicity and race in Canada, including discussion of the concept of the vertical mosaic and multiculturalism; examines Canadian race and ethnic relations and how this is played out in Canadian-based organizations; and looks at current debates on ethnicity, race and organizational analysis, including the concept of the "ethnicity paradigm" and the "ethnocentric organization". The chapter concludes with a discussion of ethnic relations in work organizations and suggestions for further research.

October 29th, 2003 Former boxer seeks apology, compensation from
Halifax police for discrimination

> *HALIFAX – Final arguments were heard on Wednesday at a high profile inquiry in Nova Scotia, where world ranked boxer Kirk Johnson is accusing the Halifax Regional Police of racial discrimination.*
>
> *"I don't know when the decision is going to happen, but the truth of the matter is that racism is in that case and was proven here, and the bottom line is people [have] got to know," said Johnson.*

Johnson represented Canada at the 1992 Olympics in Barcelona. He now divides his time between his training camp in Texas and his home in North Preston, N.S., a black community outside Halifax where Johnson is a local hero.

Five years ago, on one of his visits home, Johnson was stopped by police. He was driving a 1993 black Mustang with tinted windows and a Texas licence plate.

Police said they thought the car was stolen. They questioned Johnson for two hours, until finally they impounded his car and handed him a fine of nearly $1000. The next day they returned the car, paid the towing fees, waived the fines and apologized.

But Johnson wasn't willing to let it go. He said he believed he was stopped because he was black. He complained to the provincial human rights commission and began one of the toughest fights of his life.

"When it comes to people's human rights, that's a right. And when you violate that, that's hatred. And we've been going through that for 450 years of slavery, or what have you, and we don't want to go back to that."

The inquiry into the incident started in July and testimony revealed that Johnson's licence plate had been run through police computers 20 times in 11 months. Police apologized on the first day of the inquiry, but still insist that race was not an issue.

Johnson also wants an apology from the police (CBC News Online staff, 2003).

INTRODUCTION

How important is the topic of race and ethnicity to the study of organizations? If you look over the contents of any of the major OB or OT textbooks, you may be forgiven for concluding that these topics are of little importance to organizational studies. Until recently most OB and OT texts made little or no reference to non-White, non-Anglophone individuals, or to individuals whose national origins are different from the mainstream White Anglo-Saxon Protestant culture.[1]

Yet clearly, the topics of race and ethnicity continue to be of great importance in plural societies, such as Canada and the U. S., the populations of which have been drawn from a variety of different racial, ethnic and national backgrounds.[2] Indeed, the very history of these New World societies has been the history of different population groups who have been thrown together through the processes of immigration and colonization.[3]

Unfortunately, the history of racial and ethnic relations in Canada and the US has frequently been characterized by conflict and inequality, and even violence. Racial intolerance is nothing new in Canada and can be traced back to the earliest period of settlement and colonization.

Chinese immigrants, for example, were subjected to discriminatory head taxes around the turn of the twentieth century, and were later completely prohibited from entering Canada during the years 1923-1947, under the Chinese Immigration (Exclusion) Act. Another example of early racial discrimination in Canada was that practised against the Black Loyalists, who emigrated from the US to Nova Scotia after 1776, and who were refused land grants which had been promised them in return for their support of the Crown. There is no shortage of other examples of racial intolerance in Canada. The summary internment and confiscation of the personal property of Japanese Canadians during World War Two; the colonial administration of the aboriginal peoples under the Indian Act – including denial of their voting rights until 1960; the refusal of landing rights to Jewish political refugees from Nazi Germany and of East Indian passengers of the Komagata Maru in 1914; are only some of the more shameful cases of officially sanctioned racial intolerance in this country.

In addition to the particular history of racial discrimination against non-White groups, however, there have been numerous other examples of ethnic discrimination against "foreign" White immigrants in Canada.[4] The historical reluctance of English Canadians to acknowledge the legitimate language and cultural rights of French Canadians, both inside and outside of Quebec, contributed to the long-term inequality of Francophones in terms of their educational rights, employment opportunities and cultural development.

Other ethnic groups have, at different times, also experienced prejudice and discrimination at the hands of the Anglophone majority, including such groups as Ukrainians, Italians, and others once classified as "non-preferred" immigrants. The history of many ethnic groups in Canada, therefore, has been marked by struggles for greater justice and equality within the institutions and organizations of the majority culture.

In the 1980s, in an attempt to address the issue, the government of the day established a number of commissions and official inquiries into racial discrimination in Canada, including a Special Committee on Visible Minorities (1984) and the Royal Commission on Equality in Employment (Abella, 1984). The

Abella Commission identified four groups that suffered discrimination in the workplace – women, native people, disabled persons, and visible minorities. Native people were defined as "Status and non-Status Indians, Métis, and Inuit" and the Abella Commission found that, the "aeverage employment income in 1980 for non-native men was 60.2 per cent of the average income for non-native men; for native women it was 71.7 per cent of the average for non-native women" (Abella, 1984: 33). Visible minorities are, in the terms of the Abella Commission (1984: 46), "non-white." Admitting that race and ethnicity were ambiguous categories at best, through the term visible minorities the Abella Commission set out to "attempt to ascertain the extent to which people who were visibly non-white where excluded thereby from employment opportunities available to whites" (ibid). The Commission found that "non-whites all across Canada complained of racism" and concluded that visible minorities "undeniably face discrimination, both overt and indirect" (Abella, 1984: 46-47). Although the Commission lacked general comparisons between whites and visible minorities due to the fact that Statistics Canada did not collect data classified by race it was able to make some comparisons based on selected "ethnic or cultural" ancestry. It found that "the highest male unemployment rates were reported by native, French, Indo-Chinese, and black males, while the lowest was reported by Japanese, Pacific Islander, and European males other than British and French" (Abella, 1984: 84). It also found that women "reported higher unemployment rates than men, with the highest rates reported by native women, and by women of French, Indo-Chinese, and Indo-Pakistani origin. The lowest female unemployment rates were reported by Pacific Islanders, Japanese, and Chinese (ibid). In terms of income, "native people of both genders had the lowest incomes of all groups [followed by] the Indo-Chinese, Central and South Americans, and blacks. Average earnings reported by Indo-Chinese were two-thirds of the national average […] Among females, the lowest incomes were those of native and Central and South American women – women in each of these groups earned 77 per cent of the national female average"(Abella, 1984: 84-85).

Despite a number of improvements over the past two decades racism remains a vital issue in Canadian life in the 21ˢᵗ century. As the opening quotation shows, institutional racism remains a factor in Canadian society.[5] This is not only reflected in policing practices but in workplace practices. In 1996 45% of Aboriginal people had less than high school education and this figure actually dropped to 39% in 2001. Aboriginal people with post secondary training had an employment rate of 38% compared to 33% in 1996. Yet most of these jobs were in the construction trades for men and office administrators for women (Statistics Canada 2001). On average non-whites in Canada continue to experience a much higher jobless rate than whites and, contrary to expectation, the unemployment disparities between whites and non-whites in Canada and the US are at very similar rates (Jedwab, 2003). In terms of wage disparities, visible minorities earned 11% less than the Canadian average in 1991 and this gap grew to 14.5% in 2000 (Conference Board of Canada, 2004).

Media representation and depiction of visible minorities also continues to be problematic. For example, a major review of the literature on racism in the Canadian print media over the last two decades of the 20th century found that:

- People of colour are underrepresented and largely invisible in the media;
- When people of colour do appear in media coverage, they are often misrepresented and stereotyped;
- The corporatist nature of the media influences the kind of news that is produced and disseminated;
- Despite the claims of objectivity and neutrality by journalists, editors, and publishers, their individual and organizational beliefs, values and interests impact on the production of news discourse (Henry and Tator, 2000b: 4).

The study went on to state that: "Most significantly, there appears to be a lack of awareness, understanding or concern on the part of those who work in the media that they may be contributing to racism. While the press feels free to critique other institution, they are resistant to criticism of their own standards and practices" (ibid. See also Henry and Tator, 2002). Some observers have commented that this may also be linked to the fact that 97.3 per cent of Canadian journalists across the media are white (Pritchard, Sauvageau and Centre d'études sur les médias, 1999).

Given disparities in the media and the workplace it is perhaps not surprising that a number of Canadians who belong to visible minority groups report that they feel discriminated against. A 2003 Statistics Canada survey of "Ethnic Diversity" found that of those in visible minority groups more than 33% reported that they had experienced some form of racism, mostly in the workplace but also in stores. Half of those interviewed referred to skin colour as the trigger for their discrimination, both at work and when applying for jobs. One in three of those reporting discrimination had experienced racist responses in stores, banks, or restaurants. While 18 per cent of Chinese Canadians reported some form of discrimination, 32 per cent of black respondents said they had experienced racism in the past five years (Statistics Canada, 2003).

In 2000 the Federal Government introduced a new programme, "Embracing Change," in order to address the under representation (6.9 percent) of visible minorities in the Canadian Public Service:

> Meeting the challenges set out in the Task Force's Action Plan requires active support at all levels, particularly among deputy heads and managers. Embracing Change means eliminating systemic barriers, fostering a favourable corporate culture and assuming direct responsibility for the achievement of the benchmarks aimed at building a representative and inclusive federal Public Service (Treasury Board of Canada Secretariat, 2003).

There can be little doubt, therefore, that the topic of ethnicity is of burning interest to the study of organizations. Without some knowledge of how different ethnic and racial groups are represented in the labour force, in the education system, in law enforcement statistics, in housing surveys, and in other strategic areas of public life, and important part of our picture of Canadian society and its institutions is missing. More specifically, by excluding the topic of ethnicity from organizational studies, and thus rendering the experiences of visible minority people invisible (and inaudible), we are all the more tempted to succumb to the myth of Canadian tolerance: that racism is something you find in the United States and Great Britain, but not here in Canada.

NOW TURN TO EXERCISE 6.1 AT THE END OF THE CHAPTER.

THE POLITICALIZATION OF RACE AND ETHNIC RELATIONS

Studies of race and ethnicity in Canada have remained closely influenced by government policy, and by the debates and controversies that have frequently surrounded major changes of policy. Over the past several decades, but especially since the 1960s, the Canadian government has focused on three broad areas of concern in the field of race and ethnic relations policy: Francophone-Anglophone relations, Immigration and Multiculturalism, and Indian Affairs. Together, these areas have encompassed the major priorities of government policy, and are representative of much of the academic research undertaken on the topics of race and ethnicity in recent years.

The Evolution of Government Policy

One of the landmark events in the study of ethnicity in Canada was the creation of the Royal Commission on Biculturalism and Bilingualism (B&B) in 1965. This Commission was set up to inquire into the continuing separation of Francophone and Anglophone communities in Canada, and to examine the implications of this split for national unity. Some of the recommendations contained in the Report of the B&B Commission were later adopted by the Liberal government of the day, and became the basis for the Official Languages Act which, for the first time in Canadian history, established both French and English as official languages of the Federal government and its agencies. Beyond these immediate ramifications for Federal policy, however, the B&B Report provided a major incentive for further research into Francophone-Anglophone relations in this country, an initiative that has resulted in a growing proliferation of such studies.

The B&B Commission Report also opened the door to further studies of other ethnic groups in Canada. With the publication in 1969 of Book IV entitled *The Cultural Contribution of other Ethnic Groups*, a political climate was created to extend to non-charter ethnic groups (i.e., groups other than English and French) some public recognition of their importance in Canadian society. This recognition was further reinforced in 1971, when the then-Prime Minister Trudeau formally introduced the policy of Multiculturalism.[6] The declared intent of this policy was to provide official recognition and support to those ethnic groups who sought to preserve their distinctive cultural heritages and ethnic identities within the framework of a pluralistic society. This aspect of the B&B Commission Report inspired a new wave of research into the status of non-charter ethnic groups in Canada. If bilingualism was the Federal government's answer to demands for Quebec sovereignty, Multiculturalism was its answer to the demand of non-charter groups for greater recognition and respect. It seemed, at the time, a neat and elegant solution to the problem of how everyone fit into Canadian society.[7]

Over the past four decades, other events have also led to a renewal of interest in the study of Canadian ethnic and race relations. In 1974, for example, the Federal government released its Green Paper on Immigration and Population, a document that was intended to serve as a discussion paper for a national review of Canadian immigration policy. While the Green Paper proved to be a controversial document, it contributed to a renewed interest in studies of non-White, (i.e., visible minority), immigrants in Canada. Although certain parts of the Green Paper presented a highly provocative (many would say irresponsible) discussion of Third World immigration to Canada, in its own way it also motivated a new wave of Canadian ethnic studies into the status of visible minority groups. This tradition was further strengthened in 1984 with the publication of the Report of the Special Committee on the Participation of Visible Minorities in Canadian Society (1984). The Report, entitled "Equality Now," provided a contemporary picture of race relations in Canada focused on the problems of institutional racism, and on measures for addressing and alleviating these problems. This was followed by the Abella Commission Report (1984), which sought to address the issues of institutionalized discrimination against minority groups, including women, visible minorities, Native peoples and the physically handicapped… Since the publication of these reports, several significant pieces of legislation have been passed, including the Employment Equity Act in 1986 and various amendments (Department of Justice Canada, 2003), and the Canadian Multiculturalism Act in 1988 (cf. Canadian Heritage, 2003).

The other major area of ethnic studies in Canada has been that of Native studies. In 1966-67, a landmark study of Native peoples was published entitled, "A Survey of Contemporary Indians in Canada." Commissioned by the then-Department of Indian Affairs, this report became known as the Hawthorn Report, after its primary author Harry Hawthorn. It has remained until recently the singular, most comprehensive report on the status of Indian people in Canada, and has drawn much attention to the problems of poverty, unemployment and general neglect which have long confronted so many Native communities across this country. Two years later, in 1969, the Federal government released a White Paper on Indian Policy entitled, "Statement of the Government of Canada on Indian Policy." This document, which advocated among other things the repeal of the Indian Act, the abolition of the Department of Indian Affairs, the termination of universal aid programs, and the ending of any special status for Indians, was met with almost universal opposition from all Native communities across the country. In the face of this opposition, the White Paper was withdrawn in the Spring of 1971, and none of its recommendations were ever implemented. The defeat of the White Paper marked the end of an era: from this point on, it would no longer be possible for any Federal government to pursue an overt policy of forcible assimilation of Native peoples.

More recently, in November 1996, the final report of the *Royal Commission on Aboriginal Peoples* was published (cf. Indian and Northern Affairs

Canada, 2004). Established in 1991 by the former Federal Progressive Conservative government of Brian Mulroney, this was the first comprehensive survey of Indians in Canada to be commissioned since the Hawthorn Report of 1966-67.[8] The Commission's recommendations broke with earlier notions of "assimilation", arguing that the assimilation of native culture into mainstream Canadian life is "a denial of the principles of peace, harmony and justice for which this country stands". The Commission recommended that Canada should recognize aboriginal government as "one of three orders of government in Canada", and spend an extra $2 billion per year to help native peoples establish an aboriginal parliament, or House of First Peoples, with "national" powers over citizenship and membership; elections and referenda; final say regarding access to and residence in the territories; family matters such as marriage, divorce, adoption and child custody; health; education; housing; policing; and the administration of justice (Western Report, 11(47), December 9, 1996).[9]

These, then, are some of the landmark studies of ethnic and racial minority groups in Canada which were completed over the past three decades. Together, they help to define the big picture of race and ethnic relations in Canada, and the political context in which these studies were undertaken.

Academic Theory

In Canada, as we have seen, studies of race and ethnicity have traditionally been related to three major areas of concern for Canadian public life: Francophone-Anglophone relations, Immigration and Multiculturalism, and Native Peoples. These concerns have helped to chart the course of much of the work that has been done in the area of race and ethnic studies in Canada. However, unlike their American counterparts, most Canadian scholars have not been strongly motivated by the ideology of assimilationism and integration.[10] In matters of race and ethnicity, Canadians have traditionally distinguished themselves quite sharply from their American cousins; in place of the melting pot, Canadian society has more often been seen as an ethnic mosaic which, for over two decades now, has been influenced by the government policy of Multiculturalism.

One of the most influential studies of ethnic relations ever published in Canada was that undertaken by sociologist, John Porter in *The Vertical Mosaic* (1965). This study, which was developed as a critique of the dominant model of ethnic (or cultural) pluralism in Canada, established a critical framework for Canadian ethnic studies, and set the direction of subsequent research or many years to come.

In his study, Porter documents the extent of ethnic inequality in Canada through an analysis of census data covering a twenty-five year period from 1931-1951. Porter found that there were major inequalities between different ethnic groups in terms of their average levels of income, education and occupation. According to Porter's research, Canadians of British background tended to be overrepresented in the higher socio-economic strata, while Canadians of Southern and Eastern European backgrounds fell consistently into the bottom of the social class structure. These, and other findings, led Porter to question the value of the policies of ethnic pluralism in Canada, (or what later came to be called, Multiculturalism), and to challenge the image of Canada as an "ethnic mosaic." Although the passage of more than a quarter of a century has necessarily dated the conclusions of this analysis, it remains unsurpassed as a comprehensive study of Canadian society in which the fundamental themes of ethnicity and social class are analyzed in the classical sociological tradition.

According to John Porter, therefore, Canada has always been a hierarchically-organized society in which there has been very little mobility from one socio-economic level to another. Different ethnic groups, because of their different entrance statuses, became trapped into segregated occupations within the labour force. The highest positions in the structures of wealth and power were occupied by those of British descent, followed by those from Northern and Western Europe. Those from Eastern and Southern Europe occupied the lower levels of the stratification system, while those of French-Canadian and Native descent found themselves at the very bottom of the social pyramid. This is why Porter referred to Canadian society as a "vertical mosaic": a society made up of a mosaic of different ethnic groups, but rigidly arranged in a vertical hierarchy of wealth and power.

Since the appearance of *The Vertical Mosaic* in 1965, there have been other studies of ethnicity, class and social mobility in Canada, although none has equalled the breadth and scope of Porter's original study. The general conclusion of many of these studies has been that the structure of ethnic relations in Canada is characterized by a much greater degree of social mobility than was indicated in Porter's research (cf. Heap, 1974; Henry and Tator, 2000a; Tepperman, 1975; Tepperman and Curtis, 2004). While British and American groups have remained overrepresented at the top of the socio-economic system in comparison to groups from other ethnic backgrounds, these differences have tended to diminish over several generations. Other ethnic groups have not, for the most part, remained trapped in their original en-

trance statuses as Porter had concluded. Over a period of several generations, the rate of social mobility within many of these ethnic communities has begun to approach the Canadian norm. This does not invalidate Porter's evidence of an Anglo-American domination of the system of ethnic stratification in Canada, but it does suggest that the system displays a much greater degree of social mobility than he had acknowledged.

However, as other researchers have pointed out, evidence that the stratification of traditional ethnic groups has diminished does not mean that ethnicity is now no longer related to socio-economic status in Canada. It only means that the inequalities that Porter observed have progressively declined. But it should be remembered that Porter's analysis was based largely on the comparative status of White ethnic groups – that is, those of European descent – whether from continental Europe, or from Britain or the United States. This limitation of Porter's "ethnicity model" prevented him from analyzing the social status of long-established non-White racial groups in Canada, rendering them "invisible subjects" of Canadian ethnic studies.

Since 1967, however, with the introduction of the universal points system, there has been a spectacular increase in the percentage of immigrants originating from non-European source areas. Based on the evidence of this "new immigration," more recent studies have shown that although many of these new immigrants (from the Caribbean, India, Hong Kong, the Philippines, etc.) came to Canada with higher levels of education than their previous European counterparts of the 1950s and early 1960s (those from Italy, Spain, Portugal, Greece, etc.), many often have difficulty in obtaining employment commensurate with their higher education and qualifications (cf. Kunz, Milan and Schetagne, 2000).[11] This is because many visible minority immigrants face problems of prejudice and discrimination in the workplace which seriously impede their occupation mobility, and trap them into lower paying job ghettos. Indeed, the notable disparity between the earnings and the educational attainments of many non-European immigrants in Canada has led some researchers to conclude that the institutionalized ethnic discrimination faced by the earlier generation of European immigrants (which has all but disappeared as a significant social force)[12] has now been replaced by an institutionalized racial discrimination against the current generation of Third World immigrants (cf. Agócs, Jain and Canadian Race Relations Foundation., 2001; Greenhalgh, 2000; Ighodaro, 2004; Mighty, 1997; Ramcharan, 1982; Satzewich and Li, 1987).

Public Reaction and Debate

If the political climate of the 1970s and 1980s proved more responsive to the concerns of racial and ethnic minorities in Canada than in earlier decades, this momentum appears to have slowed down since the 1990s and 2000s when there have been numerous indications of the growing unease with which many Canadians seem to view present policies of Multiculturalism.[13] For example, in a national public opinion survey undertaken during the Winter/Spring of 1990-91, the Citizen's Forum on National Unity, chaired by Keith Spicer, reported that a significant proportion of its informants and respondents were critical of how policies of Multiculturalism had been administered. Many people believed that Multiculturalism had become an unnecessary extravagance which the nation could no longer afford at a time of economic recession. The ascendancy of a neo-conservative agenda in many parts of the country, preoccupied with the politics of the debt crisis, also began to threaten the Multicultural vision of Canadian society and the public consensus upon which this vision depended.[14]

Others had more pointed criticisms that reflected a belief that Multiculturalism increasingly favoured the rights of ethnic minority groups over those of the dominant cultural majority. During the past couple of years, several well-publicized cases may have served to reinforce some of these anxieties and frustrations. Among many Canadians, for example, the decision to permit the wearing of turbans by Sikh officers, or the wearing of braids by Aboriginal officers in the RCMP, was an unpopular one. Rather than welcoming these changes as evidence of the removal of cultural barriers to the recruitment of minority groups into the Federal law enforcement service, many Canadians appeared to see these changes as unreasonable concessions to the pressures of visible minority communities. Similarly, plans announced by some public school trustees to allow baptized Sikh students to wear kirpans, (that is, ceremonial daggers) in public schools aroused opposition and protest in some quarters.[15] For many Canadians, these and other measures which were designed to enable ethnic minorities to fully participate in the institutions of Canadian society without necessarily having to sacrifice their own traditions – particularly when the maintenance of these traditions was seen as a matter of religious conscience – have not always evoked sympathy or understanding.

Even some scholars have expressed misgivings about the role of Multiculturalism in Canadian public life. In a book entitled, *Mosaic Madness*, sociologist Reginald Bibby (1990) has lamented what he sees as some of the more unfortunate consequences of Multiculturalism. He suggest that Multiculturalism has contributed to a destructive relativism and individualism in the attitudes of many Canadians. Because of the need to extend legitimacy to a diversity of cultural viewpoints, Bibby suggests that we have lost sight of any overriding common vision that would serve as a basis for national unity and integration.

> To encourage individual mosaic fragments may well result in the production of individual mosaic fragments – and not much more. The multi-culturalism assumption – that a positive sense of one's group will lead to tolerance and respect of other groups – has not received strong support, notes McGill University sociologist Morton Weinfeld. The evidence, he says, "suggests a kind of ethnocentric effect, so that greater preoccupation with one's own group makes one more distant from and anti-pathetic to others." [...] If we view Canadian society as a group of cultures that co-exist like tiles in an art piece, we have nothing but parts beside parts. Socially, such a view translates into mosaic madness [...], Bibby, (1990: 177).

Bibby is also concerned that those who see themselves as members of the cultural majority in Canada, now find it increasingly difficult to express opposition to Multiculturalism without being labelled as "racists," "sexists," or "bigots," of one kind or another.

> In keeping with the communication rules, if Natives feel they are being discriminated against when they are trying to obtain housing, they can call a news conference to register their concern. If a Jewish organization believes that anti-Semitism is on the increase, it can issue a press release. If women feel that they are experiencing discrimination in the workplace, they can hold a press conference. If Sikhs want to wear turbans in the workplace, they can turn to the media to express their concern over the opposition they encounter. However, the communication is all one-way. If the majorities involved do not agree with the claims of the minorities, they are labelled racists or bigots [...] Canadians do not allow majorities to speak out. And we don't encourage minorities and majorities to speak to each other (Bibby, 1990: 169-70).

For Bibby, and others like him (e.g., Zolf, 1982), Multiculturalism has left us without a common frame of reference; it has encouraged ethnic and cultural groups to pursue their own particular agendas without regard for the wider needs of the national collectivity. According to this view, Multiculturalism has encouraged the fragmentation of public life in Canada, and has made more difficult the task of creating national unity through consensus-building and compromise.

In many ways, this is a profoundly conservative critique of Multicultural-ism, one which seeks to invoke the idea of a "national interest" over what is often seen to be the divisive interests of a highly relativistic and individualistic society. Conservative thinkers have, at least since the time of the French Revo-lution, stressed the importance of the social collectivity over its individual parts. They have also emphasized the integrative functions performed by such tradi-tional institutions as the church, the family, the community, and so on. There is, notwithstanding Bibby's efforts to remain even-handed in his judgements, a strongly conservative sentiment expressed in this type of social criticism. Per-haps it is unsurprising that this type of thinking on multiculturalism character-ises the new Conservative Party of Canada.

Not all criticisms of Multiculturalism have come from the political right, however. Some have originated from the very groups whose interests were sup-posedly served by Multiculturalism. Thus, some ethnic leaders and spokesper-sons have dismissed Multiculturalism as having very little relevance to the ma-jor problems presently confronting racial and ethnic minorities in Canada to-day. Instead of combating racial prejudice and discrimination in employment, housing, education, and other strategic areas of public life, some critics believe that Multiculturalism has remained preoccupied with the politically safer issues of preserving ethnic heritages, and fostering traditional ethnic identities. Instead of using the resources of Multiculturalism agencies to fund employment equity programs, organize campaigns against racial hatred, or for other aggressive pro-grams for social justice and equality, it sometimes seems as though Multicultur-alism has concentrated largely on funding Heritage Day events, ethnic dancing groups, and other cultural fringe activities which do little to challenge the in-stitutional forms of racial and ethnic discrimination in our society.

> Although members of visible minorities appreciate government assistance in the multiculturalism area, they tend to see this as government fostering cul-tural patterns but not dealing with the key issues of multiracialism or dis-crimination. What they want are strong government measures not only to en-hance their cultural origins but also to enhance their ability to integrate eco-nomically, despite their cultural origins. Multiculturalism programs do little to assist in their economic integration or to confront racism (Abella, 1984: 51).

This focus upon, what at least one politician of the left has described as "the singing and dancing syndrome,"[16] has been accomplished at the expense of pro-moting full economic, social and political development for visible minorities.

Whereas for conservatives, Multiculturalism has gone too far, for more radical critics, it has not gone far enough.

> Despite the intention, there is little indication that racial prejudice has been less prevalent, or ethnic inequality less evident. The policy has failed to combat racism and discriminatory practices. Indeed, the persistence of ethnic inequality in the labour market is well documented by the report of the Royal Commission on Equality in Employment (1984). It is also interesting to note that there is no mention of the multicultural policy in the entire report – an omission that would imply the ineffectiveness of the policy to combat racism […] "the irony of multiculturalism is that it furnishes Canadian society with a great hope without having to change the fundamental structures of society. Multiculturalism is the failure of an illusion, not of a policy (Li, 1990: 9).

RACE AND ETHNIC RELATIONS IN ORGANIZATIONAL THEORY

The Silence of Organizational Theory

When attempting to explain the traditional silence(s) of organization theory and organizational behaviour towards the subjects of race and ethnicity, (as well as those of gender and class), it is necessary to examine both the ideological content of OT and OB and the ethnocentric culture from which it has emerged.

One of the characteristics of most OT and OB textbooks has been the focus on general principles. This focus has grown quite naturally out of the administrative and managerial interest that have underlined the major traditions of organizational studies. Managers are, after all, primarily interested in learning a set of techniques, which can be used to promote organizational effectiveness. The fewer the number of techniques to be learned, and the broader the range of application, the more efficient becomes the development and utilization of specialized managerial knowledge. One of the problems with this generalizing approach, however, is that it has tended to overlook many of the distinctive aspects of organizations that are rooted in particularities of their external or internal environments.

The systematic neglect of gender, race and ethnicity may be partly attributed to this generalizing approach which has until now, excluded these issues from mainstream organizational analysis. The image of the organization that appears in standard OT and OB textbooks is an image from which all references to gender, race, ethnicity, class, nationality or history are largely absent. The models and theories developed in these texts are intended to be universal in their application, and to be used to analyze organizations in any part of the industrial world. However, because many of the general principles underlying modern organizational analysis have been developed in the United States, and based upon American cultural experiences, there is an important sense in which the much-touted universality of these models is open to question. All organizations are located within a larger society possessing its own distinctive history, culture, and social relations. No organization is free from the influences of this external environment, and many aspects of the internal environment of the organization are shaped by these external factors. What is often portrayed as a generalized model of organizational analysis, therefore, turns out in reality to be an American model, informed by the particular need and experiences of American managers.[17]

In an important sense, therefore, the silences of OT and OB have continued to reflect the traditional worldview of the American corporate culture which has remained ethnocentric, androcentric and elitist in outlook. The consequence of this ethnocentrism for organizational studies has been to obscure the multicultural and multiracial reality of many organizations in Canada and the US for much orthodox OT and OB has been based upon what one critic (Rich, 1979: 306) has called "white solipsism," which refers to the tendency to "think, imagine, and speak as if whiteness described the world." White solipsism, however, is "not the consciously held belief that one race is inherently superior to all others, but a tunnel vision which simply does not see non-White experience or existence as precious or significant" (ibid). It is this ethnocentrism which has rendered ethnic minorities invisible in contemporary organizational studies, and which has overlooked the special problems that many members of these groups face in the modern organization world. The result, as several recent authors have suggested (e.g., Bell, 1989; Nkomo, 1992) has been to "whitewash" the modern organization by refusing to acknowledge the depth and breadth of institutional prejudice and discrimination against members of racial and ethnic minority groups.

> If one were to review much of the literature on organizations, one would assume that racism takes place somewhere else, outside of the workplace; or when the possibility is acknowledged at all, it is framed as an affirmative action issue. It is rarely acknowledged that race relations are reproduced in organizational, behavioural and structural systems (Bell et al., 1992: 22).

In trying to understand why the topics of race and ethnicity have been so neglected in organizational studies, we sooner or later have to face the inescapable fact that the problem of institutional racism, which is generally widespread throughout North American society,[18] is also present in OT, OB, and other organizational disciplines. Problems of race and ethnicity in organizations have been neglected for various reasons, but, in particular, due to the fact that the great majority of organizational researchers are White (males) and operate within a network of ideological factors that have served to reproduce the status quo in which other White males dominate organizations and their representation. The academic press, for instance, is a key factor in reinforcing ideological conformity. The editorial boards of scholarly publishing houses exercise considerable control over what is accepted for publication within their journals and textbooks, serving in effect as the legislators of what are acceptable research problems, methodologies, and standards of argumentation. They have acquired the status of "gatekeepers" of knowledge, letting in those who conform to the cannons of orthodoxy, and refusing entry to those who don't (Crane, 1967; De la Mothe and Paquet, 1997; Jauch and L., 1989; Morgan, 1985). Other ideological controls within academia include internal controls related to the certification process of new academics – the graduate programs, which shape, direct, and approve the research proposals and dissertations of graduate students.

The impact of these ideological controls in regard to race and ethnicity has been to reproduce colour-blind research that reflects the prevailing priorities of the North American corporate culture. A stark example can be seen in the comments of one distinguished contributor to a 1990 special issue of the *Journal of Organizational Behaviour* on race and ethnicity:

> I am unaware of a mainstream journal in organizational behaviour ever before devoting a special issue to the subject of race, authorizing a black scholar to be in charge of the issue, and publishing a complete set of papers by black authors (Alderfer, 1991: 493).

The situation was, in the words of Alderfer, "an historic event" but one that took until the 1990s to happen. Until this point the great majority of journal articles and texts in organizational and management disciplines have had little or nothing to say on race and ethnicity (cf. America and Anderson, 1978; Cox and Nkomo, 1990; Davis and Watson, 1982; Dickens and Dickens, 1991; Fernandez, 1975; Prasad et al., 1997). Until recently, with the development of postcolonist theorising (cf. Prasad, 1997a; Prasad and Prasad, 2002) there has been virtually nothing written from the perspective of non-White workers, or which has focused on minority workers as subjects in their own right.

It is only very recently that the silence on race and ethnicity has been broken by a new generation of minority group scholars whose work has inspired fresh attempts to include the experiences of ethnic and racial minorities in the tradition of organizational research. A number of these scholars are also women, and in their writings they have focused on the "double jeopardy" of racism and sexism faced by many minority women within the workplace (cf. Bell, 1990; Denton, 1990; Mighty, 1991; 1997; Nkomo and Cox, 1989). Nonetheless, it remains true that organizational theorists with an interest in pursuing research into race and ethnicity face a number of institutional obstacles within their respective disciplines (Cox, 1990). Scholars, including minority group scholars, have been discouraged from pursuing these subjects for fear of being perceived as overly specialized in fields that have remained marginal to mainstream OB and OT research. Similarly, as Cox (1990: 10) also documents, some OB and OT faculty members and departments have not hesitated to use what can only be described as outright intellectual harassment and intimidation to prevent their graduate students from selecting research topics on race and ethnicity. These pressures to marginalize and exclude racial and ethnic research have been exerted through a network of different control agencies within the academic community – through university hiring committees and, of course, through interpersonal contacts. All of these pressures have succeeded in defining race and ethnicity as taboo subjects in the mainstream tradition of organizational research.

> [C]ompared to most other topics related to organization management, work on racioethnicity is both more difficult to perform and more difficult to publish, at least in the leading academic journals. Much of this difficulty exists because American society has never really resolved problems of racioethnic relations and racioethnic heterogeneity, including those related to racism (Cox, 1990: 19).

The Influence of American Assimilation Theory

Although traditional research in OT has remained largely silent on the issues of race and ethnicity, this does not mean that no organizational research has been undertaken in these areas. As Alderfer and Thomas (1988) have shown, even during the earlier part of the twentieth century, the issues of race and ethnicity had already acquired significance in several sectors of organizational life in the United States. They certainly had significance for business organizations at a time when immigrants from all parts of Europe were coming to America in search of work and prosperity. The period of mass immigration, which lasted well into the first quarter of the twentieth century produced a labour force with an increasingly ethnic and cultural heterogeneity. Interestingly enough, this ethnic transformation of the labour force was even recorded in the Hawthorne Studies of the Western Electric plant – studies that gave birth to the Human Relations School of Management Theory. Roethlisberger and Dickson (1939: 6), for example, allude to the ethnic diversity of the work force in their sample of respondents:

> In 1927, when the studies commenced, the company employed approximately 29,000 workers, representing some 60 nationalities. About 75% […] were American born. The Poles and Czechoslovakians were by far the largest foreign groups; there was a fair sprinkling of Germans and Italians.

Given this recognition of the importance of the ethnic work force, why was it, then, that the Human Relations researchers paid so little attention to ethnicity in the course of their research on the Western Electric plant? This passing reference to ethnicity was never expanded into a topic of research interest. The answer, as Alderfer and Thomas (1988: 27) suggest, lies in the ideological world-view held by the researchers, themselves, at this time. In common with many other Americans of the period, the leading researchers subscribed to a radical assimilationist vision of society, in which differences of race and ethnicity were perceived as temporary impediments to the eventual achievement of a democratic cultural uniformity and homogeneity throughout the United States. Such a view was essentially inimical to focusing on the differentia speciae of race and ethnicity. This is well illustrated in an autobiographical fragment from Roethlisberger's (1977: 14-15) own self-portrait:

> I was an American – an isolationist by factors then unknown to me […] who was not going to have anything to do with battles fought in Switzerland […] or with the Franco-Prussian War. This was America, where race, creed, birth, heredity, nationality, family and so forth, did not count and where individual merit, skill, competence, knowledge, freedom, and so on did. I believe it with all my heart and in a crazy way, in spite of many subsequent experiences to the contrary, I still do.

Part of the silence on race and ethnicity, therefore, especially in studies of business organizations, may well derive from a disinclination to focus on these issues for ideological and political reasons. Organizations, after all, were expected to be melting pots for the American work force.

In other organizations, however, the strongly assimilationist creed of the times succeeded in motivating, rather than inhibiting, some of the earliest studies of ethnicity in American organizations. This was especially true of the military after President Harry Truman's 1948 executive order desegregating the armed forces. Samuel Stouffer's monumental study, *The American Soldier*, included a chapter on "Negro Soldiers," which illustrated in some detail the racial dynamics of the armed forces. Similarly, in educational organizations, studies of race played an important part in the legal and constitutional battles to desegregate the US public school system. As Alderfer and Thomas (1988: 10) record, the research of Clark and Clark (1958), which examined the racial preferences of Black children for White over Black dolls, played an important role in influencing the Supreme Court decision to abolish the "separate but equal" doctrine of education in the United States, in the case of Brown versus Board of Education. Again, the motivating force behind the development and use of this type of racial research in the educational system was the strong assimilationist commitment to equality and integration, which began in the 1950s – and later erupted into the Civil Rights movement of the 1960s.

Subsequent research, which has since been carried out in military, educational and, finally, also in business organizations in the United States, has continued to build upon this early legacy of assimilationism. Common to most of these assimilationist studies has been the assumption that for most organizational research, it is almost always the racial minority group that is problematized, rather than the organization, or majority culture. In most contemporary studies, race is typically defined as a "problem" which more and more organizations have to deal with in the course of their day-to-day operations. Indeed, this perspective of race as a problem is apparent from much of the substantive research that has been undertaken on race and ethnicity in organizations. This is very much the case in the newer diversity management literature that assumes that "diversity" is what non-whites and women possess and which managers need "to manage" (Foldy, 2002; Prasad et al., 1997). Studies in the area of job satisfaction have invariably compared levels of satisfaction between Black and White workers, often with inconsistent, inconclusive or even tautological results (see for example, Agócs et al., 1992; Jones,

James, Bruni and Shell, 1977; Konar, 1981; Slocum Jnr. and Strawser, 1972; Vecchio, 1980).

Earlier studies of race and ethnicity more typically focused on the evidence of discrimination in the occupational distribution of jobs. To what extent have Blacks remained overrepresented in lower socioeconomic jobs? (Franklin, 1968) Or have there been systemic disparities between the recruitment and selection of Blacks and Whites in selected occupational areas? (Brown and Ford, 1977; Newman, 1978; Stone and Stone, 1987; Tepstra and Larse, 1985).

A growing number of studies have investigated evidence of bias in the performance ratings of Black and White ratees. Several comprehensive literature reviews have appeared on this subject (Dipboye, 1985; Kraiger and Ford, 1985; Landy and Farr, 1980). While there appears to be some inconsistency between these findings, several of the more influential of these studies have reported rates that tend to receive higher ratings from raters of the same race, and that these effects were more pronounced in field studies than in laboratory ratings (see Kraiger and Ford, 1985).

By far the largest number of studies in the US, however, has concentrated on the legal and administrative aspects of how organizations could comply with the Civil Rights legislations – specifically Title VII Guidelines requiring them to develop affirmative action programs to increase minority representation. Much of this research has centred on the validity of various measures that have been designed to test the effectiveness of these programs (see, for example, Arvey and Faley, 1988; Schmidt, Pearlman and Hunter, 1980).

THE ETHNICITY PARADIGM

In a prominent critical review of OB and OT, Nkomo (1992) has argued that much current organizational research has remained dominated by what she calls the "ethnicity paradigm."

Derived in large part from the ideology of assimilationism, the ethnicity paradigm provides a framework for interpreting the significance of race and ethnic relations in organizations, and for focusing on the areas of priority in current organizational theory and research. According to Nkomo, however, the ethnicity paradigm has remained locked into an ethnocentric view of the world: a view in which minority individuals are expected to conform to, and to assimilate into, the organizational culture of the racial and ethnic majority – that is, of the White, Anglo-Saxon, (or in Canada, Anglo-Celtic) Protestant majority. This Eurocentric and latently racist view of minority individuals is constructed from several theoretical and methodological assumptions that are implicitly contained in the ethnicity paradigm:

1. Race and ethnicity are commonly perceived as essential properties of individuals – whether these are biological, cultural, or social psychological properties. Problems of race relations, therefore, are frequently related to some of these essential properties, and to the need to change those that are amenable to change (such as attitudes, motivation, work ethnic, etc.). This essentialist view of race and ethnicity overlooks the extent to which racial categories have always been imposed on the politically weak by the politically powerful, and in this sense represent socially constructed categories that are often legacies of conquest, colonization, slavery or economic exploitation.

2. Studies of race and ethnicity in organizations typically focus on the individual rather than on the organization or culture of the racial majority. Because of their individualistic focus, most studies of race and ethnicity in organizations are primarily concerned with psychological or social psychological variables, but remain silent on the socio-historical dynamics of the capitalist system. The major emphasis of this kind of research, therefore, is how to get the minority individual to fit into the organization, or how to rid the majority individual of prejudiced attitudes. The legitimacy of the status quo is rarely challenged, and questions regarding the dominance of racial majorities are never asked.

This focus on the individual absolves the researcher from problematizing the dominant culture of the racial majority. Indeed, it is only non-Whites who are seen as having a racial status; the terms race or ethnic are rarely applied to members of the majority culture. The result of this individualistic focus has been to assume that the problems of racial discrimination, segmentation or exclusion in organizational life are reducible to problems of individual prejudice and intolerance. Traditionally, the roots of such prejudice have been sought in attributes of the individual – whether in terms of authoritarian personality (Adorno, 1969) or in terms of other cognitive processes but rarely in the social system itself, or in the structures of power and domination. Consequently, the solution to problems of racism is always understood to lie in the reform of individuals, rather than in the restructuring of organizations, or other significant parts of the social order. This tendency to psychologize the issues of race and ethnicity has been a characteristic of the ethnicity paradigm.

3. Inequality is accepted as a natural feature of industrial societies in general, and of organizations in particular. In common with the long-term tradition of

OB and OT, hierarchy is accepted as an inevitable feature of all large-scale organizations; the problem is to prevent a concentration, or overrepresentation, of visible minority members at the bottom of the organization. By accepting the inevitability of hierarchy and inequality, in society and in its institutions, the problem(s) of racial minorities are invariably defined in terms of: Why aren't they like us, and what will it take for them to become like us?

4. The model of assimilation which as traditionally been used to explain the successful integration of White ethnic groups (such as Italians, Poles, Jews, etc.) into the institutions of the majority culture is also seen as the appropriate model for bringing about the assimilation and integration of currently disadvantaged visible minority groups. In other words, the historical experiences of European immigrants in the US (and Canada) are presumed to provide an appropriate framework for understanding the experiences and social patterns of non-White minorities. There is an unspoken assumption that the processes that worked to integrate European groups into the institutions of the majority culture will also work to integrate currently disadvantaged visible minority groups.

Notwithstanding the fact that several social scientists (Blauner, 1972; Omi and Winant, 1994; Said, 1979; 1993), have argued that because of their histories of conquest, colonialism, slavery, and other forms of unfreedom, the experiences of many non-White groups have differed significantly from those of traditional European immigrant groups, much of the research undertaken within the ethnicity paradigm has ignored this distinction (Prasad, 1997a; Prasad and Mills, 1997). It has been assumed that conclusions based on the experiences of White ethnic groups are generalizable to the case of non-White groups. As Nkomo,(1992: 500) observes,

> [C]onspicuously absent from these articles is any suggestion or recognition of the different socio-historical experience of Afro-Americans or other racial minorities in the United States.

Taken together, these orienting assumptions have ensured that the prevailing paradigm for studying race and ethnicity in organizations – the ethnicity paradigm – has remained ethnocentric (that is, Eurocentric), and paternalistic in its view of race relations. It has typically defined racial status, itself, as a problem in need of a solution: Do racial and ethnic minorities have what it takes to succeed in organizations; or more concisely, why aren't they like us? Much of this work is often characterized by what has been labelled as the "deficit hypothesis"(Nkomo, 1992: 499): the assumption that in order to succeed in typical organizations, minority individuals need to overcome a deficit in "motivation," "education," "mentors," "human capital," and so on. Because of this tendency to problematize race, much current research within the ethnicity paradigm has focused on how to incorporate minority individuals into typical organizations by rectifying, or compensating for, any "deficits" in their cultural or psychological backgrounds. Again, this appears to form much of the trust of diversity management research.

What is conspicuously absent from these studies is any reference to the structures of power and domination that have resulted in the minoritization and marginalization of some racial and ethnic groups, and in the dominance of others. Similarly, most of these studies never examine how it is that the dominant values of organizational culture represent the attitudes and interests of the dominant ethnic group. These are some of the deafening silences of mainstream OB and OT when it has turned its attention to the issues of race and ethnicity.

The Ethnicity Paradigm and Canadian Research

At first glance, it might seem reasonable to expect that the problems associated with the ethnicity paradigm had been avoided in the Canadian literature of organizational theory and research. After all, the ideology and policy of assimilationism has long been officially rejected in this country in favour of ethnic pluralism, or Multiculturalism, as it has come to be known. However, the truth is that Canadian research has so far failed to take the lead in the study of race and ethnicity in organizations. Much traditional research on minority groups in Canada has focused on (White) ethnic groups to the virtual exclusion of (non-White) racial groups.

It has only been in the last decade or so that any serious academic attention has been paid to problems of racial prejudice and discrimination, and to the contentious issues of racial and ethnic inequality in Canada (cf. Agócs et al., 2001; Bolaria and Li, 1988; Hazell, 2002; Henry and Tator, 2000b; Li and Tsui, 2002; Li, 1990; Mighty, 1997; Ramcharan, 1982; Razack, 1998). For the most part however, Canadian organization and management studies have paid remarkably little attention to the more vexatious questions of race and ethnic relations.

Notwithstanding the history of official Multiculturalism in Canada, organizational theory and research in this country has remained as much locked into the ethnicity paradigm as that in the US. There are several reasons for this:

1. In its own way, Canadian research has exhibited an overly individualistic definition of ethnicity. This is true even though Canadian studies have frequently included research on ethnic communities, and ethnic group relations. The focus of much of this research, however, has remained psychological or social psychological in nature: language retention, identity, intergenerational attitudes, etc., have all continued to be popular topics in the literature of Canadian research.

2. In common with assimilationist studies, most Canadian research has defined ethnicity in terms of some essential properties such as nationality (or homeland), language or religion. This essentialist view of ethnicity is similar in its results to that employed in assimilationist studies, and suffers from the same drawbacks and limitations as those already discussed in the previous section.

3. If assimilationist studies have tended to accept the inevitability of inequality in race and ethnic relations, this is even more so for multiculturalist research. In their celebration of difference and diversity, many Canadian scholars have turned their backs on the legacy of John Porter and have avoided asking troubling questions about ethnic inequality – either in organizations, or in society at large. This lack of any critical perspective, with its attendant blindness to the issues of power, conflict, and inequality, has rendered the Canadian tradition of ethnic studies particularly susceptible to government influence through direct funding for policy-oriented research.

4. Although the Canadian tradition of ethnic studies has normally eschewed the strong assimilationist undertones of much American research, in its own way, it has also remained ethnocentric (i.e., Eurocentric) in terms of its basic assumptions. Instead of preaching the sermon of assimilation, integration, and homogenization, Canadian scholars have accepted ethnic difference and diversity. However, the unspoken assumption of the multiculturalist view of society implies that ethnic diversity be necessarily contained within the framework of a standardized, civic culture: that of the ethnic majority. This is especially true of organization studies, in which the management of diversity is normally assumed to take place in the context of a typical corporate or business culture. Perhaps more significant is the fact that the acceptance of difference and diversity in multicultural studies is rarely linked to questions of equality. For clearly, any acceptance of difference and diversity in a system based on inequality can be little more than a sanctification of the status quo.

There has, therefore, been little significant difference between Canadian and American studies of race and ethnicity in organizations. The larger political climate of multiculturalism does not appear to have advanced the study of race or ethnicity in organizations.

In part, this may reflect the traditional reluctance of a corporate culture to acknowledge the importance of multicultural or multiracial differences in the workplace. On the other hand, as the sociologist Karl Peter (1981: 57, 59), has suggested, the ideology of multiculturalism, itself, has sometimes served to inhibit the study of race and ethnic relations, especially where the issues of power and inequality are involved.

> The denial of any economic and political significance to ethnic groups, which is the essence of the government's policy on Multiculturalism, has been adopted by Canadian sociologists and has largely prevented them from analyzing Multiculturalism in terms of power and politics […] The reluctance of many leading liberal Canadian sociologists to deal with ethnicity in terms of power and politics, it seems, is proportionate to their commitment to the policies of bilingualism and Multiculturalism, and ultimately to the concept of Canadian unity as proposed by the Liberal government.

Beyond the Ethnicity Paradigm

Today, however, a growing number of researchers in Canada and in the United States have begun to employ a more multiculturalist approach to the study of race and ethnicity in organizations in order to distance themselves from earlier assimilationist studies. This has resulted in a crop of studies focusing on diversity in the workplace (cf. 2002; Agócs et al., 2001; Alderfer, 1991; Bell and Nkomo, 2001; Kirchmeyer and McLellan, 1991; Mighty, 1991; Mighty, 1997; Nkomo, 1992; Nkomo, Fottler and McAfee, 2005; Prasad and Prasad, 2002; Prasad, 1997b).

In a 1991 review of the literature on ethnic diversity in the workplace, Kirchmeyer and McLellan concluded that most organizations have attempted to assimilate minority individuals into the corporate culture of the majority group. This has typically been done through a process of "cultural homogenization," whereby "cultural differences are ignored and suppressed so that potentially valuable perspectives remain unexplored," (Kirchmeyer and McLellan, 1991: 75). The consequence of these homogenization pressures can be very harmful to members of minority groups:

> Members of ethnic and racial minorities may be most vulnerable to organizational pressures to conform because they tend to have the least status […] For

these minorities, conforming to corporate values can also mean denying their own culture, and even turning against others of their own category, (ibid).

Similar findings were also reported by Mighty (1991), who suggested that many organizations in her study resorted to a form of "cultural imperialism," in which the dominant group would seek to homogenize non-dominant cultures in an effort to transform them into a single majority culture. According to Mighty, (1991: 66), "In ethnocentric organizations the usual mode of maintaining stability is through the social influence process of conformity."

For the management of many organizations, therefore, the norms and values of the majority group are those that define the normal standards of the corporate culture, and any minority or divergent values are necessarily defined as aberrant or deviant. For minority members of organizations, however, the pressures of homogenization can be onerous in their psychological and cultural consequences. In reporting these results, Mighty (1991: 69) observes that minority members of an organization who feel victimized on account of their racial or ethnic status may suffer from an "internalized oppression" which leads them to model their behaviour on the (idealized) behaviour of the majority culture, while simultaneously de-valuing fellow minority members who continue to display minority cultural characteristics. In this way, minority individuals become alienated not only from their own ethnic groups, but – perhaps more ominously – from themselves.

These, and similar findings, have persuaded some researchers that the ethnocentric practices of many organizations are extremely harmful to minority individuals working within them. However, beyond the simple concern for the welfare and equity of minority employees, there is a growing body of evidence to suggest that the adoption of more multicultural management policies and workplace practices brings rewards, not just for minorities, but for the organization as a whole. Burke (1991), for example, argues that multiculturalist approaches to the management of workplace diversity may have a number of benefits for the organizations involved. Nelson (1988) contends that, at the very least, these new approaches help organizations to harness the full potential of their diverse workforces and that "proper management" of ethnic diversity can also provide an organization with a competitive edge, in an increasingly multicultural and international market. As well as these advantages, however, a more equitable treatment of racial and ethnic minorities in an organization may, according to Burke (1991: 120), also bring benefits to members of the majority group:

> Interestingly, attempts to make organizations more supportive of the career aspirations of minorities may also have benefits for the white majority and the organization itself. The development of a more objective performance or potential appraisal system would benefit both; the development of a more comprehensive career management process would benefit both.

Kirchmeyer and McLellan (1991: 77) add that among the other instrumental benefits of a more multicultural management of ethnic diversity in organizations is the possibility that,

> In ethnically diverse workshops, an appreciation of various cultures not only heightens mutual understanding, but ... can also facilitate the group's understanding.

At the same time, however, as Mighty (1991; 1997) and Alderfer (1991) are at pains to point out, the benefits of racial and ethnic diversity in the workplace are only likely to be realized in a setting which encourages mutual respect between members of different groups. To achieve this, it is necessary for diverse groups, not only to respect each other's cultural differences, but for them also to occupy equal statuses within the organization. This is very important, as the status of minority groups within the traditional ethnocentric organization has always been institutionally inferior to that of the majority group. A long-term condition for the successful management of workplace diversity, therefore, is the disappearance of all forms of ethnic stratification within the organization. But, as Prasad and Mills (1997: 3) (1997: 3), contend, this will be difficult to achieve within the framework, or paradigm, of "diversity management" which is primarily concerned with *managing* rather than *understanding* diversity:

> Despite the proliferation of research on discrimination, the value of diversity and multiculturalism in organizations, the literature fails to address the more serious dimensions of difference in organizations. In particular, we suggest that more attention must be paid to some common dilemmas of diversity, such as the backlash against any commitment to multiculturalism, the continuing anger and disappointment of women and minorities, and the systematic institutional resistance within organizations to difference.

Although the corporate cultures of most organizations in North America have remained resolutely ethnocentric (and androcentric) there are an increasing number of organizations today that have introduced more enlightened polices for the management of diversity. Mighty (1991: 68) records that Avon Products Inc., has implemented regular management sensitivity programs for dealing with issues of race and ethnicity which have resulted in a dramatic reduction in the turnover rate for minority employees. Similarly, the Municipality of Metropolitan Toronto has developed its "Kingswood Management Training Programme" to enable managers to respond more effectively to the problems of women, and of racial and ethnic minorities. Several other corporations, including Shoppers Drug Mart, Northern Telecom Canada, and the Canadian Imperial Bank of Commerce, now have programs that place Aboriginal peoples into entrepreneurial training internships for six months of the year. These, and other examples, serve to illustrate how many organizations have begun to see the light, and are attempting to turn the ethnic diversity of their respective workforces into an asset.

There can be little doubt that the new focus of some organizations on more effective management of ethnic diversity represents a definite advance over earlier practices. Any programs that increase interracial or intercultural sensitivity and respect among members of an organization are to be applauded, whether these are implemented by government agencies, or by private corporations. In this respect, it is clear that Multiculturalism has something to offer, both to the study of managing workforce diversity. At the same time, however, we should not expect too much from this approach. As we have already suggested, Multiculturalism is also limited by inherent individualism, psychologism, and its acceptance of organizational hierarchy. The sudden appearance of management strategies for optimizing the advantages of workplace diversity owes as much to the need for greater labour productivity, and the need for competitive advantage in a global market, as it does to any profound regard for human rights (Prasad et al., 1997).

While a fresh perspective on ethnic diversity may make it easier for some minority individuals to scale the corporate hierarchy, it in no way questions the need for hierarchy, nor does it point towards other, more humanized forms of corporate organization. Because they both take the present structures of power and domination as given, neither variants of the ethnicity paradigm provide a critical alternative to the status quo. For although Multiculturalism is an improvement over the Assimilation perspective, it still falls short of being a radical critique of race and ethnic relations in organizations. While it has made it easier for some minority individuals to move up the class system inside the organization, the existence of the class system itself is never open to question. Much as John Porter suggested, some three decades ago, multiculturalism (or what he called "ethnic pluralism") simply facilitates the growth of ethnic elites within their own communities, and within the organizations of a larger society. But as far as the conditions of most racial and ethnic minority individuals are concerned – especially the conditions of minority women – not much has changed.

WHAT DOES THE FUTURE HOLD?

Whenever we leave our office at the end of a particularly full day and beat a hasty retreat through the empty hallways and corridors of the deserted campus buildings, we encounter members of a community who are largely invisible during the day. Like the legendary Owl of Minerva, they only seem to emerge when the shades of night are falling. We are talking, of course, about the evening workforce of cleaners and janitors whose job it is to scrub the floors, polish the tables, empty the trash cans and ashtrays, long after the daytime population of staff and students have gone home. They are the graveyard shift, and together they form their own small nocturnal community.

It is a community largely made up of women, many of who are from minority ethnic backgrounds. Some are visible minority women: West Indians, South Asians, Filipinos, Chileans, and other non-European nationalities. Others are from European countries. Many of these seem to be recent immigrants judging from their styles of dress and modes of speech. But within this community of women the only men to occasionally be seen are the supervisors or foremen who periodically come to inspect the work that is done.

In one way or another, this scene – or one like it – is replayed every evening in the hospitals, airports, shopping malls and other large work organizations in our society. It is in places like these that women and ethnic minorities are employed to perform some of the most menial and low-paid jobs in the labour market. These workers are also more likely to suffer the disadvantages of temporary, part-time and shift work, all of which comes without the security, opportunity and benefits associated with permanent, full-time employment.

For most Canadians, these are the invisible workers in our society who may remain trapped at the lowest levels of the labour force, sometimes because of their lack of skills and education, but often because they are working-class women, or people of colour. In this respect, Canada is no different from many other Western societies where women and ethnic minorities are often employed in what one writer (Bonacich, 1972), has called the "split labour market," to fill the lowest paying, least secure, most menial dead-end jobs that nobody else really wants. Today, this type of labour market segmentation has become a fact of life in many countries, and may be seen in such cases as North African workers in France; Turkish and Yugoslav workers in Germany; Italians in Switzerland; West Indians and Asians in Great Britain; and immigrant and visible minority workers here in Canada (cf. Castles and Kosack, 1985, for a review of the immigrant labour market in Europe).

Many of these minority workers, especially those who happen to be non-White women, have continued to face special problems of discrimination and exploitation in the workplace. This has been especially true for those workers who have remained trapped at the lowest ends of the occupational ladder, for it is here that the forces of sexism and racism combine to perpetuate the existence of a cheap labour force which has remained largely invisible to the larger society.

> One has only to look at the employment practices of police departments, fire departments, government services, universities, the media and private companies to see that visible minorities are consciously or unconsciously denied full participation in almost all Canadian institutions. Visible minorities are, in fact, the invisible members of our society (Canada. Parliament. House of Commons. Special Committee on Participation of Visible Minorities in Canadian Society., 1984: 1).

Of course, not all minority workers end up at the lowest levels of the labour force. Some succeed in obtaining relatively well-paid, secure and prestigious jobs in public services or private corporations. However, many of these middle-class managers, bureaucrats and professionals have also faced special problems of discrimination and prejudice in their workplaces. But because little attention has been paid to these problems in mainstream studies of organizations, they also have remained largely invisible to the public eye.

It is only recently that OT/OB and public policy have begun to address the special problems experienced by minorities within workplaces, and other organizational settings. In the past, members of disadvantaged minority groups have been excluded from many forms of employment, and today, they still face institutional discrimination and prejudice in many organizations. Not all of these barriers have been deliberate, however. Some, like the traditional height and weight requirements for certain jobs, often represent residual ethnocentric (and androcentric) standards established at a time when only White males were seen as suitable candidates for these jobs, and which have never been revised to take account of the changing composition of the labour force. Many of these institutional barriers can be removed once the needs and cultural sensitivities of minority groups have been recognized and accommodated. Although it has proven to be a controversial decision, the amendment of the RCMP dress code to permit the hiring of women, Sikhs and Aboriginals is just one example of how organizations can move with the times. If we are serious about offering equal access to employment for all members of our society, regardless of gender, ethnic or racial background, the institutional barriers that have traditionally excluded these groups must be removed.

> It is not that individuals in the designated groups are inherently unable to achieve equality on their own, it is that the obstacles in their way are so formidable and self-perpetuating that they cannot be overcome without intervention. It is both intolerable and insensitive if we simply wait and hope that the barriers will disappear with time. Equality in employment will not happen unless we make it happen (Abella, 1984: 254).

Today, however, the political climate has shifted away from the welfare liberalism of the 1960s, 1970s and 1980s, to the neo-conservatism of the 1990s and 2000s. With this shift has come a weakening of popular and political support for minority rights, including such programs as Multiculturalism and employment equity. The prevailing preoccupation with the debt crisis has brought with it a backlash against many minority rights concerns and programs. The evidence of this backlash may be seen in negative public attitudes towards minorities, and in a weakening of political support for the protection of minority rights.

Notwithstanding these temporary setbacks, however, which are typical of troubled economic times, most of the evidence suggests that the struggles of ethnic and racial minorities for social justice and greater equality will continue to move ahead. The literature of OT and OB has finally begun to acknowledge the presence of minorities in organizations, and to examine their special problems of institutional prejudice and discrimination. With the demographic trend towards increasing ethnic and racial diversity in the workplace, the issue of minority rights is here to stay, and the effective management of this issue has become a matter for the operational effectiveness and welfare of the organization.

KEY TERMS

Americanization of organization research

racism	*androcentrism*	*ethnic mosaic*
tokenism	*assimilationism*	*ethnocentrism*
vertical mosaic	*biculturality*	*glass ceiling*
visible minorities	*discrimination*	*institutionalized discrimination*
race relations	*ethnicity*	*multiculturalism*

REVIEW QUESTIONS

Q1. Briefly define each of the following terms, and say how an understanding of each can help us to understand organizations.
- androcentrism
- discrimination
- ethnocentrism
- racism

Assignment: Now turn to the glossary at the end of the book and compare your definitions.

Q2. What does the "Americanization of organizational research" refer to?

Assignment: First, read the introduction of any mainstream US OT or OB text and then compare it with the introduction of one of the few mainstream Canadian OT (e.g., Das, 1998) or OB (e.g., McShane, 2001) texts. What are the main similarities? What are the main differences? Secondly, read and compare any one of the Canadian accounts of race/ethnicity in organizations? Third, reread the section in this chapter on "The Influence of American Assimilation Theory". What is the main difference between mainstream accounts and accounts focused on race/ethnicity? How do US and Canadian accounts differ? What general conclusions do you draw?

Q3. Define "institutionalized or systemic discrimination". What does this tell us about the design and processes or organizations in Canada? Identify four groups in Canada who have been the victims of institutionalized discrimination.

Assignment: In answering this question, read the first section of the Abella Commission Report on Equality in Employment (1984). Who are the four main disadvantaged groups focused upon by the Abella Commission? What groups does the term "visible minorities" refer to? Distinguish three visible minority from three invisible minority groups in Canada.

Q4. Briefly define each of the following terms and say what impact they are likely to have on "visible minority" persons in "majority settings":

- biculturality
- glass ceiling
- tokenism

Assignment: Now turn to the glossary at the end of the book and compare your definitions.

Q5. Who is in favour of, and who is opposed to, the policies of multiculturalism in society, generally; and in the workplace, in particular?

Assignment: Make a list of all groups and individuals you know who support multiculturalist policies, and all those who oppose those who oppose them? On what basis do those different sides support or oppose those policies?

INTERNET EXERCISES

Q1. Look up the employment equity acts of Canada, the UK and Australia. How do they differ and how are they similar?

Q2. Go to the website of the Canadian Armed Forces and the RCMP. What specific policies do they have in place to recruit visible minorities?

Q3. Find the websites for the major political parties in Canada. What, if anything, do they say that reflects their views on bilingualism in Canada?

EXERCISE 6.1

This exercise is designed to make you think about the significance of race and ethnicity for an understanding of organizations. Do the tasks individually and then discuss your findings in small groups.

A. Obtain information on the composition of visible minority and Native peoples in your region (i.e., what percentage of the local population are Native and what percentage from non-White heritage).

Your University/College, or public library will have Statistics Canada material that will help you with this exercise. As you do this exercise take notes on, (i) the level of difficulty you encountered on making the assessment, and

(ii) what this tells you about the problem of assessing the impact of race/ethnicity in the workplace.

B. Compare and contrast the race/ethnic composition of two local organizations.

1. The class should meet in small groups to coordinate the division of labour for studying local organizations. A number of options are possible, (i) the group could agree to collectively study two organizations, or (ii) each group member could undertake to study one or two different organizations, or (iii) half the group members could study one organization while the other half studies a different organization.

2. Choose which organizations are to be studied. Organizations should be chosen according to the following criteria: (i) access – you should be able to have relative access to the organization (e.g., a church of which you are a member, a department store, a college, a political party to which you are affiliated), and (ii) public information – it should be relatively easy to obtain public information (e.g., corporate brochures, advertisements, etc.) on the organization, from the organization itself or from a public library.

3. Gather as much data on the ethnic composition – particularly the employment of visible minorities and Native peoples – of the organizations as possible, using observation, and other data collection. Focus upon the visible, and public image of the organization. Does it have visible minorities and/or Native people in its work force? At what levels are visible minorities and/or Native people employed? Do visible minorities and/or Native people feature in the public materials (e.g., advertising materials, brochures, etc.) of the organizations? To what extent are visible minorities and/or Native peoples in any obvious position of power and authority?

4. Now, rank the order of all the organizations studied in terms of the extent to which Native and visible minority peoples are evident (a) in the organization per se, (b) in the higher ranks of the organization, and (c) in the public image of the organization – with the best organization ranked #1 downward.

This exercise should be done over the course of a week (but longer may be taken if the class agrees).

C. Now, as a group discuss your findings and prepare a report for class discussion, focusing on the following questions:

1.(a) How many of the local organizations studied can be said to include a significant and representative number of Native and visible minority peoples at all levels?

(b) How would you define significant and representative, and why?

2. To what extent, in your estimate, is the employment of Native and visible minority peoples representative of the percentage of those peoples in the local region?

3. In what types of jobs are Native and visible minority peoples most commonly found?

4. From you rank ordering, (a) which organizations are better and which worst in regard to the employment of Native and visible minority peoples? (b) how do you account for the differences between organizations?

5. What is your overall assessment of the contribution of local organizations to the maintenance and/or development of institutionalized racism?

D. As a class take group report-backs and then discuss the implications of the actual race/ethnicity composition of local organizations on how we should approach organizational research. Pay attention to one or more of the following topic areas – motivation, organizational culture, communication, organizational structure, leadership, organizational conflict.

USEFUL INTERNET SITES

<www.crr.ca>
<http://www.cic.gc.ca/english/department/legacy/>
<http://www.chrc-ccdp.ca/default-en.asp>

FURTHER READING

Critiques of OT AND OB for their neglect of race and ethnicity:

JOURNAL OF ORGANIZATIONAL BEHAVIOR, VOL.11, 1990.

Marta Calás, (1992). AN/OTHER SILENT VOICE? REPRESENTING "HISPANIC WOMEN IN ORGANIZATIONAL TEXTS"

Ella Bell and Stell Nkomo, (1992). REVISIONING WOMEN MANAGERS' LIVES

E.L.Bell, T.C.Denton and S.M.Nkomo, (1992). WOMEN OF COLOR IN MANAGEMENT

P. Prasad et al., (1997). MANAGING THE ORGANIZATIONAL MELTING POT: DILEMMAS OF WORKPLACE DIVERSITY

P. Prasad and A. Prasad, (2002). OTHERNESS AT LARGE: IDENTITY AND DIFFERENCE IN THE NEW GLOBALIZED ORGANIZATIONAL LANDSCAPE

K. Mirchandani, (2004). WEBS OF RESISTANCE IN TRANSNATIONAL CALL CENTRES: STRATEGIC AGENTS, SERVICE PROVIDERS AND CUSTOMERS

Analyses of race/ethnicity in Canadian organizations:

F. Henry and C. Tator, (2000a). FROM THE COLOUR OF DEMOCRACY: RACISM IN CANADIAN SOCIETY

A. Fleras and J.L. Elliott, (1992). MULTICULTURALISM IN CANADA: THE CHALLENGE OF DIVERSITY

A. Fleras and J.L. Elliott, (2003). UNEQUAL RELATIONS: AN INTRODUCTION TO RACE AND ETHNIC DYNAMICS IN CANADA

Tania Das Gupta, (1995). RACISM AND PAID WORK

Linda Carty, (1991). BLACK WOMEN IN ACADEMIA

Joy Mighty, (1997). TRIPLE JEOPARDY: IMMIGRANT WOMEN OF COLOR IN THE LABOR FORCE

C. Agócs, (2002). WORKPLACE EQUALITY: INTERNATIONAL PERSPECTIVES ON LEGISLATION, POLICY AND PRACTICE.

Canadian Journal of Administrative Sciences, (1991). SPECIAL ISSUE ON DIVERSITY, 8(2)

END NOTES

1. Over the past decade OB and OT textbooks have included race and ethnicity under the general banner of "diversity" and "diversity management". This approach has tended to problematize people of colour, viewing *their* management as an important issue for organizations (Foldy, 2002; Prasad and Mills, 1997).

2. According to the 2000 US census, 23 percent of the US population was non-white (Grieco, 2001). By 2005, the ethnic minority share of the workforce is expected to grow to 28 percent, up from 18 percent in 1980 and 22 percent in 1990 (Minehan, 2004). In Canada, by 2001, visible minorities comprised 13 percent of the population (Statistics Canada, 2001). Yet by 2004 visible minorities were the fastest growing part of the labour force in Canada, accounting for one-third of the economic growth in the past 10 years, even though they make up only 11 per cent of the labour force (Stinson, 2004).

3. Blauner (1972; 2001) has distinguished between what he call, "immigrant minorities" of European background who came voluntary to the US, and have been successfully assimilated into American society; and "colonized minorities" of non-European background – Aboriginals, Blacks, Chinese, Mexicans, etc. – who were forcibly incorporated into American society through conquest and colonization, and have remained marginalized and disadvantaged. there is, in other words, an important difference in the way that white and non-white peoples entered the New World.

4. The 2001 Canadian census reported that the jobless rate for new immigrants to Canada is double the national average. Despite being highly skilled, half of the new immigrants who are employed are in low skilled jobs (Canada.Com, 2003).

5. In 2001, 39% of Aboriginal people had less than high school education compared to 45% in 1996 and Aboriginal people with post secondary training had an employment rate of 38% compared to 33% in 1996. Yet most of these jobs were in the construction trades for men and office administrators for women (Statistics Canada 2001). In terms of wage disparities, visible minorities earned 11 per cent less than the Canadian average in 1991 and this gap grew to 14.5 per cent in 2000 (Conference Board of Canada, 2004).

6. Prime Minister Pierre Trudeau formally announced the policy of Multiculturalism on October 8, 1971, in the House of Commons with the following statement:
    "A policy of Multiculturalism within a bilingual framework commends itself to the government as the most suitable means of assuring the cultural freedom of all Canadians".

7. One of the more lyrical endorsements of the new policy was provided by the Liberal Senator, Paul Yuzuk, in 1975. It accurately portrays the sense of optimism that many politicians around this time felt towards the concept of Multiculturalism: "It is fortunate that

Canadian governments have rejected the "melting pot" theory with its colourless uniformity and have promoted a "mosaic-type" of Canadian culture based on the voluntary integration of the best elements of the cultures of the component ethnic groups. The development of a composite Canadian culture, rich in variety, beauty and harmony, reflects the principle of "unity in continuing diversity" and the democratic spirit of compromise inherent in the Canadian Confederation" (Anderson and Frideres, 1981: 101).

8. In late August, 1991, Prime Minister Mulroney gave a mandate to a seven-member Royal Commission on Aboriginal Issues to deal with, "an accumulation of literally centuries of injustices." The Commission was headed by Georges Erasmus, former national chief of the Assembly of First Nations, and Rene Dussault, a Justice of the Quebec Court of Appeal. Four of the seven members of the Commission were Indian, Inuit, or Métis; the first time that aboriginal people have played a dominant role on a Royal Commission.

9. Ovide Mercredi, national chief of the Assembly of First Nations, welcomed the report as "the best chance we have in this century." Ron Irwin, Indian Affairs Minister, however refused to endorse the conclusions (Western Report, 11 (47), December 9, 1996).

10. A notable exception was John Porter (1975), who continued to believe that the policies of ethnic pluralism resulted in the persistence of ethnic stratification and inequality. According to Porter, the best guarantee of ending ethnic inequality was to eliminate any notion of group rights, and emphasize the supremacy of individual rights and equality before the law. This, he believed, entailed a policy of individual assimilation into the majority culture.

11. See also Jan Wong's weekly series "Tales from the Towers", (Globe and Mail, Feb 20-Apr. 3, 2004) which follows the trials and tribulations and job searches of residents of Thorncliffe Park, an area in north Toronto, which has been described as being home to Canada's most highly educated immigrants.

12. The exception to this seems to be the persistence, and maybe even the strengthening of anti-semitism in some quarters. The well publicized trials of Jim Keegstra in Alberta and Ernst Zundel in Ontario, and the dismissal of Malcolm Ross in New Brunswick, as well as the activities of such groups as the Ayran Nations, are evidence of the fact that anti-semitism is far from dead in Canada.

13. A 1990 Angus Reid-Southam News Poll, for example, found that 59% of Canadians want ethnic minorities to abandon their customs and language and become "more like most Canadians." At that time, according to Reid, whose Winnipeg polling firm has conducted several polls for the federal Immigration Department, Canada was on the brink of a backlash against Multiculturalism. "What Canadian's are saying is that they're sick and tired of being asked to be tolerant," Reid told a meeting in Toronto in 1990, *Edmonton Journal*, May 13th 1990. In a later Canadian parliamentary report that

discussed the three phases of the implementation of the multiculturalism policy (Leman, 1999) , it was noted that: "Quebeckers have expressed uneasiness about, or even resistance to, federal multiculturalism policy since its inception. This uneasiness is largely explained in terms of their perception of it as another intrusion by federal authorities into their province's internal affairs. Many are inclined to view multiculturalism as a ploy to downgrade the distinct society status of Quebeckers to the level of an ethnic minority culture under the domination of English-speaking Canada. Multiculturalism is thus seen as an attempt to dilute the French fact in Canada, weakening francophone status and threatening the dual partnership of English-speaking and French-speaking Canadians. For many Quebeckers, the idea of reducing the rights of French-speaking Canadians to the same level as those of other ethno-racial minorities in the name of multicultural equality is inconsistent with the special compact between the two founding peoples of Canada"

14. When the Canadian Alliance Party and the Conservative Party were discussing their merger and areas of concern in 2002, multiculturalism and immigration policies were a major issue: "Eliminating official multiculturalism was one of the Reform Party's founding principles and there is no question this policy attracted some racists to the party. However, the Canadian Alliance has modified its position somewhat. For example, a 2002 policy declaration by Stephen Harper states that multicultur-

alism is a personal choice and should not be publicly funded. However, it also acknowledges that multiculturalism is a basic feature of Canadian society, and one with positive benefits. This is consistent with the PC position outlined in their 2000 policy platform, that 'While they cherish their diversity, most Canadians believe that institutionalized multiculturalism should no longer be publicly funded.' Like multiculuralism, the CA's immigration policy has been modified since Reform Party days. The party still believes new immigrants should not receive national government-funded assistance. However, it does commit to helping new immigrants receive provincial support. With respect to choosing immigrants, the party believes immigration should be merit-based, with the main criteria being Canada's economic needs. Laws against illegal immigrants should be toughened. The PC party platform on immigration is more moderate. Its guiding principles state that immigration should be based on humanitarian concerns and social needs, as well as Canada's economic needs. However, it also stresses the economic value of immigration" (Mapleleaf Web, 2004). On biligualism Stephen Harper the current leader of the Conservative Party told the Calgary Sun that "As a religion, bilingualism is the god that failed. It has led to no fairness, produced no unity, and cost Canadian taxpayers untold millions." Three years later he softened his tone during the 2004 general election, vowing to respect provincial rights and protect Quebec language and culture if he became prime minister (Bailey, 2004). Harper was responding to remarks made by the Party's critic for official languages, Scott Reid, that a future Conservative government would remove the federal government's obligation to offer bilingual services in some areas of the country. Reid later resigned following Harper's remarks.

15. Discrimination against Sikhs seems to have come to a head in 1991. In another turban-related incident, Mr.Ram Raghbir Singh Chanal, secretary of the Alberta wing of the Federal Liberal Party, was barred from entering the Red Deer Legion hall on his way to attend a speech by Ontario Liberal M.P., Sheila Copps on August 13th, 1991. Mr. Chanal was apparently also subjected to verbal abuse and told to remove his turban.

16. In a speech to the National Association of Canadians of Origins in India, held in Edmonton in September 1987, Ray Martin – the leader of the Alberta NDP – told the convention that the Alberta Government's focus on the "singing and dancing syndrome" had obscured more important multicultural issues, such as equal access to employment, and career advancement for new Canadians. *Edmonton Journal*, Sept.8th., 1987.

17. There are those who argue that "the logic of industrialization" has created general trends throughout industrial societies; that industrialization has rendered cultural differences obsolete (Galbraith, 1978).

18. This includes Mexico where deep-rooted racism discriminates against people the more native born, and the less like the gringos of the US, they appear to be.

CHAPTER 7

Knowledge and Power in Theories of Organization: The Organizational World and the Managerial Paradigm

This chapter sets out to explain why OT and OB continue to be dominated by managerialist thinking – arguing that mainstream OT and OB should be viewed not so much as a paradigm but as a field of discourse. The chapter goes on to detail the rise of critical theories of organization and suggest ways forward in developing organizational research that can address the needs of persons in the new Postmodernist, yet continually problematic, organizational world.

INTRODUCTION

The underlying purpose in writing this book has been to argue for a radical rethinking of theories of organization. By "radical," however, we are not proposing that serious theoretical analysis be abandoned in favour of political sloganeering. What we are suggesting is that it is now time for Organization Theory and Organizational Behaviour to return to their intellectual roots to renew themselves and to come to terms with the contemporary needs of organizational analysis. This, after all, is the original meaning of the word, "radical": a return to the roots in search of regeneration.[1]

To go back to its own roots, Organization Theory and Organizational Behaviour need to re-establish their ties to the classic tradition of social theory, and to the general theories of society represented in this tradition. Indeed, this book has been written very much in the belief that it is neither possible nor desirable to divorce the study of organizations from the broader study of society. This is because organizations are part of the history and culture of their respective societies and cannot meaningfully be analyzed in isolation from these larger influences.

Although the relationship of organizations to the history and culture of their respective societies may seem self-evident, the fact remains that much mainstream work in Organization Theory and Organizational Behaviour have consistently overlooked the extent to which organizations – and organizational theorizing – are shaped by influences from the larger society.

To argue for the return of OT and OB to their classical roots in more general theories of society, is, of course, to run counter to the direction in which these subject areas have evolved over the past fifty years or so. In common with the general tendency for increasing specialization in academia – as in most other institutions of the modern world – the emergence of OT and OB as independent disciplines have taken them farther and farther away from their root in classical social theory.

FROM PARADIGM TO DISCOURSE: UNDERSTANDING THE MANAGERIALIST DOMINANCE OF OT AND OB

Superficially, it may even appear as though the development of OT and OB have followed the pattern of growth of other modern scientific disciplines. According to Thomas Kuhn (1970), an eminent historian of science, most of the modern sciences came into existence through a process of "scientific revolution," whereby a number of traditionally competing schools of thought were replaced by a single powerful scientific "paradigm." The new paradigm succeeded in unifying a previously fragmented community of scholars around a common conceptual framework. This is how the modern sciences of chemistry and physics emerged from the rival schools of alchemy and natural philosophy. In each case, a powerful and new scientific paradigm – whether Daltonian atomic theory, or Newtonian mechanics – served to unite the community of scholars, and to render obsolete the traditional rivalries which had characterized the earlier pre-scientific schools of thought. Once the new paradigm was fully accepted by the scientific community, it began to function as a common framework for all scientific inquiry undertaken within the discipline. The adoption of this common framework for theory and research put an end to the earlier debates which had traditionally preoccupied the pre-scientific schools of thought. With the entrenchment of a single scientific paradigm, scientific enquiry entered a stage of "normal science," in which problem-solving research within a common conceptual framework replaced the more philosophical and fundamental debates of earlier, pre-scientific days.

In most disciplines, this period of normal science has lasted for as long as the prevailing paradigm has continued to provide an effective framework for solving the ongoing problems of research. Only when confronted by a growing number of "anomalies" which defy explanation through the procedures of normal science have scientific paradigms finally lost their credibility and legitimacy. At these times of "revolutionary crisis," a discredited paradigm has sometimes been displaced by a number of new and rival conceptual frameworks which may compete with each other for acceptance within the scientific community. This state of affairs has only been concluded with the emergence of a new paradigm which has reunited the scientific community around another common framework.

For some social scientists, Kuhn's theory of the growth of scientific knowledge has been accepted only as a description of the way in which modern sciences emerged from their pre-scientific origins. For others, however, Kuhn's theory has been interpreted as a prescription of the path that any discipline must follow to attain the status of a modern science. According to this latter, positivist view – positivist in the sense that it seeks to imitate the development of the natural sciences – it is only through the development of a single unifying paradigm of theory and research that any discipline can ever reach scientific maturity.

The fact that Kuhn, himself, rejected any suggestion that paradigms could be artificially imposed or "legislated" on scientific communities, and even questioned the applicability of his analysis to the social sciences, has not prevented positivist readings of Kuhn from being adopted by some social scientists. In these readings, the development of a single, dominant paradigm has always carried with it the promise of a "takeoff" into sustained scientific development, and to the eventual consensus of the scientific community around a unified set of theories and methods of social scientific research.

When we look back over the past several decades at the development of OT and OB as independent disciplines of applied social science it is apparent that, until very recently, a dominant view of organizational analysis prevailed within these disciplines. Whether this view has constituted a "paradigm" in the strict Kuhnian sense remains debatable, but there can be little doubt it has exercised a controlling influence within OB and OT, and has become recognized as an orthodoxy by a majority within the community of organizational theorists. That orthodoxy has been termed "functionalist" by Burrell and Morgan (1979), who – using a Kuhnian-type approach – attempted to conceptualize the field of organizational analysis as being comprised of four main paradigms (or ways of viewing reality): a dominant, "functionalist" paradigm, and competing "interpretive," "radical humanist" and "radical structuralist paradigms." Burrell and Morgan's intention was to "expose" the dominant paradigm as but one way of viewing the world, one way of several potential ways of viewing reality; and, in the process of exposing "functionalism" so as to weaken its dominance and open the field to new ideas. Morgan (1996b)has extended the idea by attempting to expose views of organizations as a series of competing metaphors – each one of which is at least partially true, none of which is completely valid.[2] As useful as the exercise of exposure has proved to many radical scholars within the field of OT and OB, the dominant, "functionalist" or managerialist approach – despite the protestations of some to the contrary[3] – still continues to hold sway like a dead hand on the discipline, a fact that needs to be explained as well as countered.

In many ways, it may be more useful to analyze the dominant view of OT/OB as a (Foucauldian) field of discourse than as a (Kuhnian) paradigm. For in Foucault's analysis, the emergence of a dominant, or hegemonic field of discourse is inseparable from the institutionalized practices and relations of power and authority that serve to privilege some forms of knowledge over others. In other words, to understand how particular fields of discourse have come to constitute certain domains of knowledge it is always necessary to examine the institutions which are linked to these new ways of thinking and speaking about the social (or natural) world.

OT/OB as a field of discourse is derived from a number of different intellectual traditions. Its origins, as we have already seen, date back to the schools of classical social theory, most notably to Weber's theory of bureaucracy (1948), but also, as Gouldner (1954), has suggested, to the work of Saint-Simon and Compte. Later sociological writers such as Parsons, Selznick, Gouldner, Kanter, and others, have continued to work within this sociological tradition of OT/OB.

However, it is only with the rise of management theory at the turn of the century that the study of organizations began to acquire a distinctly administrative focus, one which has remained its hallmark until the present time. It was through the contribution of such "classical" management theorists as Taylor (Rose, 1978; Taylor, 1911), and others, as well as the later contributions of Human Relations theorists (Mayo, 1933; Roethlisberger and Dickson, 1939) that a managerial perspective became firmly entrenched within organizational discourse.

When, after World War Two, OT and OB finally emerged as independent disciplines, drawing on a number of different fields of discourse which included not only social systems theory (from Sociology), but also decision theory (from mathematics), rational choice theory (from economics), and information theory (from psychology), it was the managerial perspective which served as a common point of reference, and as a framework for the assimilation and synthesis of these diverse traditions within a distinctive discourse of OT/OB.

Organization Theory and Organizational Behaviour, therefore, emerged as successors to the earlier schools of management theory and incorporated many of their insights into their fields of discourse. Its language and concepts were used by managers to legitimize their authority within the modern organization. Within the academic community, the dominant managerial perspective of OT/OB became fully institutionalized through the proliferation of management schools, standard textbooks, disciplinary journals and professional associations. Notwithstanding the polyglot origins of modern OT and OB, therefore, these powerful institutions of thought control have successfully combined to impart a dominant managerialist perspective to these disciplines, one which has continued to provide a common problem-solving framework for ongoing theory and research. In this sense, we may say that in spite of their interdisciplinary origins and diverse conceptual frameworks, OT and OB can be characterized by a highly orthodox approach to the study of organizations, and one which has remained distinguished by its managerialist orientation. This is the closest we can get to saying that OT has developed a "paradigm" which has served to give some unity and coherence to the field of organizational discourse, as well as some basis for intellectual consensus within the academic community of organization theorists.

INSIDE THE MANAGERIALIST VIEW OF REALITY

More than anything else, the prevailing paradigm of OT and OB have continued to assume that *rational* action within organizations is primarily, (if not exclusively), associated with the functions of management. This is an assumption which has helped to integrate such otherwise diverse theoretical schools as Scientific Management, Human Relations and neo-Weberian studies of bureaucracy, with more recent traditions of decision theory, rational choice theory, game theory, contingency theory, and process (TQM, BPR) and mathematical (Six Sigma, Balanced Scorecard) perspectives on change. In earlier schools of management theory the assumption, that the only rational functions in the organization were those that were performed by managers, was generally stated openly and explicitly. For Scientific Management theorists, it was axiomatic that managers had a rational interest in maximizing the efficiency of work, while workers maintained an irrational interest in "soldiering." Similarly, Human Relations theorists also distinguished between what they saw as a "logic of efficiency" which informed the actions of managers within an organization, and a "logic of sentiment" which motivated the actions of workers. In this respect, as in many others, early management theorists were united in their belief that only managers fully identified with the formal goals of the organization, but workers were more typically motivated by their own self-interests. It is easy to see how these beliefs contributed to the general assumption that the rationality of the organization resided exclusively in the functions of management.

Later theorists, such as Chester Barnard (1938), Herbert Simon (1976) and others, revised their conceptions and definitions of organizational rationality. Whereas, for Taylor, rationality was manifested in the "scientific" reclassification of work tasks and in the redesign of work processes, later theorists located rationality in other dimensions of the organization: in communication structures, information processes, rational choice designs, and so on. Common to virtually all these traditions, however, is the basic assumption that organizations may be viewed, first and foremost, as instrumental tools, (variously conceptualized as "machines," "organic structures," "social systems," "cybernetic systems," etc.) for the accomplishment of rational goals, and that primary responsibility for the formulation and realization of these goals remains with a specialized group of rational decision-makers, i.e., managers.

It is only recently that contemporary critics of OT and OB – especially feminist critics – have shown how this apparently objective, neutral and universalistic assumption of organizational analysis is based on a highly gendered view of the organization. For, as Kanter (1977) has suggested, the identification of "rationality" as the primary attribute of any organization also implies a corresponding rejection of such other attributes as "emotionality," "subjectivity," and so forth. In other words, the concept of "rationality" which has remained so central to most traditions of OT/OB, is based on a strong identification with stereotypical masculine values, and an equally strong rejection of stereotypical feminine values. This "masculine ethic" of rationality has had lasting theoretical and practical consequences for the participation of women (and other so-called minorities) in organizational life.

At a theoretical level, it has centred organizational analysis around the masculinized ideals of rationality and hierarchy, and has overlooked the experiences and values of other groups which not conform to these ideals. At a practical level it has helped to typify the ideal manager according to heavily masculinized criteria, thereby legitimating the long-term exclusion of women from positions of management.

WHAT IS TO BE DONE? THE CHALLENGE AND LIMITATION OF RADICAL THEORIES OF ORGANIZATION

Karl Marx once wrote that, "Philosophers have only interpreted the world, the point is to change it." By this he was saying that it is not enough merely to analyze uncomfortable realities but that we need to find ways of challenging and changing those realities. The "uncomfortable realities" that we have documented in this book include organizations that are dominated by white, able-bodied men; that, more often than not, either exclude women and visible minorities or relegate them to the lower echelons; that have a morality which is guided more by the needs of profitability and efficiency than by social need and responsibility; and that, all too often, are places and experiences which inhibit human growth, sociability, and the potential for warmth and creativity. The "uncomfortable realities" also include the disciplines of Organization Theory and Organizational Behaviour which, far from questioning the darker realities of organizations, more often than not reflect those realities – in the process contributing to and strengthening them.

So what is to be done? What is the role of radical OT/OB in the process of change and, equally to the point, what is the role of change in the development of radical theories of organization? Organization Theory and Organizational Behaviour have, as we have argued in earlier parts of the book, tended to reflect much of the times in which they were located. Not as a simple mirroring of reality but, at one level, as an interpreter of aspects of reality;

those aspects that serve a managerialist focus. At another level, OT/OB has developed as a "field of discourse" – a living element in the process of producing and reproducing managerialist views of reality. In the 1930s, which were characterized by mass unemployment, widespread poverty, and preparations for war, management control was the major emphasis in the theories and practice of organizations. Managers needed little more than the threat of unemployment to control their work-forces. It was in the looming shadow of the Second World War that the key leadership study of Lewin, Lippitt, and White (1939) emerged, with its appropriate characterization of different leadership styles whose names – democratic, authoritarian and *laissez faire* – referenced the actual international political concerns of the time. The immediate post-war era was shaped by a number of forces including – particularly in North America – rising expectations, high levels of employment, rising educational standards, and a rapid shift from blue- to white-collar work. This had its impact on the new breed of professional manager who, by inclination – they too were part of the changing ways of seeing the world which emerged after 1945 – and by the force of the new circumstances, sought different ways to achieve coordination and control; new ways that turned to more humanistic theories of motivation, and leadership styles to manage the work of the growing white-collar and professional workers whose ranks were growing rapidly. These forms of "hegemonic" control (Clegg, 1981) where applied in the white-collar sphere, but traditional "technical forms of control" still seemed to hold sway in those blue-collar or more routinized white-collar work (Edwards, 1979).

The ghost of the Cold War hung over much of the post-war era of organizational thinking and practices that characterized industrial societies, East and West. The Cold War was no idle fantasy and was experienced in a number of institutional ways. It was a discursive practice; a set of institutionalized relationships that has shaped the way we saw the world. It was manifest in the proliferation of Cold War institutions (NATO, the Warsaw Pact, The Pentagon, the Red Army, the KGB, the CIA, etc.) which dominated the lives of millions of people until recently. It was manifest in McCarthyism in the West and Stalinism in the East that led to the purging of persons from (government, military, media, school, and trade union) organizations. It was manifest in the strengthening of conservative and bureaucratic forces both in the East and the West. It was manifest in funding priorities that focused on military and space development, espionage, arm's manufacture and other war preparations (Robin, 2001). It was manifest in the social, military and political links between the top managers of the large corporations and government bodies (from ITT's link to the 1974 coup in Chile – see Sampson, 1973, through to the Irangate disclosures of the late 1990s). It was manifest in the government polices of the US, (for example, the US involvement in the Vietnam War, designed to protect US corporations), and of the Soviet Union, (for example, their involvement in the Afghanistan War, designed to retain Soviet influence, or "hegemony," in the region). And, no doubt, it was manifest in the multitudes of ordinary workplace practices (in particular management, industrial relations, the maintenance of hierarchical relations) that went to shape management thinking to the present time (Mills and Helms Hatfield, 1998; Mills et al., 2002).

In the same way the Cold War has served as a framework – sometime background, often foreground – for the development of radical theories of organization. In the East, where the dead hand of Cold War orthodoxy excluded the possibility of alternative theories of organization, critiques of organization appeared in literary form – the books of Solzenitzen, for example, that attacked much of the institutions of oppression (the Gulags, the KGB, etc.). In the West, George Orwell's *1984,* Ken Kesey's *One Flew Over the Cuckoo's Nest,* and Margaret Atwood's *Handmaid's Tale,* have carried on a similar tradition.

It was a sharp reaction against the Cold War that led many persons – East and West – to protest on the streets throughout much of the late 1960s and well through the '70s. The year of 1968 was in many ways pivotal. In Paris during May of that year workers and students were barricading the streets, and a nationwide strike and series of sit-ins threatened radical change. In Vietnam the National Liberation Front was planning a key military offensive – the "Tet Offensive"- against the US forces in their country, and in Czechoslovakia the people were celebrating a "Prague Spring" under a communist leader – Alexander Dubcek – who promised "Socialism with a Human Face." (Six years later Edward Heath, the Conservative Prime Minister of Britain, was promising "Capitalism with a Human Face.")

The "May '68" events ended in defeat for the French Left, and the Czechoslovak Spring was crushed under the weight of Soviet tanks. Only the TET Offensive achieved a measure of success in embarrassing the US military and helping to push them further on the road towards political defeat. Ironically, this era was also marked by a "thaw" in the Cold War, and the development of a coherent body of radical theories of organization. In the East – still under great danger – a limited number of challenging work appeared (cf. Djilas, 1982). In the West a number of radical critiques appeared. Works such as that of Ivan Illich (1981) and David Dickson (1977), which challenged the whole notion of organization and called for a radical restructuring of key social institutions (e.g., the schools) and of work. These were joined by a series of books and key articles (within the organizations and management literatures) – which owed much to the traditional Marxist perspective – including Allen (1975), Clegg (1975), Benson (1977), Hydebrand (1977), and Clegg and Dunkerley (1980). In some ways these works reflected the growing schism in the traditional Marxist Left between those who saw the need for a radical restructuring of society and those argued for a new type of "non-organizational thinking." Interestingly, these works were joined by a new orthodoxy in the work of Althusser (1970; 1971; 1971; 1977; 2003) who provided a new framework for the old Marxist concept of organization, with its notion that the economy is "in the last analysis" determinate. They were also joined by new, feminist writers who were beginning to challenge to sexist character of organizations (cf. Acker and van Houten, 1974; Kanter, 1977).

By the end of the 1970s the work of Burrell and Morgan (1979) and Clegg and Durkerley (1980) signified a new level of analysis in the development of radical organization theories. Burrell and Morgan set out, in summarizing developments of several schools of radical and alternative thought, to challenge the prevalent managerialist orthodoxy of the time. In other words, to "educate" new generations of organizational analysts of the possibilities of alternative ways of viewing organizational analysis. Where Burrell and Morgan stopped short of explicitly encouraging the development of a radical theory of organization, Clegg and Dunkerley (1980), set out to provide educators with a text that would present the radical alternative to conservative theories of organization. Clegg and Dunkerley's text had a considerable initial impact on the field of organization studies but it is the Burrell and Morgan work that has had the greater impact. This is due to Burrell and Morgan's open-ended approach – suggesting that each of four major paradigms has something to offer: this appeals to those who see a need for change in "the ethos" of management but not a radical change in the character of organizations and organizational control. Ironically, it is on the development of interpretive and radical humanist approaches to organization that Burrell and Morgan seem to have had the most impact; a factor no doubt encouraged by Morgan's (1996b) next book which offered managers a smorgasbord of "images of organization" from which to chose. It is likely that the potential of

Clegg and Dunkerley's work was inhibited by subsequent events in the development of the Cold War. While Clegg and Dunkerley's work is by no means an apologia for the Soviets the general demise of East European communism – from glasnost to the fall of the Berlin Wall – seems to have thrown much of the broad left forces into a kind of doldrums, where they have remained ever since.

In an atmosphere of near euphoria where the conservative anti-Communist forces were loudly proclaiming victory in the Cold War, the Left became introspective. While the large multinational companies are moving into Eastern Europe with undue haste, people on the Left are half-heartedly debating "the future of Socialism"; for the time being socialist thinking has disappeared as a force within radical organizational thinking. So too has some of the more radical elements of so-called Radical Humanism. The Cold War framework, against which East European people's rebelled, has been rapidly transformed into a drive for the development of "market economies" losing much of its focus on a rethinking about the structure of society and its central institutional forms.

Over the same period, feminism has continued to have a strong and growing presence within organization theory. An increasing number of works over the last two decades has challenged the male domination of organizations and the gender-blindness of organization theory (Mills and Tancred, 1992). The growing strength of feminist theory has been due to three factors, (i) the fact that it was relatively untroubled by the Cold War – in as much as many of the Cold War institutions and practices could be translated as manifestations of a type of male-associated organizational behaviour; (ii) given the changing character of the work-force and the increasing numbers of women in the labour force in general, and in management in particular; and (iii) because a significant element of feminist theory has been co-opted and adapted to mainstream OT/OB, in the form of much of what is called women-in-management approaches. Such approaches set out to locate more women in management positions rather than challenging the nature of the positions themselves. The existence of a strong and growing body of women-in-management theory has not been a bad thing. It has almost certainly helped to strengthened those organizational discourses which question the gendered character of institutions and it has helped to keep alive a broad discourse in which more radical feminisms are able to raise issues and to continue to question.[4]

It is only in the last decade or so – after years of Black struggle, with the changing demographics of North America, and with the development of the notion of the "global economy" – that we are getting "racioethnicity" (Cox, 1990) critiques of OT and OB, many of which are primarily concerned with getting people of colour into greater numbers of management positions but a growing number of which question the "imperialist" roots of modern organizational thinking (cf. Prasad, 1997a; Prasad and Prasad, 2002; Prasad, 1997b).

And what of the future? A vital feature of the current debate about radical theories of organization is a growing interest in postmodernist and poststructuralist theory (cf. Alvesson, 2002; Alvesson and Skoldberg, 2000; Boje, 1996; Boje et al., 1996; Hancock and Tyler, 2001; Hassard and Parker, 1993; Hatch, 1997; Styhre, 2003). We can see this as very much a reflection of our time when we see that postmodernism questions not only the rationale behind much of traditional institutional thinking (questioning notions of progress, rationality, objectivity, etc.), but also any potential "truth claims" (e.g., philosophies of change based on ideas of truth, or "the right way forward," etc.) which set out to change the world by replacing existing power structures with new ones. These approaches tend to be highly introspective and focus on the relationship between organization and different forms of subjectivity. Postmodernism currently has a growing following across a broad cross-section of OT and OB theorists – uniting previously socialist theorists with those who, in other times, may have been attracted to humanist managerialism, interpretive approaches and radical humanism.

Today, postmodernism is providing a rich and challenging debate within the discourse of OT/OB but it is a debate which seems destined to be short-lived in a field that traditionally seeks clear answers and in the face of potential changes in the organizational world. Within postmodernism there appears to be two main trends regarding the development of opposition and change. One trend – the main tendency – focuses largely on critique by explaining current organizational discourse; frowning upon any attempt to go beyond explanation, to strategies for change. The other tendency – exemplified by Burrell (1984) and Ferguson (1984) – argues that postmodernism is impotent if it acts as a break on challenge to existing forms of oppression. This approach takes the difficult but necessary road of arguing for the development of alternative discourses but discourses that question their own truths as part of a wider agenda of challenging discourses of oppression.

In the period ahead the world is being reformed into new power blocs – this time along competing capitalist entities. Thus, we see the consolidation of the European Common Market (EC), with the Maastricht Treaty, and the consolidation of the North American Free Trade Agreement (NAFTA) with the inclusion of Mexico; some of the more developed South East Asia countries (Thailand, Singapore, Korea) are already operating as an informal trading bloc. Many of the former East European countries have either joined or applied to join the EC. In these circumstances, those who question the notion of modernity might find themselves swamped by the creation of new subjectivities in which people sink into old ways of thinking and rivalries and resort to traditional forms of organizational control.

Of course, it is not that simple. The world is also troubled by many new questions and much new questioning. Some of it is negative as in the development of a new "post 9/11" era in which fear of communism has been replaced by fear of terrorism in the west and has led to a curtailing of civil liberties particularly in the United States. It is an era marked by an emerging discourse of domination whereby the United States, Britain and their allies feel able to ignore world opinion and established institutions of international law (e.g., the United Nations assembly) to invade any country they deem a threat to their national interest. Some of it is a renewal of old capitalist values of entrepreneurship – as in the wave of interest sweeping Eastern Europe in entrepreneurial skills and values. Much of it is potentially positive – as in the widespread questioning of and opposition to the US-led war and occupation of Iraq. It is a time when new discourses are developing. New frameworks of thinking and organizing are developing. In this, radical theories of organization have a crucial role to play: not only in providing a radical critique of existing organizational frameworks but also in developing a discourse of opposition and change (Mills, 1998b) and a self-critical discourse which seeks to avoid replacing one group of truths with a new set of (oppressive) truths. We need to see a radical theory of organization as a process of change, rather than a prescription of change – a journey rather than a destination, a permanent revolution in which our vision is a constant striving for change rather than of a blueprint of change. That is the challenge of radical organization theory.

END NOTES

1. The need for a radical rethinking of OT and OB has been expressed by a number of authors from different perspectives, including Aldrich (1988), Clegg (2002), Donaldson (1988), and Hinings and Greenwood (2002).

2. Burrell and Morgan (1979) have since been taken to task for failing to include feminist ways of viewing the world as part of the paradigmatic landscape of organizational analysis (see Hearn and Parkin, 1983; Mills and Murgatroyd, 1991).

3. See Lex Donaldson (1985; 1988; 1996) who, believing that the functionalist orthodoxy was under threat, felt compelled to wrote a defence of organization theory and positivism.

4. This should not, however, be over-stressed. The influence of feminism on OB and OT can be seen in the changing character of business textbooks over time. Most North American textbooks that were published since the mid-1990s give some attention to women and "diversity" but the treatment is still somewhat cursory (Mills, 2004; Mills and Helms Hatfield, 1998). Compared to any other approach to management feminist research takes longer to be disseminated through the OB and OT textbook (Mills, 2004).

Integrated Case:
The Westray Mine Explosion*

Caroline J. O'Connell
Albert J. Mills

INTRODUCTION

It was the sixth of February 1996. Carl Guptill sat at his kitchen table nursing a cup of coffee. He was a beefy man with long hair, often tucked through the back of a baseball cap. The next day he would testify at the Commission of Inquiry into the Westray Mine explosion, and friends had been phoning to offer their support. One caller, a geologist from nearby Antigonish, hadn't been in touch since working with Guptill at a mine in Guysborough County more than five years ago, but he wanted Carl to know he was thinking of him.

Carl Guptill's thoughts drifted back to a longtime friend – Roy Feltmate. Roy had worked on B crew at the Westray Mine. In April of 1992, three months after he had left his job at Westray, Guptill met up with Roy and four other members of B crew, at Feltmate's home. Talk quickly turned to safety at the mine. Conditions had continued to deteriorate and the men believed that an explosion or a cave-in was inevitable. They calculated their odds of being the crew underground when it happened at 25 per cent. The men made Guptill promise that if they died in the mine, he would "go public" and tell the world what he knew. Mike MacKay implored him to "do it for our widows."

---

* The winning case in the 2003 Academy of Management Critical Management Studies/ Management Education "Dark Side III" case writing competition.

On May 9, 1992, a few short weeks after that kitchen meeting, the odds caught up with Roy Feltmate, Mike MacKay, Randy House, Robbie Fraser and twenty-two other members of B crew. At 5:20 am an explosion ripped through the Westray Mine. All twenty-six miners underground died. Fifteen bodies were recovered but eleven bodies, including Roy Feltmate's and Mike MacKay's remained in the mine. Guptill would keep his promise to them.

ONE MINER'S TALE

Carl Guptill had worked in hard rock mines in Nova Scotia prior to hiring on at Westray. At the Gay's River Mine, he had chaired the health and safety committee and at the Forest Hill Mine he'd been a shift supervisor to a crew of 35 or more men. He had completed an advanced management course at Henson College, the continuing education arm of Halifax's Dalhousie University. He was mine rescue certified and had been captain of a mine rescue team. As both a miner and a supervisor, he'd enjoyed a good working relationship with Albert McLean, the provincial mine inspector. Guptill had ended up working at Westray more by happenstance than by design. He had offered to drive his buddy to the mine site to fill out an application and had ended up hired on himself. Guptill put safety first and believed he'd made that clear to Roger Parry, underground manager at Westray, when Parry interviewed him for a job. He demonstrated that commitment by joining the safety committee.

After only a few shifts, Guptill began to question safety practices at Westray. On his very first day, Bill MacCullogh, the mine's training officer, wasn't able to answer some of his questions. He noticed that farm tractors, which should not be used underground, were loaded beyond their capacity. Combustible coal dust was allowed to build up underground; the rock dust that should be spread to neutralize it wasn't anywhere to be found; levels of explosive methane gas were too high and the methanometers that detected the gas were rigged to circumvent their intended purpose of warning miners when gas levels were dangerous. In addition, miners worked twelve hour shifts, often without breaks. The batteries for miners' headlamps could not sustain their charge and were often dim or out by the end of a shift. There were no underground toilets and miners relieved themselves in unused corners of the mine.

Complaints fell on deaf ears. One supervisor answered Guptill's concerns with the comment that "they got a few thousand applications up on top, men willing to come down here and take your place." On only his thirteenth shift, Guptill's supervisor ordered him to continue working after his lamp had dimmed. In the dark, Guptill stumbled and a steel beam he was attempting to move landed on him and injured him. After three days in hospital, he called Roger Parry. The conversation quickly turned into a shouting match. Guptill then contacted Claude White, the provincial director of mine safety. White, in turn, sent him to mine inspector Albert McLean. Shortly thereafter Guptill met with McLean, John Smith, the man responsible for inspection of electrical and mechanical equipment in mines, and Fred Doucette, in charge of mine rescue. In this meeting Carl Guptill spoke of his accident and of the many safety violations he had observed in his short time working at Westray. Guptill expected that his report would result in a shutdown of the mine and a complete investigation. Weeks later, having heard nothing, he again called inspector Albert McLean. The two met once more, this time in a local motel room, instead of the labour department's offices. McLean kept the television on high volume throughout the meeting. Puzzled, Guptill later concluded that McLean was fearful he would tape the meeting. McLean told Guptill that the other men had not backed up his complaints and he could do little. He did offer to "put in a good word" for Guptill with management if he wanted to return to work. This was the story Carl Guptill told the Commission of Inquiry.

A SNAPSHOT OF MINING IN PICTOU COUNTY

The four communities of Trenton, New Glasgow, Westville and Stellarton run into each other to make up Pictou County, Nova Scotia. All told, 25,000 people live there, descendants of Scots that landed with the ship *Hector* and immigrants from the other British Isles and Europe that followed Britain's General Mining Association oversees in the early nineteenth century. Hardy stock, they had mined the county's twenty-five seams of coal for generations. One historian estimated that nearly six hundred residents lost their lives in coalmines, as many as had been killed in both world wars. Although full of coal, the seams were considered among the most dangerous in the world; the beds were uneven and the ash content was high. The mines were subject to rock falls and flooding. Most significant were the high levels of explosive methane gas.

At its peak in 1875, Pictou coalmines produced 250,000 tons of coal a year and employed over 1600 men and boys. The last mine operating in Pictou was the small, privately operated Drummond Mine that closed in 1984. By the mid-eighties, the only coalmines left in Nova Scotia were operating under heavy federal subsidy in Cape Breton, an economically depressed area in the northernmost part of the province. Cape Breton mines might have met the same fate as those in Pictou had they not been in the territory of a powerful federal Member of Parliament as the oil crisis in the Middle East dominated headlines and economies in the 1970's. Under OPEC, oil from the Middle East was subject both to price hikes and embargoes. This rejuvenated the dying Cape Breton coal industry and coal rebounded as a source of energy in Nova Scotia. In the late 1980's and early 1990's, a similar opportunity presented itself to the industry in Pictou. An evolving environmental agenda was driving power generation. The provincial electrical utility, Nova Scotia Power Corporation, was seeking to lower its sulphur dioxide emissions. It needed an alternative to high-sulphur Cape Breton coal. Enter Clifford Frame.

POLITICS AND BIG GUNS

Clifford Frame, a big man who drove big cars, raised cattle and smoked expensive cigars, was a self-made tycoon in the style of a previous era. In his youth he turned down a chance to play for the New York Rangers farm team. Instead he got a degree in mine engineering and worked his way from the pit to the corner office. After rising to the post of president of Denison Mines, he'd been fired in 1985 after a very public project failure in British Columbia. He formed Curragh Resources in 1985 and had early success reviving a lead-zinc mine in the Yukon. In 1987, the industry publication the *Northern Miner* named him "Mining Man of the Year." That same year he incorporated Westray Coal and a year later, in 1988 he bought out Suncor's coal rights in Pictou County. In his time at Denison, Frame had come to know key political players in Ottawa. Through these connections he was introduced to Elmer MacKay, then federal representative for Pictou, and Minister of Public Works. Frame aggressively sought federal and political support for his operation. Pictou County was burdened by a 20 per cent unemployment rate and Frame promised that his mine would employ at least 250 people in jobs paying $35,000 – $60,000 for 15 years. Economic spin-off in neighbouring communities would total in the millions of dollars. Politicians, including then Premier John Buchanan, supported Frame. Perhaps the project's greatest advocate was local provincial MLA (Member of the Legislative Assembly) Donald Cameron who became minister of economic development as the project evolved and ultimately was elected Premier, his position at the time of the explosion. Frame successfully negotiated a $12 million equity loan with the Provincial government as well as an $8 million interim loan when federal negotiations lagged. He also struck a so-called "take or pay" agreement that guaranteed a market for Westray coal. Under this contract, the Nova Scotia government would buy 275,000 tons of coal if other buyers did not materialize. Westray would pay back any revenues from this agreement without interest at the end of fifteen years. The federal government proved a tougher sell and discussions dragged out over three years. Ultimately the federal government came through with a loan guarantee of $85 million and an interest buy down of nearly $27 million. This was much less than the amount originally sought by Frame and much more than the government's policies usually allowed for such projects. Harry Rogers, a federal deputy minister, was involved in the negotiations and would later describe Clifford Frame as "…personally abrasive and abusive … probably the most offensive persona I have met in business or in government." However a deal was struck and in September of 1991, at Westray's official opening, politicians at both levels lined up to congratulate each other. Nor did they hesitate to parlay their support into jobs for constituents. One phone call from a politician's assistant could result in the hiring of an inexperienced young man with the right family connections. Indeed, Bill MacCullogh had been able to jump from the development agency where his job included lobbying government to support the mine's development directly onto Westray's payroll. In August of 1991 he became the company's training officer.

RULES OF THE GAME

Mining is dangerous work. The first regulations to protect the safety of miners date back to 1873 and provided for the inspection of mines. In 1881 legislation allowed for the certification of miners and mine officials. The new rules also called for gas testing and banned smoking underground. This legislation, following a disaster in which sixty miners died, made Nova Scotia mines the safest in the world, according to one mining historian. In 1923 the age limit for working underground was raised from 12 to 16. (It would not be raised to age 18 until 1951.) By 1927, the maximum allowable level of methane in a mine was 2.5 per cent. At the time of the Westray explosion, a methane reading of 2.5 per cent required the removal of all workers from the site, while a reading of 1.25 per cent mandated the shutdown of electricity that could spark an explosion.

At the time the Westray mine exploded, the regulation of coal mining in Nova Scotia fell primarily under the *Coal Mines Regulation Act*, a 160-page piece of legislation considered thirty years out of date. An example of its anachronisms could be found in section 94 that outlined the duties of stablemen who tended the horses underground. The section provided for care of the horses and cleanliness of the stables. A further indication of just how out of date the legislation was, and how limited was its power to deter unsafe behaviours, was the fine schedule. The maximum fine that could be levied under the Act was $200. It also regulated the qualifications required for various levels of mining competency, including miners, managers, owners and inspectors. Most significantly, for Westray, the legislation regulated maximum allowable levels of methane. It also stipulated the removal of highly combustible coal dust and the spreading of limestone dust to neutralize its effects. The Act included provisions for roof supports and the prohibition of tobacco products and matches underground; it permitted worker inspections of the mines and limited shift duration to eight hours. All would become issues for public scrutiny after the explosion.

Operating in parallel was the provincial *Occupational Health and Safety Act* enacted in 1986. It imposed on employers the obligation to ensure workplace safety and to provide appropriate training, equipment, facilities and supervision. This legislation also required employees to take safety precautions, to wear appropriate clothing or equipment and to cooperate with employers, regulators and other employees in these goals. The Act also mandated joint occupational health and safety committees for workplaces with designated numbers of employees. These committees made up of both employer and worker representatives were charged with educating on safety issues, maintaining records, inspecting the workplace and responding to complaints. A key element of this legislation was a worker's right to refuse unsafe work and not to be discriminated against, or punished for doing so. The Act also provided that the legislation itself must be available for inspection by workers so that they might be aware of their rights. It also required employers to report to the regulators any accident resulting in an injury.

When the occupational health and safety legislation was passed, responsibility for enforcement was transferred from the provincial department of Mines and Energy to the department of Labour. Inspectors also retained jurisdiction over the *Coal Mines Regulation Act*. Both *Acts* authorized inspectors to order a work stoppage and the *Coal Mines Regulation Act,* under section 64, specifically empowered an inspector to order a dangerous mine closed.

TRAINING AT WESTRAY

William (Bill) MacCulloch began his job as the training officer at Westray on August 1, 1991, just over a month before the official opening of the mine. He had been on the job nine months when the mine blew up. Previously, he had worked as an economic development officer with the local municipality, providing information and support to the business community. In particular, he helped companies from outside the area that were considering investing in Pictou County. In this capacity he had brokered relations between Curragh executives and local contacts; he had lobbied government for funding and had promoted the project prior to the mine's opening. His connections in the community were extensive. Earlier in his career he'd worked both as a bank teller and radio personality. He had a high school diploma and a certificate in economic development acquired through part-time studies at the University of Waterloo, along with some accounting courses. He had no mining experience.

In his time at Westray, MacCulloch attempted to create a comprehensive training package that included certification in underground skills and equipment operation, mine rescue, health and safety, first aid and the handling of hazardous materials. Much of the training protocol was already enshrined in legislation. This was reflected, for example, in the employee manual that included, among other provisions the following:

Health and Safety Philosophy:
It's the personal responsibility of each member of the management team to ensure that the necessary education and training to equip all employees, to encourage a zero accident rate while reducing possible threats to good health and safety is provided…
…It's the personal responsibility of each supervisor to ensure that employees receive adequate training in work procedures so maximum productivity can be achieved within a safe work environment.

MacCulloch understood his job to be that of administrator of the program, ensuring schedules and facilities as well as sourcing materials and expertise.

Of particular importance at Westray was the training of inexperienced miners. Legislation stipulated a 12-month progression, under a "black tag" (certified) miner. In this time a miner would begin with basic labour and would gradually be introduced to and trained in the safe operation of the bolter, the continuous miner and other equipment. This period could be shortened to six months if systematic training took place at a work face in the mine designated as a training area.

MacCulloch developed a three day orientation program, building on a handbook already in existence when he began the job. He envisioned classroom modules on gas levels and safe ventilation, and practical demonstrations with equipment like the self-rescuer. His plan was forwarded to the provincial labour department as required.

THE UNION DRIVE

Bob Burchell had been a miner and mine inspector for almost a decade. In his current role with the United Mine Workers of America he organized union drives, lobbied for political and social reform, negotiated on behalf of miners and advocated for safe mining practices. He had trained at the Mine Safety and Health Administration (MSHA) Academy and returned annually to maintain and upgrade his credentials. He was unabashedly zealous in his work and could, on occasion, be loud, aggressive and profane.

Burchell had been on what he termed a "scouting" mission at Westray over the summer months of 1991. Some of his contacts had passed on the word that conditions underground were not optimal. Burchell positioned himself near the mine's entrance, hoping to catch miners coming or going. Early response was less than encouraging. He had to jump out of the way of the miners' cars as they raced on or off the property. "They knew who I was," he said. It wasn't long before management also delivered a message. Having refused Burchell access to the men at shift change, they sent a police officer to remove him. When Burchell persisted, management drove down the access road, parked nearby and either watched him silently or engaged him directly in conversation. One day, Gerald Phillips even sent his wife down to chat. To the miners, management presence at the entrance was a clear message.

Undaunted, and continuing to hear rumors of unsafe practices, Burchell established a base in nearby New Glasgow. A few emboldened miners stopped one day and talked to him. They told him about the use of farm equipment underground. They expressed concern for their safety but were pessimistic about the union's potential for a successful certification drive. They told

Burchell that many miners had moved to take jobs at Westray and would have to repay their relocation expenses if they stayed less than a year. Despite the miners' fears of repercussions, the union drive progressed slowly and under a cloak of secrecy. The men asked Burchell not to take notes at their meetings. A local woman, who owned the restaurant where Burchell often met the men, told him that she'd received a call from Bill MacCulloch at Westray. He had asked her, "as a long-time friend," to "keep tabs" on who was coming and going at the restaurant and to report back to him. Offended, she refused.

Burchell received permission from his Washington superiors to send union cards out in the mail instead of delivering them in person. Miners could sign them in the privacy of their homes and return them by mail. Meanwhile, information continued to accumulate painting a picture of ill-trained miners working without adequate safety knowledge. In one meeting, Burchell listened as one young man, a new miner, described his high-quality, stainless steel first-aid kit, issued to him with the words, "Here, this is in case of an emergency. Burchell realized the young man was unwittingly referring to his self-rescuer – the only thing between the miner and death in the event of a cave-in. "It blew my mind" said Burchell.

Ultimately, the union lost the certification drive by twenty votes.

A DAY IN THE LIFE[1]

The continuous miner roared, cutting coal from the face of the mine and loading it into shuttle cars for transport to a conveyor belt. A huge machine, it allowed previously unheard of quantities of coal to be mined in day. Pictou miners knew it was a far cry from the pick and shovels of their grandfather's mines and the explosives of their father's mines. The men at work that day were the usual mixed bag of experienced miners and untried "greenhorns." Like most days at Westray, even those with underground experience had gained it in hard rock mines, not coal mines. There were simply not enough certified coal miners in the area to fill the jobs. Claude White had granted the company an exemption under the *Coal Mines Regulation Act* to use hard rock miners in their place. Lenny Bonner and Shaun Comish were old friends and veterans of hard rock mining. They had been hired together and their pit talk this morning centred on a recent accident in the mine. A young kid, Matthew Sears, had his leg crushed when he tried to replace a roller on the conveyor belt. As he stood on the belt, it started up without the usual warning and his leg was jammed in a large roller. The men in the mine at the time had reported that Ralph Melanson kept pulling the safety cable to stop the belt, but it kept restarting. Sears had been through five surgeries since the accident and would be months off work. "Poor kid," said one to the other, "he told me that his first day on the job he didn't even know how to turn his lamp on." Roger Parry had sent him down alone to meet his crew and he'd stood there, shocked by how dark it was. Both Bonner and Comish recalled their first day at Westray. Without any orientation, they'd been issued their self-rescuers and sent underground. At the time they had laughed because neither of them understood much of what Roger Parry said to them. Between his British accent and his wad of chewing tobacco, they were lucky to catch half of what he said. Both men had progressed quickly underground from installing arches on the roadway and roof supports in the rooms being mined to operating equipment – drills, the bolter, the shuttle car. Neither had received any specific instruction. As Comish put it, "I got on it and [he] showed me what levers to move and what was your brake and what was your throttle and away you go." He recalled with some nostalgia the mine in Ontario where he had learned to drive a scoop tram in a designated training are, away from production. Both men knew that at Westray, the more equipment a miner could operate the higher his pay.

The continuous miner had come to a stop. This meant the methanometer or "sniffer" had detected too much gas. Comish pressed the reset button a few times to no effect. Bonner was running the shuttle car and waited. Comish overpowered the trip switch and kept filling the shuttle car. He disliked overriding a safety measure that was really for his own protection but he'd been shown how to do it and he understood what was expected. The mine's bonus system was simple: more coal meant more money. As he did every four days when he was back underground, Comish thought about quitting; he thought again about the roof over his family's heads and the food on their plates, sighed and got back to work. Some days, there was no need to override the sniffer. Comish recalled working in the Southwest section of the mine one shift when the methanometer wasn't working. Comish had turned to Donnie Dooley and joked, "If we get killed, I'll never speak to you again." Despite the jokes and the camaraderie, Comish couldn't escape the feeling that things weren't quite right. He decided that this day he just didn't want to be in the mine. He planned to tell his supervisor that he had to leave at five to get his car fixed – a harmless white lie.

Some of the men underground that day wondered when Eugene Johnson would be back from Montreal. His name had been selected from a draw to go to a ceremony where the industry association would give out the John T. Ryan award honouring Westray as the safest coal mine in Canada. The award was based on reported accident statistics. The men had laughed off the award since they knew management had "jigged" the accident stats to ensure a good record. Nonetheless, they didn't begrudge their co-worker and friend a trip to the big city. Johnson and his wife were scheduled to see the Toronto Maple Leafs play. They were having a big night out with Clifford Frame and his wife. The men were sure Eugene would have some good stories from his trip.

Bonner asked Comish if Wayne Cheverie was underground that day. Neither could recall seeing him at the beginning of the shift. With no tag system in the deployment area, at any given time there was no way of knowing who or how many people were underground. Lenny Bonner thought back to his time at the Gay's River Mine. The tag system there had been stringently enforced. One day, he'd forgotten to tag out, meaning that his tag was on the board and therefore, he was officially still underground. Although his shift boss had watched him leave the property, he could not remove a miner's tag from the board. Instead, Bonner had driven back, tagged out and his shift boss had been required to wait since he could not leave until all men under his charge were accounted for.

The men were interested in Wayne Cheverie because he was making a lot of noise about safety lately. Even back in September at the official opening of the mine, he had buttonholed Albert McLean after the ceremonies. Cheverie reported that he had told McLean many of his concerns about roof conditions and the lack of stone dust and asked him point blank if he had the power to shut the mine down. McLean told him no. Cheverie knew the outcome for other miners who had complained – harassment and intimidation. However, it was well known among the men that Cheverie was coming to the end of his rope. He was not only talking about complaining to the department of labour, but he was also threatening to go to the media. Recently, after refusing work, Cheverie had been told by Arnie Smith, his direct supervisor, that if he left the mine, he'd be fired. His response, "fired or dead, Arnie, that's not much of a choice, is it?" Bonner understood how Cheverie felt. A chunk of the mine's roof had fallen on his head one day. Bonner had gone home with a sore leg and back and an egg on his head. He'd had to fight with management to get paid for the day. Roger Parry had said, "We don't pay people for going home sick." Bonner had replied, "If you call the roof coming in and chunks of coal hitting you on the head and the back and almost killing you, you call that "going home sick!" Eventually he had been paid for the shift. He reflected that at least he was better off than that poor kid Todd MacDonald. On MacDonald's first day of work, there'd been a roof fall and the kid had been buried up to his waist. He was flat on his back, facing the roof, as if he'd watched it fall instead of running the hell out of there.

Bonner and Comish and a few of the other men stopped work for a quick and belated break. They often didn't get to their lunches until after their shifts. Bonner sat down with his lunch pail but jumped up again quickly. He had picked a spot too close to a pile of human waste but in the dark had not noticed it until the stink hit him. Back when he'd first started work at the mine, Bonner had spoken to mine manager Gerald Phillips about installing underground toilets. Phillips had told him that he was considering a number of different models. In the meantime, Bonner felt demeaned, like an animal forced to crouch on the ground like a dog. As it turned out, their lunch break was short lived anyway. Shaun Comish had warned the others that he saw a light approaching and the men had scattered like rats, fearing that Roger Parry was on his way down. With his usual profanities he would send them back to work. End of shift couldn't come soon enough.

★ ★ ★

DISASTER AND AFTER

Within minutes of the explosion, neighbours and family members began to gather at the mine site. Within hours local, national and international media had set up equipment and reporters in the community centre that served as their hub. Family members, in an arena directly across from the centre, where they awaited news of their loved ones, resented the prying cameras and intrusive questions. For six days they waited, they cried, they drank coffee; they smoked cigarettes and comforted their children and each other with hopes for a triumphant rescue. Each silently held close the tale of the Springhill mine disaster of 1958. After eight days, the last men there were taken alive out of the mine after the explosion or "bump." Their story remains that of the longest that men underground have ever survived in a mine disaster and the lore of their dramatic rescue resonated with fearful families.

Family and community, producers and reporters, along with viewers everywhere grew to know Colin Benner as the "face of Westray." He had been appointed to the position of President of Operations in April and had been responsible for the Westray Mine less than one month when it blew up. He had just barely begun the processes that he hoped would help dig Westray out of its financial hole. Production was short with the mine failing to provide the 60,000 tons a month to Nova Scotia Power for which it had contracted. Sales in the previous six months had reached $7.3 million but costs had exceeded $13 million. Benner had also heard rumblings about safety, about discontent among the miners and about the heavy-handed techniques of Gerald Phillips and Roger Parry.

All this however, was put aside as he dealt with the crisis. He served as media liaison, updating on the progress of the rescue efforts. By the sixth day he was showing the strain – his tie off, his sleeves rolled, his shirt creased and sweaty as his hands raked through his hair. On May 14th, with obvious sorrow, he announced the search was being called off. There was no hope that anyone could have survived the blast. It was simply too dangerous for the rescue crews to continue.

THE SEARCH FOR TRUTH

On May 15th, just the day after Colin Benner had announced that the search for the miners had been suspended, Premier Donald Cameron appointed Justice Peter Richard as a Commission of Inquiry into the explosion. His terms of reference were broad and mandated him to look into all aspects of the establishment, management and regulation of the Westray Mine. They specifically empowered the Inquiry to determine if any "neglect had caused or contributed to the occurrence" and if the events could have been prevented. A tangled web of legal proceedings held up the Inquiry for more than three years. In that time both provincial health and safety charges and federal criminal charges were laid, then withdrawn against the company and its managers. The Inquiry heard its first testimony on November 6, 1995. Justice Richard also undertook substantial study on coal mining and mine safety to prepare for the task. He visited mines in Canada and the United States and consulted with experts in South Africa, Great Britain and Australia. He commissioned technical reports from six experts in subjects that included mining ventilation and geotechnology. He commissioned academic studies in history, economics, psychology and political science. These reports provided him with insight into the history of mining in Pictou, the multiplier effect of large-scale employment on the communities, the impact of production bonuses on miners' behaviour and the role of ministerial responsibility in the public sector. The Inquiry heard seventy-one witnesses in seventy-six days of testimony and produced 16,815 pages of transcripts; it entered 1579 exhibits into evidence after examining eight hundred boxes of documents. The total cost of the Inquiry was nearly $5 million.

More than 20 miners testified before the Inquiry. All told similar tales of life underground with little training and less respect. They told of accidents never documented and management promises never kept. They told of conversations with Inspector Albert McLean that he testified never happened. The Inquiry questioned McLean about his response to Carl Guptill's complaints. McLean authenticated a memorandum to his director in which he stated, "in conclusion, I find no flagrant violation of regulation in this case." In a dramatic moment of testimony, shown repeatedly on television news, McLean admitted that he did not know what the word "flagrant" meant. Bill Burchell of the United Mineworker testified that prior to Westray he had felt great respect for Albert McLean, calling him responsible and efficient – "one of the best inspectors I've ever worked with." He said that his response to McLean's inaction was similar to the betrayal felt by a cuckolded spouse. Another pivotal moment in the Inquiry was the examination of former Premier Donald Cameron who blamed the accident on miners who smoked underground. Bill MacCulloch, Westray's training officer, acknowledged that he could produce no records of completed training and that he had assumed that the required supervised progression underground had occurred. He also testified that he had misrepresented to the board of mine examiners the hours of classroom training miners had received.

The Inquiry also felt the presence of a group that came to be known as "The Westray Families Group." Legal counsel represented the group and had standing to question all Inquiry witnesses. The group exerted its influence to ensure that the testimony of the miners would be heard "at home" in Pictou County but lost an application to have the entire Inquiry take place there rather than Halifax, the provincial capital and seat of government. Media coverage of the proceedings often focused on their taut faces and passionate pleas.

Justice Richard's findings are contained in a three-volume, 750-page report entitled, "The Westray Story: A Predictable Path to Disaster." He released his report on December 1, 1997. His key conclusion was that the explosion was both predictable and preventable. He acknowledged the 20/20 vision that accompanies hindsight but in specific, detailed and readable prose he isolated the many factors that contributed to an explosion that cost twenty-six men their lives, left over twenty women widows and over forty children fatherless. He set he tone of his report by quoting the French sociologist and inspector general of mines, Frederic Le Play (1806-1882) who said, "The most important thing to come out of a mine is the miner." In dedicating the report to the memory of the lost miners, Justice Richard, in the preface, stated, "the *Westray Story* is a complex mosaic of actions, omissions, mistakes, incompetence, apathy, cynicism, stupidity, and neglect." He noted with some dismay the overzealous political sponsorship of Westray's start-up but he clearly implicated management as the entity most responsible through its arrogance, its lack of training, its tacit and overt support of unsafe practices and its production bonus system. Only Colin Benner and Graham Clow, an engineering consultant to Westray, were singled out for praise. Each had attended the Inquiry without subpoena and at his own expense. They were the only Curragh executives to testify after numerous attempts to subpoena Clifford Frame, Gerald Phillips and Roger Parry had failed. Benner, in particular, offered key testimony on his plans for the mine. He had struck a Mine Planning Task Force to address the safety and production problems in the mine. His goal had been to design a safe and achievable mine plan that incorporated human relations and mutual respect among workers and managers. His plans had been cut short by the explosion. Justice Richard also noted the many failures of the provincial inspectorate, describing it as "markedly derelict." He singled out inspector Albert McLean for his incompetence and lack of diligence, but did not spare his supervisors to whom McLean's failings should have been obvious. Finally, he vindicated Carl Guptill. He concluded that McLean's treatment of him was a "disservice to a miner with legitimate complaints."

EPILOGUE

In 1993 a review by Coopers and Lybrand of Nova Scotia's Labour Department's management and practices recommended sweeping changes that included staff training, development and performance reviews. In 1997, a revised *Occupational Health and Safety Act* became law. In 1995, all criminal charges against Westray and mine officials were stayed for procedural reasons. In 1998, in embarrassed response to the findings of the Commission of Inquiry, the Canadian Institute of Mining, Metallurgy and Petroleum (CIM) rescinded the John T. Ryan award for safety, presented to the late Eugene Johnson on behalf of Westray on the eve of the explosion. In 1999, Alexa MacDonough, the federal leader of the New Democratic Party, an opposition party in the federal parliament, introduced a private member's bill in the House of Commons to amend the *Criminal Code* to hold corporations, executives and directors liable for workplace deaths. The bill died on the order paper after an election call. In 2001 the Nova Scotia Court of Appeal denied the Westray Families Group the right to sue the provincial government, concluding that such a lawsuit contravened provincial workers' compensation legislation. The Supreme Court of Canada upheld this in 2002. In May of 2002, ten years after the explosion and despite all lobbying and legislative efforts, Parliament was still considering the issue of corporate criminal liability.

Albert McLean and others were fired from their positions in the Department of Labour. Donald Cameron won a provincial election in 1993 but was defeated in 1998. Shortly thereafter he accepted a posting in Boston as Consul General to the United States. It was reported that Gerald Phillips had been charged with attempted homicide in Honduras as a result of an injury to a young man caught up in a protest to prevent a mine operation that threatened his village. A Vancouver based mining company subsequently hired Phillips in 1998. Although Curragh Resources dissolved into bankruptcy as a result of the explosion, Clifford Frame continued to attract investors and at last report was still developing mines. Roger Parry was last known to be driving a bus in Alberta. Many miners left Pictou County and looked for work in western and northern Canada. Carl Guptill operates an aquaculture business on Nova Scotia's Eastern Shore. Some of the "Westray widows" have moved, remarried and rebuilt their lives while others remain frozen in loss. The bodies of eleven miners remain underground.

END NOTE

1. All events described in this section are based on the sworn testimony of miners and other witnesses to the Commission of Inquiry. They are told here as if they happened on one workday. Except for this change in chronology they are an accurate depiction of work underground at Westray as described by the parties.

The Westray Mine Explosion
Teaching Note

TEACHING AND LEARNING OBJECTIVES

- To explore complex organizational behaviour at both the individual and group level. In particular, to examine motivation, decision making, conflict and culture;
- To identify the contextual realities within which the modern organization operates by encouraging students to integrate political, economic and social concerns in organizational analysis;
- To apply behavioural constructs beyond the specifics of case personalities, industry and geography
- To offer an alternative critical approach to analysis which will introduce students to a discursive framework and dialectical format;
- To challenge the assumptions of the market imperative, private ownership and the presumption that human behaviour can be "managed";
- To problematize power, truth, gender and culture as they inform organizational analysis in the case study format.

PEDAGOGY

The case is suitable for either an introductory undergraduate or MBA level course in Organizational Behaviour (OB). Sections may also be used in courses in Human Resource Management, Industrial Relations and Business Ethics. It may be used disjunctively in identified topic modules or may be used in complete form.

The case will sustain a 75-minute class on any of the individual topics or on a combination of related topics. Choice of approach may depend on time constraints and the depth with which a topic is covered. If the case were to be used throughout a course, familiarity with recurring facts and cumulative student knowledge would permit it to be used for a portion of a class (25-50 minutes). The case in its entirety may also be used as an end of term case assignment, a take-home examination or an in-class final examination of 2-3 hours.

The case is evaluative, rather than decision-oriented as must be all cases that reflect retrospectively on an event; however, it permits extrapolation to industries and organizations facing similar challenges. The incorporation of the social and political framework within which the Westray Mine was opened, and the inclusion of selected findings of Justice Richard's Commission of Inquiry, makes it an interesting case for instructors seeking rich material to explore various aspects of organizational behaviour in context. The case is divided into two parts. In the first part, topic modules have been linked to typical chapter breaks identified in popular OB texts. The focus is on group/organizational content, however individual constructs including learning, motivation and job satisfaction are also integrated. In Part 2, an optional (or complementary) critical approach provides students with an opportunity to challenge the more traditional and structured modes of case study in an integrative way.

Much of the information about the mine, the company, corporate structure and the Inquiry is now public record and is accessible to students in libraries and online through newspaper and magazine accounts as well as the transcripts of testimony and findings of the Inquiry. A bibliography and ancillary reading list are provided to direct students to some of these sources. The case itself provides sufficient information to permit wide-ranging application of OB theory as students evaluate the organizational events, decisions, actions and people involved in the Westray drama. However, also included are a number of optional questions and exercises that are beyond the immediate scope of the outlined case but which can be dealt with through exploration of website material. These optional questions/exercise, indicated with a double asterisk (★★), are designed for the instructor who wants to engage students in the process of researching case materials.

Part 1 of the teaching note begins with a summary of the case, followed by an introductory discussion on OB topics identified in a first reading of the case. Structured modules based on individual and related topics follow. Each topic includes a general guide to opening discussion, proposed questions and suggested responses. Also included are a number of group exercises intended to encourage more in-depth student analysis and experiential learning.

KEY ISSUES

Individual Behaviour and Processes

Learning:
- Explicit and tacit knowledge
- Behaviour modification and reinforcement

- Feedback

Motivation, applied motivation and outcomes:

- Motivation and rewards
- Job satisfaction
- Organizational commitment

Group/Organizational Behaviour and Processes

- Team processes
- Power and politics
- Conflict management
- Decision making and employee involvement
- Leadership
- Ethics
- Organizational structure and design
- Organization culture
- Organizational change

CASE SUMMARY

On May 9, 1992 the Westray mine in Plymouth, Nova Scotia (Canada) blew up, taking the lives of 26 miners working at the time. Shortly thereafter, the premier of the province appointed Justice Peter Richard to sit as a Commission of Inquiry, empowered by broad terms of reference, to look into the causes of the explosion. At the Inquiry miners, safety experts, engineers, Westray supervisors, union representatives, members of provincial and federal government and two former Westray senior managers testified. Justice Richard's report, released in 1996, described a workplace characterized by unsafe practices and an overriding concern for productivity. He did not spare Curragh Resources, Westray's parent company, its executives and managers in his assessment. He cited the company's tough negotiating stance to secure government backing, its autocratic style of management, management's contempt for miners who complained about safety and both tacit and overt encouragement of unsafe practices in the interest of production. Justice Richard was equally condemnatory of provincial mine inspectors who disregarded the complaints of miners and operated in a bureaucratic system unable to follow up, manage or enforce its own regulations.

The case provides introductory material on the social, economic and political contexts of Nova Scotia and Pictou County intended to situate analysis within a framework that may not be familiar to many students. Pictou's long history of mining the dangerous Foord seam of coal, its disproportionately high unemployment rates and its lack of alternative job opportunities provide a partial explanation why miners continued to work in conditions that many recognized to be unsafe. (Most behavioural analysis and virtually all writing on the mine attempt to answer this question.) In addition, the case explicates a complex series of political relationships among the company, the provincial government and the federal government. Zealous intervention by elected politicians led to controversial decisions by the province to invest $12 million in equity and to buy coal from the company for the provincial electrical utility and by the federal government to guarantee a $100 million loan.

The case tells the story in the words of many of the key players, primarily through their inquiry testimony and interviews conducted by a number of researchers subsequent to the explosion.

The case describes the interplay of these and other key players through the negotiations to establish the mine, its brief period of operation, the explosion and rescue and recovery efforts. The case concludes with commentary on the findings of the Commission of Inquiry and its fallout.

Supplementary material in reproducible format may be found in appendices at the end of Part 1 of the Teaching Note. These include:

Appendix 1: Summary of key players
Appendix 2: Resource list
Appendix 3: Industry note

PART 1: INTRODUCTION

Westray may be used as a recurring case throughout the course. An introductory class may be used to explore the multiplicity of OB topics raised. The instructor may begin with a very general question e.g., "what happened here?" To take students beyond event chronology, ask what OB topics they can identify, using the sub-topics of this teaching note to channel and prompt. It may increase context relevance to ask if any student comes from an area that is currently or was previously a mining community and to ask if students or family members have worked in mines or alternatively in primary industries or those characterized by physical labour and danger. Students from such communities may be prompted to recount what is particular about the nature of such work. If students minimize the relevance of this primary industry, note the increased role of technology in mining and the economic impact. (See Appendix 3 – Industry Note)

To extend the value of the case beyond its specific industrial context, return to the list of topics generated previously by students and inquire which of them only apply to mining. This will help students recognize that case studies serve as exemplars but apply beyond the organization/ industry studied.

TOPIC MODULES

I. Learning

This module flows naturally from the introductory session in which the events and industry were introduced. Consider opening the discussion by asking students about their own job-related experience. Why were they selected for a particular job and how did they learn how to do it? If the instructor has access to bio-data (e.g., introduction index cards or similar), prompt to elicit varying examples: retail, hospitality, manufacturing, construction or family-businesses.

Questions:

1. How did Westray management select, orient and train miners? Propose an outline for an orientation/training program that links learning theory to organizational outcomes at Westray.
2. Give examples of both explicit and tacit knowledge communicated at Westray.
3. Consider the relationship between behaviour and consequences to explain miners' actions.
4. What are the characteristics of effective feedback? What role did feedback play in Westray's operation?

II. Motivation, Applied Motivation and Outcomes, Stress Management

This module includes many of the elements of individual behaviour. In this section, students will address the complex question of why miners who knew just how dangerous this workplace was continued to go to work. In addition to assigned text reading, students should read: "Risk awareness and risk acceptance at the Westray Coal Mine: An attempt to understand miners' perceptions, motivations and actions prior to the accident" by Professor Gerald Wilde. He was commissioned to prepare this report for the Westray Mine Public Inquiry. The report is available at <http://pavlov.psyc. queensu.ca/faculty/wilde/ westray.html>. It has also been adapted and included in a collection of articles and essays on Westray edited by Christopher McCormick and noted in the case bibliography.

Instructors may begin the class with the broad question, "Why did these men continue to mine?" Students will cite the miners' need to sustain themselves and their families and may introduce the concept of greed arising from the production bonus scheme. They may be inclined to dismiss any possible psychological states/rewards to the job and will therefore need to be encouraged to consider that the job would hold inherent meaning to miners. This will provide a foundation for the later module on culture. The following questions may be used to link theory to this pivotal question; however, students should also be encouraged to identify the limits of the theories in addressing a complex, multi-dimensional case.

Questions:

1. How might a content theory and a process theory of motivation help to explain miners' decisions at Westray?
2. Propose a reward structure for Westray that you believe might have prevented the disaster.
3. Consider the role stress played in the Westray explosion. Which stressors might have been minimized at Westray? Is it possible, or desirable to eliminate stress?
4. What role, if any, did job satisfaction and organizational commitment play at Westray?

III. Team Processes – Power and Politics, Conflict and Negotiation

This module will provide a transition to group behaviour in a course that includes both individual and group processes or will provide an opportunity for introductory analysis in a separate course devoted only to the group elements of OB. In the latter instance, if the case was used for a prerequisite course in individual behaviour, it may be appropriate to provide a brief summary of issues considered at the individual level of analysis. This will remind students who worked previously with the case and will provide a bridge for students new to the case.

An understanding of the factors that influence team effectiveness is critical to meaningful analysis of this case, as the employees' failure to develop cohesiveness and their perpetuation of dysfunctional team norms underlie the inability of the miners to have acted in concert to speak out against unsafe practices. However, this inaction must be contextualized within an organization that was characterized from the outset by politics and conflict.

Questions:
1. Why did the first union drive at Westray fail?
2. **Why didn't the Health and Safety Committee have any effect at Westray?
3. Consider the five sources of power. For each source, identify a "player" in the Westray drama that exhibited the capacity to influence others through the power source.
4. Contingencies of power may limit the ability to exercise power. Use two of the contingencies to argue that Westray's miners lacked power.

IV: Decision Making and Employee Involvement, Leadership and Ethics
This unit continues to address the fundamental questions asked by many observers of the Westray Story:

- Why did miners decide day after day to enter the mine after consciously calculating that they had a 25% chance of dying there?
- **How did two levels of government justify ongoing commitment to the Westray project?

Students may express confusion and dismay at the miners' decision to work in unsafe circumstances, but will also often readily admit to having made poor decisions under imperfect conditions. The instructor may solicit examples of such decisions, for example, the choice of school or major, or a decision to drive or to engage in a dangerous sport after consuming alcohol. This may permit a fuller discussion of the frailties of the rational model and the distinction between decision theory in an economic or mathematical framework and in a context that incorporates human behaviour. In the case of Westray, two particularly salient concepts are escalation of commitment to a failing proposition and "groupthink" by all parties at all levels. Students may return to motivation theories in addressing these questions. As well, they may incorporate team processes and previous reflections on the failed union drive as they attempt to understand the complete lack of employee involvement in the mine. A particular challenge to the instructor will be to encourage students not to jump immediately to negative conclusions in evaluating leadership style and ethical standards of behaviour exhibited by Westray management. They may be encouraged to consider the challenges of operating under the time, financial and political constraints that guided much of the Westray chronology. The case indicates that despite the guaranteed market provided by Nova Scotia Power, the mine had lost nearly $6 million in the previous six months. Colin Benner, in his short time responsible for the operation, had recognized the effects of previous decisions and was seeking to implement a program to balance productivity problems against human resource issues including training and safety deficiencies.

Questions:

1. **The Commission of Inquiry into the explosion of the Westray Mine might be considered an elaborate exercise in evaluating decision outcomes. Using concepts rooted in decision theory, attempt to understand and evaluate the following decisions:

   (a) The decision of the Nova Scotia government to enter into the "take or pay agreement" to buy coal from Westray.

   (b) The decision of Carl Guptill not to return to work at Westray.

   (c) The decision of Albert McLean not to shut down the mine.

2. How would you characterize leadership at Westray and what impact did it have on the eventual disaster?

3. After the explosion, many expressed moral outrage at management practices at Westray. The Report of the Commission of Inquiry adopted a similar tone. Use the ethical principles of utilitarianism, individual rights and distributive justice to provide alternative evaluations of the organization.

V. Organizational Structure, Culture and Change

This is an integrative module that builds on previous material while incorporating capstone principles. It is critical in this module for students to understand the interrelationships between structure and culture as well as the influence on these issues of other preceding topics including conflict negotiation and leadership styles. Students will be challenged to incorporate previous material on team processes and employee involvement, as well as to consider how timely change might have prevented the explosion.

Questions:

1. Describe the main features of the structure at Westray and discuss how this may have contributed to the disaster.

2. Identify cultural artifacts that characterized the organization.

3. Discuss the role socialization played in the communication of organizational culture at Westray.

4. Contrast espoused and enacted values at Westray. Support your analysis with specific examples. (See expanded model and questions in Part 2.)

5. Colin Benner, in his testimony to the Westray Inquiry implied that had he been given the opportunity, he had intended to be an agent of change at Westray. Using Lewin's framework and other OB theories and concepts, write a memorandum to Mr. Benner proposing a plan for effective change.

GROUP ACTIVITIES

A: Systems and Knowledge at Westray

Break students up into small groups (3-5). Give them approximately 10 minutes to begin an analysis of Westray within a systems framework. Ask them to identify inputs, subsystems and outputs, as well as external environmental influences, and to identify key stakeholders in the Westray story. After a group reporting and the assembly of a "master list" of players on either slides or a board, ask the class to consider the issue of knowledge management as an alternative perspective. As a traditional industry, mining offers a classic opportunity for systems analysis and may appear unsuited to a knowledge-based perspective. However, have students consider critical junctures at which either formal or informal knowledge sharing might have prevented the explosion. What was the intellectual capital at Westray? Were communities of practice in evidence? This may provide a "jumping-off point" to the more specific questions asked in the Learning Module.

B: Theory in Action – The Job Characteristics Model

Divide the class into small groups (3-5). Half the class will be asked to use the Job Characteristics Model to demonstrate that lack of motivation and job dissatisfaction were inevitable outcomes at Westray. The other half will use the model to propose a program of work redesign that would have addressed many of the issues identified by miners, experts (and students) as having contributed to the explosion. Regardless of which side is argued, students must demonstrate a link between job design and organizational outcomes while using case facts to support their proposition. Students proposing redesign should identify the core job characteristics and focus on autonomy and feedback while those arguing for inevitable dissatisfaction will demonstrate that skill and task variety and task significance are less open to redesign. Students favouring redesign should provide specific recommendations to increase all three critical psychological states while those arguing against may focus on the difficulties inherent in making such work meaningful . Students should consider the relationship between Westray's lack of training and the concepts of job rotation, enlargement and enrichment. The instructor may choose to assign this one class ahead and have students come to class with a spokesperson identified and prepared to present and defend the groups' position. Randomly select one group representing each view, and have them present their thoughts in 5-7 minutes. Have other students evaluate the debate and contribute the conclusions of their groups. Debrief with a discussion of the value of theoretical models, and with discussion of the ambiguity of using "textbook" solutions and 20/20 hindsight to "solve" organizational problems.

C: Sources and management of conflict at Westray **

This role-play exercise is intended to give students the opportunity to place themselves in the positions of Westray miners, management, promoters, lenders and regulators. *Note that it requires additional preparation beyond case materials. In particular, it will require students to read transcripts of Inquiry witnesses available online.* The class will be divided into six groups of six or more students. (Note: The exercise may be adjusted to accommodate varying class sizes by including more or fewer parties in each group or by selecting among the groups and having students role-play only some of the situations.) Each group should be able to extract from the case sufficient information about their assumed roles to identify a point of conflict. Each group will then hold a meeting out of class time (either videotaped or with instructor present as observer, if possible) and attempt to address the conflict. It is important for students to understand that *a resolution to the conflict is not the goal of the exercise.* Rather, they should seek to identify the source(s) of the conflict, to recognize their own (in role) conflict management styles and those of others and finally, to create a plan for eventual conflict resolution. The case will provide the starting point for the process but students may be encouraged to access other resources in the case bibliography, in particular, the report of the Commission of Inquiry. This will assist them in understanding the complex relationships of the various players and incorporating realistic details into their portrayals.

In debriefing the exercise in class, a key point of discussion will be the multitude of examples of conflict in this story and the many opportunities for this conflict to be managed or mismanaged. The role assignments will overlap so more than one student may assume the role of a key player (e.g., Industry Minister, Donald Cameron or mine manager, Gerald Phillips). Students assuming either the same role, or those with overlapping interests should be encouraged to meet prior to the scheduled conflict meeting to share information and to enhance their understanding of the role(s). They may ultimately choose different approaches; however, this will invite valuable discussion after the exercise. (Note: The composition of the industry, of the company and governments of the day lead to an unfortunate dearth of roles for women. We suggest that this not be any consideration when roles are randomly assigned and that it be used as a discussion point in debriefing.)

Group One will include Westray management and members of the provincial government. The instructor will randomly select three students to assume the roles of Pictou MLA (and then minister of Industry, Trade and Technology) Donald Cameron, Deputy Minister for Industry, Trade and Technology, Tom Merriam and legal counsel to the department of mines and energy, Nancy Ripley-Hood. Three other students will assume the roles of the Westray Management team, Gerald Phillips, Marvyn Pelley and Clifford Frame. Remaining students may be evenly divided into advisors to each group.

Issue: The negotiation of the provincial government's contract to buy coal from Westray

Group Two will include Representatives of the United Mine Workers of America (UMWA) and miners who are considering signing union cards to certify the union. The instructor will randomly select three students to assume the roles of Bob Burchell of the UMWA and two representatives of the union's headquarters. All other students will assume the roles of miners both for and against a prospective union.

Issue: The certification of the union to represent Westray miners

Group Three will include miners and management. The instructor will randomly select three students to assume the roles of Arnie Smith, Roger Parry and Gerald Phillips; the other students will assume the role of miners. They may take on specific roles gleaned from the case and any other sources accessed.

Issue: Twelve-hour shifts and their effect on safety

Group Four will include miners and regulators from the Department of Labour. The instructor will randomly select two students to assume the roles of Albert McLean and Claude Smith; the other students will assume the role of miners. One student will be randomly selected to assume the role of Carl Guptill. Others may take on specific roles found in the case and adjunct resources.

Issue: Safety violations in the Westray Mine

Group Five will include Westray management and members of the media. The instructor will randomly select three students to assume the roles of Roger Parry, Gerald Phillips and Colin Benner; the other students will assume the role media personnel including print and broadcast reporters, editors and producers.

Issue: The lack of access to miners and their families throughout the rescue and recovery effort

Group Six will include the Westray Families Group and the Commission of Inquiry. The instructor will randomly select three students to assume the roles of Commissioner Mr. Justice Peter Richard, Associate Commission Counsel, Jocelyn Campbell and Families Group Counsel Brian Hebert. The other students will assume the roles of members of the Families Group, including spokesperson Kenton Teasdale and widow, Colleen Bell.

Issue: The Commission's decision to move the inquiry to Halifax upon completion of the Miners' testimony

Assignment Outcome

Each group will prepare a 5 -7 page reflection paper that outlines the experience of addressing the conflict. It should include identification of the source(s) of conflict, the styles of conflict management and how the conflict might be ultimately resolved (or why students have concluded that it is not resolvable). Finally, students should reflect on their experiences as they stepped into the shoes of the key players in the Westray drama. Did they feel a sense of identification? Did they come away with a sense of the complexity of organizational conflict?

APPENDIX I – KEY PLAYERS

- **Colin Benner**, the public "face" of Westray in televised coverage after the explosion and the only senior company executive to testify before the Inquiry. He was responsible for the mine operation for a very short time before the explosion and later testified that he had begun an action plan to address production and HR issues in the mine.

- **Donald Cameron**, a member of the provincial cabinet and active promoter of the mine in its infancy and Premier at the time of the explosion. In his testimony before the Inquiry he suggested that miners caused their own death in their failures to adhere to safety standards, in particular by smoking in the mine.

- **Clifford Frame**, the charismatic and persuasive CEO of Curragh Resources who exercised political know-how in bringing Westray to Pictou. His persona is that of the tycoon, or "rugged individualist" of earlier days.

- **Carl Guptill**, a Westray miner from a hard rock mining background, who was injured on the job and ultimately fired from Westray after complaining to Albert McLean about safety violations. McLean denied that Guptill had expressed concern but Guptill's version was accepted by the Inquiry and his experience vindicated. In testifying, Guptill believed he was upholding a sacred trust to the dead miners.

- **Alexa McDonough**, the leader of the federal New Democratic Party who attempted unsuccessfully to introduce legislation to criminalize corporate malfeasance like that identified at Westray.

- **Elmer MacKay**, the Member of Parliament for Pictou County, he was a congenial and popular politician who worked to exploit his personal and political connections to bring Westray to his area.

- **Albert MacLean**, a provincial mines inspector who was authorized to shut down the mine for safety violations and failed to do so. He was also found to have ignored the complaints of miners, noting that his "hands were tied". His disregard for the safety of Westray miners was in sharp contrast to his reputation among miners and unions as a professional and safety-conscious inspector. The Inquiry clearly did not accept his version of events.

- **Roger Parry**, the profane and authoritarian underground manager who threatened miners with termination when they expressed safety concerns.

- **Gerald Phillips**, the mine manager at Westray who cultivated an environment of risk in his subordinate managers as well as miners, in the interest of meeting production schedules.

- **Justice K. Peter Richard**, the judge appointed to sit as a Commission of Inquiry, conducted extensive research and became somewhat of an expert himself in coal-mining processes. He attempted in his proceedings to balance many competing interests and to maximize the information available to himself. He wrote a comprehensive and readable report that "pulled no punches" in affixing the responsibility for the explosion on the company, the government and the regulators.
- **Claude White**, the provincial director of mine safety and Albert McLean's boss, he appeared incapable of holding his inspector to legislative standards and excluding himself from political influence.
- **Westray Miners**, including Lenny Bonner, Wayne Chevarie, Shaun Comish, Matthew Sears, testified (along with many surviving co-workers) to the deplorable state of underground operations at Westray and the company's disregard for safety rules.
- **Westray Families Group**, brought together surviving family members to ensure their voice in the Inquiry.

APPENDIX 2 - RESOURCE LIST

Reading

Comish, S., (1993). *The Westray Tragedy: A Miner's Story*, Halifax: Fernwood.

Dodd, S.,(1999). "Unsettled Accounts After Westray," pp 218-249 in *The Westray Chronicles*, edited by C. McCormick. Halifax: Fernwood.

Glasbeek, H. and E. Tucker., (1999). "Death by Consensus at Westray," pp.71-96 in *The Westray Chronicles*, edited by C. McCormick. Halifax: Fernwood.

Goff, C., (2001). "The Westray Mine Disaster: Media Coverage of a Corporate Crime in Canada," pp.195-212 in *Contemporary Issues in Crime and Criminal Justice: Essays in Honour of Gilbert Geis.*, edited by H. Pontell, N. Shicho, and D.Shicho. Upper Saddle River: Prentice Hall.

Hynes, T. and P. Prasad,(1997). "Patterns of 'Mock Bureaucracy," in *Mining Disasters: An Analysis of the Westray Coal Mine Disaster.*" Journal of Management Studies, 34 (4), 601-623.

Jobb, Dean, (1994). *Calculated Risk: Greed, Politics, and the Westray Tragedy.* Halifax, NS.: Nimbus Publishing.

McCormick, C., (1999). "Preface to disaster," pp. 12-39 in *The Westray Chronicles*, edited by C. McCormick. Halifax: Fernwood.

McMullan, J., (2001). "Westray and After: Power, Truth and News Reporting of the Westray Mine Disaster," pp. 130-145 in *[Ab]using Power: The Canadian Experience*, edited by S.C. Boyd, D.E. Chunn, and R. Menzies. Halifax: Fernwood.

McMullan, J. and S. Hinze, (1999). "Westray: The Press, Ideology, and Corporate Crime," pp. 183-217 in *The Westray Chronicles*, edited by C. McCormick. Halifax: Fernwood.

O'Connell, C.J. and A. Mills, (2003). "Making Sense of Bad News: The Media, Sensemaking and Organizational Crisis." *Canadian Journal of Communication*, 28 (3): 223-239.

Richard, Justice K. Peter, (1997). *The Westray Story: A Predictable Path to Disaster*. Report of the Westray Mine Public Inquiry. Executive Summary: Province of Nova Scotia.

Richards, T., (1996). "The Westray Mine Explosion: An Examination of the Interaction Between the Mine Owner and the Media." *Canadian Journal of Communications*, 21 (3), 339-363.

Wicks, D. , (2001). "Institutionalized Mindsets of Invulnerability: Differentiated Institutional Fields and the Antecedents of Organizational Crisis." *Organization Studies*, 22 (1), 659-693.

Wilde, G.J.S., (1997). *Risk Awareness and Risk Acceptance at the Westray Coal Mine: An Attempt to Understand Miners' Perceptions, Motivations and Actions Prior to the Accident*. Report to the Westray mine public inquiry.

Websites

The following list comes with the caveat that websites change. A "Google" search for the term "Westray Mine" turned up over 1500 references, many pointing to a single published article or research paper. This list attempts to provide links to durable and reliable sources. Note that for some (marked with an asterisk★), entering the address will not always produce the site; however, linking from a broader search will often permit entry into the desired site.

• <http://libmain.stfx.ca/newlib/collections/westray/welcome.htm>. This site allows access to a complete and searchable set of Inquiry transcripts and is maintained by Saint Francis Xavier University. Justice Richard donated his entire collection to this library so it also lists all documents and exhibits available onsite at the library.

- <http://www.alts.net/ns1625/wraymenu.html>. ★This site is community led and acts as a gateway to many linked sites with wide perspectives on the disaster including news coverage and stories and poems. It is a site best reached by linking from a broad search.
- <http://pavlov.psyc.queensu.ca/faculty/wilde/westray.html>. This site provides the text of Professor Wilde's report to the Inquiry on risk and motivation of Westray miners.
- <http://www.newsworld.cbc.ca/flashback/1992/westlinks.html>. This site, hosted by the Canadian Broadcasting Corporations all-news channel provides archival coverage of the disaster, links to other sites (some live, some not at the authors' last check) as well as a link to a lesson plan for using Westray in grades 10-12 that is amenable to adaptation for undergraduate students.
- <http://www.cbc.ca/news/features/westray.html>. ★Again, this site is hosted by the Canadian Broadcasting Corporation and links much archival footage and radio broadcast available in streaming audio. This site also appears to be best reached by linking from a broader search.
- <http://www.littletechshoppe.com/ns1625/950013index.html>. This site is also a searchable set of Inquiry transcripts hosted by a community site. The authors have found the St.F.X. site above to be more complete.
- <http://www.infomine.com>. This site is a comprehensive database of information on coal mining worldwide with many useful and interesting links by country.
- <http://www.umwa.org>. This is the site of the United Mine Workers of America; it has many useful links organized by topic including links to legal sites governing mine safety in the US.
- <http://www.msha.gov>. This is the site of the Mine Safety and Health Administration where Bill Burchell of the UMWA trained.

Film

"Westray," directed by Paul Cowen, released in 2002 in recognition of the 10th anniversary of the explosion and available through the National Film Board of Canada. This film follows surviving miners and widows as they recount their lives since the explosion.

APPENDIX 3 - INDUSTRY NOTE

(Abridged from "Mining and Quarrying: Significant points" - US Department of Labor)

Mining is the process of digging into the earth to extract naturally occurring minerals. There are two kinds of mining – surface and underground. Underground mining is used when the mineral deposit lies deep below the surface of the earth. When developing an underground mine, miners first must dig two or more openings, or tunnels where they believe the coal is located. Tunnels may be vertical, horizontal or sloping. One opening allows the miners to move in and out of the mine with their tools and also serves as a path for transporting the mined coal by small railroad cars or by conveyor belts to the surface. The other opening is used for ventilation. Entries are constructed so that miners can get themselves and their equipment to the coal and carry it out while allowing fresh air to enter the mine. Once dug to the proper depth, a mine's tunnels interconnect with a network of passageways going in many directions. Long steel bolts and pillars of unmined coal support the roof of the tunnel. Using the room-and-pillar method, miners remove half of the coal as they work to the ore seams from the tunnel entrance at the edge of the mine property, leaving columns of ore to support the ceiling. This process is then reversed, and the remainder of the coal is extracted as miners work back out. In the case of long-wall mining of coal, self-advancing roof supports, made of hydraulic jacks and metal plates, are moved ahead, allowing the ceiling in the mined area to cave in as the miners work back towards the tunnel entrance.

In the US, in 2000, there were approximately 1450 mining operations in 28 states. About three-quarters of thee are located in three states – Kentucky, Pennsylvania and West Virginia. The United States remains highly dependent on coal as a source of energy as it is the cheapest and most abundant fossil fuel and accounts for half of the electricity production in the country. However, environmental regulations requiring cleaner burning coal with lower sulfur emissions is resulting in a regional shift from the eastern states to the west. There were approximately 77,000 jobs in coal mining in 2000. These included managers, geologists, technicians and engineers; however, the majority of jobs were in construction and extraction. Average earnings in mining and quarrying were significantly higher than the average for all industries. In 2000, production workers throughout private industry average $13.74 an hour, compared to $19.40 in coal mining. Wage and salary employment in mining is expected to decline by 14 percent through the year 2010 compared with 16 percent projected growth for the entire economy. This continuing long-term decline is due to increased productivity due to technological advances, as well as downsizing, stringent environmental regulation and international competition. Approximately 22.5 percent of mineworkers are union members or are covered by union contracts, compared to about 13.5 percent of workers throughout private industry. This number is slightly higher again for coal miners as about 24 percent of them are represented, primarily by the United Mineworkers of America, the United Steelworkers of America and the International Union of Operating Engineers.

Work conditions in mines are dangerous as a result of low roofs, darkness, damp and heat as well as the presence of combustible coal dust and gases. The rate of work-related injury and illness in coalmines was 7.4 per 100 full-time workers, compared to 6.3 for the private sector. The number of fatalities in coalmines continues to decline from its high of 3242 in 1907 to 27 in 2002. However, it is interesting to note that in 1992, the same year in which the Westray Mine exploded, 55 coal miners perished. The federal *Mine Safety and Health Act* of 1977 mandates that each US mine must have an approved worker-training program in health and safety issues. Each plan must include at least 40 hours of basic safety training for new miners with no experience in underground mines. In addition, each miner must receive at least eight hours of refresher safety training a year and miners assigned to new jobs must receive safety training relating to the new job. A miner with at least five years experience, or a degree in mining engineering, may qualify as a mine safety inspector. Before miners are allowed underground such inspectors check the work area for loose roofs, dangerous gases and inadequate ventilation. If the inspector finds sub-standard conditions, production is prohibited.

Once the coal has been extracted, the mine and its surrounding environment must be restored to the condition that existed before mining began. Mine operators, and environmental engineers must ensure that groundwater is uncontaminated and that abandoned mines will not collapse. The reclamation process is highly regulated by federal, state and local laws.

WESTRAY - A CRITICAL APPROACH

The purpose of this appendix is to assist instructors who wish to use the Westray case in the classroom and would like to incorporate a critical approach to case discussion. The material in this appendix may be used in conjunction with the primary teaching note to augment and enrich a more traditional case framework or may be used on its own to incorporate critical pedagogical methods.

An instructor teaching from this view will have already introduced the premise of a critical perspective. This is presumed to take a discursive approach to organizations in which the specific incidents of this case present a context in which to challenge the underlying foundations of traditional organizational thought. Instructors may use this perspective at the undergraduate level as counter-point to a traditional approach, as well as at the graduate level for students of management, sociology, philosophy or political science.

KEY ISSUES

The critical approach to Westray is organized around three theoretical issues:

- The problem of control;
- The implications of truth; and
- The question of culture.

This appendix provides guidance in structuring classroom discussion around each of these three "jumping off points." In contrast to the main teaching note, which reflects typical chapters and topics from mainstream OB textbooks, the primary text resource for this approach is *Reading Organization Theory: A Critical Approach to the Study of Organizational Behaviour and Structure, Third Edition* (2005) by Mills and Simmons. This appendix does not follow the text's specific chapter structure but rather includes conceptual material from throughout the text organized around the themes noted above. As such, the case may be used disjunctively as themes are uncovered, or may be used as a capstone assignment or examination case.

The Problem of Control

This theme facilitates an approach that focuses on the definition of and historical development of capitalism as the underlying assumption of organizing. It encourages students to challenge the market imperative while understanding the contextual growth of both private ownership and organization studies rooted in the model's prevalence. Sub themes may include Weber and the bureaucratic structure of organizing; Taylorism and the principles of scientific management; Marx and class struggle; Braverman and deskilling. This may be accompanied by a critique of the fields of OB/OT characterized by the "myth of objectivity" and a management focus that excludes the worker perspective from meaningful analysis. Ultimately, students will address the issues of control and power that characterize organizations and their members, including Westray management, miners, federal and provincial governments, unions, the public prosecution service, the Commission of Inquiry and the Westray Families Group. It will also encourage students to consider the discourse of safety and its marginalized role in management.

Ancillary Reading:

Edited version of "Death by Consensus at Westray?" by Harry Glasbeek and Eric Tucker (in *The Westray Chronicles*).

Group Exercise A: Organizing Around Westray

A starting point of discussIon might be to have students identify groups "organized" around the issue of the explosion. Students may need encouragement to consider this question, first at its broadest and then, more narrowly – for example, a subset of the provincial government organized around the promotion of the project, while another, the labour department, organized around the task of regulating the workplace safety of the mine. The instructor may construct a "master list" of identifiable organizations. Break students into groups (group size depending on both class size and the number of groups identified after encouragement). Have them meet as a group for approximately 15 minutes and, while assuming the perspective of the "organization" they represent, attempt to answer the following question in one sentence "What caused the mine to explode?"

Assemble a master list of the one-sentence responses. Debrief their responses with a view to uncovering the assumptions that inform them and the construction of these assumptions as a function of group membership. The class should be able to identify the vested interests of many of the groups including the deflection of blame and responsibility, the preservation of reputation and validation of the very existence of the organization.

Group Exercise B: Dialectical Tension in Theory and Practice

This exercise will encourage students in dialectical debate. Divide students into two groups and introduce as a proposition Weber's claim that bureaucracy favours the leveling of social class and the elimination of class privilege. Prior to class, instruct students to prepare a two to three page position paper either in support of or in contention to this premise. Students taking the opposing position should become familiar with Marx's views that bureaucracy protected the interests of the capitalist ruling class and that only through worker ownership of the means of production could class, and the bureaucracy be eliminated. Whatever position taken, students should use evidence from Westray in support. Randomly select students to present their positions in a debate format for the class.

If more structured support of discussion is needed, or as guiding questions for use of the case as an assignment or examination, the following questions may be offered:

1. Provide evidence that Westray was (or was <u>not</u>) a bureaucracy.
2. Apply the principle of "calculability" to analysis of Westray.
3. Discuss "the myth of consensus at work" and its application to Westray.
4. Consider Edwards' typology of control and characterize the control exerted at Westray.
5. Evidence at the Commission of Inquiry suggests that had the mine explosion not occurred, Colin Benner would have introduced more "humanistic" management at the mine. Would this have prevented the explosion? Why or why not?

The Implications of Truth

This section introduces students to the concept of truth claims. Post-modern in approach, this material is primarily intended to help students to identify the underlying assumptions of their own beliefs. They will also be encouraged to consider the dialectical tension of competing truths and to develop the analytical skills to question those who dominate the public agenda in putting forth their constructions of organizational reality.

Ancillary Reading:

Edited version of "Unsettled Accounts after Westray" by Susan Dodd (in *The Westray Chronicles*).

Edited version of "The Road to Recovery is Long" by Shaun and Shirley Comish (in *The Westray Chronicles*).

Executive Summary and Consolidated Findings of "The Westray Story: A Predictable Path to Disaster." Report of the Westray Mine Public Inquiry.

In addition to the Summary and Findings of the Inquiry, each student should also read an excerpt of testimony of any witness to the Inquiry.

To start discussion the instructor may want to return to the opening exercise in which students answered the question "what caused the explosion?" from various perspectives. (Alternatively, the exercise may be introduced here) The instructor may now facilitate a deeper discussion of how the identity assumed helped to construct the responses. Discussion may ensue around the partiality of each truth when taken individually and the amorphous nature of truth even when all perspectives are considered. Instructors may encourage students to think about the relationships of each party to structures of social power and how that informs an understanding of various events that comprise what we now know as "Westray." They should also consider the unspoken conventions and norms of behaviour that support each of these disparate accounts.

A key theme of this unit is consideration of the findings of the Commission of Inquiry. This has become the definitive narrative of the Westray story. Students must differentiate the critical stance clearly articulated by Justice Richard about the company's management from a critical analysis of the case, which must itself include Justice Richards' own words as a text available for examination. Instructors may use the formation of the Commission and its findings as themselves exemplary of the "disciplinary practices" of social response to the explosion. This may be juxtaposed to the Dodd article and its privileging of the families' narratives.

Questions:

1. Discuss the relationship between power and truth.

2. The Dodd article claims that consideration of marginalized voices has "rhetorical strength" and "symbolic potency". Do you believe that rhetoric and symbolism can unsettle dominant narrative? Why or why not?

3. Dodd uses the metaphor of accounting to support her premise. Does this metaphor enhance your understanding of her position? Identify a metaphor of your own and consider how it might explicate the puzzle of Westray and uncover "truth".

4. ★Each witness who testified at the public inquiry swore an oath "to tell the truth". Consider the nature of truth as it is defined in a courtroom setting and contrast it to your understanding of truth.

5. Does the contrast above influence your acceptance of the Inquiry's findings as "truth"?

The Question of Culture

This unit provides a more complex understanding of culture than that of the mainstream texts. It will question some of the traditional thinking on culture, in particular as it informs a discussion of masculinity and ethics. The approach taken here also challenges the functionalist premise that culture is amenable to managerial manipulation for the maximization of organizational performance. It presents a model that juxtaposes espoused and enacted values to help students understand how a culture of danger developed at Westray. This allows students to explore worker behaviour and how it contributed to the explosion without the normative implications of blame that characterized some previous analyses of miners' behaviour.

Figure 1

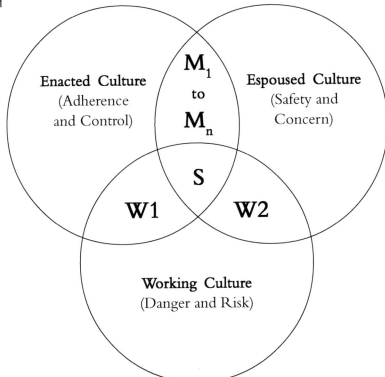

Figure 1, may be used as a framework to explore the disconnect between espoused and enacted values and the role this disconnect played in constructing a working culture in which miners and other underground workers appeared to accept a culture of danger and risk. The large circles show espoused and enacted values. The overlap signified by **M** illustrates the cultural space of management (e.g., its acceptance of the John T. Ryan award for safety while disregarding any role of a safety committee and threatening dismissal for workers that refused unsafe work.) The areas of overlap **W** illustrate the disjunctive response of workers. **W1** represents the worker(s) who confronted their dissonance but remained at Westray, contributing to the ongoing construction of the culture of danger and risk-taking. By living this working culture, they unconsciously shared it with new, less experienced miners and perpetuated it despite the continuing awareness of its potential for disaster. **W2** represents the worker(s) who responded to the cultural disconnect by leaving. (e.g., Carl Guptill) Finally, the space occupied by **S** represents that of supervisors who experienced the value collision of safety versus production. They ostensibly shared the cultural landscape of management in title and in their legislated responsibility for worker safety, but were impotent to act. Simultaneously, they worked underground with workers, sharing the experience of danger. The model disputes the mainstream view that culture may be imposed and managed. Students may suggest that the acceptance of danger to the benefit of production is exactly the culture sought by Westray management. However, this would not account for the more complex awareness of most workers. Nor, does it account for some supervisory acceptance of managerial approbation for lower production. A traditional, or integrationist perspective would identify those aware (e.g.,those at the breakfast meeting at Roy Feltmate's home) as a sub-culture and those that protested, and/or left employment, as a counter-culture. (e.g., Carl Guptill) This perspective fails to account for inconsistencies in behaviour such as articulating knowledge of danger, expressing a desire to stay home, yet ultimately going to work.

Such behaviours may also be explored through the lens of a study of masculinity. The case presents opportunities to consider the gendered nature of some work. Westray miners have spoken of mining as being "in their blood." They refer to father, grandfather and uncles who worked in mines and the work is seen not as a job but as a cultural legacy of demanding, physical work with the rewards of camaraderie and male community. Others have disputed this, claiming no such romanticized view existed. However, these miners often instead explained their actions within the equally gendered context of the family provider. The dignity of employment and the ability to care for a family were repeated often in explanations of Westray miners' choices.

An exploration of culture also permits the opportunity to discuss the role of ethics in corporate life. Recent ethical upheavals in the financial sector will illustrate the currency of this issue and its broad application. The approach proposed here is that ethics, and codes of ethics, have become window dressing to enhance a corporation's instrumental value. In the case of Westray, concern for worker safety was a manifestation of such ethical pretense. The ensuing failure of criminal prosecution of Westray management provides a context in which to consider overlapping concepts of morality, ethics and legality as they are played out in corporate construction.

Group Exercise C: Life or Death in the Dark[1]

In this exercise students will attempt a familiar manual task in the dark. This presents an interactive but safe opportunity to simulate an underground environment.

Students will each be given a package containing commercially manufactured cracker snacks containing crackers and spreadable cheese. They will receive no instructions at the beginning of class other than not to touch or open the package. In the midst of class and with no warning, shut off the classroom lighting. (If there is natural light, make every effort to block it prior to class or plan ahead to relocate the class to a room without windows.) Instruct students to open the package and remove two crackers; spread the cheese on one cracker and top it with the other like a sandwich. The first person to do so should indicate by calling out "finished" at which point the instructor may turn on the lights, indicate the number of seconds taken to complete the task and evaluate the quality of the finished product – is the spread on evenly? Are the crackers lined up with each other? How much mess did the worker make of both the workspace (desk) and her/his hands?

In debriefing, acknowledge that such an example may trivialize the genuine dangers and challenges of underground work but that it may for a moment have given students insight into the challenges of intricate work in the dark. (Note the questionable ethics of attempting to simulate danger with students.) A key failing of Westray was the lack of training given to miners in donning their self-rescuers (emergency breathing devices). Clive Bardauskas, a British miner, testified that in the UK his training had included simulations in which a new miner had to demonstrate competence in putting on the self-rescuer in 15 seconds. Mine management reinforced this with a program of annual training refresher drills. This illustrates for students both the real and ethical implications of the failure to train Westray miners, and the failure to inculcate a real culture of safety.

Questions:

1. Consider an event or experience in which your espoused and enacted values were in conflict. What did you do? If you acted contrary to your espoused values, what were the repercussions? Do you believe that such behaviour affected (or might affect) others around you?

2. Using the example of a job you have worked in, characterize it as "masculine," "feminine" or "neither". How did this manifest and what were the implications both for you and for others?

3. Go to the website of the Canadian Centre for Ethics and Corporate Policy. <http://www.ethicscentre.ca>

    (a) What is the purpose of the organization? Evaluate this purpose critically.

    (b) What does the Centre say about Westray?

    (c) Locate a similar organization dedicated to corporate ethical behaviour in the US Would its standards have helped to prevent an accident like Westray?

4. Do you believe that corporate criminal liability for managers would prevent another Westray? Why or why not?

END NOTE

1.   The authors thank Terrance Weatherbee, Saint Mary's University for assistance in this section, in particular with the culture model and the exercise.

For Your Eyes Only[1]

Gina Grandy

A CAREER DECISION

For Your Eyes Only (FYEO) is a large chain of exotic dancing clubs operating in the United Kingdom and internationally. FYEO markets itself as a "gentlemen's club" with upscale entertainment and surroundings. In this manner it distinguishes itself from competitors with its policy of escorting customers to their seats, table-side waitressing, elaborate and comfortable surroundings with plush chairs, no contact policy imposed upon both dancers and clients, and protection provided to dancers (e.g., escorting them to their cars, taxis). Some of the clubs provide both topless and full nude dancing (e.g., London) while others (e.g., Newcastle) offer only topless dancing.

It is February 2004 and Sherry,[2] who has been working at FYEO in Newcastle since it began operations in November 2002, is contemplating her future. Prior to her time at FYEO she danced for a year in London. She feels it is now time for a change and plans to start looking for a job relevant to her degree in accounting over the next few months so as to leave FYEO in the spring. She is not really interested in working in accounting and would rather work in public relations. However, she views her degree in accounting as the means that will allow her to make the transition from FYEO to another career path, after which she can then consider the direction of her future career. She is worried that if she does not leave soon, within five years from now, she will still be in the industry. Sherry started in the industry for financial reasons. She saw an advertisement in the paper for hostessing, and was not aware at the time that the organization was actually looking for exotic dancers. She became aware of the nature of the job at the interview, but thought she would give it a try, and has stayed in the industry ever since. The financial benefits from dancing afford her a comfortable life to be able to go out when she wants, live where she wants, and she has gained an overall sense of independence. Her thoughts of leaving the industry have been stirred by several events. Firstly, she has lost interest in the work and feels it has become monotonous. Secondly, it has become less busy during the week, making it difficult to earn as much, and this has affected her motivation. This time last year on a Tuesday night she might make £200 but now she struggles to make £100. Management maintained the same number of dancers working nights despite the decreased business. Now, before she comes to work, she tries to do anything she can to get out of it, for example calling other dancers to cover her shift. Sherry also feels there have been changes in management recently and this has stirred a lot of discontent. Over the last few months the club has doubled the house fees dancers have to pay every night in order to work. Some dancers have been fired, or have decided to leave due to problems with management. With no real options in the exotic dancing industry in the Newcastle area, other than a full nude establishment, the dancers can stay and accept it as is, or leave.[3] Circumstances in her personal life also play a role in her consideration of changing jobs. While her fiancé has been supportive of her working as an exotic dancer, when she told him she was thinking of leaving he was delighted. His reaction reinforced her stirring thoughts of leaving the industry. Leaving however, is not as easy as it appears. In a new job she will likely only earn a quarter of what she presently earns at FYEO. Some dancers continue to work part time while developing a career elsewhere, but Sherry does not want to do this. Working in the industry part time will only draw her back into the industry rather than serve as a mechanism to facilitate her shifting career paths.

The Industry

Some dancers, managers and owners make distinctions between exotic dancing and other forms of sex work, but these establishments can be broadly categorized as falling under the sex industry. Sex work is defined as a form of sexual or erotic labour that entails a variety of activities including prostitution, "gogo" dancing, stripping, phone sex, pornographic video production and dominatrix work. Sex work is, and occurs within, a complex network of social, political, cultural and economic space in which prescribed sexual and gender roles are often (re)created and sustained. The sex industry includes the organizations, workers, managers, and owners involved in sex work. Exotic dancing is defined as a form of sex work that involves either topless or nude dancing. These exotic dancers are referred to and refer to themselves as strippers, entertainers, "go-go" dancers, lap dancers and dancers. The term "sex work," however is often used to overgeneralize without acknowledging differences between and within categories of "sex work." Within exotic dancing there are a variety of contexts in which workers may be expected to work (e.g., no contact/contact, topless/nude). And even organizations that offer seemingly similar services, there are likely to be differences in the "culture" of the organizations and in the experiences of different individuals. For example, FYEO establishments in South Hampton and Newcastle only offer topless dancing while in London, FYEO offers both topless and full nude dancing. In London the competitive environment is more intense, and this in turn affects the nature of the job for dancers, managers and customers.

While tableside dancing in the United States has been around since the early 1970s, in the UK it is a relatively recent phenomenon with the first club opening in 1994. The industry is still in its infancy and highly fragmented in the UK, but most major cities have some form of exotic dancing establishments operating. The influence of the US has been, and continues to be, significant on the industry. One of the first lap-dancing clubs, Cabaret of Angels at Stringfellows, was opened in London by Peter Stringfellow. Stringfellow operated a club in New York for three years before launching the idea in the UK. Recently, the intensity of rivalry is increasing and Spearmint Rhino, a large US chain, has played a crucial role in defining the rules of the industry. Spearmint Rhino, starting with two clubs in the London in 2001, has plans to open 20 to 30 clubs in the UK over the new few years. The industry has also seen shifting norms from topless only to full nudity, even in its "gentlemen's" clubs. FYEO, a topless only club since its inception in the mid 1990s, now operates with a license for full nudity in its clubs, although not all clubs have implemented full nudity (e.g., South Hampton, Newcastle). Licensing bodies have become more relaxed in issuing licenses (i.e., full nude licenses). Felix, a manager in London, feels that the competitive environment in London is different from the rest of the UK, and changes rapidly. In order to keep up with competition, the club had to implement full nudity or the customers would go elsewhere.

A Gentlemen's Club

In 2003 the family-run Ladhar Group acquired four of the For Your Eyes Only (FYEO) table dancing clubs, part of a larger chain of FYEO clubs in the United Kingdom and internationally. The Ladhar is a diversified company with its portfolio including nursing homes, cafés, restaurants, houses, pubs, clubs and hotels.

FYEO markets itself as a "gentlemen's club" with "upscale" entertainment and surroundings. While the clientele is primarily heterosexual males, females are often included in its broad spectrum of clients. Overall, most dancers at FYEO prefer to work in a "gentlemen's" club and claim that workplace arrangements are better than the experiences, directly or indirectly, they have had with less "upscale" establishments.

THE NATURE OF EMPLOYMENT

Employment arrangements: Common to the industry, FYEO dancers are self-employed. They pay house fees to FYEO on a nightly basis in order to dance at the establishment. In general, FYEO requires the dancers to pay FYEO a start-up fee at the beginning of the night and the rest of the house fees towards the end of the night. The amount varies depending upon the week night and the level of business. Overall, on any night approximately one quarter of their earnings are paid to FYEO. Some establishments in the industry can charge the dancers up to half of their earnings on a given night. While all dancers pay the same amount, there are nights where some dancers find it difficult to pay the required amount because they may not have had many dances during a shift. In these circumstances management will often allow the dancer to pay the outstanding house fees on the next shift. While the dancers themselves may have some concern over the fee structure there is no real mechanism through which their voice can be expressed. Any dispute about paying house fees will likely result in the dancer losing her job.

Working schedules: The dancers can decide on a monthly basis how often and when they prefer to work during the month. Management tries to regulate and monitor this by insisting that the dancers balance their schedule to include shifts on less busy (e.g., early week nights) as well as busy evenings (e.g., Thursday onwards). Management is constantly trying to ensure that the pool of dancers is growing. This is necessary for at least two reasons. First, turnover in the industry is relatively high, with dancers frequently moving to other establishments or leaving the industry. Second, a lot of the dancers are friends and request time off (e.g., for holidays) during the same periods. A large pool of dancers provides management with flexibility and better control of the dancers they employ, and the number working on any given night.

House rules: FYEO also employs a set of house rules, some enforced more stringently than others. Dancers must be at work at a certain time to ensure that they are on the club floor as soon as it opens for early clients. If not, monetary fines (e.g., £10) are issued. Excess drinking is also seen as an issue to be monitored by management. Management requires dancers to drink in moderation. It is expected that dancers engage with clients, which often entails accepting offers for drinks. Clients are more often willing to buy dancers a drink than a dance from them. Dancers that are seen to be inebriated will be fined or suspended up to a month. The fine system is not viewed as a profit making exercise by management, rather as a deterrent for unwanted behaviour.

Dancers that prefer to moderate their drinking, or not drink at all, develop strategies for limiting their intake of alcohol, while not refusing any offers of drinks, by asking the waitress to give them non-alcoholic drinks without the client's knowledge.

Recruitment: Given that turnover is relatively high in the industry, FYEO is constantly hiring new dancers. While most recruitment is through word-of-mouth, the club does advertise auditions from time to time. Auditions are generally run weekly, whereby dancers come in and perform on stage briefly for management members. Selection is based primarily upon the physical appearance and stage presence of the individual. The objective for management is to ensure that they always have a balanced mix of dancers (e.g., height, hair colour, race) in their pool to meet customer demand. Dancers are also referred to the club by managers of FYEO, doormen of FYEO and other clubs, as well as by others dancers. Krissy had been working elsewhere when it was suggested to her by the doormen of the club where she was working, that she should audition at FYEO. The doorman contacted FYEO and inquired about an audition on her behalf.

Pole dancing classes are also used as a mechanism through which individuals are recruited to FYEO. In London, FYEO operates a pole dancing school whereby individuals can participate in classes taught by dancers of FYEO. The participants for these classes have different motives for attending, ranging from a desire to become a pole dancer to those wishing to increase their confidence. With celebrities such as Danny Minogue, Britney Spears, and Kate Moss participating in these classes, pole dancing may become a growing trend. A group of fifteen attendees to a dance class will result in three or four auditioning at FYEO.

Management: The exotic dancing industry is a male-dominated field. Management at FYEO, and across the industry, consists primarily of males. Some locations have a "House Mother" whose responsibility is to act as a go-between the dancers and management. The effectiveness of such positions is debateable. Management feels it is sometimes useful for the dancers to have someone with whom they can feel comfortable discussing personal issues. However, there is some concern that the "House Mother" serves the interests of the dancers at the expense of the management (of which she is considered a part). Some dancers advocate the need for more female managers or owners as a means through which clubs could better balance the needs of the dancers and the customers. Felix, a manager in London, feels that about 90 per cent of management in the industry are males and that the females that come into management generally do so with an agenda to open their own club and eradicate the issues they experienced as a dancer or manager in the industry. He also feels that females in management in the industry face a paradox. As a manager they make far less money than the dancers themselves and are constantly faced with the lure of dancing rather than managing. In addition, while he does know of successful female managers in the industry, in his experience the dancers tend to be more critical of female managers than they do of male managers, and this often deters females from entering and staying in management.

THE DANCERS

Demographic Profile and Motivations: The demographic profile of dancers is diverse. There is no typical dancer. Generally, in the UK, dancers range from 18 to 30 years of age. Most identify economic reasons as the primary motive for entering and continuing dancing. Their backgrounds are varied, with an increasing number of students working at FYEO as an alternative to working in restaurants or clubs earning minimum wage.

University students feel dancing provides them with higher income, more flexibility and less working hours than other employment options, such as waitressing, bartending, etc. Krissy, for example, was tired of working for £4.50

an hour in a demanding job and decided to go to the audition without giving much serious consideration to whether she would be hired. Krissy emphasises the financial motivator over any other. For her, the job is not something most people would find particularly enticing. She likes the idea of the money, and cannot understand any other reason for dancing, " who likes getting dressed up and talking to sleazy men?" Her view is not held by all dancers. Some dancers enter the industry partly due to the glamour associated with the job, while others find the job empowering and rewarding beyond the purely financial. Elizabeth is motivated both by the financial benefits and the corresponding lifestyle that the increased income facilitates.

> I think it was the lifestyle really. I mean I was a student when I first started doing it and I worked part time in a call centre and it was kind of like the lifestyle. My friend used to come in and she used to be out all weekend and come back with all this money and all these nice clothes and stuff and I thought well if she can do it, I can do it.

Some dancers are working at FYEO while working elsewhere and for some it is their sole form of income. Jenny earns more in one night dancing than she did in her fulltime job on a weekly basis. Amy started dancing as a means to finance her world travels. She wanted to travel around the world, so she decided to earn money dancing as a means to finance her travels without long term saving. She said she dances for a few consecutive weeks, travels for a couple of months, then dances again for a few weeks, travels again, and so on. Overall, a feeling of financial security generating a sense of freedom and control over their lives emerges from the stories of the dancers.

For many dancers, financial "freedom" is also complemented with feelings of empowerment through increased confidence and control. Maddy attributes her career in dancing to increasing her levels of confidence in her physical appearance, interpersonal relations and sense of self.

> Stripping has completely changed my life, apart from being more confident and less, like you know, ashamed or embarrassed or trying to cover your body up in swimming on beaches or at the gym, now I just go around naked and I absolutely think nothing of it. One of the most major things really is men. Out on the streets before, if a man was to like harass me in some kind of way, like all women get at one point or another, I would, like other women, get really scared or just a bit embarrassed, or a bit angry or whatever. Now like, I feel so strong, really above men. Before I didn't feel like that at all.

Not all dancers, however feel empowered by their employment. Jenny feels the job is demoralising. She is disgusted by the fact that she has an anthropology degree, cannot find relevant work, and is dancing instead. She has great contempt for the industry, co-workers, clientele and herself for being a part of it. In addition, as in the case of Maddy, while many are empowered in some way by their jobs, dancers also experience a plethora of emotions at different points of their times as a dancer.

Stigmatization: The sense of freedom is challenged by the stigmatisation that dancers confront on numerous sides from family, friends, partners, customer, managers, and the public. There is a lot of diversity in the extent to which dancers are "open" about the nature of their employment. The dancers that are completely "open" about their jobs to their friends, family and partners are rare. Both Amy and Elizabeth have told everyone of significance to them about their work. However, both these women still use stage names as a means of separating themselves from their jobs. It is more common that dancers confide in close friends and partners, but not confide in their parents. Reasons for not openly discussing their occupation seem to be underpinned by public perceptions of the image of dancers, dancing and the sex industry as a whole. Some dancers find their relationships with partners strained because of the nature of their job. Maddy met her present boyfriend since she started dancing. Her job is often a cause of disagreement between them. Her partner appears not bothered by the nature of her job for a couple of weeks and then the topic surfaces again. She has real concern and a resulting sense of insecurity over the strain her job has on their relationship. Perceptions of the image of dancers, the organisations and the sex industry as a whole affect dancers' sense of self. In addition, the stigma affects their relationships with friends, family and partners. Interestingly, the stigma associated with the industry also affects dancers' perceptions of men associated with the clubs.

The dancers sometimes experience negative reactions from customers and men in general, given the image of dancers as promiscuous, cheap, and as objects of beauty but no brains. Some men are disgusted by the dancers and think they are "dirty," while other clients assume that the dancers are also prostitutes and inquire as to how much it costs for sexual services beyond the table-side dancing. Krissy and Elizabeth feel that men view and treat them differently once they know they are strippers. Furthermore, dancers feel that customers often push the line because they feel the dancers are not the sorts of people they would meet on the street. Customers inquire about far more intimate details of the dancers' personal lives because customers have preformed conceptions of the "types" of individuals that dance.

Some dancers feel that the stigma associated with the industry affects the way managers view and treat them. Dancers recall incidents where managers come into dressing rooms and linger in order to see the dancers naked. This disturbs the dancers because of the assumption that because they are dancers their bodies are there to be exploited by anyone at anytime. Amy worked at one club where the managers use vulgar language when addressing the dancers and treat the dancers like prisoners. At this particular establishment the dancers are not allowed to go out for any reason after work hours, and overall, management are very controlling. Comparing that establishment to FYEO, Amy feels the managers at FYEO are really respectful and treat the dancers well. She does feel, however that there are real concerns about the structure of the sex industry as it pertains to exotic dancing and with management attitudes and perceptions of dancers.

Truths about exotic dancing and sex work in general appear to be created, negotiated and sustained by various stakeholders and structural conditions. Dancers themselves enact stigma constituted by power relations in their demonstration of contempt for customers of exotic dancing, as well as for their fellow dancers and across the industry as a whole. The whole industry is fraught with stigma and the dancers often sustain this stigma.

The dancers [re]create a hierarchy amongst themselves in more than one respect. Firstly, students distinguish themselves from the dancers who dance fulltime, that is, those who dance as a fulltime, permanent job. Most students emphasise the fact that they work only to fund their education, thus deeming it a legitimate reason, and that they do not intend to remain once they finish their degrees. While most student/dancers do not say they feel there is something abnormal about working in the industry, they do feel the need to set themselves apart from the rest of the dancers. Many of the student dancers also feel that they, too, will only dance for a short period and plan to go back to university full time in the near future. Other dancers emphasize the temporality of their employment to serve as a means to travel, save money for future investments, pay off debts, etc. to separate themselves from "the others." It appears that dancing as a means to an end is therefore more legitimate than dancing for its own sake or as a long term career decision.

Disciplining the body: The exotic dancing industry places heavy emphasis upon the appearance of the dancers, including their weight, dress, make-up, breasts, and hair. Many dancers are very aware of the temporality of their jobs as dancers given the impact of ageing on their appearance (e.g., weight, breasts, agility). Felix has worked with dancers that were up to 43 years of age, however this is rare. It is more likely that after 30, for various reasons, individuals do not continue dancing. Elizabeth was unsuccessful in her first attempts at an audition, even though she had taken a diploma course in pole dancing from FYEO. She was told that she needed to lose weight to become a dancer. She then came back two weeks later after having lost weight, auditioned again and was successful.

The dancers are also expected to dress in custom made dresses and change outfits several times during a shift. The ceremony of achieving the appropriate appearance involves a range of activities that vary from dancer to dancer, from applying make-up, having tanning sessions to surgically enhancing their breasts. The importance of appearance is also evident in the selection requirements at FYEO. Felix feels that the "standard" of dancer has dwindled since the industry went fully nude. He attributes it partially to the turnover of many dancers who were dancing while modelling part-time, doing print work and promotional material. Many of these dancers were unwilling to dance fully nude and likely have gone back to what they were doing part-time rather than continue dancing as a means of income.

Emotion Management: Most dancers liken their work to that of performers, such as professional dancers, actors, and so on. For them, dancing involves putting on an act in order to fulfil the fantasy of customers, primarily men. Notions of emotional management through assessing whether customers want you to be extroverted or introverted, demonstrating interpersonal skills and even detachment while engaging clients are integral components of their jobs. While clients vary greatly, dancers describe typical clients as men who are lonely or depressed and looking for attention. Dancers are there to fulfil fantasies of men who otherwise would not have such individuals giving them attention.

Some of the dancers and management use the notion of fantasy to distinguish table-side dancing from other parts of the sex industry (e.g., contact clubs, prostitution). Firstly, the notion of "gentlemen clubs" as a positioning strategy is a means through which dancers, management and organisations alike differentiate themselves from others. Establishments where dancers are well-dressed, made-up, well spoken and presented, where managers are dressed in suits, where waitresses come to your table rather than you going to the bar, and fine wines and champagnes are on offer serve to create the "gentlemen's" fantasy. In addition, the no-contact premise reinforces the notion of "gentlemen" and creates a distinction between reality and fantasy – you can look but not touch.

FYEO EXPANSION?

FYEO had establishments operating in other locations in the UK prior to opening its doors in Newcastle in November 2002, but the community discontentment surrounding its opening was high. On its opening night, demonstrators took pictures of customers as they entered or left the club. The reactions from various stakeholders, including licensing magistrates, city councillors, members of Christian groups, Rape Crisis centre, students' unions, employees, management and owners, are varied and complex. They range from claims of increasing violence against women, to causing marital problems, to exploiting women in an area plagued by low wages, to providing more flexible working arrangements, to empowering women.

FYEO was the centre of debate again in the fall of 2003, when it was granted a license request for an additional FYEO in Newcastle only after an appeal decision. Various groups, including city councillors and other community groups, expressed concerns over another club operating in Newcastle. Glenn Nicie, FYEO director, at the time hoped the public involvement would be less controversial than when they opened their first establishment in Newcastle two years prior.

> I hope they'll not be any objections this time. Last time we made an application there were a lot of fears but we understood those as we'd faced them and they have proved to be unfounded. We provide a safe, friendly environment. It takes time and attention to get it right. You need the right management, staff, dancers and customers. We are discreet, we do think of the public and the city centre. We liaise with the police and councillors. There is not intention to cause offence to anyone.

Two requests for licenses, one by FYEO owners and one by the owners of Sugar, a nightclub in Newcastle, were filed in July 2003 and denied in September 2003 by the local city council. FYEO heard their appeal in November and the appeal from Sugar, renamed Privilege, was heard by licensing magistrates in February 2004. Both licenses were eventually granted but not without re-ignited interests.

City councillor, Nigel Todd, who objected to the first application to FYEO said he felt that it was a

> "pretty sad kind of man who'd want to go to this kind of thing. I think this kind of club presents women in a way that puts back all the work done to secure equality. It presents them as sexual object and that increases all sorts of risks for women in terms of safety on the streets and how they're seen in public".

Furthermore, Wingrove councillor Joyce McCarty objected to the licenses because the locations were part of the cultural quarter as well as the gay quarter of the city.

> We have a responsibility to ensure that area remains safe. My concerns were that under-the-influence heterosexuals standing in the same queue as gay people might cause problems. I am morally opposed but you can't object on those grounds.

However, Glenn Nicie was keen to emphasise that Northumbria Police had no complaints about the management of the premises, nor had there been any reports of indecency in the area since it opened.

In February 2004, around the same time that Sherry contemplated a career change, FYEO owners in Newcastle, were again at the centre of a heated discussion. They awaited a decision from the Magistrate's Course for permission to open on Sundays from noon to 12:30 am and to stay open until 2 am on Sundays before bank holidays weekends. Christian groups and women's rights groups were outraged by the request. This is not the first time, and likely not the last time the Newcastle location faced controversy.

Questions:

1. What sources of power are evident in the case?
2. Using the sources of power you highlight in your answer to question one, identify how these sources inform your understanding of power relations given a particular conceptualisation of power. Do a comparative analysis using at least two different conceptualisations of power (i.e., one-dimensional, two-dimensional, three-dimensional, four-dimensional).
3. How does the way in which power is exercised in the case affect individual and group behaviour? What are the individual, organizational and social outcomes of such power relations?

4. Compare and contrast two of the following perspectives of power to explore power relations in the case:
   - A systems rationality perspective
   - An interpretative perspective
   - A critical perspective
   - A feminist perspective
   - A poststructuralist perspective
5. What role does resistance play in the operations of FYEO? How does this resistance relate to power relations within and surrounding the organization?
6. What forces affect dancers identity and how does this manifest itself?

REFERENCES

"Baring all in public gives us a real thrill," *The Evening Chronicle*, September 5, 2003.

Cartmell, A., (2003). "Moves for topless clubs," *The Evening Chronicle*, August 21, 2003.

Chapkiss, W., (1997). *Live Sex Acts: Women Performing Erotic Labour*. Toronto: Women's Press.

Ford, C., (2001). "Lapping it up," *Sunday Sun*, November 11, 2001.

For Your Eyes Only website <http://www.fyeo.co.uk>

Hastings, V., (2002). "Table dancing club fights for new licence," *The Journal*, May 25, 2002.

Mcmillan, P., (2003). "Lap dance club goes to appeal," *The Evening Chronicle*, December 2, 2003.

Oliver, S., (2003). "Pair reveal all on plans," *The Evening Chronicle*, September 18, 2003.

"Pole position in the fitness league," *The Journal*, February 2002.

"Putting it on the table," *The Observer*, February 11, 2001.

"Sunday dance plan outrage," *Newcastle Herald and Post*, February 25, 2004.

"Table dancing club opens to cries of 'shame,'" *The Journal*, November 8, 2001.

Walker, H., (2003). "Ladhar aims for the top table after buying chain," *The Journal*, September 17, 2003.

Weitzer, R., (2000). "Why We Need More Research on Sex Work, in R. Weitzer (ed.), *Sex for sale: Prostitution, pornography and the sex industry, 1-16*. New York: Routledge.

Wesley, J.K., (2002). "Growing Up Sexualized: Issues of Power and Violence in the Lives of Female Exotic Sancers. *Violence Against Women*, 8(10): 1182-1207.

END NOTES

1. This case was a finalist in the Academy of Management Critical Management Studies/Management Education "Dark Side III" 2004 case writing competition. It is intended as a basis for discussion and not as an illustration of either good or bad management practice.

2. The individuals described are based largely upon interviews conducted with various dancers at FYEO over a six-month period in 2003 for doctoral work. Their stories and descriptions have been slightly altered so as maintain their anonymity, however the accounts described are real. The individuals described however may not symbolize one individual but a culmination of accounts from different dancers and managers. The accounts of Glenn Nicie, FYEO director, and that of councillors Nigel Todd and Joyce McCarty are those as reported by secondary sources.

3. Another club, Privilege, has just been granted a license to operate a table-side dancing club in Newcastle, so this may open up other avenues for dancers in Newcastle.

Glossary of Terms

Americanization of organizational research – the tendency of most mainstream texts in OT and OB to uncritically adopt American organizational models and principles, and the generalization of these ideas over different cultures and societies. With few exceptions (cf. Das, 1990), OB and OT texts used in Canadian universities have made little if any reference to such specifically Canadian policies as Bilingualism, or Multiculturalism. For a much earlier protest over the neglect (and distortion) of Canadian reality in Americanized research, see John Seeley (1967). Some attempt has been made to address this problem through the Canadianization of existing US textbooks. Here the author(s) use the US book's basic structure and add Canadian content – see for example Robbins and Langton (2003; 2004). We have also seen the successful introduction of Canadian OB and OT textbooks in recent years – see for example McShane (2001).

Androcentricism – male centred; a way of viewing the world exclusively from the perspective of men.

Assimilationism – the doctrine, first popularized in the United States, which emphasized the desirability and the inevitability of the process whereby overseas immigrants relinquished their own cultures in favour of that of the host country – America. In popular parlance, American society became seen as a huge "melting pot" which stripped immigrants of their original cultural identities (sometimes over a period of several generations) before transforming them into standardized (or fully homogenized) American citizens.

Besides attaining the status of an unofficial national doctrine in the US, assimilationism also influenced the work of a generation of early American race relations researchers, most notably, Robert Ezra Park (1950). In Canada, however, although the doctrine of assimilationism was initially supported by many powerful groups, it has long been rejected in favour of the policy of cultural pluralism, or what in the 1970s became known as the policy of Multiculturalism.

Authoritarian personality – term devised by Adorno (1969) to describe a person with a set of authoritarian characteristics. In some "potentially fascist" people there are a number of characteristics which form an authoritarian pattern or syndrome. The defining characteristics of the syndrome are a fear of strangeness and resort to authority. The authoritarian personality is someone who fears strangeness and persons who are culturally, ethnically, politically, and/or religiously different from themselves. The authoritarian personality is manifest in anti-Semitic, ethnocentric, and politically conservative behaviour.

Authority – the social power that a person or social group believes to be *legitimate*. The important point here is the stress on legitimacy of the power exercised. In other words those who recognize the "authority" believe that it is justified and proper, and for these reasons the exercise of this authority tends to be effective in achieving its aims. It is directly opposed to the exercise of social power which relies on the coercive consequences of non-compliance for its effectiveness (definition from Weeks, 1978: 13).

Bio-power – a term developed by Foucault to describe the relationship between power, knowledge and the body. Foucault contends that we live in a world that concerns itself with understanding and controlling the human body. Many organizations have come into being whose purpose is to collect data on the body and its functions; in the process there had been developed an understanding of the body which ultimately controls the way we view life. Medicine, education, public health and prisons, for example, all contribute to the way we view "normalcy" and this has a controlling influence – or bio-power – over the way we think and act.

Budgeting – this refers to one of the universal principles of management identified by the early American management theorist Lther Gullick (1937). Gullick defined as "budgeting, those activities which relate to the financial planning, accounting and control of the fiscal life of the organization. Today, budgeting is widely acknowledged to be one of the key elements in the practice of management. Without budgetary control no manager can exercise real authority within an organization.

Bureaucracy – to many people, the term, "bureaucracy" has become synonymous with "red tape," over-regulation, wastage and general organizational inefficiency. To the sociologist, however, the term has a more technical (and a more neutral) meaning. It can best be defined as "a large, complex, formal organization which is organized through an elaborate division of labour, under an hierarchical structure of authority and which operates according to explicit rules and procedures." The actual word, "bureaucracy," means "rule by officials, or office holders," and is often associated with the use of written files as part of the apparatus of administration. Although large organizations have existed for over a thousand years (for example, the Roman Catholic Church), the first writer to study the modern bureaucratic organization was the sociologist Max Weber, who described the typical characteristics of the bureaucracy (Gerth and Mills, 1974; Weber, 1947; 1948).

Bureaucratic systems of control – according to Richard Edwards (1979), the bureaucratic system is the most recent system of managerial control to emerge in the modern workplace. Unlike earlier systems of workplace control, which relied on direct supervision or on the technical control of the workplace through technological means, bureaucratic systems of control regulate the workplace through company rules and policies. Bureaucratic forms of control, therefore, include collective agreements, job descriptions and designations, wage and salary scales, work rules and so on.

Calculability – one of the characteristics of bureaucratic organizations is their tendency to subject all activities to precise measurement and calculation. Whether this involves a government case worker calculating an applicant's eligibility for social assistance payments, or the worker in a fast food industry who is obliged to carefully measure levels of coffee dispensed to customers, all bureaucracies try to ensure that their activities are subject to strict calculation and measurement.

Charismatic authority – this is a term used by the sociologist Max Weber to describe the type of authority which is based upon some extraordinary or outstanding personal qualities of a leader, or authority figure. Examples of charismatic authority vary from those of religious prophets (Jesus, Mohammed, Buddha, etc), to political or demagogic figures (Hitler, Mao Zedong, etc). In each of these cases, however, it was the individual qualities of the charismatic leader that formed the basis of his (or her) authority. Although the word "charisma" originally meant "magical" (in Greek), it has more commonly been used in a theological sense to refer to "the gift of grace".

Class – refers to a group of people with a shared relationship to social and economic aspects of society. For Marx, "ownership of the means of production" (by which he meant whether or not a person was a business owner) was the most important defining characteristic of class. The two main classes in capitalist society are the owning class and the working class (those who do not own a business and who need to work to earn a living). Marx believed that these two classes stand in an antagonistic relationship to one another, leading to economic conflict which will eventually result in the revolutionary transformation of society. For Max Weber, on the other hand, "life chances" (by which he meant the ability to advance socially due to income, skills, market assets, and/or property) is the defining characteristic of class. Nowadays, many sociologists take account of both "life chances" and a person's relationship to "the means of production" to attempt to predict future events.

Classical approach – the classical approach to any field of study is usually associated with those writers who have attained recognition in the area, and whose works are commonly acknowledged to have an enduring and permanent value within the field. The classical approach is often synonymous, therefore, with the established tradition, or the received wisdom, within an academic or professional discipline. The classical approach to the study of bureaucracy, for example, normally includes such writers as Marx, Weber and Michels; while the classical approach to management studies normally includes such writers as F. W. Taylor and Henri Fayol, among others.

Commanding – refers to one of the key activities involved in the practice of management which was first identified by the French management theorist, Henri Fayol, and later elaborated more fully by the American management theorist, Luther Gullick. "Commanding," or "directing," refers to the practice of setting goals, and of decision making within an organization.

Confessional practices – a term developed by Foucault to refer to the influence of psychological and psychoanalytical practices on notions of the self. Foucault contends that certain practices within society exert a powerful influence on the way we come to view our self and the selves of others. Take, for example, the influence of psychology on the legal system – in particular, modern notions of guilt and innocence. Psychological explanations of human growth and development have helped to shape the widespread belief that a person is not fully responsible for their actions: if it can be proven that a person had a bad upbringing the law is likely to be more lenient on the person charged with a crime. [see also disciplinary practices]

Consensus view of management – this expression refers to a conception of management which views the organization as a set of mutually interrelated parts linked together by strong underlying common interests. The manager, according to this view, is seen as a catalyst for bringing together the different physical and human resources in order to achieve the commonly desired goals of the organization. Because of its overemphasis on shared interests and commonly held goals, the consensus view overlooks, to a large extent, the existence of opposed interest groups, as well as conflict, power and inequality within the organization.

Controlling – this refers to another of the key activities involved in the practice of management, which was also identified by the French management theorist, Henri Fayol. It also refers to the regulation of all aspects of work processes within the organization.

Coordinating – this refers to another of the key activities involved in the process of management, originally identified by the French management theorist, Henri Fayol and later more fully elaborated by the American management theorist Luther Gullick. According to Gullick, coordination refers to the integration of the different parts of the organization in an effort to ensure the fulfillment of organizational goals.

Corporate culture – this refers to the prevailing set of values which are typically reflected in the managerial practice of most large corporations. Among other things, the corporate culture of many large organizations has been characterized by strong personal ambition, aggressive competition, and an all pervading individualism. While these values have traditionally been represented as desirable and necessary for the efficient performance of managers, more recent critics (especially feminists) have suggested that these values have more to do with patriarchal attitudes than with corporate efficiency. Indeed, even the most central values of the bureaucratic organization: those of rationality and hierarchy – inherited from the time of Max Weber, have been seen by some writers as no more than the institutionalization of patriarchal attitudes and practices. (See Ferguson, 1984; Morgan, 1988; Kanter, 1977).

Decisional roles – this concept was introduced by Henry Mintzberg (1973; 1975)(1975) in his efforts to distinguish between the variety of roles performed by managers in the everyday practices of management. Decisional roles refer to those activities which relate to the efficient deployment of resources within the organization.

Deskilling – this concept is often associated with the work of Harry Braverman (1974)(1974) who was one of the earliest labour process theorists to question the optimistic conclusions of the post industrialism thesis. Unlike many theorists of the late 1960s, Braverman did not believe that the new technologies of industry would necessarily eliminate the need for unskilled labour nor bring about the expansion of a new highly skilled middle class. Instead, Braverman suggested that the new technologies have often been used by managers to strip workers of their traditional craft skills and to cheapen the value of their labour power in the workplace.

Directing – see *Commanding*

Disciplinary practices – a term used by Foucault to refer to those practice concerned with knowledge and control of the body. Medicine, education, public health, prisons, schools and many other organizations have developed sets of practices which combine to control how we view the world and how we behave as a result. The school system, for example, involves a series of practices which require that as children we attend school at certain ages, and during specified periods of time. The school system also helps to create the viewpoint that being schooled is the mark of a "normal" person: as a reaction against the disciplinary nature of schools Illich (1981) has suggested that we "deschool" society. (See also bio-power.)

Discourse – refers to a set of ideas and viewpoints, experienced in and through a series of communications, which influence the behaviour and thinking of the persons involved. Organizing, for example, is a discourse that is reproduced daily through sets of practices. From religion to sport, from physical activity to music, when ever we want to achieve something in the modern world we usually think of organization. We rarely stop to think whether an activity is best left unorganized. Organizing is a powerful discourse which influences the way we think.

Discrimination – refers to the process or processes whereby some individuals are deprived of equal access to rights and opportunities generally available to others. Individuals who face discrimination in such areas as employment, housing or educational opportunities are frequently members of particular minority groups (whether racial/ethnic, women, physically handicapped, etc.).

Division of labour – refers to the specialization of tasks within the process of production. Popularized by Adam Smith during the eighteenth century in his economic writings, the term originally indicated the breakdown of the production process into a series of separate and distinct technical tasks. However, the term was later used by Emile Durkheim in a broader sense to describe the social division of labour: that is, the specialization of different occupational groups in any given society.

Dominance – a personality characteristic which involves a striving to exert control over others. In some persons – due to the effects of socialization – this can be experienced as a need to be dominated.

Efficiency – the concept of efficiency implies the selection of the most appropriate means in order to achieve certain predetermined ends. In organizational terms, efficiency implies the effective utilization and allocation of physical and human resources for the achievement of organizational goals. The standard measurement of efficiency in most organizations (in both private and public sectors), are those of productivity and profitability.

Ethnic mosaic – refers to the pattern of social relations in a society whereby different ethnic groups maintain their distinctive ethnic identities and their separate cultural heritages. In Canada, (unlike the US, which still espouses the goal of assimilating all ethnic groups into the dominant North American culture), the maintenance of ethnic diversity has been officially supported by the Federal Government's policy of Multiculturalism.

Ethnicity – refers to the social categorization of persons according to their cultural background. Factors taken into account can include a person's national, cultural, and language heritage. The term is utilized by some people to build pride in their heritage (e.g., as in the various heritage and cultural celebrations that take place throughout Canada's provinces). In recent years the term has been used by some as a political weapon to proclaim white supremacy (e.g., such people never use the term "ethnic" to describe their own white, Anglo-Saxon heritage), to create an ethnic hierarchy of peoples (e.g., references to "ethnic food" or "ethnic people") and to attack people of colour (for example, references to black people as "ethnics").

Ethnocentricism – refers to the tendency of many, if not most, individuals to centre their beliefs and attitudes around the cultural values and practices of their own particular ethnic group. In practice, this usually means that the values and practices of one's own group are seen as superior to those of other groups, or that elements of one's own culture have universal validity across all cultures. Unlike a fully developed racist ideology, however, the biases of ethnocentrism are usually implicit and taken-for-granted.

Femininity – characteristics associated with "being a woman"; culturally specific notions of what physical and behavioural features constitute females. What is seen as feminine changes over time and depends on a number of factors, including female resistance to patriarchal rules. In Victorian Britain, for example, it was not considered "feminine" for a woman to have the vote. In today's Britain some people still consider it unfeminine for women to go out to work. Notions of femininity vary not only with time but with context. In Northern Holland, for example, the working woman is a fact of life but in Maastricht, in the South of Holland, it is still regarded as unfeminine.

Formalization – refers to the process by which informal social relations are gradually replaced by social relations governed by explicit rules and regulations oriented towards the realization of officially defined goals. In organizational terms, the modern bureaucracy, with its highly specialized division of labour and differential allocation of authority represents a high level of formalization

Gender – culturally shaped characteristics associated with being a man or a woman. Gender is often confused with sex. While sex refers to a person's biological constitution (i.e., specifically the genitalia) gender refers to socially constructed understandings of what it means to be a man or a woman. The biological features that a person is born with serve only as a basis for categorization as male or female. The characteristics of manhood and of womanhood are dependent on cultural notions and have to be learned. People spend most of their lives learning what it is to be masculine or feminine, to be a "real man" or a "real woman." Historically notions of gender have been constructed in male-dominated contexts and as a result are made up of a series of discriminatory ideas. For example, the notion that men are "strong" and women are "weak" is a culturally devised idea which has been used in a number of discriminatory ways, including preventing women from gaining the vote or serving in the armed forces, or being employed in a range of occupations. (See also femininity, masculinity.)

Glass ceiling – concept invented by Morrison et al. (1987) to describe a situation where companies statements encourage women to enter senior management but their practices prevent them from doing so. Thus, women can see the top of the management ladder but as seemingly invisible ceiling prevents them from climbing above the middle rungs.

Goal displacement – a term used to describe how a commitment to the goals of particular sectors of an organization may sometimes become more important to the individuals and groups within these sectors than the larger goals of the entire organization. Thus, competition between officials from different departments may result in their losing sight of, or displacing, the more central goals of the organization. This problem was first clearly articulated by Robert Merton (1940), in his discussion of "bureaucratic ritualism."

Hierarchy – virtually all large organizations are characterized by a differential allocation of authority, status and prestige. Which is to say, that all large organizations are based upon a principle of inequality: those at the top have more authority and prestige than those at the lower levels. Most organization theorists have traditionally assumed that hierarchy is a necessary condition of organizational efficiency. Today, however, opinions are changing on this issue. Some theorists may believe that hierarchy in bureaucracies contributes to poor communication, poor motivation and reduced efficiency. Others have argued that the principle of hierarchy simply reflects an entrenchment of patriarchal attitudes.

Identity – the psychological experience of sameness over time. Through various processes of socialization and other experiences a person comes to believe that they are a certain, and unique, person. This belief plays an important part in the way a person orients his or her actions.

George Herbert Mead argues that the self – a crucial aspect of identity – is socially constructed; that we develop a sense of self through interaction with others. Mead contends that we acquire a sense of self through social contexts involving the organized attitudes of others (the "me") and our reflections on those attitudes (the "I"). Mead's view suggests that the self is never finally formed but is always to some degree in a state of flux and mediation. Leonard (1984) argues that Mead's theory lacks an understanding of the concrete situations in which identities are formed; contexts in which people are not equal in their power and ability to shape how other persons are viewed. For the large majority of working people, for example, the self is developed in contexts in which the "I" is confronted by more powerful symbols and actors.

Some theorists argue that as we develop into adults we acquire a fix and unchangeable identity – Flax (1990), for example, refers to the "core identity" which we have acquired by the age of three years. Postmodernist theorists, on the other hand, argue that people develop "multiple identities" which depend on the person's location in and experience of a number of social discourses (cf. Dreyfus and Rabinow, 1982).

Impersonality – this term describes the kind of social relations which typically exist between members of a bureaucracy and their clients. Impersonality implies, on the one hand, that all clients are treated alike without preference or favouritism; but on the other hand, impersonality may also imply a lack of personal feeling or empathy with the other person. Although impersonality has often been seen as a necessary condition for efficiency and equity in bureaucratic transactions, it has been recognized as a problem in interpersonal relations.

Informational roles – this concept was introduced by Henry Mintzberg (1975) in his effort to distinguish between the variety of roles performed by managers in the everyday practice of management. Informational roles refer to those activities which relate to the communication of ideas (both their transmission and their receipt) within the organization.

Institutionalized, (structural, or systemic) discrimination – refers to indirect discrimination that occurs as a by-product of the normal functioning of bureaucratic organizations. In this sense, institutionalized discrimination may often be unintended, and often results from the entrenchment of selection criteria, or other job-related qualifications, which have failed to keep up with the changing composition of the workforce in particular, and of society in general. Examples would be physical requirements for jobs which may well exclude some ethnic groups, as well as women. (For a useful discussion of institutionalized discrimination in Canada, see Abella, 1984.)

Instrumental reason – a term developed by Max Weber to characterize modern thinking based on means and ends calculations. According to Weber, the success of bureaucracy as an enduring and widespread form of organization is due, in large part, to instrumental reasoning. People accept bureaucratic rules and authority because it accords with their own way of measuring the world; people are motivated to act by judging whether what they will put into a situation will be balanced by what they get out of it. Bureaucracies offer employees a system in which they can advance according not to the whim of the employer or by dint of personality but to the effort and commitment of the employee his- or herself. Ferguson (1984) and Morgan (1988) challenge this perception and argues that patriarchal discourse intervenes to inhibit the advancement of female employees of bureaucracies. Martin (1990) questions whether instrumental reason can be said to be characteristic of both men *and* women; arguing that it is more likely a part of male thinking.

Interpersonal roles – this concept was introduced by Henry Mintzberg (1975) in his effort to distinguish between the variety of roles performed by managers in the everyday practice of management. Interpersonal roles refer to those activities associated with the leadership functions of management, whether these are understood in ritualized, symbolic, or in wholly practical terms.

Life instincts/Eros – a term developed by Freud who argued that people are born with a drive for species survival. The drive has two main elements (i) self-preservation, and (ii) sexual instincts. In other words, we act in certain ways because of an unconscious striving to ensure the survival of humankind. The problem is, according to Freud, that this striving is shaped by family and social influences which can lead to personality disorders.

Managerial revolution – term developed by James Burnham (1941) to refer to the twentieth century rise and development of professional managers as a new, and powerful class in the day-to-day running and control of organizations.

Managerial viewpoint – see *Managerialist*

Managerialist – an analysis of organizations which takes the needs and the perspectives of management as its starting point.

Masculinity – characteristics associated with "being a man"; culturally specific notions of what physical and behavioural features constitute males and maleness. What is seen as masculine changes over time and depends on a number of factors. In eighteenth century Britain, for example, it was considered masculine in some quarters to wear long hair and brightly coloured clothing. It was quite the opposite in the Britain of the mid-twentieth century. Notions of masculinity vary not only with time but with context. In the US, for example, there are some communities which view masculinity as the ability to cry ("new age man") while in other communities the ability to avoid crying is viewed as a sign of manhood.

Mirroring – a psychoanalytic term referring to the process where the actions of certain others becomes reflected (or mirrored) in the thoughts and behaviour of a person. Kets de Vries (1989; 1989; 1991) argues that an unreflective and psychologically weak person is in danger of over identifying with a strong other; he contends that, in the workplace, mirroring is facilitated by excessive dependency between executives and subordinates. Organizational success often depend on a mirroring of appropriate behaviour and in such situations in subordinates can come to identify excessively with the leader. This can lead to situations of moral uncertainty and corruption as employees attempt to mirror rather than reflect upon executive decisions. In a patriarchal world mirroring helps to reproduce discriminatory practices against women.

Multiculturalism – refers to the official policy of ethnic pluralism in Canada which was introduced in October, 1971 by the Liberal Government of Prime Minister Trudeau. This policy has supported the right of ethnic groups in Canada to preserve their ethnic identities and cultural heritages, and has provided government funding for this purpose. Recently, however, Multiculturalism has come under attack from a number of directions. Some groups and individuals have argued that Multiculturalism policies should no longer be financed through public funds. Others have suggested that Multiculturalism has eroded our sense of national identity and national unity (Bibby, 1990); still others have argued that Multiculturalism has not gone far enough in combating racial prejudice and discrimination. Multiculturalism has become a divisive issue in Canadian politics.

Narcissism – a Freudian term for a psychological condition of having an exaggerated love of self; it involves the development of an idealized and unrealistic image of self which becomes the object of the person's love.

Organizing – refers to another of the key activities involved in the practice of management. Originally identified by the French management theorist, Henri Fayol, it was later elaborated more fully by the American management theorist, Luther Gullick. According to Gullick, planning refers to the process of identifying tasks and how to complete them in order to fulfill the goals of the organization.

Planning – refers to another of the key activities involved in the practice of management. Originally identified by the French management theorist, Henri Fayol, it was later elaborated more fully by the American management theorist, Luther Gullick. According to Gullick, organizing refers to the establishment of a formal structure in an organization, and to the implementation of an efficient division of labour in the workplace.

Postmodernism – the postmodernist approach argues that there is not one central knowledge waiting to be uncovered, but that there are several, often competing, "truths" in any given situation. Whether a person believes one "truth" or another will, according to postmodernism, depend on a number of factors such as the beliefs they bring to a situation, their relationship to others in the situation, and how they and others define the situation. With that in mind the Postmodernist theorist seeks to *expose* the underlying assumptions of organizational theories and practices as being rooted in particular, and thus partial, views of reality. The postmodernist does this in order to encourage people to free themselves from different forms of organizational control. From a conservative or mainstream postmodernist perspective this type of analysis can assist managers to identify outmoded attitudes and behaviours which inhibit their ability to question and challenge themselves and others. The "enlightened" manager is then in a better position to develop more innovative ways of working – ways that may even challenge and question the way the organization does business and the power structures of the organization.

From a radical postmodernist perspective this type of analysis sets out to reveal organizational and management studies as "disciplinary practices," or powerful sets of ideas – rooted in workplace assumptions and associated practices – that serve to define what is ideal or appropriate workplace behaviour. The radical postmodernist is centrally concerned to expose the impact that theories of workplace behaviour have on people's sense of self and their ability or power to influence their sense of worth, self-esteem and identity.

Power – the control which a person has over other people; the ability of a person to exact compliance or obedience of other individuals to his or her will. Persons in positions of authority have power by dint of the fact that they hold legitimate office; people usually comply with the will of an office holder because it is assumed that they have legitimately attained the post and therefore have a certain level of competency. But not all people with power are in positions of authority. The unofficial trade union organizer, the charismatic "rabble-rouser," and the well respected member of a social group can also exercise power due to their character or attributes. It used to be argued that power corrupts and absolute power corrupts absolutely but Kanter (1979) argues that *a lack* of (organizational) power can be more corrupting. For example, the person with no organizational autonomy or discretion often resorts to the rules in dealing with problems. Postmodernist writers of recent years argue that power is "decentred" in that it we all contribute to practices and discourses which bestow different elements of power (and powerlessness) on each of us. The US airline industry of the 1960s, for example, restricted the recruitment of flight attendants to "pretty," young, white females. This practice originated from top management in the business but was also supported by a travelling public which accepted the practice as "normal" and by the tens of thousands of female applicants who attempted to join the business. The problem with the post modernist version of power, however, is that it underestimates the range of power involved in any given context. Clearly, airline executives were powerful in the creation of sexist recruitment practices and in their maintenance. Other actors helped to support those practices, but individually would have found it difficult to have changed them. It took a concerted action on the part of the modern women's liberation movement before some of the airlines' sexist practices were changed.

Psychic prison – metaphor developed by Gareth Morgan (1996) to characterize the way that people can experience organizations as confining and dominating; that people can actually become imprisoned or confined by the images, ideas, thoughts, and actions to which organizational processes give rise.

Race – the categorization of persons – usually according to skin colour and ethnic origin – into sub-species of humanity. The development of the concept of race is bound up with the development of imperialism and this is reflected in its usage, which suggests that some peoples are biologically inferior to others. The concept, which owes more to belief and political use than to biological fact, has for centuries been invoked to discriminate against and suppress people of colour. (See also ethnicity.)

Race relations – this refers to the pattern of social relations existing between members of different visible minority groups and the dominant (i.e., white) groups in society. The state of race relations between different groups may be variously defined as harmonious, antagonistic, etc., depending upon a number of different factors. The greatest threat to the existence of harmonious race relations is often the presence of sharp inequalities of power and/or wealth, especially when differences in socioeconomic status are reinforced by differences in racial or ethnic background.

Racioethnicity – a term coined by Taylor Cox, Jr. (1990) to describe an approach which seeks to identify and address the discriminatory aspects of organizational practices that serve to exclude people of colour from professional and managerial positions within organizations. Some racioethnicity research accepts the underlying managerialist assumptions of organizational study – seeking to find places within the system for people of colour. Much of this work has found a place in the recent "diversity management" fad. Other racioethnicity research is focused on challenging the racist (or "post-colonialist") notions inherent in the concept and power structures of organizations – seeking to establish different, non-racist, ways of organizing.

Racism – refers to a set of beliefs which are based on the assumption that differences in racial or ethnic background correspond to differences in social, cultural, intellectual or even moral development. Implicit in this assumption is the belief that some "races" have a higher potential for development than others; in other words, that some "races" are superior to others in terms of their innate abilities. Racism can also be expressed as a set of practices which are consistent with the above beliefs. Unlike ethnocentric beliefs, therefore, which are often held naively without conscious reflection, racist beliefs are often codified into self-conscious ideological frameworks. The historical function of racist beliefs and practices has typically been that of denying to certain minority groups equal access to strategic resources (such as employment, housing, education, voting rights, etc.,) while protecting and rationalizing privileges enjoyed by a dominant group (or groups).

Rational-legal authority – this is the term used by Max Weber to describe the type of authority which is based upon a system of explicitly defined rules and regulations in which authority derives from the status of the office held rather than from any personal or traditional qualities of the individual. Bureaucratic organizations represent the most complete example of a system of rational-legal authority. Authority within a bureaucratic system may either come from appointment (as in private corporations) or from election (as in many public bodies).

Re-engineering – developed by Hammer and Champy, re-engineering is a theory which emphasizes the restructuring of the workplace through a focus on workflow or process; companies are encouraged to "organize around outcomes not tasks" (Hammer, 1990; 1995; 1996; Hammer and Champy, 1993). Heralded as a "revolutionary" approach, re-engineering advocates argue that companies should not change in a piecemeal fashion but that they should entirely change their work practices from top to bottom; completely rethinking the way work is undertaken.

Reporting – refers to another of the key activities involved in the practice of management. Originally identified by the American management theorist, Luther Gullick, reporting refers to the processes of information gathering, storage and retrieval through such activities as research, inspection and record keeping.

Repression – in psychoanalytical theory this refers to the psyche's main defence mechanism which acts unconsciously to exclude from memory unpleasant experiences: the ego pushes unwanted memories into the unconsciousness. According to psychoanalysts, repressed thoughts, memories and experiences not only continue to exert an influence on thoughts and behaviour but, because they are repressed, can be the major cause of thoughts and actions.

Rigidity – refers to the fact that bureaucracies can sometimes appear inflexible and inefficient when dealing with unusual, exceptional or atypical cases. This is because bureaucracies are established to process large amounts of information, and large numbers of people, as efficiently as possible. When confronted with unusual cases which cannot be processed according to standard procedures, those who administer the rules and regulations within bureaucracies can sometimes appear to be rigid, insensitive and singularly unimaginative.

Routinization – refers to the process whereby regularly recurrent patterns of social interaction acquire the status of relatively stable and objective elements of social structure. All social structure, including organizational relations, is based upon the routinization of particular forms of social interaction.

Scientific Management – refers to the movement established early in the twentieth century by the American management theorist F. W. Taylor. Scientific Management, or Taylorism, comprised a system of principles and practices which rapidly transformed workplace relations during the opening decades of the twentieth century. Ventral to Taylorism was the idea that increased workplace efficiency depended upon a greater divisions of labour, and on the systematic analysis and redesign of jobs. Taylor believed that every work process could be analyzed systematically and broken down into its constituent parts, thus reducing each worker's job to a simple, single task. He also believed that the planning and conception of work should remain the sole responsibility of management, while the actual performance and execution of work tasks remained the responsibility of workers. Taylor's ideas led to a revolution in workplace relations enabling managers to acquire a new monopoly of knowledge and control over most industrial work processes, and also enabling them to progressively replace higher-waged skilled workers with lower-waged unskilled workers. In historical terms, therefore, Scientific Management directly contributed to the cheapening and to the de-skilling of the modern industrial labour force (see Braverman, 1974).

Sexual preference – reference to a person's choice of sexual orientation, from a range of sexual possibilities that include heterosexuality, homosexuality and bisexuality. The term was developed in recent years as a reaction against heterosexist assumptions and terms which labeled non-heterosexual orientation "abnormal". The term sexual preference, as opposed to earlier terms (e.g., sexual deviancy) suggests choice rather than biological abnormality; "sexual preference" suggests that all forms of sexual orientation are equally acceptable.

Simple control – according to Richard Edwards (1979) the earliest system of managerial control to emerge in the modern workplace was that of "simple control." Largely associated with small owner-operated firms, this form of control was characterized by highly personalized and paternalistic systems of supervision where the workplace was small, and the bosses were close and powerful.

Specialization – refers to the division of labour which has accompanied the growth of large bureaucratic organizations in the modern world. Modern organizations are characterized by the elaborate division of occupational roles into separate and distinct spheres of competence and responsibility. Functional specialization and structural differentiation have become the hallmarks of the modern bureaucracy.

Staffing – refers to all aspects of personal and human resource management including the recruitment, evaluation, promotion and dismissal of employees within an organization.

Standardization – refers to the tendency for the modern bureaucracy to reduce many of its activities to simple, easily reproducible tasks which help to fulfill the goals of the organization. This standardization of functions is one aspect of what Max Weber termed the growing "rationalization" of organizations in the modern world.

Subjectivity – a person's sense of themself as a person; a set of understandings about what constitutes the human subject. In early times it was generally believed that people were ordained to occupy a certain status or position in life: people spoke, for example, of "the divine right of kings." This influenced how people viewed themselves and humanity in general. In South Africa, how people understand themselves and others was shaped by the policy of Apartheid; a person's subjectivity was constructed out of a society that was sharply divided along racial lines. Today, subjectivity is being shaped differently in a South Africa rocked by economic and political crises.

Systematic soldiering – this is the term used by F.W. Taylor, and other managers and business people of his generation, to designate the way many workers deliberately regulated the pace of their work, and often restricted their productivity and output. For Taylor and his associates, the tendency for workers to produce below their optimal speeds constituted a major "problem" for the efficient organization and supervision of work. Taylor's system of Scientific Management was designed to strip workers of any effective control over their work processes, and to return this control exclusively to managers.

Systemic discrimination – term developed by the Abella Commission (1984) to characterize forms of discrimination which arise out of the ways in which organizations are structured. (See also Institutionalized *discrimination*.)

Technical control – according to Richard Edwards (1979), the emergence of systems of technical control in the workplace correspond to the growth of big business and to the introduction of new forms of technology. With the installation of assembly lines, workers became subject to the control of the new machinery which directed not only their pace of work, but also their rates of pay. Under these new conditions, the role of management became more related to the monitoring and evaluation of work, than to its initiation and direction.

Time and motion studies – refers to those studies undertaken by management researchers and consultants, such as F. W. Taylor and his followers, which were designed to increase the efficiency of work. Time and motion "experts" were primarily interested in clocking speeds at which workers completed their assigned work tasks, and in exploring ways in which these tasks could be performed more efficiently by redesigning them for greater specialization.

Tokenism – refers to the practice of hiring a single, or small number of, individual(s) from underrepresented minority or disadvantaged groups (often racial, ethnic, gender, or physically challenged), as evidence of any lack of institutional discrimination against these groups. Rather than demonstrating any serious commitment to employment equity, however, tokenism usually implies the "show-casing," or "window-dressing" of a few minority individuals as a minimal way of fulfilling moral, political or even legal obligations for fair employment practices.

Traditional authority – is a term used by Max Weber to describe the type of authority which is based upon a system of long-lasting beliefs and practices passed down from one generation to the next. Such authority derives its legitimacy from the continuity which links it to previous generations, as in the customary status accorded to hereditary chiefs in traditional societies, or in the institution of the monarch in modern societies.

Uniformity – refers to the tendency of the modern bureaucracy to impose a common format on many of its products and services. Large bureaucracies have often tended to discourage diversity or variety in the mass production of goods and services. Uniformity has often been seen as a logical consequence of technical efficiency.

Universalist tradition – is a term normally used to describe the tradition of management studies which emerged at the beginning of this century, and was associated with the work of the French management theorist, Henri Fayol, among others. Many of these early theorists begun their careers as engineers which accounts for their tendency to view organizations much as they viewed machines. Because of this, universalist theorists focused almost exclusively on the formal structure and design of organizations, and in their writings, they sought to discover a universal set of management principles which could be applied to any organization. Their general aim was to develop a universal "science" of management.

Vertical mosaic – is a term that was introduced by the Canadian sociologist, John Porter (1965), to describe the degree of ethnic inequality in Canadian society. From his research, Porter found that ethnicity had traditionally played an important role in determining the occupational and socioeconomic status of early immigrants upon their arrival in Canada. He concluded that the historical legacy of ethnic stratification had contributed to the low rates of social mobility, and to the lack of any genuine equality of opportunity in Canadian society.

Visible minorities – is a term which has replaced that of "racial minority" as a way of describing non-white people, or people of colour, in multicultural societies. Visible minorities refer to those communities who come from other than a European ethnic background.

Bibliography

Aaltio, I. and Mills, A.J. (eds.), (2002). *Gender, Identity and the Culture of Organizations.* London: Routledge.

Aaltio, I., Mills, A.J. and Helms Mills, J.C. (eds.), (2002). *Special Issue on "Exploring Gendered Organizational Cultures."*

Aaltio-Marjosola, I. and J. Lehtinen, (1998). "Male Managers as Fathers? Contrasting Management, Fatherhood and Masculinity," *Human Relations*, 51 (2), pp. 121-136.

Abella, R.S., (1984). *Equity in Employment: A Royal Commission Report.* Ottawa: Ministry of Supply and Services Canada.

Acker, J. and D.R. van Houten, (1974). "Differential Recruitment and Control: The Sex Structuring of Organizations." *Administrative Science Quarterly*, 9 (2), pp. 152-163.

Adorno, T.W., (1969). *The Authoritarian Personality.* New York: Norton.

Agócs, C., (2002). *Workplace Equality: International Perspectives on Legislation: Policy and Practice.* New York: Kluwer Law International.

—— (1989). "Walking On The Glass Ceiling: Tokenism in Senior Management," *Annual Meeting of the Canadian Sociology and Anthropology Association,* Univerisité Laval, Quebec.

Agócs, C., C. Burr and F. Somerset, (1992). *Employment Equity: Co-operative Strategies for Organizational Change.* Toronto: Prentice-Hall Canada.

Agócs, C., H.C. Jain and Canadian Race Relations Foundation, (2001). *Systemic Racism in Employment in Canada: Diagnosing Systemic Racism in Organizational Culture.* Toronto: Canadian Race Relations Foundation.

Alderfer, C.P., (1991). "Changing Race Relations in Organizations: A Critique of the Contact Hypothesis," *Canadian Journal of Administrative Sciences*, 8 (2), pp. 80-89.

Alderfer, C.P. and D.A. Thomas, (1988). "The Significance of Race and Ethnicity for Understanding Organizational Behaviour," in C.L. Cooper and I.T. Robertson (eds.), *International Review of Industrial and Organizational Psychology*, pp. 1-41. 2. New York: Wiley.

Aldrich, H., (1988). "Paradigm Warriors: Donaldson Versus the Critics of Organization Theory," *Organization Studies*, 9 (1), pp. 19-25.

Allen, V.L., (1975). *Social Analysis: A Marxist Critique and Alternative.* London: Longman.

Allport, G.W., (1979). *The Nature of Prejudice.* Reading, MA: Addison-Wesley Pub. Co.

Althusser, L., (1970). *For Marx.* New York: Vintage Books.

——— (1971). *Lenin and Philosophy and Other Essays.* London: New Left Books.

Althusser, L. and E. Balibar, (1971). *Reading Capital.* New York: Pantheon Books.

——— (1977). *Reading "Capital."* London: Nlb.

Althusser, L., F. Matheron and G.M. Goshgarian, (2003). *The Humanist Controversy and Other Writings (1966-67).* London: Verso.

Alvesson, M., (2002). *Postmodernism and Social Research.* Buckingham: Open University.

Alvesson, M. and Y.D. Billing, (2002). "Beyond Body Counting: A Discussion of the Social Construction of Gender at Work," in I. Aaltio and A.J. Mills (eds.), *Gender, Identity and the Culture of Organizations,* pp. 72-91. London: Routledge.

——— (1997). *Understanding Gender and Organizations.* London: Sage.

Alvesson, M. and S. Deetz, (1996). "Critical Theory and Postmodernism Approaches to Organizational Studies," in S.R. Clegg, C. Hardy and W. Nord (eds.), *Handbook of Organization Studies,* pp. 191-217. London: Sage.

——— (2000). *Doing Critical Management Research.* Thousand Oaks, CA: London: SAGE.

Alvesson, M. and K. Skoldberg, (1999). *Reflexive Methodology: New Vistas for Qualitative Research.* Thousand Oaks, CA, London: SAGE.

——— (2000). "Poststructuralism and Postmodernism," in M. Alvesson and K. Skoldberg (eds.), *Reflexive Methodology: New Vistas for Qualitative Research,* pp. 148 – 199. London: Sage.

American, R.F. and R. Anderson, (1978). *Moving Ahead: Black Managers in American Business.* New York: McGraw-Hill.

Anderson, A.B. and J. Frideres, (1981). *Ethnicity in Canada: Theoretical Perspectives.* Toronto: Butterworth.

Argyris, C., (1957). *Personality and Organization.* New York: Harper and Row.

Armstrong, P., H. Armstrong, J. Choiniere, E. Mykhalovskiy and J. White, (1997). *Medical Alert: New Work Organizations in Health Care.* Toronto: Garamond Press.

Arnold, J., C.L. Cooper and I. Robertson, (1998). *Work Psychology: Understanding Human Behaviour in the Workplace* Harlow, UK, New York: Financial Times/Prentice Hall.

Arvey, R.D. and R.H. Faley, (1988). *Fairness in Selecting Employees.* Reading, MA: Addison-Wesley.

Ashcraft, K.L. and D.K. Mumby, (2004). *Reworking Gender. A Feminist Communicology of Organization* Thousand Oaks, CA: Sage.

Astley, W.G. and A.H. Van de Ven, (1983). "Central Perspectives and Debates in Organization Theory," *Administrative Science Quarterly,* 28, pp. 245-273.

Bahra, N., (2001). *Competitive Knowledge Management.* New York: Palgrave.

Bailey, S., (2004). "Harper softens stance on bilingualism." Montreal, CNews, <http://cnews.canoe.ca/CNEWS/Politics/CanadaVotes/2004/05/25/472392-cp.html>

Bannerji, H., L. Carty, K. Dehli, S. Heald and K. McKenna, (eds.), (1991). *Unsettling Relations: The University as a Site of Feminist Struggle.* Toronto: Women's Press.

Barnard, C., (1938). *Functions of the Executive.* Cambridge, MA: Harvard University Press.

Beattie, C., (1975). *Minority Men in a Majority Setting: Middle-level Francophones in the Canadian Public Service.* Toronto: McClelland and Stewart.

Bell, E.L., (1989). "Racial and Ethnic Diversity: The Void in Organizational Behaviour Courses," *The Organizational Behavior Teaching Review*, 13 (4), pp. 56-67.

—— (1990). "The Bi-cultural Life Experience of Career Oriented Black Women," *Journal of Organizational Behavior*, (11), pp. 459-477.

Bell, E.L., T.C. Denton and S. Nkomo, (1992). "Women of Color In Management: Towards an Inclusive Analysis," in L. Larwood and B. Gutek (eds.), *Women and Work: Trends, Issues and Challenges*. Newbury Park, CA: Sage.

Bell, E. and S. Nkomo, (1992). "Re-Visioning Women Managers' Lives," in A.J. Mills and P. Tancred (eds.), *Gendering Organizational Analysis*, pp. 235-247. Newbury Park, CA: Sage.

—— (2001). *Our Separate Ways: Black and White Women and the Struggle for Professional Identity*. Boston: Harvard Business School Press.

Bendix, R., (1974). *Higher Civil Servants in American Society: A Study of the Social Origins, the Careers, and the Power-position of Higher Federal Administrators*. Westport, CN: Greenwood Press.

Benn, T., (1988). *Office Without Power: Diaries 1968-72*. London: Hutchinson.

—— (2000). *The Speaker, the Commons and Democracy*. Nottingham: Spokesman Books.

Benn, T., I. Allende, British Broadcasting Corporation and Parliamentary Films, (1995). *Westminster Behind Closed Doors*. S.L., Parliamentary Films for BBC.

Bennis, W.G., (1966). *Changing Organizations: Essays on the Development and Evolution of Human Organization*. New York: McGraw-Hill.

Benschop, Y. and H. Doorewaard, (1998). "Six of One and Half a Dozen of the Other: The Gender Subtext of Taylorism and Team-based Work," *Gender, Work and Organization*, 5 (1), pp. 5-18.

Benson, J.K., (1977). "Organizations: A Dialectical View," *Administrative Science Quarterly*, 22, pp. 1-21.

Benson, S.P., (1978). "The Clerking Sisterhood": Rationalization and the Work Culture of Saleswomen in American Department Stores, 1890-1960," *Radical America*, 12, pp. 41-55.

—— (1981). "The Cinderella of Occupations: Managing the Work of Department Store Saleswomen, 1900-1940," *Business History Review*, LV (1), pp. 1-25.

—— (1986). *Counter Cultures: Saleswomen, Managers, and Customers in American Department Stores, 1890-1940*. Urbana: University of Illinois Press.

Berle, A.A. and G.C. Means, (1967). *The Modern Corporation and Private Property*.

Best, S. and D. Kellner, (1991). *Postmodern Theory. Critical Interrogations*. New York: The Guildford Press.

—— (1997). *The Postmodern Turn*. New York: The Guildford Press.

Beynon, H. and R.M. Blackburn, (1972). *Perceptions of Work: Variations Within a Factory*. University Press.

Bibby, R.W., (1990). *Mosaic Madness: The Poverty and Potential of Life in Canada*. Toronto: Stoddart.

Blackler, F., (1992). "Knowledge and the Theory of Organisations: Organisations as Activity Systems and the Reframing of Management," *Knowledge Workers in Contemporary Organisations* Vol., pp. 1-23. Lancaster, UK.

Blauner, B., (1964). *Alienation and Freedom: The Factory Worker and His Industry*. Chicago: University of Chicago Press.

—— (1972). *Racial Oppression in America*. New York: Harper and Row.

—— (2001). *Still the Big News: Racial Oppression in America*. Philadelphia: Temple University Press.

Blustein, D.L., L.E. Devenis and B.A. Kidney, (1989). "Relationship Between the Identity Formation Process and Career Development," *Journal of Counselling Psychology*, 36(2), pp. 196-202.

Boje, D., (1996). "Lessons From Premodern and Modern for Postmodern Management," in G. Palmer and S.R. Clegg (eds.), *Constituting Management*, pp. 329-345. Berlin: de Gruyter.

Boje, D.M. and R.F. Dennehy, (1992). *America's Revolution Against Exploitation: The Story of Post-modern Management*. Dubuque, IA: Kendall/Hunt.

Boje, D.M., R.P. Gephart, Jr. and T.J. Thatchenkery, (eds.), (1996). *Postmodern Management and Organization Theory* Thousand Oaks, CA: Sage.

Bolaria, B.S. and P.S. Li, (1988). *Racial Oppression in Canada*. Toronto: Garamond Press.

Bonacich, E., (1972). "A Theory of Ethnic Antagonism: The Split Labor Market," *American Sociological Review*, 37, pp. 547-559.

Boone, L.E., D.L. Kurtz and R.A. Knowles, (1999). *Business*. Toronto: Harcourt Brace and Company, Canada.

Borger, J. and L. Harding, (2004). "Rumsfeld: I won't quit," *The Guardian*, Manchester, May 8, pp. 1.

Borisoff, D. and L. Merrill, (1985). *The Power to Communicate: Gender Differences As Barriers*. Prospect Heights, IL: Waveland Press, Inc.

Bradshaw-Campball, (1991). "Canadian Women on Boards: Excellence in a Box." Paper Presented at "Current Canadian Research on Women in Management," Winnipeg.

Bratton, J., J. Helms Mills, T. Pyrch and P. Sawchuk, (2004). *Workplace Learning*. Toronto: Garamond Press.

Braverman, H., (1974). *Labor and Monopoly Capital*. New York: Monthly Review Press.

Brindley, J.E. and P. Frick, (1990). *Gender Differences in Management: A Study of Professional Staff in Registrars' Offices in Canadian Universities*. Athabasca: Athabasca University.

Brown, H.A. and D.L. Ford, (1977). "An Exploratory Analysis of Discrimination in the Employment of Black MBA Graduates," *Journal of Applied Psychology*, (62), pp. 50-56.

Brown, L.D. and J.G. Covey, (1987). "Development Organizations and Organizational Development: Towards an Expanded Paradigm for Organization Development," in R.W. Woodman and W.A. Pasmore (eds.), *Research in Organizational Change and Development* Greenwich, CT: JAI Press.

Bufton, M.A., (2004). "Women on the Move," Ottawa, Carleton University, February, <http://www.now.carleton.ca/2004-02/144.htm>.

Burawoy, M., (1979). *Manufacturing Consent: Changes in the Labor Process Under Monopoly Capitalism*. Chicago; London: University of Chicago Press.

—— (1985). *The Politics of Production: Factory Regimes Under Capitalism and Socialism*. London: Verso.

Burke, R.J., (1991). "Managing an Increasingly Diverse Workforce: Experiences of Minority Managers and Professionals in Canada," *Canadian Journal of Administrative Sciences*, 8 (2), pp. 108-120.

Burman, P.W., (1988). *Killing Time, Losing Ground: Experiences of Unemployment*. Toronto: Wall and Thompson.

Burnham, J.,(1941). *The Managerial Revolution*. New York: Putnam.

Burrell, G., (1984). "Sex and Organizational Analysis," *Organization Studies*, 5 (2), pp. 97-118.

—— (1988). "Modernism, Postmodernism and Organizational Analysis 2: The Contribution of Michel Foucault," *Organisation Studies*, 9, pp. 221-235.

—— (1994). "Modernism, Postmodernism and Organizational Analysis 4: The Contribution of Jürgen Habermas," *Organization Studies*, 15 (1), pp. 1-19.

Burrell, G. and G. Morgan, (1979). *Sociological Paradigms and Organizational Analysis*. London: Heinemann.

Burrough, B., E. Peretz, D. Rose and D. Wise, (2004). "The Path To War," *Vanity Fair* (525), pp. 228-245, 281-294.

Burton, C., (1992). "Merit and Gender: Organizations and the Mobilization of Masculine Bias," in A.J. Mills and P. Tancred (eds.), *Gendering Organizational Analysis*, pp. 185-196. Newbury Park, CA: Sage.

Butler, C., (2002). *Postmodernism. A Very Short Introduction*. Oxford: Oxford University Press.

Calás, M.B., (1992). "An/Other Silent Voice? Representing "Hispanic Women in Organizational Texts," in A.J. Mills and P. Tancred (eds.), *Gendering Organizational Analysis*, pp. 201-221. Newbury Park, CA: Sage.

Calás, M.B. and L. Smircich, (1992a). "Re-writing Gender into Organizational Theorizing: Directions From Feminist Perspectives," in M. Reed and M. Hughes (eds.), *Rethinking Organization: New Directions in Organizational Theory and Analysis*, pp. 227-254. London: Sage.

—— (1992b). "Using the 'F' Word: Feminist Theories and the Social Consequences of Organizational Research," in A.J. Mills and P. Tancred (eds.), *Gendering Organizational Analysis*, pp. 222-234. Newbury Park, CA: Sage.

—— (1996). "From 'The Woman's' Point of View: Feminist Approaches to Organization Studies," in S.R. Clegg, C. Hardy and W.R. Nord (eds.), *Handbook of Organization Studies*, pp. 218-257. London: Sage.

Caley, D., (1988). "Part Moon, Part Travelling Salesman: Conversations with Ivan Illich," *Montreal: CBC Transcripts*.

Campbell, M., (1973). *Halfbreed*. Halifax: Goodread Biographies.

Canada, Parliament, House of Commons. Special Committee on Participation of Visible Minorities in Canadian Society, (1984). *Equality Now!: Report of the Special Committee on Visible Minorities in Canadian Society*. Ottawa: Queen's Printer.

Canada.com, (2003). "High skill immigrants drive labour force growth," *The Canadian Press*, CanWest Communications, May 26, <http://www.canada.com/national/features/census/story.html?id=4219B381-7FE0-40CD-ADD7-1F63220F8E6B>.

Canadian Association of University Teachers, (2004). "CAUT Almanac of Post-Secondary Education in Canada," *CAUT Bulletin*. Ottawa: January.

Canadian Heritage, (2003). "Canadian Multiculturalism Act," Ottawa: Canadian Heritage, <http://www.pch.gc.ca/progs/multi/policy/act_e.cfm>.

Carlsson, S., (1951). *Executive Behaviour: A Study of the Workload and the Working Methods of Managing Directors*. Stockholm: Strombergs.

Carr, A., (2003). "Managing in a Psycho-analytically Informed Manner," Special Issue, *Journal of Managerial Psychology*, 17 (5).

Carty, L., (1991). "Black Women in Academia: A Statement From The Periphery," in H. Bannerji, L. Carty, K. Dehli, S. Heald and K. McKenna (eds.), *Unsettling Relations: The University as a Site of Feminist Struggles*, pp. 13-44. Toronto: Women's Press.

Castles, S. and G. Kosack, (1985). *Immigrant Workers and Class Structure in Western Europe*. New York: Oxford University Press.

Catalyst, (2003). "2003 Catalyst Census of Women Board Directors of Canada," Toronto: Catalyst, <http://www.catalystwomen.org/>.

Cava, R., (1988). *Escaping the Pink Collar Ghetto: How Women Can Advance in Business*. Toronto: Key Porter Books.

CBC News Online Staff, (2003). "Former boxer seeks apology, compensation from Halifax police for discrimination," Ottawa: CBC, <http://www.cbc.ca/stories/2003/10/29/kirkjohnson031029>.

Chandler, A., (1977). *The Visible Hand*. Cambridge: Harvard University Press.

—— (1984). "The Emergence of Managerial Capitalism," *Business History Review*, 58 (Winter), pp. 473-503.

Chandler, J., J. Barry and E. Berg, (2004). "Reforming Managerialism? Gender and the Navigation of Change in Higher Education in Sweden and England," in R. Thomas, A.J. Mills and J. Helms Mills (eds.), *Identity Politics at Work: Resisting Gender, Gendering Resistance*. London: Routledge.

Chapman, B., (1961). "Facts of Organized Life," *Manchester Guardian Weekly*, January 26.

Cheng, C. and Men's Studies Association, (1996). *Masculinities in Organizations*. Thousand Oaks, CA: Sage.

Clark, D.L., (1985). "Emerging Paradigms in Organizational Theory," in Y.S. Lincoln (ed.), *Organizational Theory and Inquiry: The Paradigm Revolution*. Beverley Hills, CA: Sage.

Clark, K.B. and M.P. Clark, (1958). "Racial Identification and Preference in Negro Children," in E. Macoby and T.M. Newcomb (eds.), *Readings in Social Psychology*. New York: Holt, Rinehart and Winston.

Clarke, R., (2004). *Against All Enemies: Inside America's War on Terror*. New York: Simon and Shuster.

Clegg, S., (1975). *Power, Rule and Domination*. London: Routledge and Kegan Paul.

—— (1981). "Organization and Control," *Administrative Sciences Quarterly*, 26, pp. 532-545.

—— (1989). *Frameworks of Power*. Newbury Park, CA: Sage.

Clegg, S. and D. Dunkerley, (1980). *Organization, Class and Control*. London: Routledge and Kegan Paul.

—— (1990). *Modern Organizations*. Newbury Park, CA: Sage.

—— (1998). "Foucault, Power and Organizations," in A. McKinlay and K. Starkey (eds.), *Foucault, Management and Organization Theory*, pp. 29-48. London: Sage.

—— (2002). "Lives in the Balance": A Comment on Hinings and Greenwood's "Disconnects and Consequences in Organization Theory," *Administative Science Quarterly*, 47, pp. 428-441.

Clegg, S.R., C. Hardy and W.R. Nord (eds.), (1996). *Handbook of Organization Studies*. London: Sage.

Coch, L. and J.R.P. French, (1948). "Overcoming Resistance To Change," *Human Relations*, 1, pp. 512-532.

Cockburn, C., (1985). *Machinery of Dominance*. London: Pluto Press.

—— (1991). *Brothers, Male Dominance and Technological Change*. London: Pluto Press.

Collinson, D.L., (1988). "Engineering Humour: Masculinity, Joking and Conflict in Shopfloor Relations," *Organization Studies*, 9 (2), pp. 181-199.

Collinson, D.L. and M. Collinson, (1989). "Sexuality in the Workplace: Domination of Men's Sexuality," in J. Hearn, D.L. Sheppard, P. Tancred-Sheriff and G. Burrell (eds.), *The Sexuality of Organization*, pp. 91-109. London: Sage.

Collinson, D.L. and J. Hearn, (1994). "Naming Men as Men: Implications for Work, Organization and Management," *Gender, Work and Organization*, 1 (1), pp. 2-22.

—— (eds.), (1996). *Men as Managers, Managers as Men*. London: Sage.

Conference Board of Canada, (2004). "One-Third of Labour Force Contribution to GDP Growth Provided by Visible Minorities, Despite Gap in Wages," Ottawa: Conference Board of Canada.

Consultation Group on Employment Equity for Women, (1995). *Looking to the Future: Challenging the Cultural and Attitudinal Barriers to Women in the Public Service*. Ottawa: Minister of Supply and Services Canada.

Cooke-Reynolds, M. and N. Zukewich, (2004). "The Feminization of Work," *Canadian Social Trends*, Catalogue No. 11-008 (Statistics Canada), pp. 24-29.

Cooper, C. and M. Davidson, (1984). *Women in Management*. London: William Heinemann Ltd.

Copeland, L., (2004). "Prison Revolt," Washington: Washington Post.com, Monday, May 10, <http://www.washingtonpost.com/ac2/wp-dyn/A13114-2004May9?language=printer>.

Corman, S.R. and M.S. Poole (eds.), (2000). *Perspectives on Organizational Communication*. New York: The Guildford Press.

Cox, M.G., (1986). "Enter the Stranger: Unanticipated Effects of Communication on the Success of an Organizational Newcomer," in L. Thayer (ed.), *Organization-Communication: Emerging Perspectives*, pp. 34-50. Norwood, NJ: Ablex Publishing Corp.

Cox, Jr., T.H., (1990). "Problems With Organizational Research on Race and Ethnicity Issues," *Journal of Applied Behavioral Sciences*, 26, pp. 5-23.

Cox, T.J. and S. Nkomo, (1990). "Invisible Men and Women: A Status Report on Race as a Variable in Organization Behaviour Research," *Journal of Organizational Behavior*, (11), pp. 419-431.

Crane, D., (1967). "The Gatekeepers of Science: Some Factors Affecting the Selection of Articles for Scientific Journals," *American Sociologist*, 2, pp. 195-201.

Crozier, M., (1964). *The Bureaucratic Phenomenon*. Chicago: University of Chicago Press.

Cullen, D., (1992). "Sex and Gender on the Path to Feminism and Self-Actualization," *Administrative Sciences Association of Canada*, Quebec.

—— (1997). "Maslow, Monkeys and Motivation Theory," *Organization*, 4 (3), pp. 355-373.

Daft, R.L., (2001). *Essentials of Organization Theory and Design*. Cincinnati, OH: South-Western.

Dagg, A.I. and P.J. Thompson, (1988). *MisEducation: Women and Canadian Universities*. Toronto: OISE Press.

Dahrendorf, R., (1959). *Class and Class Conflict in Industrial Society*. London: Routledge and Kegan Paul.

Daily News Staff, (2004). "Pin-up Put-down," *The Daily News*. Halifax, pp. 1, 3.

Dale, E., (1973). *Management: Theory and Practice*. New York: McGraw-Hill.

—— (1978). *Management: Theory and Practice*. Toronto: McGraw-Hill.

Das, H., (1998). *Strategic Organizational Design*. Toronto: Prentice-Hall Canada.

Das Gupta, T., (1995). *Racism and Paid Work*. Toronto: Garamond Press.

Davidson, M.J. and R.J. Burke (eds.), (1994). *Women in Management: Current Research Issues*. London: Paul Chapman Publishing.

Davies, S., (1990). "Inserting Gender in Burawoy's Theory of the Labour Process," *Work, Employment and Society*, 4 (3), pp. 391-406.

Davis, G. and G. Watson, (1982). *Black Life in Corporate America: Swimming in the Mainstream*. Garden City, NY: Anchor Press/Doubleday.

Davis, K. and W.G. Scott, (1964). *Readings in Human Relations*. New York: McGraw-Hill.

De la Mothe, J. and G. Paquet, (1997). *Challenges Unmet in the New Production of Knowledge*. Ottawa: PRIME.

Delbridge, R., (1998). *Life on the Line in Contemporary Manufacturing*. Oxford: Oxford University Press.

Delgado, R. and J. Stefancic, (2000). *Critical Race Theory: The Cutting Edge*. Philadelphia: Temple University Press.

Deming, E., (1986). *Out of the Crisis*. Cambridge: MIT-CAES.

Denton, T.C., (1990). "Bonding and Supportive Relationships Among Black Professional Women: Rituals of Restoration," *Journal of Organizational Behavior*, (11), pp. 447-457.

Department of Justice Canada, (2003). "Employment Equity Act." Ottawa:

Department of Justice, <http://laws.justice.gc.ca/en/E-5.401/49886.html>.

Dickens, F. and J.B. Dickens, (1991). *The Black Manager: Making it in the Corporate World*. New York: American Management Association.

Dickson, D., (1977). *The Politics of Alternative Technology*. New York: Universe.

Dierkes, M., (2001). *Handbook of Organizational Learning and Knowledge*. New York: Oxford University Press.

Dipboye, R.L., (1985). "Some Neglected Variables in Research on Discrimination on Appraisals," *Academy of Management Review*, 10, pp. 116-127.

Disabled Women's Network Ontario, (2004). "Equal Pay: Making Politicians Make Better Choices for Women," North Bay, ON: DAWN Ontario, <http://dawn.thot.net/election2004/issues.htm>.

Djilas, M., (1982). *The New Class*. SanDiego, CA: Harvest Books.

Donaldson, L., (1985). *In Defence of Organization Theory*. Cambridge: Cambridge University Press.

—— (1988). "In Successful Defence of Organization Theory: A Routing of the Critics," *Organization Studies*, 9 (1), pp. 28-32.

—— (1996). *For Positivist Organization Theory*. Thousand Oaks, CA: Sage.

Donnelly, J.H., J.L. Gibson and J.M. Ivancevich, (1987). *Fundamentals of Management*. Plano, TX: Business Publications, Inc.

Doyle, M.K., (2000). *Mentoring Heroes: 52 Fabulous Women's Paths to Success and the Mentors who Empowered Them*. Batavia, IL: 3E Press.

Drane, J.W., (2001). *The McDonaldization of the Church: Consumer Culture and* the Church's Future. Macon, GA: Smyth and Helwys Pub.

Dreyfus, H.L. and P. Rabinow, (1982). *Michel Foucault: Beyond Structuralism and Hermeneutics*. Hemel Hempstead: Harvester Wheatsheaf.

Drucker, P., (1986). *The Practice of Management*. New York: Harper.

Duff, C.S., (1999). *Learning From Other Women: How to Benefit From the Knowledge, Wisdom, and Experience of Female Mentors*. New York: AMACOM.

Durkheim, E., (1957). *Professional Ethics and Civic Morals*. London: Routledge and Kegan Paul.

—— (1964). *The Division of Labour in Society*. New York: Free Press.

Easterby-Smith, M. and M.A. Lyles, (2003). *The Blackwell Handbook of Organizational Learning and Knowledge Management*. Oxford: Blackwell.

Edwards, R., (1979). *Contested Terrain: The Transformation of the Workplace in the Twentieth Century*. New York: Basic Books.

Ellis, S. and P. Dick, (2000). *Introduction to Organizational Behaviour*. Maidenhead: McGraw-Hill.

Fayol, H., (1949). *General and Industrial Management*. London: Pitman Publishing.

Federal Bureau of Investigation, (1954-1968). *Subject: Abraham H. Maslow, File Number: 100-HQ-415677*. Washington, DC: FBI.

Feldberg, R.L. and E.N. Glenn, (1979). "Male and Female: Job Versus Gender Models in the Sociology of Work," *Social Problems*, 26(5), pp. 524-538.

Ferguson, K., (1994). "On Bringing More Theory, More Voices, and More Politics to the Study of Organization," *Organization*, 1(1), pp. 81-99.

Ferguson, K.E., (1984). *The Feminist Case Against Bureaucracy*. Philadelphia: Temple University Press.

Fernandez, J.P., (1975). *Black Managers in White Corporations*. New York: Wiley.

Feyerabend, P.K., (1975). *Against Method: Outline of an Anarchistic Theory of Knowledge*. London.

Flax, J., (1990). *Thinking Fragments: Psychoanalysis, Feminism and Postmodernism in the Contemporary West*. Berkeley, CA: University of California Press.

Fleras, A. and J.L. Elliott, (1992). *Multiculturalism in Canada: The Challenge of Diversity*. Toronto: Nelson Canada.

—— (2003). *Unequal Relations: An Introduction to Race and Ethnic Dynamics in Canada*. Toronto: Prentice Hall.

Foldy, E.G., (2002). "'Managing' Diversity: Identity and Power in Organizations," in I. Aaltio and A.J. Mills (eds.), *Gender, Identity and the Culture of Organizations*, pp. 92-112. London: Routledge.

Fondas, N., (1997). "Feminization Unveiled: Management Qualities in Contemporary Writings," *The Academy of Management Review*, 22 (1), pp. 257-282.

Foucault, M., (1972). *The Archaeology of Knowledge*. London: Routledge.

—— (1979). *Discipline and Punish: The Birth of the Prison*. New York: Vintage.

—— (1980). *Power/Knowledge*. New York: Pantheon.

Francis, D., (1996). "The Feminine Mystique in the Front Office." *Maclean's*, pp. 15.

Franklin, R., (1968). "A Frameowrk for the Analysis of Inter-urban Negro-White Economic Differentials," *Industrial and Labour Relations Review*, 2, pp. 209-223.

French, J.R.P., J. Israel and D. Aas, (1960). "An Experiment on Participation in a

Norwegian Factory," *Human Relations*, 13, pp. 3-19.

Friedan, B., (1983). *The Feminine Mystique*. New York: Dell.

Fukuyama, F., (1989). "The End of History," *The National Interest*, Summer Issue.

Galbraith, J.K., (1978). *The New Industrial State*. Boston: Houghton Mifflin.

Giglio, M., (2003). *The Effects of Affirmative Action on Rationalizing Sexual Harassment*. Ottawa: National Library of Canada/Bibliothèque Nationale du Canada.

Gilligan, C., (1982). *In A Different Voice: Psychological Theory and Women's Development*. Cambridge, MA: Harvard University Press.

Gillis, J., (2005). "SMU bans campus sales of pinup calendar." *The Halifax Herald*, Halifax.

Goldenberg, S., (2004a). "From Heroine to Humiliator," *The Guardian*, Manchester, May 8, pp. 5.

—— (2004b). "Pentagon braced for wave of abuse images," *The Guardian*, Manchester, May 10, pp. 4.

Goldenberg, S., D. Leigh and R. Norton Taylor, (2004). "Bush sinks deeper into trouble," *The Guardian*, Manchester, May 10, pp. 1.

Gorber, T.A., (2001). *Equality in the Federal Public Service, the Intersections of Identity Visible Minority, Immigrant Women and Multiple (Dis)advantage*. Ottawa: National Library of Canada/ Bibliothèque Nationale du Canada.

Gouldner, A., (1954). *Patterns of Industrial Bureaucracy*. Glenco, IL: Free Press.

Grant, J. and P. Tancred-Sheriff, (1992). "A Feminist Perspective on State Bureaucracy," in A.J. Mills and P. Tancred-Sheriff (eds.), *Gendering Organizational Analysis*. Newbury Park, CA: Sage.

Greene, A.-M., P. Ackers and J. Black, (2002). "Going Against the Historical Grain: Perspectives on Gendered Occupational Identity and Resistance to the Breakdown of Occupational Segregation in Two Manufacturing Firms," *Gender, Work and Organization*, 9 (3), pp. 266-285.

Greenhalgh, P., (2000). *Women and Work the Labour Market: Experiences of Recent Immigrant Women*. Ottawa: National Library of Canada/Bibliothèque Nationale du Canada.

Gregory, J., R. Sales and A. Hegewisch, (1999). *Women, Work and Inequality: The Challenge of Equal Pay in a Deregulated Labour Market*. New York: St. Martin's Press.

Grieco, E.M.C., (2001). "The White Population: 2000." Washington, DC: US Census Bureau, <http://www.census.gov/prod/2001pubs/c2kbr01-4.pdf>.

Griffin, R.W., R.J. Ebert and F.A. Starke, (2002). *Business: Fourth Canadian Edition*. Toronto: Prentice Hall.

Griseri, P., (2001). *Management Knowledge: A Critical View*. New York: Palgrave.

Gross, B.M., (1985). *Friendly Fascism: The New Face of Power in America*. Montreal, Black Rose Books.

Gulick, L. and L. Urwick, (eds.), (1937). *Papers on the Science of Administration*. New York: Institute of Public Administration.

Gutek, B. (1985). *Sex and the Workplace* (San Francisco, Jossey-Bass).

Gutek, B. and A. Cohen, (1992). "Sex Ratios, Sex Role Spillover, and Sex at Work: A Comparison of Men's and Women's Experiences," in A.J. Mills and P. Tancred (eds.), *Gendering Organizational Analysis*, pp. 133-150. Newbury Park, CA: Sage.

Gutek, B.A. and L. Larwood, (eds.), (1987). *Women's Career Development*. Newbury Park, CA: Sage.

Halberstam, D., (1986). *The Reckoning*. New York: Morrow and Co.

Hall, M., (1989). "Private Experiences in the Public Domain: Lesbians in Organizations," in J. Hearn, D.L. Sheppard, P. Tancred-Sheriff and G. Burrell (eds.), *The Sexuality of Organization*, pp. 125-138. London: Sage.

Hammer, M., (1990). "Reengineering Work: Don't Automate, Obliterate," *Harvard Business Review*, 68 (4), pp. 104-112.

—— (1995). *The Reengineering Revolution*. New York: Harper and Collins.

—— (1996). *Beyond Reengineering: How the Process-centred Organization is Changing our Work and our Lives*. New York: HarperBusiness.

Hammer, M. and J. Champy, (1993). *Reengineering the Corporation*. New York: HarperCollins.

Hancock, P. and M.J. Tyler, (2001). *Work, Postmodernism and Organization: A Critical Introduction*. London: Sage.

Hardy, C. and S.R. Clegg, (1996). "Some Dare Call it Power," in S. Clegg, C. Hardy and W. Nord (eds.), *Handbook of Organization Studies*, pp. 622-641. London: Sage.

Harriman, A., (1985). *Women/Men, Management*. New York: Praeger.

Harrington, H.J., (1991). *Business Process Improvement* (McGraw-Hill, New York).

Harris, C., (1991). Configurations of Racism: The Civil Service, 1945-1960, *Race and Class*, 33, pp. 1-30.

Hassard, J. and M. Parker, (1993). *Postmodernism and Organizations*. London: Sage Publications.

Hatch, M.J., (1997). *Organization Theory: Modern Symbolic and Postmodern Perspectives*. Oxford: Oxford University Press.

Hatton, M.J., (1990). *Corporations and Directors*. Toronto: Thompson.

Hayes, D. and R. Wynyard, (2002). *The McDonaldization of Higher Education*. Westport, CT: Bergin and Garvey.

Hazell, R., (2002). *Interrogating the Social Construction of Race and Difference in Ontario Public Schools*. Ottawa: National Library of Canada/Bibliothèque Nationale du Canada.

Heap, J.L., (1974). *Everybody's Canada: The Vertical Mosaic Reviewed and Re-examined*. Toronto: Burns and MacEachern.

Hearn, J., (1985). "Men's Sexuality at Work," in A. Metcalf and M. Humphries (eds.), *The Sexuality of Men*, pp. 110-128. London: Pluto Press.

—— (2002). "Alternative Conceptualizations and Theoretical Perspectives on Identities and Organizational Cultures: A Personal Review of Research on Men in Organizations," in I. Aaltio and A.J. Mills (eds.), *Gender, Identity and the Culture of Organizations*, pp. 39-56. London: Routledge.

—— (2004). "Personal Resistance Through Persistence to Organizational Resistance Through Distance," in R. Thomas, A.J. Mills and J. Helms Mills (eds.), *Identity Politics At Work: Resisting Gender, Gendering Resistance*. London: Routledge.

Hearn, J. and P.W. Parkin, (1983). "Gender and Organizations: A Selective Review and a Critique of a Neglected Area," *Organization Studies*, 4 (3), pp. 219-242.

—— (1987). *"Sex" at "Work" – The Power and Paradox of Organizational Sexuality*. Brighton: Wheatsheaf.

—— (1991). "Women, Men and Leadership: A Critical Review of Assumptions, Practices and Changes in the Industrialized Nations." in N.J. Adler and D. Izraeli (eds.), *Women in Management Worldwide*. New York: M.E. Sharpe.

Hearn, J., D. Sheppard, P. Tancred-Sheriff and G. Burrell, (eds.), (1989). *The Sexuality of Organization*. London: Sage.

Held, D., (1980). *Introduction to Critical Theory*. London: Hutchinson.

Helms Mills, J.C., (2002). Employment Practices and the Gendering of Air Canada's Culture During its Trans Canada Airlines Days, *Culture and Organization*, 8(2), pp. 117-128.

—— (2003a). *Making Sense of Organizational Change*. London: Routledge.

—— (2003b). *Making Sense of Organizational Change*. London: Routledge.

Helms Mills, J.C. and A.J. Mills, (2000). "Rules, Sensemaking, Formative Contexts and Discourse in the Gendering of Organizational Culture." in N.M. Ashkanasy, C.P.M. Wilderom and M.F. Peterson (eds.), *Handbook of Organizational Culture and Climate*, pp. 55-70. Thousand Oaks, CA: Sage.

Henry, F. and C. Tator, (2000a). *From the Colour of Democracy: Racism in Canadian Society*. Toronto: Harcourt Brace.

—— (2000b). "Racist Discourse in Canada's English Print Media," Toronto: The Canadian Race Relations Foundation, <http://www.crr.ca/en/Publications/ResearchReports/ePub_ RR20000330_full.htm>.

—— (2002). *Discourses of Domination: Racial Bias in the Canadian English-Language Press*. Toronto: University of Toronto Press.

Hersh, S.M. (2004). "Annals of National Security. The Gray Zone," *The New Yorker,* May 17.

Hinings, C.R. and R. Greenwood, (2002). "Disconnects and Consequences in Organization Theory," *Administative Science Quarterly*, 47, pp. 411-421.

Hochschild, A.R., (1983). *The Managed Heart*. Berkeley, CA: University of California Press.

Hoffman, E., (1988). *The Right To Be Human. A Biography of Abraham Maslow*. New York: St.Martin's Press.

Hofstede, G., (1980). *Culture's Consequences: International Differences in Work Related Values*. London: Sage.

Hollway, W., (1989). *Subjectivity and Method in Psychology: Gender, Meaning and Science*. London: Sage.

Hudson, J., (2003). "It's Not Fair, It's Not Right, But It's Fact," Wolfville, NS: Acadia University Student Union, December 2, <http://www.theath.ca/issues/12.02.03/news/newsp1.htm>.

Husu, L., (2001). *Sexism, Support and Survival in Academia: Academic Women and Hidden Discrimination in Finland*. Helsinki: University of Helsinki.

Hydebrand, W., (1977). "Organizational Contradictions in Public Bureaucracies: Towards a Marxian Theory of Organization," *Sociological Quarterly*, 18, pp. 83-107.

Iacocca, L., (1984). *Iacocca – An Autobiography*. New York: Bantam.

Ighodaro, M. (2004). *Understanding African Refugees' Resettlement Experiences in Canada Through a Critical Anti-racist Paradigm*. Ottawa: National Library of Canada/Bibliothèque Nationale du Canada.

Illich, I., (1981). *Deschooling Society*. London: Calder Boyars.

Indian and Northern Affairs Canada, (2004). "Royal Commission on Aboriginal Peoples," Ottawa: <http://www.ainc-inac.gc.ca/ch/rcap/index_e.html>.

International Committee of the Red Cross Report – Edited Extracts, (2004). "Violations were 'tantamount to torture.'" *The Guardian,* Manchester, May 8, pp. 4.

Irwin, J., Gay and Lesbian Rights Lobby (N.S.W.) and Australian Centre for Lesbian and Gay Research, (1999). *"The Pink Ceiling is Too Low": Workplace Experiences of Lesbians, Gay Men and Transgender People.* Sydney, NSW: Australian Centre for Lesbian and Gay Research: NSW Gay and Lesbian Rights Lobby.

Jackall, R., (1988). *Moral Mazes.* Oxford: Oxford University Press.

Jacques, R., (1996). *Manufacturing the Employee: Management Knowledge From the 19th to 21st Centuries.* London: Sage.

—— (1997). "The Unbearable Whiteness of Being: Reflections of a Pale, Stale Male," in P. Prasad, A.J. Mills, M. Elmes and A. Prasad (eds.), *Managing the Organizational Melting Pot: Dilemmas of Workplace Diversity*, pp. 80-106. Thousand Oaks, CA: Sage.

Jameson, F., (1991). *Postmodernism, or, the Cultural Logic of Late Capitalism.* Durham, NC: Duke University Press.

Jauch, L.R. and J.L. Wall, (1989). "What They Do When They Get Your Manuscript: A Survey of Academy of Management Reviewer Practices," *Academy of Management Review*, 32, pp. 157-173.

Jedwab, J., (2003). "Visible Minority Unemployment in Canada and the United States," Montreal: Association for Canadian Studies, <http://www.acs-aec.ca/Polls/Poll31.pdf>.

Johns, G. and A.M. Saks, (2001). *Understanding and Managing Life at Work: Organizational Behaviour.* Toronto: Pearson Education Canada.

Jones, A.P., L.R. James, J.R. Bruni and S.B. Shell, (1977). "Black-White Differences in Work Environment Perceptions and Job Satisfaction and its Correlates," *Personnel Psychology*, 30, pp. 5-16.

Juran, J., (1988). *Juran on Planning for Quality.* New York: Free Press.

Kane, P., (1974). *Sex Objects in the Sky.* Chicago, IL: Follett.

Kanter, R.M., (1977). *Men and Women of the Corporation.* New York: Basic Books.

—— (1979). "Power Failure in Management Circuits," *Harvard Business Review*, 57 (4), pp. 65-75.

Kaye, M., (1997). "The Best Man for the Job," *Canadian Living* (4), pp. 65-70.

Kerfoot, D. and D. Knights, (1996). "The Best is Yet to Come?": The Quest for Embodiment in Managerial Work," in D.L. Collinson and J. Hearn (eds.), *Men as Managers, Managers as Men: Critical Perspectives on Men, Masculinities and Managements*, pp. 78-98. Newbury Park, Sage.

Kets de Vries, M.F.R., (1989). "The Leader as Mirror: Clinical Reflections," *Human Relations*, 42 (7), pp. 607-623.

—— (1989). "Alexithymia in Organizational Life: The Organization Man Revisited," *Human Relations*, 42 (12), pp. 1079-1093.

—— (1991). *Organizations on the Couch: Clinical Perspectives on Organizational Behavior and Change.* San Francisco: Jossey-Bass.

Kets de Vries, M.F.R. and D. Miller, (1984). *The Neurotic Organization.* San Francisco: Jossey-Bass.

Kirby, S. and K. McKenna, (1989). *Experience, Research, Social Change: Methods From the Margins.* Toronto: Garamond.

Kirchmeyer, C. and J. McLellan, (1991). "Capitalizing on Ethnic Diversity: An Approach to Managing the Diverse Workgroups of the 1990s," *Canadian Journal of Administrative Science*, 8 (2), pp. 72-79.

Klein, N., (2004). "Jobs Down, Thumbs Up," *The Globe and Mail.* Toronto, May 13, pp. A19.

Knights, D. and G. Morgan, (1991). "Corporate Strategy, Organizations, and Subjectivity: A Critique," *Organisation Studies*, 12 (2), pp. 251-273.

Knights, D. and H. Willmott, (1999). *Management Lives: Power and Identity in Work Organizations*. London: SAGE.

Kohut, H., (1971). *The Analysis of the Self: A Systematic Approach to the Psychoanalytic Treatment of Narcissistic Personality Disorders*. New York: International Universities Press.

Konar, E., (1981). "Explaining Racial Differences in Job Satisfaction: A Re-examination of the Data," *Journal of Applied Psychology*, (66), pp. 522-524.

Konopaske, R. and J.M. Ivancevich, (2004). *Global Management and Organizational Behaviour*. New York: McGraw-Hill Irwin.

Konrad, A.M., P. Prasad and J.K. Pringle (eds.), (in press). *Handbook of Workplace Diversity*. London: Sage.

Kotter, J.P., (1990). "What Leaders Really Do," *Harvard Business Review*, May-June, pp. 103-111.

—— (1996). *Leading Change*. Boston: Harvard Business School Press.

Krahn, H. and G.S. Lowe, (2002). *Work, Industry and Canadian Society*. Toronto: Thomson Nelson Learning.

Kraiger, K. and J. Ford, (1985). "A Meta-analysis of Rated Race Effects in Performance Ratings," *Journal of Applied Psychology*, (70), pp. 56-65.

Kranz, H., (1976). *The Participatory Bureaucracy: Women and Minorities in a More Representative Public Service*. Lexington, MA: Lexington Books.

Kuhn, T.S., (1970). *The Structure of Scientific Revolutions*. Chicago: University of Chicago Press.

Kunz, J.L., A. Milan and S. Schetagne, (2000). "Unequal Access: A Canadian Profile of Racial Differences in Employment, Education and Income," Toronto: Canadian Race Relations Foundation, <http://www.crr.ca/EN/Publications/ePubHome.htm>.

Lacey, R., (1986). *Ford – The Men and the Machine*. New York: Ballantine.

Lakatos, I., (1972). "History of Science and its Rational Reconstructions," in R.C. Buck and R.S. Cohen (eds.), *Boston Studies in the Philosophy of Science*, pp. 91-135. Boston: Reidel Publishing.

Lamphere, L., (1985). "Bringing the Family to Work: Women's Culture on the Shop Floor," *Feminist Studies*, 11 (3), pp. 519-540.

Landy, F.J. and S.L. Farr, (1980). "Performance Rating," *Psychological Bulletin*, (82), pp. 72-107.

Lasch, C., (1979). *The Culture of Narcissism*. New York: Warner Books.

Lawrence, P., (1984). *Management in Action*. London: Routledge and Kegan Paul.

Leigh, D., (2004). "UK Forces Taught Torture Methods," *The Guardian*, Mancester, May 8, pp. 1,2.

Leman, M., (1999). Canadian Multiculturalism in L.o. Parliament (ed.), Ottawa: Political and Social Affairs Division.

LeMoncheck, L. and J.P. Sterba, (2001). *Sexual Harassment: Issues and Answers*. New York: Oxford University Press.

Lenin, V.I.i., (1927). *Imperialism: The Last Stage of Capitalism*. London: Communist Party of Great Britain.

—— (1992). *The State and Revolution*. London: Penguin.

Leonard, P., (1984). *Personality and Ideology: Towards a Material Understanding of the Individual*. London: Methuen.

Lewin, K., R. Lippitt and R.K. White, (1939). "Patterns of Aggressive Behavior in Experimentally Created 'Social Climates,'" *Journal of Social Psychology*, 10, pp. 271-299.

Li, J. and A.S. Tsui, (2002). "A Citation Analysis of Management and Organization Research in the Chinese Context: 1984-1999," *Asia Pacific Journal of Management*, 19 (1), pp. 87-107.

Li, P.S., (1990). *Ethnic inequality in a Class Society*. Toronto: Thompson Educational.

Li, P.S., B.S. Bolaria and Western Association of Sociology and Anthropology Conference, (1983). *Racial Minorities in Multicultural Canada*. Toronto: Garamond Press.

Linstead, S., L. Fulop and S. Lilley, (2004). *Management and Organization: A Critical Text*. London: Palgrave MacMillan.

Lipset, S.M., (1950). "Bureaucracy and Social Reform," in A. Etzioni (ed.), *Complex Organizations: A Sociological Reader*. Austin, TX: Holt, Rinehart and Winston.

—— (1971). *Agrarian Socialism: The Cooperative Commonwealth Federation in Saskatchewan; A Study in Political Sociology*. Berkeley: University of California Press.

Livingstone, D.W. and M. Luxton, (1989). "Gender Consciousness at Work: Modifications of the Male Breadwinner Norm Among Steelworkers and Their Spouces," *The Canadian Review of Sociology and Anthropology*, 26 (2), pp. 240-275.

Locke, E.A., (1982). "The Ideas of Frederick W. Taylor: An Evaluation," *Academy of Management Review*, 7 (1), pp. 14-24.

Love, J.F., (1986). *McDonalds: Behind the Arches*. New York: Bantham Books.

Lowe, G.S., (1987). *Women in the Administrative Revolution*. Toronto: University of Toronto Press.

Lowe, L., A.J. Mills and J. Mullen, (2002). "Gendering the Silences: Psychoanalysis, Gender and Organization Studies," *Journal of Managerial Psychology*, 17 (5), pp. 422-434.

Lukács, G., (1971). *History and Class Consciousness: Studies in Marxist Dialectics*. London: Merlin Press.

Maier, M., (1991). "The Dysfunctions of 'Corporate Masculinity': Gender and Diversity Issues in Organizational Development," *The Journal of Management in Practice*, Summer/Fall.

—— (1997). "'We Have to Make a Management Decision': Challenger and the Dysfunctions of Corporate Masculinity." in P. Prasad, A.J. Mills, M. Elmes and A. Prasad (eds.), *Managing the Organizational Melting Pot: Dilemmas of Workplace Diversity*, pp. 226-254. Newbury Park, CA: Sage.

Maier, M. and J.W. Messerschmidt, (1998). "Commonalities, Conflicts and Contradictions in Organizational Masculinities: Exploring the Gendered Genesis of the Challenger Disaster," *The Canadian Review of Sociology and Anthropology*, 35 (325-344).

Mainiero, L., (1993). "Dangerous Liaisons? A Review of Current Issues Concerning Male and Female Romantic Relationships in the Workplace." in E. Fagenson (ed.), *Women in Management*. Newbury Park, CA: Sage.

Mapleleaf Web, (2004). "Can the Right Successfully Unite?" Lethbridge, AB: Department of Political Science, University of Lethbridge, <http://www. mapleleafweb.com/features/party/unite-right/right-successful.html>.

Marcuse, H., (1970). *One Dimensional Man*. London: Sphere Books.

Marshall, H. and M. Weatherall, (1989). "Talking About Career and Gender Identities: A Discourse Analysis Perspective," in S. Skevington and D. Baker (eds.), *The Social Identity of Women*, pp. 106-129. London: Sage.

Marshall, J., (1984). *Women Managers: Travellers in a Male World*. Chichester: John Wiley and Sons.

Martin, J., (1990). "Rethinking Weber: A Feminist Search for Alternatives To Bureaucracy," Paper presented at the annual meeting of the Academy of Management, San Francisco.

—— (2000). "Hidden Gendered Assumptions in Mainstream Organizational Theory and Research," *Journal of Management Inquiry*, 9 (2), pp. 207-216.

—— (2002). *Organizational Culture. Mapping the Terrain*. Thousand Oaks, CA: Sage.

Marx, K., (1967). *Economic and Philosophic Manuscripts of 1844*. Moscow: Progress Publishers.

—— (1999). *Capital: A Critical Analysis of Capitalist Production*. London: Oxford University Press.

Marx, K. and F. Engels, (1940). *The German Ideology*. London: Lawrence and Wishart.

—— (1967). *The Communist Manifesto*. Harmonsworth: Penguin.

Marx Memorial Library, (1992). "Post Modernism," *Marx Memorial Library Bulletin*, 117.

Maslow, A., (1998). *Maslow on Management*. New York: John Wiley and Sons.

—— (1943). "A Theory of Human Motivation," *Pychological Review*, 50, pp. 370-396.

Mayo, E., (1933). *The Human Problems of an Industrial Civilization*. New York: MacMillan.

McClelland, D.C., (1961). *The Achieving Society*. Princeton, NJ: Van Nostrand.

McGregor, D., (1960). *The Human Side of Enterprise*. New York: McGraw Hill.

McManus, K., (2000). *Employed Mothers and the Work-Family Interface: Does Family Type Matter?* Ottawa: National Library of Canada/Bibliothèque Nationale du Canada.

McShane, S., (2001). *Canadian Organizational Behaviour*. Toronto: McGraw-Hill Ryerson.

McShane, S.L. and M.A. Von Glinow, (2000). *Organizational Behaviour*. Boston: Irwin McGraw Hill.

Meehan, E.R. and E. Riordan, (2002). *Sex and Money: Feminism and Political Economy in the Media*. Minneapolis: University of Minnesota Press.

Meissner, M., (1986). "The Reproduction of Women's Domination," in L. Thayer (ed.), *Organization-Communication: Emerging Perspectives*, pp. 51-67. Norwood, NJ: Ablex.

Merton, R.K., (1940). "Bureaucratic Structure and Personality," *Social Forces*, XVII, pp. 560-568.

Michels, R., (1949). *Political Parties*. Chicago: Free Press.

Miewald, R., (1970). "The Greatly Exaggerated Death of Bureaucracy," *California Management Journal*, Winter, pp. 65-69.

Mighty, E.J., (1991). "Valuing Workplace Diversity: A Model of Organizational Change," *Canadian Journal of Administrative Sciences*, 8 (2), pp. 64-71.

—— (1997). "Triple Jeopardy: Immigrant Women of Color in the Labor Force," in P. Prasad, A.J. Mills, M. Elmes and A. Prasad (eds.), *Managing the Organizational Melting Pot. Dilemmas of Workplace Diversity*, pp. 312-339. Thousand Oaks, CA: Sage.

Mikalachki, A., D.R. Mikalachki and R.J. Burke, (1992). *Gender Issues In Management: Contemporary Cases*.

Miller, G.E., (2002). "The Frontier, Entrepreneurialism, and Engineers: Women Coping With a Web of Masculinities in an Organizational

Culture," *Culture and Organization*, 8 (2), pp. 145-160.

Mills, A.J., (1988a). "Organization, Gender and Culture," *Organization Studies*, 9 (3), pp. 351-369.

—— (1988b). "Organizational Acculturation and Gender Discrimination," in P.K. Kresl (ed.), *Canadian Issues, X1 – Women and the Workplace*, pp. 1-22. Montreal: Association of Canadian Studies/International Council for Canadian Studies.

—— (1995). "Man/Aging Subjectivity, Silencing Diversity: Organizational Imagery in the Airline Industry – The Case of British Airways," *Organization*, 2 (2), pp. 243-269.

—— (1996a). "Corporate Image, Gendered Subjects And The Company Newsletter – The Changing Faces of British Airways," in G. Palmer and S. Clegg (eds.), *Constituting Management: Markets, Meanings And Identities*, pp. 191-211. Berlin: de Gruyter.

—— (1996b). "Organizational Sexuality," in K. Borman and P. Dubeck (eds.), *Women and Work*, pp. 323-325. New York: Garland Publishing Inc.

—— (1996c). "Strategy, Sexuality and the Stratosphere: Airlines and the Gendering of Organization," in E.S. Lyon and L. Morris (eds.), *Gender Relations In Public and Private: New Research Perspectives*, pp. 77-94. London: Macmillan.

—— (1997a). "Gender, Bureaucracy and The Business Curriculum," *Journal of Management Education*, 21 (3), pp. 325-342.

—— (1997b). "Practice Makes Perfect: Corporate Practices, Bureaucratization and the Idealized Gendered Self," *Hallinnon Tutkimus (Finnish Journal of Administrative Studies)* 4, pp. 272-288.

—— (1998a). "Cockpits, Hangars, Boys and Galleys: Corporate Masculinities and the Development of British Airways," *Gender, Work and Organization*, 5 (3), pp. 172-188.

—— (1998b). "Toward an Agenda of Radical Organizing: introduction to the Special Issue," *The Canadian Review of Sociology and Anthropology*, 35 (3), pp. 281.

—— (2002a). "History/Herstory: An Introduction to the Problems of Studying the Gendering of Organizational Culture Over Time," in I. Aaltio and A.J. Mills (eds.), *Gender, Identity and the Culture of Organizations*, pp. 115-136. London: Routledge.

—— (2002b). "Studying the Gendering of Organizational Culture Over Time: Concerns, Issues and Strategies," *Gender, Work and Organization*, 9 (3), pp. 286-307.

—— (2004). "Feminist Organizational Analysis and the Business Textbook," in D.E. Hodgson and C. Carter (eds.), *Management Knowledge and the New Employee*. London: Ashgate.

Mills, A.J. and P. Chiaramonte, (1991). "Organization as Gendered Communication Act," *Canadian Journal of Communications*, 16 (4), pp. 381-398.

Mills, A.J. and J.C. Helms Hatfield, (1995). "From Imperialism to Globalization: Internationalization and the Management Text – A Review of Selected US Texts." *A.P.R.O.S.* Cuernavaca: Mexico.

—— (1998). "From Imperialism to Globalization: Internationalization and the Management Text." in S.R. Clegg, E. Ibarra and L. Bueno (eds.), *Theories of the Management Process: Making Sense Through Difference*, pp. 37-67. Thousand Oaks, CA: Sage.

Mills, A.J. and J. Helms Mills, (2002). "Masculinity and the Making of Trans-Canada Air Lines, 1938-1940," *Proceedings of the Australia and New Zealand Academy of*

Management/International Federation of Scholarly Associations of Management (ANZAM/IFSAM) Conference.

—— (2004). "When Plausibility Fails: Towards a Critical Sensemaking Approach to Resistance," in R. Thomas, A.J. Mills and J. Helms Mills (eds.), *Identity Politics at Work: Resisting Gender and Gendered Resistance*. London: Routledge.

Mills, A.J., E. Kelley and B. Cooke, (2002). "Management Theory in Context: Exploring the Influence of the Cold War," in G. Spraakman (ed.), *Proceedings of the Business History Division of the Administrative Sciences Association of Canada*, pp. 11-20. 23 (Winnipeg,

Mills, A.J. and S.J. Murgatroyd, (1991). *Organizational Rules: A Framework for Understanding Organizations*. Milton Keynes: Open University Press.

Mills, A.J. and C. Ryan, (2001). "Contesting the Spiritual Space: Patriarchy, Bureaucracy, and the Gendering of Women's Religious Orders," *Tamara: Journal of Critical Postmodern Organization Science*, 1 (4), pp. 60-79.

Mills, A.J. and T. Simmons, (1999). *Reading Organization Theory: Critical Approaches to the Study of Behaviour and Structure in Organizations*. Toronto: Garamond Press.

Mills, A.J. and P. Tancred (eds.), (1992). *Gendering Organizational Analysis*. Newbury Park, CA: Sage.

Minehan, M., (2004). "Changing Demography and Recruitment," *Diversity Resources, Inc.*, <http://www.diversityresources.com/rc04_sample/changedem.html>.

Mintzberg, H., (1973). *The Nature of Managerial Work*. New York: Harper and Row.

—— (1975). "The Manager's Job: Folklore and Fact," *Harvard Business Review*, 4, pp. 49-61.

—— (1979). *The Structure of Organizations*. Englewood Cliffs, NJ: Prentice-Hall.

—— (1983). *Power In and Around Organizations*. Englewood Cliffs, NJ: Prentice-Hall.

Mirchandani, K., (1998). "No Longer a Struggle?": Teleworkers Reconstruction of the Work Non-work Boundary." in P.J. Jackson and J.M. van der Wielen (eds.), *Teleworking: International Perspectives*, pp. 118-135. London: Routledge.

—— (2004). "Webs of Resistance in Transnational Call Centres: Strategic Agents, Service Providers and Customers," in R. Thomas, A.J. Mills and J. Helms Mills (eds.), *Identity Politics at Work: Resisting Gender, Gendering Resistance*. London: Routledge.

Moorhead, G., R.W. Griffin, P.G. Irving and D.F. Coleman, (2000). *Organizational Behaviour. Managing People and Organizations*. Boston: Houghton Mifflin.

Morgan, D.H.J., (1996a). "The Gender of Bureaucracy," in D.L. Collinson and J. Hearn (eds.), *Men as Managers, Managers as Men: Critical Perspectives on Men, Masculinities and Managements*, pp. 43-60. Newbury Park: Sage.

Morgan, G., (1985). "Journals and the Control of Knowledge: A Critical Perspective," in L.L. Cummings and P. Frost (eds.), *Publishing in the Organizational Sciences*. Homewood, IL: Richard D. Irwin.

—— (1996b). *Images of Organization*. Thousand Oaks, CA: Sage.

Morgan, G. and D. Knights, (1991). "Gendering Jobs: Corporate Strategies, Managerial Control and Dynamics of Job Segregation," *Work, Employment and Society*, 5 (2), pp. 181-200.

Morgan, N., (1988). *The Equality Game: Women in the Federal Public Service (1908-1987)*. Ottawa: Canadian Advisory Council on the Status of Women.

Morrison, A., R. White and E. Van Elsor, (1987). *Breaking the Glass Ceiling*. Reading, MA: Addison Wesley.

Mouzelis, N.P., (1975). *Organisation and Bureaucracy: An Analysis of Modern Theories*. London: Routledge and Kegan Paul.

Mumby, D.K. and L.L. Putnam, (1992). "The Politics of Emotion: A Feminist Reading of Bounded Rationality," *Academy of Management Review.*, 17 (3), pp. 465-486.

Nahem, J., (1981). *Psychology and Psychiatry Today: A Marxist View*. New York: International Publishers.

Nehmé, M., (2001). "Equality Legislation in the Canadian Federal Public Service," Ottawa: National Library of Canada/ Bibliothèque Nationale du Canada.

Neil, C., M. Tykkyläinen and J. Bradbury, (1992). *Coping With Closure: An International Comparison of Mine Town Experiences*. London, New York: Routledge.

Nelson, D.L. and R.J. Burke, (2002). *Gender, Work Stress, and Health*. Washington, DC: Amer. Psychological Assoc.

Nelson, D.L. and J.C. Quick, (2000). *Organizational Behavior*. Cincinnati, OH: South-Western.

Nelton, S., (1988). "Meet Our New Workforce," *Business Week*, pp. 14-21.

Nemeth, M., (1993). "When the Boss is a Woman," *Maclean's*, Oct. 4, pp. 20-23.

Newell, S., (2002). *Managing Knowledge Work*. New York: Palgrave.

Newman, J.M., (1978). "Discrimination in Recruitment: An Empirical Analysis," *Industrial and Labour Relations Review*, (32), pp. 15-23.

Newson, J. and H. Buchbinder, (1988). *The University Means Business*. Toronto: Garamond Press.

Nichols, T. and H. Beynon, (1977). *Living With Capitalism: Class Relations and the Modern Factory*. London: Routledge and Kegan Paul.

Nickels, W.G., J.M. McHugh, S.M. McHugh and P.D. Berman, (1994). *Understanding Canadian Business*. Burr Ridge, IL: Irwin.

Nkomo, S., (1992). "The Emperor has no Clothes: Rewriting 'Race in Organizations,'" *Academy of Management Review*, 17 (3), pp. 487-513.

Nkomo, S. and T.H.J. Cox, (1989). "Gender Differences in the Upward Mobility of Black Managers: Double Whamming or Double Advantage?," *Sex Roles*, 21, pp. 825-839.

Nkomo, S.M., M.D. Fottler and R.B. McAfee, (2005). *Applications in Human Resource Management*. Mason, OH: Thomson/South-Western.

Nord, W. and S. Fox, (1996). "The Individual in Organizational Studies: The Great Disappearing Act?" in S. Clegg and C. Hardy (eds.), *Handbook of Organizational Studies*, pp. 148-175. Thousand Oaks, CA: Sage.

O'Connell, C.E., (1999). *Sexual Harassment in a University Workplace*. Ottawa: National Library of Canada/Bibliothèque Nationale du Canada.

Oakley, A., (1972). *Sex, Gender and Society*. London: Temple Smith.

Omi, M. and H. Winant, (1994). *Racial Formation in the United States: From the 1960s to the 1990s*. New York: Routledge.

Ondrack, D. and M. Evans, (1984). "QWL at Petrosar: A Case Study of a Greenfield Site." in J.B. Cunningham and T.H. White (eds.), *Quality of Working Life: Contem-*

porary Cases, pp. 107-136. Ottawa: Labour Canada.

Orator Magazine, (2002). "Female Dean at the Helm," Leuven and Gent, Vlerick Leuven Gent Management School, <http://www.vlerick.be/news/magazine/sep2002/people.htm>.

Orser, B., (2001). *Sexual Harassment is Still a Management Issue*. Ottawa: Conference Board of Canada.

Ouchi, W., (1990). "Interview (with William Ouchi)," *Selections*, Spring, pp. 38.

Parker, M., (2002). *Against Management: Organization in the Age of Managerialism*. Cambridge: Polity.

Parker, M. and J. Hassard, (eds.), (1993). *Postmodernity and Organizations*. London: Sage.

Parkinson, C.N., (1957). *Parkinson's Law, and Other Studies in Administration*. Boston: Houghton Mifflin.

Pearson, J.C., (1985). *Gender and Communication*. Dubuque, IA: William C. Brown.

Perrow, C., (1984). *Normal Accidents: Living With High Risk Technologies*. New York: Basic Books.

Peter, K., (1981). "The Myth of Multiculturalism and Other Political Fables," in J. Dahlie and T. Frenando (eds.), *Ethnicity, Power and Politics in Canada*. Toronto: Methuen.

Peter, L.J. and R. Hull, (1969). *The Peter Principle*. New York: William Morrow.

Peters, T. and R. Waterman, (1982). *In Search of Excellence: Lessons From America's Best Run Companies*. New York: Warner Communications.

Pfeffer, J., (1992). "Understanding Power in Organizations," *California Management Review*, 35, pp. 29-50.

Pollert, A., (1981). *Girls, Wives, Factory Lives*. London: The MacMillan Press Ltd.

Ponting, J.R., (1986). *Arduous Journey: Canadian Indians and Decolonization*. Toronto: McClelland and Stewart.

—— (1997). *First Nations in Canada: Perspectives on Opportunity, Empowerment, and Self-determination*. Toronto: McGraw-Hill Ryerson.

Ponting, J.R., R. Gibbins and A.J. Siggner, (1980). *Out of Irrelevance: A Socio-political Introduction to Indian Affairs in Canada*. Toronto: Butterworths.

Porras, J.I. and P.J. Robertson, (1992). "Organizational Development: Theory, Practice and Research," in M.D. Dunnette and L.M. Hough (eds.), *Handbook of Industrial and Organizational Psychology*. Palo Alto, CA: Consulting Psychologists Press.

Porter, J., (1965). *The Vertical Mosaic: Analysis of Social Class and Power in Canada*. Toronto: University of Toronto Press.

—— (1975). "Ethnic Pluralism in Canadian Perspective," in N. Glazer, D.P. Moynihan and C.S. Schelling (eds.), *Ethnicity: Theory and Experience* Cambridge, MA: Harvard Univ. Press.

Powell, G.N., (1994). *Gender and Diversity in the Workplace: Learning Activities and Exercises*. Thousand Oaks, CA: Sage.

—— (1999). *Handbook of Gender and Work*. Thousand Oaks, CA: Sage.

—— (2004). *Managing a Diverse Workforce: Learning Activities*. Thousand Oaks, CA: Sage.

Prasad, A., (1997a). "The Colonizing Consciousness and Representations of the Other: A Postcolonial Critique of the Discourse of Oil," in P. Prasad, A.J. Mills, M. Elmes and A. Prasad (eds.), *Managing the Organizational Melting*

Pot: Dilemmas of Workplace Diversity, pp. 285-311. Thousand Oaks, CA: Sage.

Prasad, A. and P. Prasad, (2002). "Otherness at Large: Identity and Difference in the New Globalized Organizational Landscape," in I. Aaltio and A.J. Mills (eds.), Gender, Identity and the Culture of Organizations, pp. 57-71. London: Routledge.

Prasad, P., (1997b). "The Protestant Ethic and the Myths of the Frontier: Cultural Imprints, Organizational Structuring, and Workplace Diversity," in P. Pradas, A.J. Mills, M. Elmes and A. Prasad (eds.), Managing the Organizational Melting Pot, pp. 129-147. Thousand Oaks, Sage.

Prasad, P. and A.J. Mills, (1997). "From Showcase to Shadow: Understanding the Dilemmas of Managing Workplace Diversity," in P. Prasad, A.J. Mills, M. Elmes and A. Prasad (eds.), Managing the Organizational Melting Pot: Dilemmas of Workplace Diversity, pp. 3-27. Thousand Oaks, CA: Sage.

Prasad, P., A.J. Mills, M. Elmes and P. Prasad, (eds.), (1997). Managing The Organizational Melting Pot: Dilemmas of Workplace Diversity. Thousand Oaks, CA: Sage.

Pritchard, D., F. Sauvageau and Centre d'études sur les Médias, (1999). Les Journalistes Canadiens: Un Portrait de fin de Siècle. Sainte-Foy, QC: Presses de l'Université Laval.

Pugh, D.S., (1997). Organization Theory: Selected Readings. London: Penguin.

Pugh, D.S. and D.J. Hickson, (1997). Writers on Organizations. Thousand Oaks, CA: Sage.

Pugh, D.S., D.J. Hickson and C.R. Hinings, (1983). Writers on Organizations. Harmondsworth: Penguin.

Purich, D., (1986). Our Land: Native Rights in Canada. Toronto: Lorimer.

Putnam, L., (1982). "In Search of Gender: A Critique of Communication and Sex Roles Research," Women's Studies in Communication, (5), pp. 1-9.

—— (1983). "The Interpretive Perspective: An Alternative to Functionalism," in L.L. Putnam and M.E. Pacanowsky (eds.), Communication and Organizations: An Interpretive Approach, pp. 31-54. Beverly Hills, CA: Sage.

Putnam, L. and G. Fairhurst, (1985). "Women and Organizatinal Communication: Research Directions and New Perspectives," Women and Language, IX (1/2), pp. 2-6.

Quinn, R.E., (1977). "Coping With Cupid: The Formation, Impact and Management of Romantic Relationships in Organizations," Administrative Science Quarterly, 22, pp. 30-45.

Raeburn, N.C., (2004). Changing Corporate America From Inside Out: Lesbian and Gay Workplace Rights. Minneapolis: University of Minnesota Press.

Rakow, L.F., (1986). "Rethinking Gender Research in Communication," Journal of Communication, 36 (4), pp. 11-24.

Ramcharan, S., (1982). Racism: Nonwhites in Canada. Toronto: Butterworths.

Ranke-Heinemann, U., (1990). Eunuchs for the Kingdom of Heaven: Women, Sexuality and the Catholic Church. London: Doubleday.

Rattansi, A. and R. Boyne, (1990). Postmodernism and Society. Basingstoke: Macmillan Education.

Ray, T., P. Quintas, S. Little and Open University, (2002). Managing Knowledge: An Essential Reader. Thousand Oaks, CA: Sage.

Razack, S., (1998). Looking White People in the Eye: Gender, Race, and Culture in Courtrooms and Classrooms. Toronto: University of Toronto Press.

Reinharz, S., (1988). "Feminist Distrust: Problems of Context and Content in Sociological Work," in D.N. Berg and K.K. Smith (eds.), *The Self in Social Inquiry*, pp. 153-172. Newbury Park, CA: Sage.

Reinharz, S. and L. Davidman, (1992). *Feminist Methods in Social Research*. New York: Oxford University Press.

Rich, A.C., (1979). *On Lies, Secrets, and Silence: Selected Prose, 1966-1978*. New York: Norton.

Rinehart, J., (1986). "Improving the Quality of Working Life Through Job Redesign: Work Humanization or Work Rationalization," *The Canadian Review of Sociology and Anthropology*, 23 (4), pp. 507-530.

Ritzer, G., (1996). *The McDonaldization of Society: An Investigation into the Changing Character of Contemporary Social Life*. Thousand Oaks, CA: Pine Forge Press.

Robbins, S.P., (1989). *Organizational Behavior: Concepts, Controversies, and Applications*. Englewood Cliffs, NJ: Prentice-Hall.

—— (1990). *Organizational Theory: Structure, Design and Applications*. Englewood Cliffs, NJ: Prentice Hall.

—— (1996). *Organizational Behavior: Concepts, Controversies, and Applications*. Englewood Cliffs, NJ: Prentice-Hall.

Robbins, S.P. and N. Langton, (2003). *Organizational Behaviour: Third Canadian Edition*. Toronto: Pearson Prentice Hall.

—— (2004). *Fundamentals of Organizational Behaviour: Second Canadian Edition*. Toronto: Pearson Prentice Hall.

Robin, R. (2001). *The Making of the Cold War Enemy: Culture and Politics in the Military-Intellectual Complex*. Princeton, NJ: Princeton University Press.

Roethlisberger, F.J. and W.J. Dickson, (1939). *Management and the Worker* Cambridge: Harvard University Press.

Roethlisberger, F.J. and G.F.F. Lombard, (1977). *The Elusive Phenomena: An Autobiographical Account of my Work in the Field of Organizational Behavior at the Harvard Business School*. Boston: Division of Research, Graduate School of Business Administration, distributed by Harvard University Press.

Rogers, A. (1997). *Secrecy and Power in the British State: A History of the Official Secrets Act*. London: Pluto Press.

Rose, M., (1978). *Industrial Behaviour*. Harmondsworth: Penguin.

Rozell, M.J., (2002). *Executive Privilege: Presidential Power, Secrecy, and Accountability*. Lawrence, KS: University Press of Kansas.

Runte, M. and A.J. Mills, (2002). "The Discourse of Work-Family Conflict: A Critique," Proceedings of the Gender and Diversity in Organization Division of the Annual Meeting of the Administrative Sciences Association of Canada, edited by Gloria Miller, Winnipeg, May 25-28.

Runte, M. and A.J. Mills, (2004). "Paying the Toll: A Feminist Post-structural Critique of the Discourse Bridging Work and Family," *Culture and Organization*, (in press).

Said, E.W., (1979). *Orientalism*. New York: Vintage.

—— (1993). *Culture and Imperialism*. New York: Vintage.

Sampson, A., (1973). *The Sovereign State of ITT*. New York: Stein and Day.

Sanchez, R., (2001). *Knowledge Management and Organizational Competence*. Oxford: Oxford University Press.

Satzewich, V. and P. Li., (1987). "Immigrant Labour in Canada: The Cost and Benefits of Ethnic Origin in the Job Market,"

Canadian Journal of Sociology, 12, pp. 229-241.

Saunders, D., (2004). "The Timely Exit," *The Globe and Mail*. Toronto: May 15, pp. F6-F7.

Savage, M. and A. Witz, (eds.), (1992). *Gender and Bureaucracy*. Oxford: Blackwell.

Sayles, L., (1964). *Managerial Behaviour*. New York: McGraw-Hill.

Schein, E., (1980). *Organizational Psychology*. Englewood Cliffs, NJ: Prentice-Hall.

—— (1985). *Organizational Culture and Leadership*. San Francisco: Jossey-Bass.

—— (1987). *The Clinical Perspective of Fieldwork*. Newbury Park, CA: Sage.

—— (1990). "Organizational Culture," *American Psychologist*, 45 (2), pp. 109-119.

—— (1992). *Organizational Culture and Leadership*. San Francisco: Jossey-Bass.

Schein, V.E. (1994). "Managerial Sex Typing: A Persistent and Pervasive Barrier to Women's Opportunities," in M.J. Davidson and R.J. Burke (eds.), *Women in Management. Current Research Issues*, pp. 41-52. London: Paul Chapman Publishing Ltd.

Schermerhorn, J.R., A.J. Templer, R.J. Cattaneo, J.G. Hunt and R.N. Osborn, (1992). *Managing Organizational Behavior*. Toronto: Wiley.

Schmidt, E.L., K. Pearlman and J. Hunter, (1980). "The Validity and Fairness of Employment and Educational Tests for Hispanic Americans: A Review and Analysis," *Personnel Psychology*, (33), pp. 705-724.

Schneider, B.E. (1982). "Consciousness About Sexual Harassment Among Heterosexual and Lesbian Women Workers," *Journal of Social Issues*, 38 (4), pp. 75-98.

—— (1984). "The Office Affair: Myth and Reality for Heterosexual and Lesbian Women Workers," *Sociological Perspectives*, 27 (4), pp. 443-464.

Selznick, P., (1949). *T.V.A. and the Grass Roots: A Study in the Sociology of Formal Organizations*. Berkley, CA: University of California Press.

Senge, P., (1994). *The Fifth Discipline: The Art and Practice of the Learning Organization*. New York: Doubleday.

Shawcross, W. (1979). *Sideshow: Kissinger, Nixon and the Destruction of Cambodia*. New York: Simon and Schuster.

Sheriff, P. and E.J. Campbell, (1992). "Room For Women: A Case Study in the Sociology of Organizations," in A.J. Mills and P. Tancred (eds.), *Gendering Organizational Analysis*, pp. 31-45. Newbury Park, CA: Sage.

Shields, V.R. and D. Heinecken, (2002). *Measuring Up: How Advertising Images Shape Gender Identity*. Philadelphia: University of Pennsylvania Press.

Shilts, R., (1993). *Conduct Unbecoming: Gays and Lesbians in the US Military*. New York: St. Martin's Press.

Silverman, D., (1970). *The Theory of Organizations*. New York: Basic Books.

Simon, H., (1976). *Administrative Behavior*. New York: The Free Press.

—— (1997). *Administrative Behaviour: A Study of Decision-making Processes in Administrative Organizations*. New York: Free Press.

Sinclair, A., (1995). "Sex and the MBA," *Organization*, 2 (2), pp. 295-317.

Sinha, M., (1987). "Gender and Imperialism: Colonial Policy and the Ideology of Moral Imperialism in Late Nineteenth-Century Bengal," in M.S. Kimmel (ed.), *Changing Men: New Directions in Research on Men and Masculinity*, pp. 217-231. Newbury Park, CA: Sage.

Sjoberg, G., (1983). "Afterword," in W.B. Littrell, G. Sjoberg and L.A. Zurcher (eds.), *Bureaucracy as a Social Problem*. Greenwich, CT: JAI Press.

Slocum Jr., J. and R. Strawser, (1972). "Racial Differences in Job Attitudes," *Journal of Applied Psychology*, (56), pp. 28-32.

Smircich, L., (1985). "Is the Concept of Culture a Paradigm for Understanding Organizations and Ourselves?" in P.J. Frost, L.F. Moore, M.R. Louis, C.C. Lundberg and J. Martin (eds.), *Organizational Culture*, pp. 55-72. Beverley Hills, CA: Sage.

Smith, J., (1998). *Different For Girls: How Culture Creates Women*. London: Vintage.

Spence, R.A., (1999). *Sexual Harassment Sociocultural Aspects and Organizational Policy Interventions*. Ottawa: National Library of Canada/Bibliothèque Nationale du Canada.

Stanley, J., W. Robbins and R. Morgan, (2004). "Selected Indicators of the Status of Women in Universities in Canada and Further Equity Data, 2003." Ottawa: Canadian Federation for the Humanities and Social Sciences, <www.fedcan.ca/english/policyandadvocacy/win/publications.cfm>.

Stanley, L. and S. Wise, (1983). *Breaking Out: Feminist Consciousness and Feminist Research*. London: Routledge and Kegan Paul.

Starke, F.A. and R.W. Sexty, (1995). *Contemporary Management in Canada*. Toronto: Prentice-Hall.

Statistics Canada, (2001). "Census – Population," Ottawa: Statistics Canada, <http://www.statcan.ca/english/Pgdb/popula.htm>.

—— (2002). "Gender Pay Differentials: Impact of the Workplace," Ottawa:

Statistics Canada, <http://www.statcan.ca/Daily/English/020619/d020619b.htm>.

—— (2003). "Ethnic Diversity Survey," Ottawa: Statistics Canada, 29 September, <http://www.statcan.ca/Daily/English/030929/d030929a.htm>.

Steers, R.M., (1981). *Introduction to Organizational Behavior*. Santa Monica, CA: Goodyear Publishing Inc.

Stewart, R., (1988). *Managers and Their Jobs: A Study of the Similarities and Differences in the Ways Managers Spend Their Time*. Basingstoke: Macmillan.

Stinson, M., (2004). "Visible Minorities Bulk Up the Economy," *The Globe and Mail*. Toronto: May 7, pp. B4.

Stone, D.L. and E.F. Stone, (1987). "Effects of Missing Application-blank information on Personnel Selection Decisions: Do Privacy Protection Strategies Bias the Outcome?" *Journal of Applied Psychology*, (72), pp. 452-456.

Styhre, A., (2003). *Understanding Knowledge Management: Critical and Postmodern Perspectives*. Malmö, Liber: Abstrakt.

Susman, G., (1972). "The Impact of Automation on Work Group Autonomy and Task Specialization," in L. Davis and J. Taylor (eds.), *Design of Jobs*. Harmondsworth: Penguin.

—— (1976). "Job Enrichment, Need Theory and Reinforcement Theory," in R. Dubin (ed.), *Handbook of Work, Organization and Society*. Chicago: Rand McNally.

Sweeney, P.D. and D.B. McFarlin, (2002). *Organizational Behaviour: Solutions for Management*. New York: McGraw-Hill Irwin.

Tancred-Sheriff, P. (1989). "Gender, Sexuality and the Labour Process," in J. Hearn, D.L. Sheppard, P. Tancred-Sheriff and G. Burrell (eds.), *The Sexuality of Organization*, pp. 44-55. London: Sage.

Tancred-Sheriff, P. and E.J. Campbell, (1992). "Room for Women: A Case Study in the Sociology of Organizations," in A.J. Mills and P. Tancred (eds.), *Gendering Organizational Analysis*, pp. 31-45. Newbury Park, CA: Sage.

Task Force on Barriers to Women in the Public Service, (1990). *Beneath the Veneer*. Ottawa: Minister of Supply and Services Canada, 4.

Taylor, F.W., (1911). *Principles of Scientific Management*. New York: Harper and Row.

—— (1967). *The Principles of Scientific Management*. Norton.

Tepperman, L., (1975). *Social Mobility in Canada*. Toronto: McGraw-Hill Ryerson.

Tepperman, L. and J.E. Curtis, (2004). *Social Problems: A Canadian Perspective* Toronto: Oxford University Press.

Tepstra, D. and M. Larse, (1985). "A Note on Job Type and Applicant Race as Determinants of Hiring Decisions," *Journal of Occupational Psychology*, 53 (3), pp. 117-119.

Terkel, S., (1974). *Working*. Pantheon.

The Commission for Labor Cooperation, (2003). *Work Stoppages in North America*. Washington, DC: The Commission for Labor Cooperation, October.

Theoharis, A.G., (1998). *A Culture of Secrecy: The Government Versus the People's Right to Know*. Lawrence, KS: University Press of Kansas.

Thiessen, D., N. Bascia and I. Goodson (eds.), (1996a). *Making a Difference About Difference: The Lives and Careers of Racial Minority Immigrant Teachers*. Toronto: Garamond Press.

—— (1996b). *Making a Difference About Difference: The Lives and Careers of Racial Minority Immigrant Teachers*. Toronto: Garamond Press.

Thomas, R. and A. Davies, (2002). "Gender and the New Public Management," *Gender, Work and Organization*, 9 (4).

Thomas, R., A.J. Mills and J. Helms Mills (eds.), (2004). *Identity Politics at Work: Gendering Resistance, Resisting Gender*. London: Routledge.

Thompson, P., (1991). "Fatal Distraction: Post-modernism and Organizational Analysis." Paper Presented at the "New Theory of Organizations" Conference, University of Keele.

Thompson, V., (1961). *Modern Organizations*. New York: Knopf.

Tillson, T., (1996). "She's the Boss," *Canadian Business* (11), pp. 43, 46.

Toffler, A., (1981). *The Third Wave*. Glasgow: Pan.

Treasury Board of Canada Secretariat, (2003). "Embracing Change: Leading the Way," Ottawa: Treasury Board of Canada, <http://www.tbs-sct.gc.ca/ec-fpac/ltw-adla_e.asp>.

Trist, E., (1981). *The Evolution of Socio-technical Systems*. Toronto: Ontario Quality of Working Life Centre.

Trist, E.L. and K. Bamforth, (1951). "Some Social and Psychological Consequences of the Longwall Method of Coal Getting," *Human Relations*, 4, pp. 3-38.

Tudiver, N., (1999). *Universities For Sale: Resisting Corporate Control Over Canadian Higher Education*. Toronto: James Lorimer and Co. Ltd.

Turk, J.L. (ed.), (2000). *The Corporate Campus: Commercialization and the Dangers to Canada's College and Universities*. Toronto: James Lorimer and Co. Ltd.

Vecchio, R., (1980). "Worker Alienation as a Moderator of the Job Quality-Job Satisfaction Relationship: The Case of Racial Differences," *Academy of Management Journal*, 23, pp. 479-486.

Vincent, D., (1998). *The Culture of Secrecy in Britain, 1832-1998.* Oxford: Oxford University Press.

Walter, G.A., (1983). "Psyche and Symbol," in L.R. Pondy, P. Frost, G. Morgan and T.C. Dandridge (eds.), *Organizational Symbolism,* pp. 257-271. Greenwich, CT: JAI Press.

Ward, M., (1991). *The Max Ward Story. A Bush Pilot in the Bureaucratic Jungle.* Toronto: McClelland and Stewart.

Warren, C.A.B. and J.K. Hackney, (2000). *Gender Issues in Ethnography.* Thousand Oaks, CA: Sage.

Weatherall, M., H. Stiven and J. Potter, (1987). "Unequal Egalitarianism: A Preliminary Study of Discourses Concerning Gender and Employment Opportunities," *British Journal of Social Psychology,* 26, pp. 59-71.

Weber, M., (1947). *The Theory of Social and Economic Organization.* London: Free Press.

—— (1948). *From Max Weber: Essays in Sociology.* London: RKP.

—— (1967). *The Protestant Ethic and the Spirit of Capitalism.* London: Allen and Unwin.

Weber, M., T. Parsons and A. Giddens, (1992). *The Protestant Ethic and the Spirit of Capitalism.* New York: Routledge.

Whitman, S., (2004). "Halifax University Girls: A Step Back." *The Journal,* (Saint Mary's University Student's Union Paper, pp. 1).

Wicks, D. and P. Bradshaw, (2002). "Gendered Value Foundations That Reproduce Discrimination and Inhibit Organizational Change," in I. Aaltio and A.J. Mills (eds.), *Gender, Identity and the Culture of Organizations,* pp. 137-159. London: Routledge.

Wicks, D. and A.J. Mills, (2000). "Deconstructing Harry: A Critical Review of Men, Masculinity and Organization," *The Finnish Journal of Business Economics,* 3, pp. 327-349.

Williamson, O.E., (1975). *Markets and Hierarchies: Analysis and Antitrust Implications: A Study in the Economics of Internal Organization.* New York: Free Press.

Wilson, E.M., (2001). *Organizational Behaviour Reassessed: The Impact of Gender.* Thousand Oaks, CA: Sage.

—— (2002). "Family Man or Conqueror? – Contested Meanings in an Engineering Company," *Culture and Organization,* 8 (2), pp. 81-100.

Winfeld, L. and S. Spielman, (2001). *Straight Talk About Gays in the Workplace.* New York: Harrington Park Press.

Wolf, N., (2002). *The Beauty Myth: How Images of Beauty are Used Against Women.* New York: Perennial.

Wolfe, J., (2001). *Coping With Work-Family Conflict and Perceptions of Coping Efficacy.* Ottawa: National Library of Canada/Bibliothèque Nationale du Canada.

Wren, D.A., (1994). *The Evolution of Management Thought.* New York: Wiley.

Wren, D.A. and D. Voich Jr., (1984). *Management: Process, Structure and Behaviour.* New York: John Wiley.

Zolf, L., (1982). "How Multiculturalism Corrupts," *Maclean's,* 15 November.

Zuckerman, A.J. and G.F. Simons, (1996). *Sexual Orientation in the Workplace: Gay Men, Lesbians, Bisexuals, and Heterosexuals Working Together.* Thousand Oaks, CA: Sage.

Index

consensus view of management, 80
Conservative Party of Canada 204
Consulting Group on Employment Equity for Women 189
contingency theory 93, 238
control 11, 13, 22, 46, 49, 51, 52, 57, 70, 78, 79, 80, 82, 83, 85, 86, 87, 90, 91, 95, 96, 97, 99, 100, 105, 109, 120, 122, 124, 126, 127, 128, 130, 134, 138, 139, 140, 142, 152, 170, 177, 178, 180, 236, 237, 240, 242, 245
   bureaucratic control 87
   hegemonic control 240
   simple control 85
   technical control 85, 86
Cooper, C.L. 133
coordinating 79, 99-100
corporate culture 103
corporate take-overs 49
coup d'etat (Chile, 1974) 241
Cox, M.G. 174
craft guilds 10
Crane, D. 207
critical approach to organizations 2, 3, 5, 13, 30, 33, 119
Crozier, M. 172
Cullen, Dallas 74, 133, 136, 144, 156
culture of narcissism 141
Czechoslovakia 241

Daft, R. 22

Dagg, A. 168
Dahrendorf, R. 83
Dale, E. 81
Davidson, M. 180
Davies, S. 172
Davis, G. 207
Deans of School of Business and Administrative Studies 168, 169, 189
decentralized corporate structure 84
decision-making 3, 11, 171, 172
decisional roles 102
degradation of work 28, 105
democracy 49, 62, 65
democratic work climates' 171
democratic style of leadership 172, 240
Denton, T. 38, 73, 208, 227
Department of Immigration 47
Department of Indian and Northern Development, 46
deskilling 90, 97, 105, 177
Devenis, L.E. 145
Devine, Grant 40
Dickens, F. 207
Dickson, D. 242
Dickson, W.J. 123
Dinter, Gail Gottleib 169
directing 99
disciplinary practices 139
discrimination 3, 14, 66, 119, 132, 176
DiTomaso, N. 4, 165
division of labour 50, 54, 59, 96, 98, 99

Djilas, M. 241
domination 32, 63, 134, 243
Don, Michael 41
Donaldson, L. 246
Donnelly, J.H. 92
Dreyfus, H.L. 140
Drucker, P. 94
Dubcek, Alexander 241
Due Billing, Y. 178, 187
Dunkerley, D. 173, 242
Dupont, Alfred 94
Durkheim, E. 11, 12, 122, 126
Dussault, Rene 229

Eastern Europe 50, 52, 61, 63, 243, 245
economic power 126
Edwards, R. 79, 85, 86
efficiency 27, 45, 48, 50, 51, 53, 55, 57, 58, 59, 83, 90, 91, 95, 96, 98, 120, 238
Elmes, M. 38, 111
employment equity 3, 147, 159, 173, 177
entrepreneurs 83, 84, 138
environment 119
environmental disasters 12
environmental pollution 12
environmentalists 31
Equality Now 198
Erasmus, Georges 229
ethnic domination 137
ethnic mosaic 199, 200, 223
ethnic stratification 201, 218, 229
ethnicity 3, 4, 48, 61, 64, 68, 179, 185, 192

Marcuse, H. 126, 150
Marshall, H. 145
Martin, J. 172
Martin, Ray 231
Marx, K. 11, 12, 52, 126, 130, 136
Marxists 52, 138, 149
Mary Kay Cosmetics 103
masculinity 121, 135, 143, 144, 159, 163, 175, 185
Maslow, A. 133, 134, 136, 150
mass unemployment, 240
May '68 events 241
Mayo, E. 58
MBA 3, 185, 263
McCarthyism 240
McClelland, D.C. 88
McDonald's 53, 69, 72, 97, 103, 115, 152
McGregor, D. 88
McKenna, K. 181
McShane, S.L. 113, 223
Mead, G.H. 136
Meissner, M. 174
mentors 178
Mercredi, Ovide 229
Merrill, L. 174
Merton, R.K. 58, 60
Métis 194, 229
Mexico 231, 245
Michels, R. 52, 63
middle management 100
middle-class 67
Miewald, R. 63
Mighty, J. 179, 227
Milken, Michael 41
Mills, A.J. 37, 103, 110, 163, 172, 174, 176, 178, 184, 185, 187

Mintzberg, H. 100, 102, 104
mirroring 143, 151, 239, 313
modes of production 17
monopolies 49
Montreal Polytechnique 188
Mooney, James 91
Morgan, Gareth 33, 37, 43, 71, 110
Morgan, Glenn 38, 126, 136, 137, 138, 236, 242
Morgan, Nicole 71, 172, 176
Morrison, A. 177
mother's power 144
motivation 100
multi-culturalism 68
multi-unit firm 83
Mumby, D.K. 73, 172, 174, 175, 178, 185
Murgatroyd, S. 37, 110, 143, 185

Nahem, J. 144
narcissism 132, 141, 142, 144, 149
narcissistic organizational culture 143
National Association of Canadians of Origins in India 231
National Liberation Front (Vietnam) 241
NATO 61, 240
Nazi Germany 131
Nazis 131
Nemeth, M. 164
neo-Nazism in Europe 132

networks of communication 174
neurosis 144
New Democratic Party (NDP) 231, 262, 275
Nixon administration 62
Nkomo, S. 110
Nord, W. 73, 140
normal science 235
North American Free Trade Agreement 245
Northcote Parkinson, C. 61
Northey, Margot 168
Nova Scotia 42, 43, 191, 193, 248, 249, 250, 251, 252, 259, 261, 262, 265, 266, 270, 277
Nova Scotia Power 89, 250, 259, 270
nurses 178

Official Languages Act 197
Official Secrets Act 62
oil 47, 62
oil crisis 9
Ondrack, D. 88
Ontario Human Rights Commission 188
opportunity structure 67
organization theory (OT) or organizational behavior (OB) 2, 3, 11, 13, 27, 33, 50, 52, 56, 57, 64, 78, 92, 95, 96, 98, 102, 103, 106, 122, 123, 124, 126, 133, 135, 166, 172, 233, 234, 235, 236, 237, 238, 243
organizational change 14, 98
organizational crisis 10